American Jewish Women's History

American Jewish Women's History

A Reader

EDITED BY

Pamela S. Nadell

New York University Press

NEW YORK AND LONDON

NEW YORK UNIVERSITY PRESS
New York and London

Library of Congress Cataloging-in-Publication Data

American Jewish women's history : a reader / edited by Pamela S. Nadell.
p. cm.
ISBN 0-8147-5807-X (cloth : alk. paper)—
ISBN 0-8147-5808-8 (Pbk. : alk. paper)
1. Jewish women—United States—History—20th century.
2. Jewish women—United States—Political activity.
3. Jewish women—Religious life—United States.
4. Jewish women—United States—Intellectual life—20th century.
I. Nadell, Pamela Susan.
E184.36.W64 J47 2003
920.72'089'924073—dc21   2002013020

New York University Press books are printed on acid-free paper,
and their binding materials are chosen for strength and durability.

Manufactured in the United States of America

10 9 8 7 6 5 4 3 2 1

In honor of my parents,
Irwin and Alice Shurman Nadell,
and
in memory of my grandparents,
Samuel and Anna Wecker Nadel
Abraham and Jennie Kantor Shurman

Contents

Acknowledgments

One of the great pleasures of finishing a book is recognizing those who assisted the author. In this case, my deep gratitude goes to those who graciously consented to have their work appear here: Dianne Ashton, Faith Rogow, Linda Mack Schloff, Alice Kessler-Harris, Paula E. Hyman, Joyce Antler, Jenna Weissman Joselit, Julia Foulkes, Joan Jacobs Brumberg, Riv-Ellen Prell, Marcie Cohen Ferris, and Debra L. Schultz. Ellen Smith and Jonathan D. Sarna trusted me to abridge their longer works for this reader. Shelly Tenenbaum and Beth S. Wenger contributed new articles based on their important books.

Many others responded to my queries as I read through the burgeoning literature in American Jewish women's history. I thank Maria Baader, Judith Baskin, Michael Brown, Rela Geffen, Karla Goldman, Deborah Grand Golomb, Mark Greenberg, Jeffrey Gurock, Melissa Klapper, Mary McCune, Marc Lee Raphael, Jane Rothstein, Rona Sheramy, William Toll, Phyllis Holman Weisbard, and Cornelia Wilhelm.

Those working in American Jewish history have long relied upon a group of dedicated archivists and librarians for guidance. It is my pleasure to recognize yet again Peggy Pearlstein, of the Library of Congress; Kevin Proffitt, of the Jacab Rader Marcus Center of the American Jewish Archives; Lyn Slome, of the American Jewish Historical Society; and Susan Woodland, of the Hadassah Archives, for their help in locating images for this cover.

Jennifer Hammer, an editor at New York University Press, conceived of this project and invited me to pursue it. I thank her for sending me on this journey and for her patience and keen editorial eye. Both have improved this reader.

For two decades, American University, and especially its Jewish Studies Program and Department of History, has remained my academic home. My colleagues Allan Lichtman and Valerie French, who in recent years have chaired the Department of History, and Kay Mussell, dean of the College of Arts and Sciences, have encouraged my scholarship.

To save the most important and the best for last, I thank my family. Now that they are fourteen and nine, my children, Yoni and Orly, no longer tread on the papers spread out on the floor of my study. As I cheer their passion for sports, they cheer mine for history. As he has done for more than a quarter of a century, my husband, Edward Farber, makes possible all that I achieve with humor, grace, and a great love.

Introduction

Pamela S. Nadell

Before the 1970s, readers of history "encountered a world of 'significant knowl-edge,' in which women seemed not to exist." But then, some, inspired by the new wave of feminism, turned to women's history. The pioneering historian of American women Gerda Lerner wrote: "My commitment to women's history came out of my life, not out of my head"; as she and a host of others set out to find for the majority its past.[1] Even as many began writing and teaching American women's history, some asked, "Why was the history of the Jewish woman yet to be written?"[2]

To the new women's historians, Jewish women, at least American Jewish women, did not seem, at first, a likely subject for study. By the early 1990s, as the initial decades of the writing of women's history gave way to the first syntheses of the new scholarship, Jewish women remained subsumed under the category of white—and thus largely privileged—women. In the first edition of the widely taught *Unequal Sisters: A Multicultural Reader in U.S. Women's History,* Jewish women were invisible. Multiculturalism did not then embrace them. The reader included no article on American Jewish women, but two references to Jews anywhere in the text, and none to American Jewish women in the index. When Jewish women did surface in survey histories of American women, they appeared fleetingly, as immi-grants striking for better wages or as the victims of the 1911 Triangle Shirtwaist Factory fire.[3]

By the end of the decade, however, historians of American women sought to craft "a more complex approach to women's experiences." They came to recognize that "not all white women's histories can be categorized under one label," and some explicitly called "to diversify our coverage of Jewish American women."[4] As they did, they drew upon the burgeoning scholarship on American Jewish women that appeared in the 1990s. In fact, with but two exceptions, the essays in this book were all written after 1990. They demonstrate the enormous progress made in uncovering the history of American Jewish women, an achievement reflected in the landmark publication of *Jewish Women in America: An Historical Encyclopedia* in 1997.[5]

This anthology conveys the sweep of that new knowledge of American Jewish women as it spans time and space from the colonial era to the close of the twentieth century. This book finds Jewish women living not only in New York City but also in Philadelphia and Baltimore, in the South, the Midwest, and the West. That many chapters are set in New York City reveals historians' deep interest in the city, as well as the geography of American Jewry. Not only did the first Jewish settlers land in New Amsterdam in 1654, but also New York City has remained the home of the largest Jewish community in the United States.

The chronology of this book favors the twentieth century. That pattern also discloses the inclinations of the scholars, as well as the weight of the demography of American Jewry, which in its first 220 years grew from a handful of colonists to about a quarter of a million men, women, and children. As late as 1880, they accounted for at most .6 percent of the population of the United States. But the migration of some two million Jews from Eastern Europe in the last decades of the nineteenth century and the early ones of the twentieth transformed American Jewry. By 1900, the population had already tripled; by 1920, there were 3.5 million Jews living in the United States. In 1990, the some 5.5 million American Jews constituted just under 2.5 percent of the population.[6]

These essays touch upon American Jewish women as daughters, wives, and mothers; students and teachers; workers and entrepreneurs. They find them in their kitchens and in their synagogues, at their writing tables and behind the counters of general stores, hunched over sewing machines and dancing in front of the mirror. They consider their volunteer activities and political crusades. They examine their interior lives and the stereotypes imposed on them. They take up their piety and the roles they played in shaping American Judaism. They show American Jewish women with their Christian neighbors and see them working to better their own lives and the lives of Jews everywhere. They thus convey the depth of the current knowledge in the field.[7]

What connects the Jewish matrons of colonial America with the young Jewish women of the 1960s who went South to fight for civil rights? Agency emerges as the overarching theme, that is, the ways in which Jewish women acted and exerted power to sustain and to shape Jewish life in America. Women sought to preserve Judaism and their Jewish communities in an America that not only allowed for integration but often demanded it. As a result, Jewish women defined a variety of American Jewish identities in their kitchens and synagogues, via their work and social organizations, in their politics, culture, and art. No matter where they found themselves in American Jewry, which indeed divided along class, religious, and ethnic lines, Jewish women saw themselves as empowered to act, to influence, and to define the emerging American Jewish communities.

Moreover, as these essays demonstrate, rather than collapsing all Jewish women, with the exception of the East European immigrants, into privileged, white, and middle class, this history exhibits the diversity of American Jewish women and establishes that it presents a unique narrative within the history of American women. Its diversity was shaped by the various intersections of gender with Judaism, that is, faith, and with Jewishness, that is, peoplehood, with a "complex interplay" of other factors.[8] To be sure, commonalities did exist, and many Jewish women indeed lived their lives somewhat within the rhythms of the Jewish calendar, with its Sabbaths and holidays and its life cycle ceremonies. Ties of religion and culture, community and memory, bound them together. Nevertheless, other factors, including class and race, economics, politics, sexuality, and religious expression divided American Jewry. When these essays, published over a number of years, are read together for the first time, they lay open the complexity and variety of Jewish women's syntheses of their American and Jewish identities.

By emphasizing Jewish women's agency, this book demonstrates how these women—whether colonial matrons or club women, turn-of-the-century garment workers or late-twentieth-century feminists—molded the contours of American Jewish life. Sometimes, the interplay of gender and class, religion and ethnicity, resulted in the creation of new forms of a separate female Jewish culture. At other times, Jewish women intersected with and interacted with their fathers and brothers, husbands and sons, who were simultaneously determining the trajectory of Jewish life in America. But, no matter the era, no matter the setting, American Jewish women's empowerment to define their Jewish homes and social organizations, to influence their synagogues and communities, and to construct their work, politics, and culture distinguishes their history from that of other minority women in the United States.[9]

The chapters that follow appear chronologically, but they can also be read thematically as they engage subjects historians of American women have analyzed. Yet, collectively they demonstrate that Jewish women adapted, negotiated, and reified for their Jewish families and communities currents in American life.

For example, domesticity, a theme women's historians have considered, is treated by both Ellen Smith and Marcie Cohen Ferris. Smith's study of the material culture of the homes of early American Jewish women presents a Jewish counterpart to the "pretty gentlewoman" of eighteenth-century colonial cities. Jewish homes also displayed "the accoutrements of gentility: table linens, forks, chairs, and looking glasses."[10] But, when a mustard pot became a ritual object, it affirmed that this remained a Jewish home. Ferris shows how, in twentieth-century kitchens, Jewish women constructed identity. When they cooked matzoh balls and hush puppies, they borrowed, as the colonial Jewish matrons had, from the surrounding culture, blending their Jewish and their American selves into a distinctive southern Jewish identity.

Historians of American women have written a great deal about women "pioneering in the creation of new public spaces—voluntary associations located *between* the public world of politics and work and the private intimacy of family." This book examines the gendered spaces American Jewish women created to influence their faith and their people. In "The Age of Association," when the new concept of the responsibilities of republican motherhood expected women to create institutions for the new society,[11] Rebecca Gratz worked with her Christian neighbors in Philadelphia's Orphan Asylum. But Gratz became convinced that Philadelphia's Jewish women and children needed their own associations, and she founded a number of them, including the school discussed by Dianne Ashton in "The Lessons of the Hebrew Sunday School."

Another spate of women's organizational building sprang up at the close of the nineteenth century, when women more broadly redefined "woman's place" within their communities and gave it a larger public dimension.[12] Faith Rogow's "Gone to Another Meeting," about the founding of the National Council of Jewish Women, the first of the national Jewish women's organizations, demonstrates how American Jewish women adapted the gendered expression of American public life to create a new space in which to affect not only their Jewish communities but also Judaism. Other chapters—those by Shelly Tenenbaum on Jewish immigrant women's credit networks and by Joyce Antler on Henrietta Szold, Hadassah, and American women's Zionism—reveal that, even as Jewish women created a separate female culture apart from that of Jewish men, the patchwork of Jewish women's organizations grew out of the diversity of class, ethnicity, and the political and religious visions of American Jewry.

Women's historians have long recognized that American women indeed went "out to work," as "economic and social conditions . . . pulled women into the labor market and altered their perceptions of self."[13] When they worked, the work Jewish women did defined them as Jewish women. The image of immigrant girls bent over sewing machines in turn-of-the-century New York tenements rests on the historical reality that, at the end of the first decade of the twentieth century, about two-thirds of the female garment workers were Jewish.[14] But geography, as well as generation, as Linda Mack Schloff shows for the Upper Midwest, also defined Jewish women's participation in the labor force. And changing economic conditions, like those of the Great Depression, could compel those who had stopped working for wages to resume work, even if only for a brief time, as Beth Wenger shows.

A long tradition of women's social and political activism emerges as another theme in this reader, as it has for many historians of American women. Nevertheless, while the struggle for woman suffrage was, in fact, among the very first of the subjects to which women's historians turned, comparatively little has been written about Jewish women and suffrage.[15] American women's involvements in other social movements, such as the antislavery and the temperance movements, also lie outside the history of American Jewish women.[16]

Instead, historians of Jewish women have uncovered other venues for Jewish women's activism. Alice Kessler-Harris writes of Jewish women union organizers. Paula Hyman discovers women boycotting their kosher butchers. Julia Foulkes finds politics choreographing the dances of modern Jewish women. Debra Schultz finds it propelling them South to fight for civil rights. Once again, the variety of Jewish women's historical experiences becomes evident. Jewish women were working class and middle class. Most were wives and mothers, but some remained single. Their activism took them out into the streets, across the city, and eventually across the Mason-Dixon Line.

Another theme that is engaging women's historians is how women were represented in the wider culture. They ask, for example, what cardinal virtues women's magazines and religious literature ascribe to middle-class women.[17] Consequently, historians of Jewish women have also begun to examine both Jewish women's self-images and the images of them created by others. Joan Jacobs Brumberg finds middle-class teens in the 1950s inspired by *The Diary of Anne Frank*. Riv-Ellen

Prell understands that postwar stereotypes of Jewish women framed by Jewish men disclose larger anxieties about life in America.

Finally, religion obviously distinguishes American Jewish women's history. Jonathan Sarna finds Jewish women shaping a "Great Awakening" in American Jewish life in the late nineteenth century. Jenna Weissman Joselit understands that adaptation to America compelled a reconsideration of Orthodox women's roles. Pamela Nadell sees how the same consideration led some Reform Jews to a very different conclusion about women's place in American Judaism. And Paula Hyman explains how Jewish feminism led to dramatic shifts there.

These essays reveal American Jewish women's history as deeply intertwined with the writing of American women's history, even as they convey the distinctiveness and the variety of the experiences of Jewish women. Acting to sustain Jewish life in America, Jewish women shaped their faith and their people. They cooked and marched on picket lines. They ran meetings and businesses, taught classes and preached. They wrote diaries and poems and danced on the stage. But, no matter where they found themselves or how they understood Judaism and Jewishness, as Jewish women "took possession of America,"[18] they defined new expressions of how to be simultaneously a Jew and an American and a woman. As they did, they left a record, proving "it was a world where we [too] had a history."[19]

NOTES

1. Gerda Lerner, "Women among the Professors of History: The Story of a Process of Transformation," in *Voices of Women Historians: The Personal, the Political, the Professional,* ed. Eileen Boris and Nupur Chaudhuri (Bloomington: Indiana University Press, 1999), 1–10, quotation, 1. See, for example, Gerda Lerner, *The Majority Finds Its Past: Placing Women in History* (Oxford: Oxford University Press, 1979).

2. Charlotte Baum, Paula Hyman, and Sonya Michel, *The Jewish Woman in America* (New York: New American Library, 1975, 1976), xii.

3. Vicki L. Ruiz and Ellen Carol DuBois, eds., *Unequal Sisters: A Multicultural Reader in U.S. Women's History* (New York: Routledge, 1990). *Unequal Sisters* also includes single references to anti-Semitism and to the kosher meat boycott. Although Meridith Tax's article "I Had Been Hungry All the Years" appears here (167–75) and culminates with her writing a novel about "Jews in the New York garment industry" (173), her essay focuses on her personal struggles to write, not on American Jewish women. Sara M. Evans, *Born for Liberty: A History of Women in America* (New York: Free Press, 1989), 131, 60–61. The only additional references to Jewish women in *Born for Liberty* are to the National Council of Jewish Women (212) and to the different religious groups that attended a national feminist conference in 1977 (306). Linda Gordon, *U.S. Women's History,* in *The New American History,* ed. Eric Foner (n.p.: American Historical Association, 1990), 15.

4. Vicki L. Ruiz and Ellen Carol DuBois, "Introduction to the Third Edition," in *Unequal Sisters: A Multicultural Reader in U.S. Women's History,* ed. Vicki L. Ruiz and Ellen Carol DuBois (1990; rev. 3d ed., New York: Routledge, 2000), xi, xii, xiv. This edition specifically includes Jewish women; Joyce Antler, "Between Culture and Politics: The Emma Lazarus Federation of Jewish Women's Clubs and the Promulgation of Women's History, 1944–

1989," in *Unequal Sisters: A Multicultural Reader in U.S. Women's History,* ed. Vicki L. Ruiz and Ellen Carol DuBois (1990; 3d rev. ed., New York: Routledge, 2000), 519–41.

5. Paula E. Hyman and Deborah Dash Moore, eds., *Jewish Women in America: An Historical Encyclopedia,* 2 vols. (New York: Routledge, 1997). This *Encyclopedia* includes a very impressive annotated bibliography; Phyllis Holman Weisbard, "Annotated Bibliography and Guide to Archival Resources on the History of Jewish Women in America," in *Jewish Women in America: An Historical Encyclopedia,* ed. Paula E. Hyman and Deborah Dash Moore (New York: Routledge, 1997), 1553–86. This may also be accessed at http://www.library.wisc.edu/libraries/WomensStudies/jewwom/jwmain.htm. See also Phyllis Holman Weisbard, *Annotated Bibliography, 1997–2001, on the History of Jewish Women in America: A Supplement to Annotated Bibliography and Guide to Archival Resources on the History of Jewish Women in America* (2002); available from http://www.library.wisc.edu/libraries/WomensStudies/jewwom/jwsupplement.htm.

6. Statistics come from Jonathan D. Sarna, ed., *The American Jewish Experience* (1986; 2d ed., New York: Holmes and Meier, 1997), 359.

7. For a collection that spans the same chronology but focuses specifically on religion, see Pamela S. Nadell and Jonathan D. Sarna, eds., *Women and American Judaism: Historical Perspectives* (Hanover, NH: Brandeis University Press/University Press of New England 2001). In addition to the works included here, see also Baum, Hyman, and Michel, *The Jewish Woman in America;* June Sochen, *Consecrate Every Day: The Public Lives of Jewish American Women, 1880–1980* (Albany: SUNY Press, 1981); Jacob Rader Marcus, ed., *The American Jewish Woman: A Documentary History* (Cincinnati: American Jewish Archives, 1981); Sydney Stahl Weinberg, *The World of Our Mothers* (New York: Schocken Books, 1988); Linda Gordon Kuzmack, *Woman's Cause: The Jewish Woman's Movement in England and the United States, 1881–1933* (Columbus: Ohio State University Press, 1990); Susan A. Glenn, *Daughters of the Shtetl: Life and Labor in the Immigrant Generation* (Ithaca: Cornell University Press, 1990); Barbara A. Schreier, *Becoming American Women: Clothing and the Jewish Immigrant Experience, 1880–1920* (Chicago: Chicago Historical Society, 1994); Paula E. Hyman, *Gender and Assimilation in Modern Jewish History: The Roles and Representation of Women* (Seattle: University of Washington Press, 1995); Joyce Antler, *The Journey Home: Jewish Women and the American Century* (New York: Free Press, 1997); Hasia R. Diner and Beryl Lieff Benderly, *Her Works Praise Her: A History of Jewish Women in America from Colonial Times to the Present* (New York: Basic Books, 2002).

8. The phrase comes from Paula E. Hyman, "Gender and the Immigrant Jewish Experience in the United States," in *Jewish Women in Historical Perspective,* ed. Judith R. Baskin (1991; 2d ed., Detroit: Wayne State University Press, 1998), 313.

9. Scholars argue that African American women's history is characterized by "the resistance of Black women to racial and sexual oppression and exploitation"; Darlene Clark Hine, Wilma King, and Linda Reed, eds., *"We Specialize in the Wholly Impossible": A Reader in Black Women's History* (Brooklyn: Carlson Publishing, 1995), xii.

10. Evans, *Born for Liberty,* 35.

11. Ibid., 3, 67.

12. Anne Firor Scott, *Natural Allies: Women's Associations in American History* (Urbana: University of Illinois Press, 1991), 2, 131.

13. Alice Kessler-Harris, *Out to Work: A History of Wage-Earning Women in the United States* (New York: Oxford University Press, 1982), xi.

14. Cited in Sylvia Barack Fishman, *A Breath of Life: Feminism in the American Jewish Community* (New York: Free Press, 1993), 69.

15. See, for example, Eleanor Flexner, *Century of Struggle: The Woman's Rights Movement in the United States.* (Cambridge, MA: Harvard University Press, 1959); Ellen Carol DuBois, *Feminism and Suffrage: The Emergence of an Independent Women's Movement in America, 1848–1869* (Ithaca: Cornell University Press, 1978). On Jewish women's involvement in the suffrage movement, see Elinor Lerner, "Jewish Involvement in the New York City Woman Suffrage Movement," *American Jewish History* 71 (June 1981): 442–61. Note that only one Jewish woman, Ernestine L. Rose, was well known for her suffrage work; Carol A. Kolmerten, *The American Life of Ernestine L. Rose* (Syracuse: Syracuse University Press, 1999).

16. Not surprisingly, Jewish women did not affiliate with the Women's Christian Temperance Union.

17. See, for example, Barbara Welter, "The Cult of True Womanhood, 1820–1860," in her *Dimity Convictions: The American Woman in the Nineteenth Century* (Athens: Ohio University Press, 1976).

18. Mary Antin, *The Promised Land* (1912; rpt. ed., Boston: Houghton Mifflin, 1969), 205.

19. bell hooks, *Yearning: Race, Gender, and Cultural Politics* (Boston: South End Press, 1990), 33.

Part I

Sense of Place

American Jews date the founding of their community to 1654, when twenty-three Jews (the majority of them women, young people, or children) landed in New Amsterdam, now New York.[1] The early history of American Jewry is very much a history of the waves of migration and of how these new immigrants, men and women, sought to create a "sense of place" for themselves, to make a home for Jews and Judaism in America.[2]

In 1820, only 2,700 Jewish men, women, and children lived in the United States.[3] But, in succeeding decades, 150,000 others from Germany and elsewhere in Central Europe joined them. The 250,000 Jews who lived in the United States in 1880 made up but one half of 1 percent of the nation's population and little more than 3 percent of world Jewry. In the waning decades of the nineteenth century, these men and women and their American-born children found the places they had so carefully made for themselves challenged by a new migration of Jews from Eastern Europe.

American Jewish women intuited that a "sense of place gives equilibrium. . . . It is the sense of place going with us still that is the ball of golden thread to carry us there and back and in every sense of the word to bring us home."[4] The first essays in this reader find Jewish women constructing a "sense of place," shaping how as Jews they would call America home.

The effort to broaden our understanding of colonial and early America compelled historians of women to search for new texts.[5] Ellen Smith is no exception. In "Portraits of a Community," she reads diverse sources—painted portraits, letters, names, even a mustard pot—to show how "American and Christian forms were adjusted, adapted, and reinterpreted by the Jewish community to allow early American Jews to integrate into the larger culture even as they protected and strengthened their Judaism and Jewish identity." Paying special attention to evidence from early American Jewish women, Smith reveals just how closely their lives were braided into their communities. For them, objects became "keepers of memory." Whether reading their portraits or the remarkable correspondence of Abigail Franks (Bilhah Abigail Levy Franks, 1688–1746), Smith understands how Jewish women in the colonial and the early Federal eras shared with their fathers and brothers, husbands and sons, in the project of preserving Judaism in their new homes.

In the colonial era, women's agency in shaping Jewish life centered largely on the home. But, subsequently, Jewish women extended their influence beyond the confines of the home, as the next three chapters demonstrate.

In the early national period, for the first time, although not the last, Jewish women crafted a new communal institution, the Sunday school. In "The Lessons of the Hebrew Sunday School," Dianne Ashton sets that invention against the Protestant Sunday schools meant to keep poor immigrant children, some of them Jews, from disturbing the Christian Sabbath. When Rebecca Gratz (1781–1869), the foremost American Jewish woman of her day, founded the Hebrew Sunday School, in 1838, she thought it would teach Jewish children "how to defend their Jewish beliefs" against the missionaries trying to lure them to Christianity.[6] Whereas in the past teaching had been the province of Jewish men, the Hebrew Sunday School—and the network of schools it spawned in Jewish communities all over the United States—offered Jewish women their first public role in religious education at the same time that American Protestant and Catholic women were taking on new roles in educating their children. American Jewish women thus shaped a new, and, ultimately, highly gendered, role in transmitting Judaism to their sons and daughters.[7]

Jonathan D. Sarna finds that, in the last quarter of the nineteenth century, an American Jewish "religious and cultural awakening" was well under way, and he accords a particular place in it to American Jewish women. This time, Jewish women's agency extended beyond their homes or the single setting of the Sunday school and into their Jewish and the wider American communities. Women believed—and acted upon that belief—"that through their personal efforts American Judaism as a whole could be saved." Sarna's case studies include the Zionism of the poet Emma Lazarus (1849–1887); the remarkable career of the "girl rabbi of the Golden West," Ray Frank (1861–1948); and the founding of national Jewish women's organizations. Thus, he shows late-nineteenth-century Jewish women actors already engaged in what would, in the twentieth century, become some of the most influential developments of American Jewish life—the drive for a Jewish state, the movement for women's ordination, and the harnessing of the collective power of American Jewish womanhood into an array of national associations.

One such association is the subject of Faith Rogow's "Gone to Another Meeting," about the first of the Jewish women's clubs, the National Council of Jewish Women (NCJW). The excitement generated as thousands of women read papers at the 1893 Chicago World's Fair sparked a host of new women's organizations.[8] Among them was the National Council of Jewish Women. Its founder, Hannah Solomon, believed that "defending Judaism was the primary responsibility of every Jew." In the NCJW, Jewish women upheld Judaism before their Christian neighbors by joining in social reform to combat white slavery and to protect female immigrants. As acculturating American Jewish women borrowed from the gendered ideology of the women's clubs, they fixed a new place for themselves in American and Jewish life.[9]

NOTES

1. Arnold Wiznitzer, "The Exodus from Brazil and Arrival in New Amsterdam of the Jewish Pilgrim Fathers, 1654," *Publications of the American Jewish Historical Society* 44 (December 1954): 80–97.

2. The phrase comes from Eudora Welty, "Place in Fiction," in *The Eye of the Story: Selected Essays and Reviews* (1956; rpt., New York: Random House, 1978), 116–33. I am indebted to William R. Ferris for bringing this essay to my attention. See William Ferris, "Rediscovering America: Humanities and the Jewish Experience" (Plenary at the Association for Jewish Studies, 16 December 2001).

3. These and the population estimates that follow come from Jonathan D. Sarna, ed., *The American Jewish Experience* (1986; 2d ed., New York: Holmes and Meier, 1997), 359.

4. Welty, "The Eye of the Story," 128.

5. See, for example, Laurel Thatcher Ulrich, *A Midwife's Tale: The Life of Martha Ballard, Based on Her Diary, 1785–1812* (New York: Knopf, 1990); Karin A. Wulf, *Not All Wives: Women of Colonial Philadelphia* (Ithaca: Cornell University Press, 2000). On Jewish women in colonial America, see also Holly Snyder, "Queens of the Household: The Jewish Women of British America, 1700–1800," in *Women and American Judaism: Historical Perspectives,* ed. Pamela S. Nadell and Jonathan D. Sarna (Hanover, NH: Brandeis University Press/University Press of New England, 2001), 15–45; Aviva Ben-Ur, "The Exceptional and the Mundane: A Biographical Portrait of Rebecca Machado Phillips (1746–1831)," in *Women and American Judaism: Historical Perspectives,* ed. Pamela S. Nadell and Jonathan D. Sarna (Hanover NH: Brandeis University Press/University Press of New England, 2001), 46–80.

6. Dianne Ashton, *Rebecca Gratz: Women and Judaism in Antebellum America* (Detroit: Wayne State University Press, 1997), 121.

7. Cf. Ann Douglas, *The Feminization of American Culture* (New York: Knopf, 1978), 111–12; Carol K. Coburn and Martha Smith, *Spirited Lives: How Nuns Shaped Catholic Culture and American Life, 1836–1920* (Chapel Hill: University of North Carolina Press, 1999).

8. Anne Firor Scott, *Natural Allies: Women's Associations in American History* (Urbana: University of Illinois Press, 1991), 131.

9. As the first of the Jewish women's clubs, the National Council of Jewish Women has received a great deal of scholarly attention. In addition to Faith Rogow, *Gone to Another Meeting: The National Council of Jewish Women, 1893–1993* (Tuscaloosa: University of Alabama Press, 1993), see also Deborah Grand Golomb, "The 1893 Congress of Jewish Women: Evolution or Revolution in American Jewish Women's History?" *American Jewish History* 70 (September 1980): 52–67; Seth Korelitz, " 'A Magnificent Piece of Work': The Americanization Work of the National Council of Jewish Women," *American Jewish History* 83 (June 1995): 177–204; Eric L. Goldstein, "Between Race and Religion: Jewish Women and Self-Definition in Late-Nineteenth-Century America," in *Women and American Judaism: Historical Perspectives,* ed. Pamela S. Nadell and Jonathan D. Sarna (Hanover, NH: Brandeis University Press/University Press of New England, 2001), 182–200.

Chapter One

Portraits of a Community
The Image and Experience of Early American Jews

Ellen Smith

> Your Pictures Are quite an Acceptable Pres[en]t you
> will make my Compliments of thanks to Mrs. Franks
> for those of her Family and allsoe to Mast[e]r and Miss
> Franks and the whole Family Was in raptures Your
> Father walks abouth the Parlour with Such Pleasure a
> Viewing of them As is not to be Expresst Most of your
> Acquaintance knew Your Picture but I will ingeniously
> Own I don't find that Likeness but it was designed for
> you and that Pleases me to have it.[1]

Naphtali Franks was twenty-four years old and had been living in England for nearly seven years when, in 1739, his mother, Bilhah Abigail Levy Franks, wrote him her joyful thanks for the receipt in New York City of his painted portrait. Perhaps remembering Naphtali as a child, Abigail did not readily recognize her oldest offspring in his portrait. Perhaps thrilled to see an adult visage in his son and business partner, Naphtali's father, Jacob Franks, exhibited joy beyond expression. The portrait hung in the family parlor—a private, domestic space where the family could have intimate contact with the image of the absent son and brother. Abigail would never see him again. For the rest of her life, the portrait of Naphtali through his letters and the portrait of her son on her parlor wall were all she had of him.

As with many of the comments in her surviving correspondence, Abigail Franks made astute observations about portraiture and its function in colonial and early American society. The image served in lieu of her absent son. As portraits continued to be exchanged, they became keepers of memory and images of family continuity for generations to come. Portraits were ways of meeting people with whom face-to-face contact could not take place. They were intimate private objects, commissioned for personal, not public, display.

Abigail also recognized that, beyond triggers of memory and affection, portraits were conscious constructions—commissioned by the sitter and "designed for" him or her. Naphtali's own choices of self-representation therefore pleased Abigail, even if they did not match her images of him. And the personal connection, the joy, the "raptures" that portraits brought to a family permanently separated across the Atlantic Ocean gave them a value beyond any commercial or personal exchange undertaken.

From the earliest days of European settlement in North America, portraits were brought over and, soon after, made.[2] From the earliest days of Jewish settlement in North America, painted portraits became a part of Jewish culture. Astounding numbers of them were made. Hannah London documented 185 portraits and miniatures in 1927 and documented 113 miniatures in 1953.[3] The sheer volume of surviving portraits of early American Jews speaks to the important role they played in colonial Jewish culture, though they were expensive and only the wealthier families could afford them.

Painted portraits realize a complex of interactions and decisions among the sitter, the artist, and the notion of the audience for whom the painting is intended. Whereas most early Jewish settlers in North American emigrated from European Jewish communities where portraits seem not to have been part of the Jewish cultural norm, in the American colonies, beginning in the first half of the eighteenth century, Jewish families began to imitate the tradition of commissioning portraits that pervaded the non-Jewish mercantile culture around them.[4] The portraits— painted by the same artists and based on the same models, mezzotint books, and colonial tastes—therefore looked like the portraits of non-Jewish sitters of the era. Nor was this conventional presentation—this act of self-representation—accidental. Early American Jews intended to be seen as looking like the broader community. The portraits declared the sitters' desires to be seen, and to be seen as looking like everyone else. Early American Jewish portraits were visual declarations that this small band of North American Jews were part of, rather than apart from, the colonial, mercantile society in which they lived.

But colonial and early American Jewish identity was complex, and painted portraits are only part of the picture colonial and early American Jews drew of themselves. A broad array of individual and community self-portraits were consciously constructed by the early American Jewish community. Letters and correspondence reveal less formal, more intimate, profiles of individuals. Naming patterns reinforced family connections through traditional Jewish practices, as painted portraits connected families in less traditional ways. Business records, wills, and religious and institutional documents all reveal aspects of the communities' aspirations and character. All these portrait forms, too, are self-referential and self-descriptive, conscious self-profiles for their contemporaries and future generations. The types of Jewish community and identity they describe change over time and with place. But the constancy of the great experiment of early American Jewry—establishing a functional equilibrium between being Jewish and being part of the larger colonial and early American society—informs the complex portrait of the Jewish community during their first two centuries in America.

Jews first settled in North America in 1654. But the society they brought with them had been formed in Europe and shaped again by a sojourn in Brazil. Exiled from Spain in 1492 and forced to convert and practice "underground Judaism" in

Portugal less than a decade later, many Jews, and forced Jewish converts, fled to Holland and, through the Dutch West India Company, on to Brazil. For twenty-four years there, they enjoyed economic, social, and religious freedom unparalleled in their recent European experience. When Brazil fell to Portugal in 1654, the Jews again set sail—this time for Holland, England, the Dutch West Indies, and the small Dutch community of New Amsterdam on the mouth of the Hudson River in North America.

From the beginning, Jewish identity in America was complicated. Early Jews in the colonies were refugees of trans-Atlantic traders, not intentional pilgrims; they were strangers and sojourners in many strange lands. Their stays in the colonies were often impermanent and transient, [as they moved] from city to city and between nations, as business dictated.

Jewish colonists also emigrated from many countries, bringing with them differences in religious traditions and even languages. Spanish and Portuguese Sephardic Jews, whose religious and common native language was Portuguese, were joined in almost equal numbers by Central European, German, English, and Yiddish-speaking Ashkenazic Jews, whose numbers surpassed those of the Sephardim by 1720.[5] The standard "solution" to a pluralistic pre-Revolutionary American Judaism was to establish a single synagogue-community in each location with a sufficient Jewish population. Sephardic liturgy and ritual predominated, but the congregations themselves were more usually dominated by Ashkenazim.

Business interests, which generally brought all Jews west to the New World, oriented them back to the east, to England, Europe, Africa, and the Caribbean. A national "home" identity could thus be varied and unstable. Upon what, then, could colonial Jewish identity be based? In the national and religious amalgam—the portable religious crazy quilt that defined pre-Revolutionary American Jewry—there was no stable or standard norm. European models of origin were varied and far away. And American religious and cultural patterns—pluralistic, nearby, and alluring—presented many challenges to the basic foundations of traditional Jewish identity.

Jews arriving in New Amsterdam had already begun undergoing the process that would in many ways define the social and religious history of American Jewry: the elongated experiment of building, preserving, and transmitting Jewish community in a new environment, of reconciling Jewish tradition and American realities.

The Levy-Franks portrait series captures these dilemmas and ambiguities of colonial American Jewish identity as they were lived. Two great portrait series survive of the family: a series of seven painting of three generations of the clan and a lively series of letters exchanged between Abigail Franks and her son Naphtali between 1733 and 1748.

The painted portraits, still in their original frames, are the oldest surviving portraits of colonial American Jews, and the oldest family-series portraits to survive in all of American painting. Probably executed in the mid-1730s and attributed by present scholars to Gerardus Duyckinck, the paintings look to English aristocratic models for their costume, background, and pose.[6] Patriarch Moses Raphael Levy and his son-in-law Jacob Franks are both portrayed as English gentlemen.

Similarly, the portraits of Grace Mears Levy, Moses's second wife, and Bilhah Abigail Levy Franks, wife of Jacob Franks and oldest child of Moses and his first wife, Richea, display many of the conventions of English portraiture of that period. Three portraits of the Franks children likewise emulate English models and replicate the clothing and posing of their parents, Jacob and Abigail Franks.[7]

To read the Levy-Franks portrait series, then, is to receive visual signals and confirmation that this is a well-established, mercantile family, consciously placing themselves within the representational conventions of English portraiture and the emerging English bourgeois class, and part of a broad range of early eighteenth-century colonial American portraits that represent men and women and children in similar costumes and poses. There is no symbol, no gesture, no background, no prop, that identifies these people as Jews. Their portraits in paint evaporated any overt signal that Jewishness formed part of the identity they put on display in the Levy and the Franks homes.

All these portrait conventions and prototypes fit the colonial Jewish self-image. The Levy-Franks portraits accurately represent the family's understanding of its members as successful merchants, familial partners, and European bourgeoisie. These were not mere aspirations; they were painted strokes of reality. The Levy-Franks family of the portraits, Jews or not, were comfortable as American colonials.

Still, the portraits present only half of the picture. The tensions embedded in forging a Jewish colonial identity were real and found expression in other material forms.

The Levy-Franks family lived in an early-eighteenth-century New York City inhabited by successful and long-established Dutch and English mercantile families. Their neighborhood in Dock Ward housed some of the city's most prominent families. Approximately 8,500 people lived in New York in 1731; about 10,000 in 1737. Among them, only twenty Jews were recorded in 1734.[8] The Jewish community owned a synagogue building, Shearith Israel, on Mill Street, dedicated in 1730, and a burial ground off Chatham Square, purchased in 1728. But the community was tiny, fragile, and transient.

If the Levy-Franks portraits are confident expressions of the social status and place of the family in America, their letters to their oldest son, Naphtali, in England, are not. In deeply intelligent prose, Abigail ponders the future of her family as Jewish in the colonial environment and puzzles whether its best interest ultimately reside in Europe or colonial America.

Abigail treasures the broad freedom to achieve and mingle in the colonies. Critical of England's rigid class structure—"You will not allow any thing right but wath has the Advantages of being bred amongst you"—she worries that Naphtali has accepted it too easily. She revels in the openness of New York ("It Gives me a Seceret pleasure to Observe the faire Charecter Our Familys has in the place by Jews and Christians").[9] Nevertheless, the Franks family in America never achieved the financial stability of the Franks and Levy families in England, and, one by one, Jacob and Abigail sent their children to England in order to prosper. The confident look toward England expressed in the portraits assumes a more melancholy and ambiguous gaze in the correspondence. Abigail and Jacob probably never saw their adult children after their departure, nor any of their English grandchildren.

Abigail's letters are also an extended conversation on the fit and fate of Judaism in colonial New York. The Levy and Franks families were active members of Shearith Israel and supported Jewish causes throughout the colonies. They practiced traditional Judaism, honoring the Sabbath, keeping kosher, and keeping the Jewish holidays. Abigail urged Naphtali in England to keep up with his "morning Dev[otio]ns" and cautioned him to avoid nonkosher food, warning him off even his uncle's table.[10] She rejoiced in the Sabbath and made sure her daughters and sons received instruction in Hebrew.[11] Jacob addressed Jewish interests in his letters, even conducting business correspondence in Yiddish and Hebrew as the occasion demanded.[12]

But Abigail also worried for the future of Judaism in America, and for the future of her children as Jews. In the open air of colonial America, and likely under the influence of the broad range of English philosophers and novelists she read, she yearned for a modernized Judaism. "I Must Own I cant help Condemning the Many Supersti[ti]ons wee are Clog'd with and heartly wish a Calvin or Luther would rise amongst Us," she mused in 1739.[13] On the ground, she was scathing in her critique of the New York Jewish community, calling its ladies "a Stupid Set of people" and despairing about the pool of Jewish suitors available for her daughters.[14] When David Gomez, of the powerful, successful, and, to some degree, rival New York Jewish family, showed interest in her daughter Richa, Abigail dismissed him as "a Stupid wretch." Even "if his fortune was much more and I a beggar noe child of Mine . . . Should Never have my Consent and I am Sure he will never git hers."[15]

But the cost was high. With a limited pool of Jewish marriage prospects, Abigail's disdain for most of them, and the entire Franks family's desire to be part of the larger New York community, it was perhaps inevitable that two of her children would take non-Jewish spouses. The oldest daughter, Phila, was the first. In the fall of 1742, Phila secretly married Oliver Delancey, son of a prominent and successful New York Huguenot merchant family. For six months, they kept the match secret, but, in the spring of 1743, Phila announced the deed and went to live with her husband. Abigail never recovered. Letters to Naphtali spoke of her sense of betrayal and of her pain.[16] It was not to be the last hurt she would feel. Her son David married Margaret Evans, the Christian daughter of one of Abigail's close friends, and settled in Philadelphia. Her young children seem never to have married at all. Even her sons Naphtali and Moses, who married their English first cousins (both named Phila Franks), watched as all of their own grandchildren left the Jewish faith. Of Jacob and Abigail Franks's more than two dozen grandchildren, not one of them appears to have passed on Judaism to his or her descendants.[17]

The Franks family thus defended America even as they looked to England for models of financial success and social status, and they defended their Judaism even as they sought to adapt and belong to the larger colonial American society. The self-portraits they left us suggest they never fully belonged in either place. The confident, English-gazing portraits belied the anxieties of maintaining that posture while enduring as Jews. Their colonial identity and their Jewish identity strained under the pressures of colonial and Christian realities. Neither their commissioned portraits in paint nor their self-portraits in words are complete one without the other. The conscious self-representations of the Levy-Franks family—constructed images of self created in paint and in ink—reflect the full palette of desires, demands, and loyalties that competed in forming a colonial Jewish identity.

But other paths were taken by other colonial Jews. The Gomez family were contemporaries of the Franks family in New York, more successful in business, more adapted as Jews to the colonial environment. Descended from Isaac Gomez, an exile from Spain, the family had emigrated to New York by the late seventeenth century; by the mid-eighteenth century, they were the wealthiest Jewish family, and among the wealthiest New York families, of their era.

Like most of the colonial Jewish families, the Gomezes were traders, merchants, investors in real estate, and owners of shipping fleets. They consciously expanded their trading networks through judicious marriages: in the first American generation into Sephardic families from Jamaica, Barbados, and Curaçao, and in the second through a series of first-cousin marriages that consolidated their wealth and the connections that linked family, business, and religion. This religious and economic stability, resulting from a strategy of intermarriage among themselves and other North American Sephardic families, was complemented by their economic focus on North America. Whereas the Franks family functionally existed in New York in the shadow of the family's English enterprises, the Gomez family cast their financial lot with the land to which they had emigrated. They struck deep roots, were active in the community's religious affairs, and occupied the most prominent seats and offices in Shearith Israel for nearly a century. Because they had secured—even ensured— Jewish identity within the home, the family, and the religious community, the potential dangers of the marketplace and gentile world to Jewish identity and survival were significantly lessened. The Gomezes thrived both as colonial Americans and as Jews.

Their adaptability is winsomely portrayed in a silver mustard pot owned by the Gomez family in New York. Commissioned for the family and imported from England, the piece is a fine example of late-eighteenth-century silver, with its cabriole feet, hinged lid, engraved Gomez family initials, and blue glass insert to hold condiments. But, in the New World, the piece took a new identity. Removed from access to European-made Jewish ritual objects, the Gomezes adapted the mustard pot to necessary Jewish ritual use, employing it as an *etrog* holder—a covered receptacle to protect the *etrog*, or citron, one of the four plants and fruits used in worship during the Jewish fall harvest festival of Sukkoth. The pot descended through six generations of the Gomez family with the attributed use intact, serving in its way as a portrait of the values and determination of the Gomezes to simultaneously thrive as Americans and survive as Jews.

Other objects likewise are material expressions of the efforts of colonial Jews to declare and preserve their Judaism. Headstones in Jewish cemeteries declare a variety of Jewish virtues and attest to the literal survival of the Jewish people.[18] Synagogue architecture blended local architectural exteriors with Jewish architectural interiors.[19] Jewish books were common in early American Jewish households, even if they consisted mostly of prayer books and family Bibles. Jewish books also began to appear in translation, reinforcing an emerging, if problematic, American-Jewish culture. Isaac Pinto, *hazzan* (religious leader) of Shearith Israel, despaired that Hebrew was not well understood by colonial Jews of the mid-eighteenth-century and subsequently produced *Prayers for Shabbath, Rosh-Hashanah, and Kippur* (1765–66) in English.[20]

But the central, and most sacred, printed object in any Jewish community is the Torah scroll, the hand-written parchment upon which the Five Books of Moses are written in Hebrew and set sections of which are read and studied both communally and privately each week. The earliest known Torah in America arrived in New Amsterdam in 1655. Torah scrolls were acquired by communities, large and small, throughout the colonial era. But Torah scrolls were also held privately, and their importance both to Jewish and to family identity is indicated by their unique mention and disposition in wills, even though no other Jewish objects are discussed. Lewis Gomez, of New York, for example, bequeathed to his oldest son, Mordecai, in his 1740 will "one pare of Silver Adornments [*rimonim*—silver ornaments for the top of Torah scrolls] for the five Books of Moses." David Gomez, another of Lewis's sons, likewise inherited a Torah and *rimonim* through his wife's family, which he then bequeathed in 1769 to his brother Isaac. Isaac specifically bypassed his oldest, unmarried, female child, Esther, in his 1770 will, leaving the Torah and its accoutrements to his oldest surviving son, Mattathais.[21] Rachel Luis, one of four women whose will survives, left money "to buy a Sefer Tora [Torah Scroll] for the use of the Kall Kados [Holy Congregation] of Shearith Ysraell in New York."[22] No other objects—not portraits, not plate, not furnishings—receive the unique attention in writing and succession accorded these central objects of Jewish identity.

Jewish self-consciousness declares itself in a variety of other objects as well. *Ketubbot,* traditional Jewish wedding contracts, continued to be prepared in the colonies, and a few survive from these earliest years. Rebecca Hendricks, like most young girls of her era, learned needlework and made samplers to practice her skills. One of her samplers survives, a neat counted-thread cross-stitch on twenty-count linen. Text for colonial samplers commonly derives from biblical phrases and aphorisms. But Rebecca picked a unique text, one that reflected a sense of herself not only as a colonial young lady of breeding but also as a Jew. In neatly spaced letters, her embroidery reproduces verses 1–14 of the Seventy-eighth Psalm, including the phrases "He commanded our fathers that they should make them known to their children . . . That they might [not] forget the works of God but keep his commandments" (Ps. 78: 5,7).

The most ancient sign of Jewish identity within the Jewish community is the circumcision of its males, as commanded to Abraham by the Lord in Genesis. Traditionally taking place on the eighth day after a boy is born, circumcision seems to have been widely maintained throughout the colonial era.[23] Two circumcision sets, in the collections of the American Jewish Historical Society, survive from early America.

Nevertheless, actual early American Jewish ritual objects, or records of their manufacture, sale, and use, are extremely rare. The objects that do survive, like the portraits themselves, are primarily domestic or synagogue pieces—material expressions of Jewish identity and practice nevertheless confined to the private spaces of home and Jewish worship.

Public expressions of Jewish identity and self-representation also existed, although they tend to lack a tangible quality. Naming patterns declared Jewish identity openly. While surnames are notoriously unreliable ways to identify Jews in colonial America, traditional Jewish first-naming patterns—naming children after deceased relatives—continued long after the Revolution and resisted more fashionable gentile naming trends. For example, the names Bilhah, Richea, Rebecca, and Shinah endure into the mid-nineteenth-century over four generations of the Etting-Myers-Cohen family. Perla, Rebecca, and Levi remain given names in the Sheftall family through the early national period.[24]

Wills, normally formulaic colonial legal documents, occasionally revealed insistence on public declaration, and even accommodation, to Judaism. Among forty-one surviving eighteenth-century New York City wills made out by Jews, sixteen bequeathed money to Jewish organizations, including the synagogue, cemetery, Hebrew school, and poor relief.[25] Several witnesses to wills insisted on being "Sworn upon the five books of Moses," rather than the Christian Bible.[26] Esther Benzaken dated her 1790 will by the English and Jewish calendars.[27] All of these written declarations were outside the normal Christian and legal conventions, indicating conscious intentions to integrate markers of Jewish identification into the public sphere.

Other behaviors, sometimes elusive, also indicate public, and perhaps, confident, signaling of Jewish identity. Jacob Franks and Aaron Lopez are among several merchants who strived to observe the Jewish dietary laws of *kashrut,* which mandated eating only meat butchered according to Jewish law and not mixing meat and milk products. They also refused to conduct business on the Jewish Sabbath.

All of these material and behavioral portraits suggest that "Jewishness" was not hidden in colonial America but that contemporary American and Christian forms were adjusted, adapted, and reinterpreted by the Jewish community to allow early American Jews to integrate into the large culture even as they protected and strengthened their Judaism and Jewish identity. The experiments were variously successful. But the efforts to make a living Judaism work in the broadly pluralistic and open society of early America are exhibited in the varieties of forms of self-representation—the varieties of portraits of colonial American Jews—produced by and for the community.

If the portrait of the colonial American Jewish community suggests an effort to craft a Jewish-American identity generally along conservative lines and within traditional forms, a very different portrait emerges of the post-Revolutionary community. The American Revolution marked a watershed for the American Jewish community, as it did for American society as a whole.

Colonial Jewish society had been characterized by small, often transient populations, usually engaged in trans-Atlantic trade, whose religious and economic security was often reinforced by marriage within the family. Although the colonial Jewish community was itself pluralistic, in every colonial city with a Jewish population, Sephardic and Ashkenazic families shared the same single synagogue. They were modest in their innovations to traditional Judaism, usually bending existing forms, rather than creating new ones.

Much of this changed with the American Revolution. Demographically, the war shifted traditional Jewish population centers, providing a new mix of people and a change of cities with concentrated Jewish populations. Philadelphia, Baltimore, Richmond, and Charleston were winners in the reshuffling. Simultaneously, Jewish population numbers rose, likely from higher birth rates rather than from new immigration, although the reasons are not fully understood. Overall, the postwar American Jewish population reconfigured, relocated, and grew, adding scale and, most important, more diversity to the mix.

The war also changed the nature of business traditionally conducted by colonial Jewry. Severed ties with England confounded prior patterns of trans-Atlantic trade. At the beginning of the nineteenth century, Jewish economics turned more local and become more modest in scale, with most Jewish merchants in the early Republic concentrated on domestic commerce. The young nation, engaged in establishing its own infrastructure, provided new opportunities for local manufacturing, merchandising, and trade. Jewish life incorporated this new diversity of population, space, and economic options. The era of a singular, hierarchical, East Coast Jewish merchant class was at an end.

The political theory guiding the American Revolution and the early Republic also directly affected Jewish self-understanding in the new nation. Concepts of democracy, self-determination, political power residing with the people, and written constitutions defining rights and responsibilities of the citizenry had a direct impact on the practice and structure of American Judaism. Beginning in the 1790s, synagogues began to adopt written constitutions and to structure their governance along the federal model. Multiple voices, with multiple opinions, began to characterize a formerly singular synagogue structure.

Indeed, one of the hallmarks of the post-Revolutionary Jewish community was its fracturing. Whereas before the Revolution every city with Jewish populations had but one synagogue, after the Revolution, communities generated several synagogues. Some were started by break-away groups; others were founded as new organizations representing a particular point of view, age group, or taste for a specific form of worship or liturgy. By 1795, Philadelphia became the first city in America to have two synagogues. By 1850, New York City alone had fifteen.[28] Jewish communal services and organizations formerly allied with the synagogue— including education, burial societies, poor relief, and social groups—now proliferated as autonomous institutions.[29]

This diversity within the Jewish population and a rising sense of individual identity and interests paired with the population's desire to fit in with the democratic values and behaviors of the surrounding Christian and secular worlds. Their optimism is reflected in the portraits painted of American Jews after the Revolution.

Based on European and American Romantic and neoclassical models, the portraits now display a broader range of poses, costumes, and individual expressions. The paintings reflect the growing differentiation and self-consciousness within the Jewish community itself.

The portraits move from stylized colonial images where status, occupation, and gendered relationships are revealed through common, conventional symbols to portraits that celebrate individuality. Costume and clothing aid the effort. In male sitters, dress most commonly signifies social or occupational standing. Among women, clothing appears even more distinctive, perhaps signaling perceived personalities and societal roles in lieu of occupational status. Whether the elaborated (actual) costume of Shina Solomon Etting or the more fanciful costume of Rebecca Gratz, many post-Revolutionary portraits of women move outside the family-centered, passive, gendered images that dominate colonial portraiture and continue beyond.[30]

Indeed, the sheer number of portraits of early American Jewish women can surprise. They make up a considerable proportion of the known surviving images of early American Jews. Most were commissioned as part of a husband-wife pair or as part of a family series or with their children. But, after the Revolution, a noticeable minority of portraits were commissioned of women on their own, outside a domestic context. Rebecca Gratz, one of American Judaism's most significant educators and organizational founders, remained unmarried and so had no other context. But Rachel Phillips Levy, one of twenty-one children and herself mother of ten, was also painted as a beautiful, lithely costumed, free-spirited young woman. Traditional women's roles and status did not substantially change after the Revolution; women's portraits still focused on virtue, domesticity, and status. But portraits of women also signaled that aspects of opportunity and image, aspects of individual character and achievement, did open more publicly.

So did a focus on children. In the early-eighteenth-century Levy-Franks portrait series, the children assume the same poses, costumes, and expressions as their parents. In the early-nineteenth-century portraits of the Solomons children, the context of the family portrait series is gone, and the individual characters of the children pop off the canvas. Nineteenth-century American society would become more child-focused as it progressed; the Solomons children, Adolphus Simeon and Mary Jane, painted in 1828, both herald the trend and announce that even society's youngest members were occasionally seen—and represented—as individuals slightly outside formulaic boundaries.

If the image of American Jews had changed with their identity and experience, their gaze had likewise shifted. On the walls of Monticello, Thomas Jefferson's eighteenth-century estate in Virginia, hung a series of paintings owned by Monticello's nineteenth-century owner and restorer, Uriah Phillips Levy. Among them was the spectacular portrait of his mother, Rachel Machado Phillips Levy, painted by the Swedish artist Adolph Wertmüller about 1795. Rachel, declared a great beauty in America and England, is depicted in a late-eighteenth-century shepherdess costume. Her posture and gaze are animated; the large, flowered Marlborough-style bonnet focuses attention to her face. It is very much the portrait of an individual, and one treasured by her son.

But, alongside Rachel, on Monticello's walls, hung a series of other kinds of paintings, indicative of the new kinds of visual images—historical, environmental, and religious—coming to dominate mid-nineteenth-century America. Their titles included "The Children of Israel Collecting Manna in the Desert," "Judith and the Head of Holofernes" [*sic*], "Holy Family," "David with the Head of Goliath," "A Rural Scene," and "The Wreck of the Frigate Madison."[31] These, too, Uriah valued, and he drew from them, as he did from Monticello itself, in fashioning both his deep patriotism and his strong sense of Jewish identity. Jewish identity—Jewish identification—no longer resided exclusively in the faces of family members, in portraits of the tribe. Jewish-American identity now encompassed the full range of history and metaphor that were becoming the nation's own self-created identity and myth.

By the 1840s, photography, silhouettes, and other less expensive forms of image replication had supplemented portraiture as the primary form of human representation. But temperament as well as technology had moved beyond the portrait form. Where colonial Jewish portraiture had signaled experiments with imitation and belonging, and Jewish portraiture of the early Republic had explored the growing diversity and individuation of the American-Jewish community, by 1830 portraiture itself had fallen away as a prime carrier of the American-Jewish image and experience. An explosion in American-Jewish publications, institutional development, and new immigrations lay on the near horizon. Portraits would remain part of the social fabric of nineteenth- and twentieth-century American-Jewish communities, but no longer would they be signal markers of American-Jewish identity and self-image.

Yet, in the eras they had dominated, painted portraits told the tale of the early American-Jewish community. As consciously created artifacts, they reflected the Jewish community's desire to be seen as part of the broader community—to be seen as looking like everyone else. In the daily, domestic context in which they were viewed, the portraits spoke to the felt ambiguities of melding American and Jewish life. The portraits never sat placidly on the walls. They marked the changes, tensions; and the creativity exhibited by the American Jewish community in creating an evolving American-Jewish identity. And, in the words of Abigail Levy Franks, the portraits brought "raptures" and joy "not to be Expresst."

NOTES

1. Abigail Franks to Naphtali Franks, October 17, 1739, in *Letters of the Franks Family (1733–1748)*, ed. Leo Hershkowitz and Isidore S. Meyer (Waltham, MA: American Jewish Historical Society, 1968), 66.

2. See, for example, Jonathan L. Fairbanks, "Portrait Painting in Seventeenth-Century Boston," in *New England Begins: The Seventeenth Century*, ed. Jonathan L. Fairbanks and Robert F. Trent, 3 vols. (Boston: Museum of Fine Arts, 1982), vol. 3: 413–79; Wayne Craven, *Colonial American Portraiture: The Economic, Religious, Social, Cultural,*

Philosophical, Scientific, and Aesthetic Foundations (Cambridge, England: Cambridge University Press, 1986); and Peter Benes, ed., *Painting and Portrait Making in the American Northeast* (Boston: Boston University Press, 1995).

3. Hannah R. London, *Portraits of Jews by Gilbert Stuart and Other Early American Artists* (New York: William Edwin Rudge, 1927), and Hannah R. London, *Miniatures of Early American Jews* (Springfield, MA: Pond-Ekberg Company, 1953.)

4. European Jewish portraiture does, of course, exist, but is not spread as commonly throughout the Jewish community. See, for example, Alfred Rubens, *Anglo-Jewish Portraits: A Biographical Catalogue of Engraved Anglo-Jewish and Colonial Portraits from the Earliest Times to the Accession of Queen Victoria* (London: Jewish Museum, 1935.)

5. Jacob R. Marcus, *Studies in American Jewish History* (Cincinnati: Hebrew Union College Press, 1969), 50.

6. The dating and artistic attribution of the Levy-Franks portrait series are extremely complex. See Erica E. Hirshler, "The Levy-Franks Family Portraits," *The Magazine Antiques* (November 1990): 1025–27; and Erica E. Hirshler, "The Levy-Franks Family Colonial Portraits," Exhibition brochure (Boston: Museum of Fine Arts, 1990). Abigail Franks often writes of the exchange and progress of portraits with Naphtali—and of her son Moses's training and talent in music, drawing, and painting on glass; see Hershkowitz and Meyer, *Letters of the Franks Family*, 41, 48, 49, 55. Oddly, she makes no mention of this large series of portrait commissions in her surviving letters of 1734, 1735, or 1736, possibly calling the dating of the Levy-Franks portrait series into question.

7. For a discussion of the English visual sources for the Levy-Franks portrait of "David and Phila Franks" not exhibited in this exhibition, see Norman C. Kleeblatt and Gerard C. Wertkin, comps., *The Jewish Heritage in American Folk Art* (New York: Universe Books, 1984), 31; and Erica Hirshler, "The Levy-Franks Family Colonial Portraits," Exhibition brochures, figs. 5, 6, and 7.

8. Hershkowitz and Meyer, *Letters of the Franks Family*, p. xix. New York was the third most populous colonial city, behind Boston and Philadelphia.

9. *Letters of the Franks Family*, Abigail Franks to Naphtali Franks, October 17, 1739, 65; Abigail Franks to Naphtali Franks, May 7, 1733, 4.

10. Ibid., Abigail Franks to Naphtali Franks, July 9, 1733, 7, 8.

11. Ibid., Abigail Franks to Naphtali Franks, June 21, 1741, 87, and Abigail Franks to Naphtali Franks, October 7, 1733, 13.

12. Ibid., Jacob Franks to Naphtali Franks, November 22, 1743, 125, 126, xxix.

13. Ibid., Abigail Franks to Naphtali Franks, October 17, 1739, 66. Abigail read widely, continually supplied by Naphtali. Among her favorite authors were Pope, Joseph Andrews, Fielding, Smollett, Dryden, Montesquieu, Addison, and *Gentlemen's Magazine*. She admonished Naphtali not to send her "Idle Trash"; see Abigail Franks to Naphtali Franks, November 20, 1738, 64.

14. *Letters of the Franks Family*, Abigail Franks to Naphtali Franks, December 20, 1741, 100.

15. Ibid., Abigail Franks to Naphtali Franks, December 5, 1742, 110.

16. Ibid., David Franks to Naphtali Franks, April 1, 1743; Abigail Franks to Naphtali Franks, June 7, 1743; Jacob Franks to Naphtali Franks, November 22, 1743.

17. Overall estimates of intermarriage among Jews before the Revolution are difficult to determine. Malcolm Stern estimates that almost 16 percent of marriages by Jews in America before 1840 were with Christians and that most Jews (up to 87 percent) who intermarried assimilated into Christian society. Cited in Eli Faber, *A Time for Planting: The First Migra-*

tion 1654–1820 (Baltimore: Johns Hopkins University Press, 1992). This number is lower than that for many other religious groups of the era.

18. See David de Sola Pool, *Portraits Etched in Stone: Early Jewish Settlers, 1682–1831* (New York: Columbia University Press, 1952).

19. Rachel Wischnitzer, *Synagogue Architecture in the United States: History and Interpretation* (Philadelphia: Jewish Publication Society, 1955). Only New York and Newport had colonial synagogue buildings. Post-Revolutionary synagogues proliferated, as did synagogue architectural experimentation and reform.

20. Isaac Pinto, trans., *Prayers for Shabbath, Rosh-Hashanah, and Kippur* (New York, 1765–66).

21. Leo Hershkowitz, *Wills of Early New York Jews (1704–1799)* (New York: American Jewish Historical Society, 1967), 62, 86, 125, 130, 152.

22. Ibid., 51.

23. See, for example, the "Record Book 1776–1843" of Jacob Raphael Cohen, in the Papers of Jacob Raphael Cohen, American Jewish Historical Society.

24. See, for example, the genealogical charts of colonial Jewish families in Malcolm H. Stern, *First American Jewish Families: 600 Genealogies, 1654–1988* (3d ed., Baltimore: Ottenheimer, 1991), 67, 223, 267.

25. Hershkowitz, *Wills of Early New York Jews,* 161, 186, 197.

26. Ibid., specifically the following wills: Samuel Levy, 1719, 29; Joshua Isaacs, 1744, 71; Isaac Levy, 1745, 76; Phillip Isaacs, 1756, 96; Mattathais Gomez, 1784, 154; and Manuel Myers, 1799, 211.

27. Ibid., 193, 209.

28. Quoted in Jonathan Sarna, "The Impact of the American Revolution on American Jews," in *Jews and the Founding of the Republic,* ed. Jonathan D. Sarna, Benny Kraut, and Samuel K. Joseph (New York: Markus Wiener, 1985), 67.

29. Ibid.

30. For a discussion of gender and colonial portraiture, see Deborah I. Prosser, " 'The rising prospect or the lovely face': Conventions of Gender in Colonial American Portraiture," in *Painting and Portrait Making in the American Northeast,* ed. Peter Benes (Boston: Boston University Press, 1995), 181–200.

31. Photostat copy of the "Inventory of the Personal Estate of Uriah Phillips Levy," 1862, Papers of Uriah Phillips Levy, American Jewish Historical Society. The inventory lists twenty-one separate oil paintings, but not that of Rachel Phillips Levy.

Chapter Two

The Lessons of the Hebrew Sunday School

Dianne Ashton

The sweetest memorial raised to [those who first plead for the female poor of this congregation] will be . . . this institution.

Rebecca Gratz, 1835

Throughout her life, Rebecca Gratz blended ideas drawn from her own American milieu and her personal understanding of Judaism to resolve conflicts and capitalize on her talents. The Hebrew Sunday School (HSS) exemplified that process more successfully than any other institution she led. By the time she was in her fifties, Gratz knew that, because her brothers' children did not practice Judaism, no Jew would carry the Gratz name to future generations. Her organizations provided her firmest reassurance of an American Jewish future. The school she had urged the Female Hebrew Benevolent Society (FHBS) women to found conveyed her own understanding of Judaism, an understanding shaped by the events and literature in America's women's culture and by her own religious experiences.

Growth

From 1840 to 1855, Philadelphians experienced "unprecedented civic violence" as the population mushroomed with ever growing numbers of immigrants. Debarkations at the port quintupled, from a little over three thousand to more than nineteen thousand. By 1850, almost a third of the city's population was foreign born, usually from Ireland, Germany, or England. Although the city experienced an economic depression at this time, population pressures created a housing boom that added several new neighborhoods west and north of the city: Nicetown, Germantown, Mount Airy, Chestnut Hill, Mantua, and Powelton. By 1844, the only building on the south side of Chestnut Street below 8th Street that was still used as a dwelling was converting its first floor into a store. In 1854, the city and county of Philadelphia were consolidated into one political unit.[1] As part of the effort to maintain peace among an increasingly diverse citizenry, religious groups sought new ways to bring a self-discipline grounded in faith to the general populace. Previously unenforced laws restricting public activities on Sundays found new advocates and new teeth.

Amid these pressures from immigration, poverty, and geographic dispersion, the HSS blossomed. Between 1840 and 1870, when Pennsylvania's Sunday Sabbath laws successfully restricted public activities, the HSS, like local Christian Sunday schools, tried to keep poor children from creating a nuisance on Sundays.[2] Gratz adapted the school's style and structure from those used by the Protestant American Sunday School Union (ASSU). Although the union's schools were originally designed to serve the children of the many unaffiliated Christian families, children in families who attended church regularly often preferred to join their friends in Sunday school rather than accompany their parents to church, and Sunday school teachers quickly claimed that in their schools "rich and poor meet together."

As middle-class families increasingly joined churches, smaller schools serving individual congregations replaced large, central Sunday schools.[3] Like the ASSU, the HSS was a mission school intended to reach all Jewish children and was never affiliated with any one congregation. Few antebellum synagogues could sustain an effective teacher-student ratio and usually they could be relied on only for bar mitzvah preparation tutorials. The HSS, by contrast, boasted a large, dedicated staff, taught in English, and supplemented the education synagogues offered.[4]

Isaac Leeser was distressed by the abysmal state of Philadelphia's Jewish education and at first thought it impossible for a Sunday school to deliver a truly thorough Jewish education. By 1840, however, at the HSS's second year-end exam, Leeser enthusiastically supported the HSS, approving new textbooks written by the Peixotto sisters, visiting classes, and writing his own catechism for their use. He criticized Rodeph Shalom's use of German instead of English for school instruction because he believed it prevented "fusion of the new immigrant with the native and older residents of the community." If the Jews of Philadelphia continued to be divided by language as well as national origin and class, mutual understanding and cooperation would be nearly impossible.[5]

Leeser was delighted to see women take an active role in Jewish education and advance the religious education of Jewish girls. He believed that if girls were educated with "a proper view of the duties they must perform . . . as loving mothers, the happiness of society would be placed on a much surer foundation of love and kindness."[6] Leeser's attitudes toward education reflected his personal history. After his father died in 1820, he lived in the home of Abraham Sutro, rabbi and superintendent of Hebrew schools in Munster, Germany, and its environs, accompanying Sutro on many of his visits to the area schools. In 1823, after Leeser relocated to Richmond, Virginia, he assisted Rev. Isaac Seixas, minister of the Spanish-Portuguese congregation there.[7] His personal and professional experience in Europe and in America convinced him that the HSS was a valuable new approach to Jewish education.

By 1841, with over one hundred students—approximately 80 to 90 percent of the city's English-speaking Jewish children—the school outgrew the Peixotto home. Mikveh Israel offered rooms in the synagogue, but Gratz refused to make it the school's permanent home.[8] She dreamed of a school used by all Jewish children in the city, and the Mikveh Israel synagogue on Cherry Street was too far from the neighborhoods of poorer Jews living south of Walnut and north of Spring Garden Streets. Also, Mikveh Israel's members were the elite of Philadelphia Jewry, and poorer parents and children might have been uncomfortable attending. Thus, after a brief stint in Mikveh Israel, the school moved for a short time into the Phoenix Hose Company and, in 1854, into the new Touro Hall, which became known as the Hebrew Education Society (HES) Building at 7th and Wood.[9] Judah Touro, a New Orleans philanthropist, had bequeathed twenty thousand dollars to the HES to carry out its plan for a Jewish day school that would teach both religious and secular subjects. After purchasing and renovating what was formerly a Baptist church, the HES opened its doors.[10]

In sharp contrast to the conflicts that synagogues engaged in over worship customs, language, family seating, congregational governance, and reform—subjects that divided many nineteenth-century Jewish congregations—the HSS had a broadly inclusive understanding of the nature of Judaism, and this fostered steady growth. Sabato Morais, minister of Mikveh Israel after Leeser, marveled that Gratz made the school "acceptable to hundreds of her . . . coreligionists, irrespective of their extraction or mode of worship."[11] HSS students earned prizes for synagogue attendance and no one synagogue received preferential treatment. The synagogues were acknowledged and respected, but the goals of the Sunday school went beyond support for synagogues.[12]

The HSS offered a new, American style of Judaism. Although the school's female teachers broke with the tradition of male religious leadership, few of Philadelphia's Jews objected. Established and supported by the local Jewish elite, the school offered a blend of popular American culture and Jewish tradition. Like the Protestant rhetoric that filled the public press and turned up in many conversations, the school's curriculum was bibliocentric. Its lessons focused on Jewish principles, the creed (the *Sh'ma* prayer), and biblical authority.[13] The school merely continued in a systematic, public, and authoritative way the historic tradition in which stories from Scripture had been taught informally to children by knowledgeable mothers. Like Victorian culture and feminized religion, the school emphasized the importance of domestic piety, the heart's longing for and devotion to God, and God's loving kindness—all ideas that were staples of Jewish private meditations, prayers, and mystical traditions. The HSS presented them as the core of mainstream Judaism itself, and in the school curriculum they took on a public, standardized form. By emphasizing the more individualistic elements of Jewish devotion, the school tailored Judaism to fit the common American belief that religion was a matter of personal conscience.[14]

This curriculum grew out of Gratz's religious conviction and from the fact that none of the school's founders were qualified to teach more than the Bible. Indeed, Gratz's family prayer book included a daily prayer asking God to mercifully "implant the holy law in our hearts that we may not sin," a phrase that might serve as the theme of the HSS early lessons.[15] Because no English-language Jewish textbooks or primers existed in America, the ASSU provided the HSS with copies of the *King*

James Bible and a catechism, *Child's Scriptural Questions,* both used in their Protestant schools. Gratz and her fellow teachers adapted these texts by tearing out and pasting over passages referring to Jesus. Gratz herself composed a book of daily morning prayers that were likely taught at school.[16] Rachel Peixotto Pyke wrote a Jewish version of the catechism, and Simha wrote an *Elementary Introduction to the Hebrew Scriptures.* Watching this struggle for educational materials, Leeser set to work on a catechism and his own English translation of the Hebrew Scriptures.[17]

In the Philadelphia HSS, the school day began with an assembly during which the superintendent led the opening prayer and read the Bible portion for the day. The selection most likely corresponded to the week's Torah portion read in the synagogues the day before. After the assembly, students broke into classroom groups in which teachers conducted lessons based on the assembly readings and tested students on their catechism. Each grade had its own additional educational goals, and students demonstrated their mastery of their work at the annual public exams, which, until 1876, were held on Purim. The youngest students learned to recite the creed (*Sh'ma*), middle classes studied catechisms, and older classes mastered individual books of the Bible. In 1841, for example, students were tested on Exodus, Ruth, and Esther. That highly unusual selection of Bible readings indicates the HSS's commitment to inculcating an appreciation for the importance of women in Jewish religious history. While Exodus is a foundational book for all of Judaism, Ruth and Esther point to women's contribution to Jews' understanding of their relationship to God and to each other.[18]

The HSS rewarded students for academic achievement and good conduct with colored tickets that could be traded for books or for small items made by the teachers. Teachers wrote the Ten Commandments on colored silk or illustrated a neatly written psalm. As the number of available books on Jewish topics grew, the school bought them for their library and gave them, as well as popular children's fiction, as rewards for punctuality, good behavior, and academic excellence to their best and oldest students.[19]

The annual exam included a call to young women to join the society's "labor of Love" and teach in the Sunday school. By 1861, twenty-five teachers served 250 students, and, in that year, Gratz asked for "every willing-minded among the daughters of Israel in the congregations of our people who desire to assist," promising that all who could "donate two to three hours punctually on Sunday mornings without sacrifice of their domestic duties" would find a "blessed reward in the consciousness of doing good." In addition, volunteers would "acquire while they impart a knowledge of the Laws and Customs and duties of our Holy religion as taught to Moses and our forefathers." In this plea, Gratz asked women to move their sense of duty beyond their families—not to the detriment of family life, but to improve the Jewish community and their own knowledge of their religion.

Jewish women's self-fulfillment, community service, and domestic responsibility were fused in the HSS. Gratz and her associates viewed it as an opportunity to extend their familial responsibilities and power to serve the children of the entire community. The national basis of Jewish life evident in the Bible allowed Jewish women to blend the rhetoric of patriotism, used to express the American ideal of republican motherhood, with the expectations for spiritual development expressed in the Victorian ideal of true womanhood. Because she grew up a Philadelphian in the Revolutionary era, Gratz easily absorbed patriotic rhetoric and saw that ideologies about women could serve the best interests of both Jewish women and the Jewish community as a whole. Through their work, the HSS women hoped to prompt a spiritual renewal among Philadelphia's Jews.[20]

Political and Religious Boundaries

Many Jews believed that efforts to enforce Christian morality with secular law would eventually curtail their freedom, regardless of their patriotism.[21] One way to combat Christian prejudice was for Jews to welcome openly non-Jews when they arrived on synagogue doorsteps asking to observe the proceedings. Rabbi Simon Tuska, the first American college graduate to become a rabbi, published *Stranger in the Synagogue,* providing "guidance in Jewish worship for the non-Jew."[22] But, by the 1850s, both Isaac Leeser and Isaac Mayer Wise believed the evangelical tone of American society posed a threat to American Jewish freedom.[23]

The Sunday Sabbath law cases, reported in the popular press, demonstrated that Jews could lose their right to observe Jewish religious customs.[24] Many states strictly enforced these laws. In Pennsylvania, Seventh Day Adventists were routinely fined or jailed for working on their farms on Sundays. In other states, Jews were arrested for working in their shops on Sunday.[25] In the *Occident,* Leeser kept a close watch on the progress of these cases and published case summaries, judges' decisions, and his own analyses. Two cases against Jews in Richmond and Charleston in 1846 were decided in favor of the defendants. Judges found that the offenses—working in their shops on Sunday—did not pose a threat to the order of the town and therefore the local police ordinances forbidding Sunday labor were in violation of citizens' rights to free labor and religion. In Richmond the ordinance was struck down in favor of increased security on Sunday to control any violence that might erupt between blacks and whites. But, in Charleston, the city appealed to the state supreme court and won. In his decision, Judge O'Neal insisted that, since shopkeeping on Sunday "shock[ed] the moral sense of Christians," it was "therefore an act of licentiousness." He ruled that the Sunday Sabbath should be enforced because it was basic to the Christian moral system, the only basis of good morals he knew. As such, it was basic to the morals of the country. Leeser responded immediately, saying that if O'Neal had read the Bible he would know that "Christianity has no moral order not already known to Jews"; consequently, their morality must be as "pure as the dominant church."[26]

That year, the *Occident* reprinted an article from the *Philadelphia Public Ledger* on the decision of Pennsylvania's Supreme Court in the case of *Specht v. the Commonwealth.* Specht, a farmer and Seventh Day Adventist, had been fined for "following his avocation on Sunday." The opinions of the court focused on two main points. Judge Bell explained first that the well-being of every society requires a day of rest, and, since most of the inhabitants of the state already rested on Sunday, the state could reasonably require all its citizens to do so without interfering with their religious freedom, since it did not ask them to perform any religious rites. He found the law reasonable, and therefore constitutional. However, Judge Coulter, of the same court, wrote that the law was "constitutional because [it] guard[s] the Christian Sabbath from profanation."[27]

These decisions brought a new element into the legal battle over the Sunday Sabbath, for they allowed workers to be jailed for offending the customs of their neighbors. Leeser was outraged. As the Adventists went to jail for harvesting their wheat, he wrote: "There is tyranny in this,—and . . . galling as there is no redress, the majority not likely to be willing to repeal a law, which, though evidently against the spirit of the Constitution, has been sanctioned by the Supreme Bench in deference to popular clamour."[28]

This Pennsylvania decision, and others like it, diminished Leeser's respect for judges. In 1846, under the headline "Ohio: Liberty of Conscience Triumphant," he had hailed Ohio's Sunday Sabbath laws, which exempted those who conscientiously observed Saturday.[29] But, twelve years later, when these laws were tested in *Rice v. Cincinnati,* he wrote that no government court should be deciding matters of religious law. The court found that Mr. Rice had not conscientiously observed any Sabbath, because, although he had gone to synagogue, his sons continued to work in his business, and he profited from their labor. Remembering the uses found in Europe for government courts that had become tribunals on Judaism, Leeser now saw this former hallmark of liberty as unfair and unconstitutional. It would allow Christian judges to determine matters of Jewish law.

After the *Specht* decision in 1848, Leeser ran articles on the customary and nonbinding nature of the Sunday Sabbath and its laws. These included a variety of exemptions, such as federal mail transport and cases acquitting Sunday workers whose jobs were considered essential, like Schuylkill River lockkeepers and blast furnace tenders. In 1856, Philadelphia police ignored Sunday statutes and allowed citizens to hire horses, sleighs, and drivers to enjoy the first great snowfall of winter. If these cases could override the statutes, then clearly they were founded on custom, not on constitutional or divine law.[30]

As minister of Mikveh Israel, Leeser also was in a position to fight Sunday Sabbath laws on religious grounds. After years of reading arguments among Christians and after completing his own translation of the Hebrew Bible, he felt ready to argue that the Sunday Sabbath laws had always been politically motivated, not the result of divine command. In 1858, he ran an article from a Christian paper, the *Sabbath Recorder,* in the *Occident,* asserting that the earliest Christians did not keep Sabbath on Sunday, that the Lord's Day commemorating the Resurrection was in Europe a day of recreation. When Protestants began reading the Bible, the writer noted, they found the command for a Sabbath and made it Sunday simply through custom, a custom that had been established by the Catholic Church to differentiate Christian society from Jewish society. Lesser also quoted the Christian editor of the *Cincinnati Commercial:* "If a Sabbath is at all commanded, which it surely is, the day, no less than the institution itself, is fixed by the will of God; wherefore all attempts at investing Sunday with a religious sanction must be fruitless."[31]

Once the battle began to be fought on religious ground, Leeser was on home territory. By arguing for the legitimacy of the commands of the Hebrew Bible, he could address both the right of Jews to protect their religious liberty and what he believed was the appalling trend toward nonobservance openly endorsed by some of the new reformists. He would not have to argue for absolute freedom of conscience—an argument also used by the reformists against the legitimacy of Talmudic law—but could reassert the absolute moral authority of the Bible, a position popular with both Christians and Jews. He found the greatest model for republican government in ancient Israel and so saw the ideas of American liberty rising from biblical revelation. Just as both Christianity and the reformists allowed local adherents to shirk their religious duties, so judges who allowed local custom to override constitutional liberties shirked their duty to maintain the commandment in Numbers 15:15–16: "There shall be one law for you and the stranger among you." In this way, Leeser insisted that Jews' rights were not based on tolerance by the majority but by right as citizens of the nation. Therefore Jews could never be legally required to abandon their rights as citizens in order to protect the sanctity of the majority's religion.[32]

Yet, by arguing finally for unhampered liberty, Leeser knew he was also protecting the rights of Jewish reformers to continue to grow in strength, despite his conviction that they were "false prophets." But that, after all, was an in-house matter, a problem of Jewish faithfulness to be addressed by Jews. The far more pressing problem was to protect the rights of observant Jews so that they were not encouraged by sheer economic necessity to violate so basic a commandment as the preservation of the Jewish Sabbath. This had to be done without antagonizing the Christian populace. Leeser supported the Hebrew Sunday School in part because it used the enforced Sunday Sabbath, women's spirituality, and the bibliocentrism of American culture to advance knowledge of Judaism among Jewish children and women.

Theological Sources and Perspectives

Gratz's blend of American ideas about domesticity, women's roles, and piety, along with Jewish bibliocentric spirituality, continued to shape the HSS curriculum throughout the nineteenth century.[33] From 1838 to 1900, the curriculum focused on the unity of God, the Ten Commandments, and stories from Hebrew Scriptures in translation. Teachers discussed life after death, obedience, gratitude to and love for God, the thirteen principles of the faith (written by Maimonides in the twelfth century and included in Jewish prayer books), the importance of piety, and concern for the Jewish community.

A traditionally observant commitment to Judaism is evident in the superintendent's report read at the twenty-sixth annual exam, in May 1864. It may have been read by Gratz, although she had resigned the post the previous October. "No worldly condition exempts . . . [Jews] from the . . . Holy Law. . . . In every Jews' heart, in every Jews' house, the Holy Law abides. God has given it as an inheritance to everyone born in Israel and the proud distinction of possessing such a treasure animates every heart to the faithful performance of its requirements."[34] This was a prescription for Jewish life, not a description of real Jewish devotion in Philadelphia. Gratz and the other leaders of the HSS thought the haphazard faithfulness of many Jews posed a problem for their own souls and for the future of Jewish life in America. They believed that Jews who were not proud of Jewish identity and faithful to traditional observance left themselves vulnerable to Christian missionaries. They thought poor Jewish immigrants were at the greatest risk, because they might abandon Judaism in their confusion over adjustment to American life. Gratz was also worried about conversions through marriage of Jewish Americans of her own class. Thus, the superintendent's report asserted the HSS's importance to a Jewish community in which, as her audience knew, Jewish life had not attained its goals.

Gratz personally evaluated every student and assigned each one to the most suitable class. Each school day began and ended in the same manner. At 10:00 A.M., a bell was rung and students stood as Gratz recited a brief opening prayer she had composed. After the prayer, students sat down and sang a hymn along with their teachers. Students and teachers then divided up into their separate classes, where teachers registered students' attendance. Lessons then began, during which teachers were admonished to keep the noise level as low as possible. As in many ASSU schools, several different class groups often met in separate areas of a single large room. Students could not leave the room or their places without a teacher's permission. At 11:45 the bell was rung again and books were collected. Gratz, as superintendent, then questioned students on the previous week's portion of Scripture, read a new portion, and sang another hymn with the students. Students then rose and repeated after the superintendent a hymn and a prayer. Teachers meanwhile marked lessons and distributed reward tickets to those students who had performed perfectly. Students were to be dismissed "in an orderly manner." Offering highly disciplined small classes conducted in English, the HSS presented a Jewish education light years away from the chaos reigning in congregational schools like that of Rodeph Shalom.[35]

The opening prayer recited each Sunday focused on the virtues that contributed to social order. Its three-part message was, first, that reverence and gratitude are essential to religious life; second, that orderly behavior resulted from faith in God; and, third, that students' faith in God would bring them food, clothing, and help in daily life.[36]

Rachel Peixotto Pyke's catechism, *Scriptural Questions for the Use of Sunday Schools for the Instruction of Israelites,* was especially devoted to this combination of faith and social order. It opened with a long poem titled "Rebekah Parting with Her Son Jacob." Its message was that a child's loyalty to the God of Abraham was crucial to a Jewish mother's happiness and honor. The poem left the students with the impression that children of Israel are also the children of Rebekah, and it reminded them of the familial foundation of Judaism. Pyke's catechism's twenty pages were devoted to teaching young children to control emotions and behavior while developing an idea of God as a parent. Missionaries had been focusing their attention on Jews in Philadelphia since 1824, and by 1838 the number of Jewish immigrants and indigents had mushroomed and missionaries were more active than ever. More children were bound out to tradesmen or left without parental supervision, no doubt leaving the wealthier teachers with the impression that students needed an extra reminder of maternal concern for their fidelity to Judaism. The equation of loyalty to Judaism and loyalty to one's mother presented in "Rebekah Parting with Her Son Jacob" is the heart of a child's Jewish ethnic identity. Pyke's catechism taught rudimentary principles of belief and tried to instill a sense of loyalty to, and identification with, the Jewish people.[37]

Students also used Simha Peixotto's *Elementary Introduction to the Hebrew Scriptures for the Use of Younger Children*. Peixotto adapted this from a text issued by the ASSU and gave Leeser final approval of her work. Because it was originally a Protestant book, its structure helped Jewish children respond to missionaries with some knowledge of what to expect. It began with a basic definition of English terms such as "Bible" and "Scriptures," explained English titles of biblical books, and took the students through the Hebrew Bible. The presentation was a simple question-and-answer format:

> *Q:* What is the first book of the Bible called?
> *A:* Genesis.
> *Q:* What is the meaning of the word Genesis?
> *A:* Creation.
> *Q:* Of what does the first book in the Bible give an account?
> *A:* Of the Creation.
> *Q:* Who created the heavens, the earth, and all that therein?
> *A:* God.[38]

Leeser also wrote a catechism, translated and adapted from Eduard Kley's *Catechismus der Mosaichen Religion*.[39] Leeser intended the book to be for eight-to fourteen-year-olds, but Gratz and her staff used the book with older children because his rhetoric was too adult and long winded. Divided into ten chapters with two appendices, Leeser discussed "Religion in General, The Mosaic Religion in Particular, God and His Attributes, The Relation of Man to God, The Law Revealed through Moses, The Moral Law, The Ten Commandments, The Kingdom of the Messiah, The Life after Death, Repentance and Atonement, The Ceremonial Law, and The Jewish Creed." Leeser wanted to teach Judaism while explaining its place among the religions of the world. He also wanted Jews to understand their own place in a non-Jewish, but largely Bible-based, American culture.[40] The festivals of Hanukkah and Purim, theologically of little importance but certainly the most fun for children, were celebrated annually at the school.[41]

Morning prayers composed by Gratz emphasized the children's utter dependence on God, who was presented as loving and merciful but demanding obedience. These prayers explain that God knows what is in the children's hearts, as well as what is on their lips. They ask God to help the children control their tempers both at home and in public and to help them develop faith and wisdom. In all of these respects, the prayers conform to both traditional Judaism and much of Christianity and present an understanding of God that the children could share with many of their Christian neighbors. However, the prayers are distinctive in the ways in which God is identified. Traditional Jewish appellations such as Rock, Redeemer, Creator, Savior, and Father are repeated throughout the prayers, but none of the prayers refers to God by another very common Jewish metaphor, King. A child of the American Revolution, Gratz remembered early America's vehement renunciation of earthly kings and all they stood for. To acculturate immigrants and their children, she may have felt it was best not to use the King metaphor.[42]

Ironically, although the HSS was the first step in radically changing the role of Jewish women by giving them a public, institutionalized role in Jewish religious education, women of the society opposed religious reform and viewed themselves as traditionally observant Jews. Like Leeser, they believed they adapted only the outer form of Judaism to American needs without changing traditional Jewish beliefs and women's piety. Although the HSS gave a public teaching role to women, it in no way broke with Jewish tradition by offering Talmudic study to women. By teaching in the vernacular instead of the "sacred tongue" (Hebrew) and by limiting their lessons to Bible stories, moral lessons, and principles of the faith found in any prayer book, the women stayed well within the bounds of traditional Jewish women's culture and religion. Only their formal role in a public educational institution was new.

Catechisms stirred a conceptual revolution in Jewish teaching in both Europe and America. Previously, Jewish educators used the Hebrew Bible as a reading primer. When that was mastered, students began to study its interpretations and analyses through rabbinic literature. By doing so, the sacred literature set the categories of thought by which all else was measured and analyzed. Catechisms, on the other hand, inserted Jewish answers into questions arising from categories of thought outside Judaism, especially from the philosophy of religion as taught in nineteenth-century German universities. This philosophy saw religion as a general category with many particular varieties, each with components such as faith, morality, and worship.[43]

The rules for decorum, pedagogy, and lesson planning set by the school conveyed the serious regard for religion held by Gratz and the other faculty. Gratz impressed upon the faculty that they must teach as much by example as "by precept." Through their manner they would communicate to their students the importance of the principles of Judaism. In training her faculty, Gratz advised them to be "patient, forbearing, and affectionate." She urged them to be zealous in their work and not to become discouraged by "dullness, obstinacy, . . . ill temper" on the part of students or by "the unreasonableness of parents."[44]

Gratz organized the school time—two hours each week—to enable her to control each day's program while allowing individual teachers to tailor their lessons to the abilities of their own students. Students and faculty experienced both the unity of the school and the individual attention necessary for the sort of education Gratz hoped to provide. The low teacher-student ratio, usually fewer than ten students per teacher, led to the sort of bond between teacher and student, and among students, that Gratz believed would deepen each person's emotional tie to the school and to Judaism. "If but a tenth [of your students] be impressed with the importance of divine truth—then you will not have labored in vain," she told her staff. . . . [45]

Crossing Gender Roles through Piety

Gratz and the HSS managers created a curriculum that emphasized women's importance in Judaism by drawing on many resources. Lesser preached that women must have a religious education to qualify them for the "holy . . . [and] noble task . . . [of] sooth[ing], calm[ing]) and . . . render[ing] happy the rugged career of a father, a brother, a husband, or a child."[46] His approval must have been crucial to winning the support of the many Ashkenazic (northern European) Jews, by far the majority, who were accustomed to a religious community that was, at least among its religious leadership, highly differentiated by gender, because among these Jews, female prayer leaders commonly led women in synagogue worship.[47] In addition to his theological supervision of the textbooks, his concern for promoting fledgling Jewish religious institutions and cultural resources, and the influence on him of strong women leaders such as Aguilar, Gratz, and the Peixotto sisters, Leeser also perceived Jewish standards for piety in a way that was nearly identical with those of Victorian culture.

Despite the HSS founders' personal objections to Reform, books by reformers of one stripe or another found their way into the school's library, probably because so few English-language materials existed, and the library grew into an eclectic mix of approaches to Judaism. Several nineteenth-century Reform leaders claimed a commitment to "securing perfect equality between woman and man before God," although women were not ordained until 1972.[48] Samuel Pike's 1801 *Hebrew Lexicon* was joined by Rev. Dr. Leo Merzbacher's 1855 prayer book, the first American Reform liturgy compiled by a rabbi and used in New York's Reform Temple Emanu-El.[49] An 1838 travelogue describing life in Syria was joined by an 1860 anonymous work, *Thoughts Suggested by Bible Texts,* and later by the British Rev. Abraham P. Mendes's 1870 catechism, *The Law of Moses.*[50] As late as the 1870s, the more traditional HSS used the *Hebrew Sabbath School Visitor,* a children's magazine published in Cincinnati by the Reform rabbi Max Lilienthal, as a pedagogical aid. Although the Philadelphians' contract with Lilienthal originally stipulated that they would be able to return free of charge any issues they found offensive, they renewed their subscription yearly.[51]

One regular column in the *Visitor* was "Little Nellie's Catechism." It described the efforts of Nellie, a Jewish Sunday school student, to train her younger brother and sister in Judaism by repeating to them the lessons she had learned in school. Nellie's mother listened appreciatively to her children while wishing that she herself could have attended such a school. Nellie's father was usually out of town on business. Stories in which daughters led their families in religious worship and education appeared more and more in popular literature, both Christian and Jewish, in the second half of the century. Just as in the antebellum era a mother's religious leadership was made plausible through nursing and educating her own children, the Sunday school movement that swept across the country made it plausible that both male and female children might instruct their parents on religious matters.[52]

Victorian culture in England and the United States often pulled Jewish men and women in directions opposite to those expected by Jewish tradition. While nineteenth-century Jewish men often simplified synagogue service and their domestic religious leadership, Jewish women appear to have taken on more responsibility for communal and familial religious life. Although the descriptions of piety in Victorian and traditional Jewish culture were nearly identical, in Jewish tradition women often shouldered financial duties so that men might fulfill religious obligations of prayer and study. Victorian culture presumed men to be immersed in financial responsibilities, while women led their families into piety.[53] By teaching a Victorian American Judaism, the HSS offered a way for American Jewish women, both rich and poor, to demonstrate that "true women" could be religious Jews.

In 1845, a new *Parent and Teachers Assistant* designed to aid "Jewish mothers and teachers [in] imparting . . . the first ideas of the Deity" to young Jewish children appeared. Its unknown author developed a basic theology out of images and experiences central to the lives of women. God is first explained as the Creator who, while able to create out of nothing, created "things in such a way that they can reproduce themselves."[54] While men, too, can create things, manmade things lack the power to reproduce. The author underscored the point by inviting students to consider that their own mothers were once the babies of their mothers, and so on for generations. Finally, after asserting that God can see the part of us that "thinks, feels sorry or glad, pleased or displeased," because God is "pure spirit that fills all space," the book concluded by inviting children to trust the "Holy Bible" as the source for "all that God has made known to men about himself."[55] Published in Philadelphia with an introduction by Isaac Leeser, the book was recommended to women in Jewish congregations and by teachers in the HSS.

The Women

The minutes of the Hebrew Sunday School Society show that the founders continued to direct the organization as it grew. Most were from Mikveh Israel, the city's oldest congregation, and from the educated, middle-class merchant and business families. By and large, their own education had been the "papa's study" sort, with some additional time at women's academies, but in these families home lessons included instruction to develop managerial skills.

The Gratzes, Phillipses, Peixottos, and Harts led synagogues and other community organizations, and encouraged their daughters to become involved, too. Miriam Gratz had brought her daughters with her into the Female Association at its founding in 1801. Other mothers from among these families acted similarly.[56] Gratz participated in and continued this tradition, bringing other young women of her class into the Philadelphia associations she began and guiding her niece Miriam Moses Cohen in establishing a Hebrew Sunday School in Georgia.

The founders participated in the mission that popular American culture gave them: to civilize a fledgling nation in disarray through their influence in education and religion. Gratz, Ellen Phillips, Louisa B. Hart, Simha Peixotto, and others gained self-respect and a sense of purpose from this task. It was not simply that community service gave these unmarried women an occupation they would not otherwise have had because they were not mothers. Motherhood was a rite of passage for nineteenth-century women, and this was a passage to adult status that Gratz and her unmarried cohorts did not make. The school gave single women something to do, but success such as the HSS enjoyed did not emerge from mere busywork, and these single women did not lightly choose service over motherhood. In fact, the HSS resolved conflicts in the women's own religious identities.

Victorian American culture dictated that, to be respected, women must be chaste and spiritual domestic guides, and this ideology was used by white Protestants to justify their superiority over both immigrants and nonwhites.[57] But Jewish culture claimed that God commanded Jewish women to be mothers and Jewish men to lead their families' lives. The HSS merged selected American ideas with those of Judaism and developed a structure that combined both worlds, using the Bible to both guide and instruct. In its bibliocentric curriculum, the HSS was an early expression of a genuinely American Judaism.

Gratz and her cohorts prized their independence and were proud of their accomplishments. Their association with each other involved much more than just class-time meetings; it gave them enormous satisfaction. Gratz called her work in the school "the crowning happiness of my days." Ellen Phillips and Louisa B. Hart both served as officers and board members until the end of their lives. Simha Peixotto was so attached to her work that she fought against resigning her board membership at seventy-eight, saying, "I am not a dead head and can serve in the holy cause."[58] Each of these women sat in the women's gallery at Mikveh Israel. Friendships nurtured in worship matured into the HSS.

NOTES

1. Elizabeth M. Geffen, "Industrial Development and Social Crisis, 1841–1854," in *Philadelphia: A Three Hundred Year History,* ed. Russell Weigley (New York: Norton, 1982), 307–314.

2. Isaac Leeser, "Progress of Persecution in Pennsylvania," *Occident* 13 (1855): 496–505, Free Library of Philadelphia.

3. Anne M. Boylan, "Presbyterians and Sunday Schools in Philadelphia, 1800–1824," *Journal of Presbyterian History* 58, no. 4 (1980), 299–310; Boylan, *Sunday School: The Formation of an American Institution* (New Haven: Yale University Press, 1988), passim; Robert Lynn and Elliot Wright, *The Big Little School: Sunday Child of American Protestantism* (New York: Harper and Row, 1971).

4. Minutes of the Hebrew Sunday School Society, 1838–1879, American Jewish Archives, Cincinnati, Ohio.

5. Isaac Leeser, *Occident* 9 (1851), quoted in David Uriah Todes, "The History of Jewish Education in Philadelphia, 1782–1873: From the Erection of the First Synagogue to the Closing of Maimonides College," Ph.D. diss., Dropsie College for Hebrew and Cognate Learning, 1952.

6. David Uriah Todes, "The History of Jewish Education in Philadelphia," 9.

7. Ibid., 8; Lance Sussman, *Isaac Leeser and the Making of American Judaism* (Detroit: Wayne State University Press, 1995), 23–24.

8. Diane E. King, "Jewish Education in Philadelphia," in *Jewish Life in Philadelphia, 1830–1940,* ed. Murray Friedman (Philadelphia: ISHI Press, 1983), 241; Lewis Allen wrote to Gratz: "The building back of the synagogue is being finished. . . . I have the pleasure of offering the Sunday School one or two rooms for the accommodation of the school." Gratz replied: "I will confer with the teachers . . . and inform Mr. Allen whether we can accept his kind offer." Lewis Allen to R. G., October 11, 1841, her note inserted, Gratz Family Papers, Collection no. 72, box 15, American Philosophical Society, Philadelphia, PA.

9. In a letter to Grace Nathan (October 23, 1842, Rebecca Gratz Papers, Manuscript Collection no. 236, American Jewish Archives), Gratz wrote that classes had moved into the synagogue but that this was only a temporary measure. Joseph Rosenbloom, "Rebecca Gratz and the Jewish Sunday School Movement in Philadelphia," *Publications of the American Jewish Historical Society* 47, no. 2 (1958): 71–75; Minutes of the Hebrew Sunday School Society, 1838–1875, American Jewish Archives; "Brief History of the Hebrew Sunday School Society," box 4, folder 18, MS 6, p. 2, Philadelphia Jewish Archives–Balch Institute of Ethnic Studies.

10. King, "Jewish Education in Philadelphia," 241.

11. Leon Jick, *The Americanization of the Synagogue* (Waltham, MA: Brandeis University Press, 1976); Samuel Morais, *Address to the Hebrew Sunday School on the Life and Character of Miss Rebecca Gratz* (Philadelphia: Collins, 1869), 7, American Jewish Archives; Michael A. Meyer, *Response to Modernity: A History of the Reform Movement in Judaism* (New York: Oxford University Press, 1988), 225–55.

12. R.G. to Miriam Moses Cohen, April 12, 1843, Rebecca Gratz Papers, Manuscript Collection no. 236, American Jewish Archives; Minutes of the Hebrew Sunday School Society, 1838–1879, American Jewish Archives.

13. A translation of the opening line of the *Sh'ma* is: "Hear oh Israel, the Lord our God, the Lord is One." The assertion of God's unity was considered Judaism's creed.

14. Bahya Ibn Pakuda, *Duties of the Heart* (Northvale, NJ: J. Aronson, 1996); *Meditations and Prayers,* trans. Hesther Rothschild (Original title, *Preires d'un Coeur Israelite*), revised by Isaac Leeser (Philadelphia: n.p. 1864); A. Z. Idelsohn, *Jewish Liturgy and Its Development* (New York: Schocken Books, 1975); Gershom Scholem, *Major Trends in Jewish Mysticism* (New York: Schocken Press, 1961); Ann Douglas, *The Feminization of American Culture* (New York: Avon, 1977) 143–310; Amanda Porterfield, *Feminine Spirituality in America: From Sarah Edward to Martha Graham* (Philadelphia: Temple University Press, 1980), 51–82; Carroll Smith-Rosenberg, *Disorderly Conduct: Visions of Gender in Victorian America* (New York: Knopf, 1985), 129–63.

15. David Levi, "Grace after Meat," *Form of Prayers,* 169, Mikveh Israel Archives, Philadelphia, PA.

16. "Monday Morning," "Wednesday Morning," "Morning Prayer Thursday," Gratz Family Papers, Collection no. 72, box 9, American Philosophical Society.

17. Lance Sussman, "Another Look at Isaac Leeser and the First Jewish Translation of the Bible in the United States," *Modern Judaism* 5, no. 2 (1985): 159–90; Joseph Rosen-

bloom, "Rebecca Gratz and the Jewish Sunday School Movement in Philadelphia," *Publications of the American Jewish Historical Society* 47, no. 2 (1958): 71–75; Barnett Elzas, "Leaves from My Historical Scrapbook," *Sunday News* (Charleston, SC) February 16, 1908, Rebecca Gratz Papers, Biographies File, American Jewish Archives; Simha Peixotto, *Elementary Introduction to the Hebrew Scriptures for the Use of Hebrew Children* (Philadelphia, [1839?]), Hebrew Sunday School Society Collection, Philadelphia Jewish Archives–Balch Institute of Ethnic Studies, Philadelphia, PA; Maxwell Whiteman, "The Legacy of Isaac Leeser," in *Jewish Life in Philadephia, 1830–1940,* ed. Murray Friedman (Philadelphia: ISHI Press, 1983), 26–47, esp. 41–42. By 1838, the ASSU had moved away from its early authoritarian style, which focused on memorizing the Bible passages and discipline. Sunday schools had become a children's arm of the revival movement, and children began to experience conversion. The goals of the schools changed from keeping the children from sin to actually preparing them for their conversions. Corporal punishment was dropped, Bible lessons were organized logically around central ideas, and teachers explained acceptable interpretations to the students. Students were rewarded for good work with colored tickets that could be accumulated and put toward the purchase of a Sunday school book or tract. Once the ASSU made these changes, Gratz could borrow some of the materials and style with only minor modifications. (Books like *Union Questions,* which was designed to precipitate conversion by posing unanswered questions that forced students to focus on their sins and on their need to repent, were not borrowed.) Ann Boylan, "Sunday Schools and Changing Evangelical Views of Children in the 1820s," *Church History* 48, no. 3 (1979): 320–34; Lynn and Wright, *The Big Little School,* 10–17.

18. Prayer Card, 1942, Hebrew Sunday School Society Collection, Philadelphia Jewish Archives–Balch Institute of Ethnic Studies; Joshua Block, "Rosa Mordecai's Recollection of the First Hebrew Sunday School," *PAJHS* 42 (1953): 397–406; Todes, "The History of Jewish Education in Philadelphia," 56.

19. Minutes of the Hebrew Sunday School, Philadelphia Jewish Archives–Balch Institute of Ethnic Studies.

20. Minutes of the Hebrew Sunday School, American Jewish Archives; R.G. to Miriam Moses Cohen, March 4, 1840, Rebecca Gratz Papers, P-9, American Jewish Historical Society.

21. Egal Feldman, *Dual Destinies: The Jewish Encounter with Protestant America* (Urbana: University of Illinois Press, 1990), 58–78; Naomi W. Cohen, *Encounter with Emancipation: The German Jews in the United States, 1830–1914* (Philadelphia: Jewish Publication Society, 1984), 66, 75, 79–80.

22. Hasia Diner, *A Time for Gathering: The Second Migration, 1820–1880.* (Baltimore: Johns Hopkins University Press, 1992), 167.

23. Isaac Leeser, *Discourses, Argumentative and Devotional on the Subject of the Jewish Religion* (Philadelphia, 5601 [1841]), 215–33; Isaac M. Wise, *Occident* 1 (1843): 113–20, 409–14; *Occident* 2 (1844): 280–81; *Occident* 4 (1846): 65; *Occident* 15 (1857): 120–25, quoted in N. Cohen, *Encounter with Emancipation: The German Jews in the United States, 1830–1914,* 67.

24. "Local Courts and Sabbath Laws, 1793–1833," in *The Jews of the United States, 1790–1840: A Documentary History,* ed. Joseph Blau and Salo Baron (New York: Columbia University Press, 1963), 21–25; Whiteman, "Legacy of Isaac Lesser"; Minutes of the Hebrew Sunday School Society, 1838–1874, American Jewish Archives.

25. Leeser, "Progress of Civil and Religious Liberty," *Occident* 13 (1855): 496–505.

26. Leeser, *Occident* 4 (1846): 511.

27. Leeser, *Occident 6* (1848): 299.

28. Leeser, *Occident 6* (1848): 413–15.

29. Leeser, *Occident 4* (1846): 563.

30. Leeser, *Occident 16* (1858): 269–85.; *Occident 8* (1850): 93–97; *Occident 8* (1851): 54, 51; *Occident 13* (1856): 226–27, 543–77.

31. *Occident 15* (1858): 231.

32. Sussman, "Another Look at Isaac Leeser," 159–90; Leeser, *Occident 11* (1853): 285–87.

33. For one account of the demise of Victorian culture, see Ann Douglas, *Terrible Honesty: Mongrel Manhattan in the 1920s* (New York: Farrar, Straus, and Giroux, 1995) passim.

34. "Superintendent's Report," May 1864, Minutes of the Hebrew Sunday School Society, American Jewish Archives.

35. Todes, "The History of Jewish Education in Philadelphia," 12.

36. Prayer Card, circa 1942, Hebrew Sunday School Society Collection, Philadelphia Jewish Archives–Balch Institute of Ethnic Studies.

37. Mrs. (Rachel Peixotto) Pyke, *Scriptural Questions for the Use of Sunday Schools for the Instruction of Israelites* (Philadephia, reprint 1854), Hebrew School Society Collection, Philadelphia Jewish Archives–Balch Institute of Ethnic Studies.

38. Peixotto, *Elementary Introduction to the Scriptures for the Use of Hebrew Children,* 7.

39. Michael A. Meyer, *Origins of the Modern Jew* (Detroit: Wayne State University Press, 1967), 54.

40. Isaac Leeser, *Catechism for Younger Children* (Philadelphia, 1839), 1, Hebrew Sunday School Society Collection, Philadelphia Jewish Archives–Balch Institute of Ethnic Studies.; B. Z. Sobel, "Legitimation and Antisemitism as Factors in the Functioning of a Hebrew-Christian Mission," *Jewish Social Studies* 23, no. 3 (1961): 170–86; Jonathan D. Sarna, "The American Jewish Response to Nineteenth-Century Christian Missions," *Journal of American History* 68 (1981): 35–51.

41. Todes, "The History of Jewish Education in Philadelphia," 55.

42. "Monday Morning," "Wednesday Morning," "Morning Prayer Thursday," Gratz Family Papers, Collection no. 72, box 9, American Philosophical Society.

43. Jacob Petuchowski, "Manuals and Catechisms of the Jewish Religion in the Early Period of Emancipation," in Alexander Altmann, *Studies in Nineteenth-Century Jewish Intellectual History* (Cambridge, Harvard University, Press, 1964), 47–64.

44. Todes, "The History of Jewish Education in Philadelphia," 12.

45. Ibid.

46. Isaac Leeser, "How to Educate Jewish Girls" (1835), in Jacob R. Marcus, *The American Jewish Woman: A Documentary History* (New York: Ktav, 1981) 130.

47. Thanks to Jonathan Sarna for this information.

48. Karla Goldman, "The Ambivalence of Reform Judaism: Kaufmann Kohler and the Ideal Jewish Woman," *American Jewish History* 79, no. 4 (1990): 477–99; Meyer, *Origins of the Modern Jew,* 379–80.

49. Meyer, *Origins of the Modern Jew,* 237; Samuel Pike, *A Compendious Hebrew Lexicon Adapted to the English Language* (1801), Hebrew Sunday School Society Collection, Philadelphia Jewish Archives–Balch Institute of Ethnic Studies.

50. Charles G. Addison, *Damascus and Palmyra: A Journey to the East with Sketches and Prospects of Syria under Ibrahim Pasha* (Philadelphia: Carey and Hart, 1838); *Seder Tefillah: The Order of Prayer for Divine Service,* revised by Dr. Leo Merzbacher of Temple

Emanu-El (New York, 1855); *Torah Moshe: The Law of Moses: A Catechism of the Jewish Religion,* revised by Abraham Pereira Mendes, 3d ed. (London, 1870); *Thoughts Suggested by Bible Texts Addressed to My Children* (Philadelphia: Hebrew Sunday School Society, 1860), all in Philadelphia Jewish Archives–Balch Institute of Ethnic Studies.

51. Minutes of the Hebrew Sunday School Society, 1860–1880, American Jewish Archives.

52. See, for example, "Little Nellie's Catechism," *Hebrew Sunday School Visitor,* January 1874, vol. 1, no. 1, 2, 7; vol. 1, no. 3, 10–11, Hebrew Sunday School Society Collection, American Jewish Archives.; Nina Baym, *Woman's Fiction: A Guide to Novels by and about Women in America, 1820–1870* (Ithaca: Cornell University Press, 1978; 2d ed., Urbana: University of Illinois Press, 1993).

53. For a discussion of how this Victorian ideology affected Catholic and Protestant American families see Colleen McDannell, *The Christian Home in Victorian America 1840–1900,* (Bloomington: Indiana University Press, 1986), passim.

54. *The Parent and Teachers Assistant: or Thirteen Lessons Conveying to Unformed Minds the First Ideas of God and His Attributes . . . by an American Jewess* (Philadelphia: C. Sherman Printer, 5605 [1845]), 10–12, Mikveh Israel Archives. Abraham Karp points out that the first edition of this volume identified the author as a young woman. Gratz was sixty-four in 1845. He suggests that the author was Simha Peixotto. Maxwell Whiteman suggested Emma Mordecai as the author. Personal conversations, Abraham Karp and Maxwell Whiteman.

55. Ibid., 14, 31–33, 35.

56. Marion Kaplan, "Tradition and Transition: The Acculturation, Assimilation, and Integration of Jews in Imperial Germany: A Gender Analysis," *Leo Baeck Institute Yearbook* 27 (1982): 3–35; R.G. to Miriam Moses Cohen, n.d., ca. 1840, Rebecca Gratz Papers, P-9, American Jewish Historical Society.

57. John D'Emilio and Estelle B. Freedman, *Intimate Matters: A History of Sexuality in America* (New York: Harper and Row, 1988), 85–108.

58. Minutes of Hebrew Sunday School Society, 1860–1880, American Jewish Archives.

Chapter Three

A Great Awakening
The Transformation That Shaped Twentieth-Century American Judaism

Jonathan D. Sarna

The Immigrant Interpretation

The years 1881–1914 are generally known in American Jewish historiography as the era of mass immigration, the period when Central European Jews were overwhelmed by East European Jews and the nation's Jewish population increased twelvefold. Most historians assume that whatever else happened during these years was a response to this immigration, a subsidiary consequence of the era's main theme. Leon Jick's interpretation sums up what is essentially a consensus view:

> The tidal wave of East European Jewish immigrants which began after 1881 inundated the Jewish community and transformed the confident [R]eform majority into a defensive minority. In the wake of the radically different values and attitudes of the newcomers and the problems created by their arrival, the process of adaptation and adjustment began anew. A new burst of organizational energy led to new modes of accommodation and to the creation of the complex institutional and ideological panorama of twentieth-century American Jewry.[1]

This view is not new; indeed, one finds it expressed as early as 1911 in Rabbi Solomon Schindler's famous mea culpa sermon entitled "Mistakes I Have Made." Schindler, who had by then abandoned his earlier radicalism and become a kind of born-again Jew, a *baal teshuva,* believed that post–Civil War Jews "seemed near assimilation." Anticipating contemporary scholars, he attributed subsequent changes, including his own sense of personal guilt for having formerly espoused assimilation, to what he called the "new spirit" that East European Jews had brought with them:

> A cloud came up out of the East and covered the world. It brought here to us two millions of people. Whilst they were different from us in appearance and habits, there were ties of blood between us and they brought a new spirit amongst us. They surrounded us like an army. This movement from the east to the west of this great army strong in the old ideals acting upon and changing our mode of thought, demanding from us change—this was the hand of God.[2]

The assumption, then, is that East European Jews were responsible for introducing a "new spirit" into American Jewish life. They overwhelmed the hitherto dominant Reform movement, reducing it, statistically, "to the position of a denomination of high social level representing only a fraction of the American Jews." Scholars like Nathan Glazer and Henry Feingold go so far as to argue that without this immigration American Jews might well have assimilated and disappeared.[3]

Yet, well rooted as this view is within twentieth-century American Jewish historiography, it does not stand up under close scrutiny. Nobody, of course, disputes that East European Jewish immigration had a profound historical impact. But it is extraordinarily difficult to argue that the immigration challenge is central to the whole period, sufficient in and of itself to explain all of the many changes that historians attribute to it. Three problems with the interpretation are particularly daunting.

First, the interpretation is, in many ways, anachronistic. Many of the changes attributed to mass immigration actually took place earlier, either before 1881 or before American Jews realized how portentous the immigration would be. So, for example, it is claimed that East European Jews are responsible for breathing a "new spirit" into American Judaism, resulting in a considerable movement back to tradition even among native-born Jews. Yet, in fact, that movement began much earlier, in the late 1870s, and was associated not with immigration but with a core of American-born young people, particularly in Philadelphia and New York. Reports that "genuine Orthodox views are now becoming fashionable among Jewish young America" circulated as early as 1879,[4] and that same year saw the establishment of the new journalistic voice of these young people, the *American Hebrew,* described by one of its founders as "our forcible instrument for the perpetuation and elevation of Judaism."[5] By the mid-1880s—that is, before immigration's impact had fully been felt—the new conservative trend within American Judaism was already widely in evidence.[6]

New organizational forms likewise predated mass immigration. The tremendous growth of the Young Men's Hebrew Associations, to take perhaps the most significant example, began in the mid-1870s. By 1890, some 120 of the associations had been founded nationwide, many in places scarcely affected by immigration.[7] These and other religious, cultural, and organizational changes cannot be attributed to mass immigration and are therefore not explicable according to our current understanding of late-nineteenth-century developments.

Second, besides being anachronistic, the current interpretation is also extraordinarily simplistic. It assumes that a wide array of late-nineteenth-century developments can all be explained by a single factor, mass migration, and that this one factor was sufficient to trigger a full-scale cultural revolution in American Jewish life. Yet, accounts of the founding of such new nationwide organizations as the Jewish Publication Society (1888), the American Jewish Historical Society (1892), Gratz College (1893), the Jewish Chautauqua Society (1893), and the National Council of Jewish Women (1893), as well as the ambitious project to produce a *Jewish Encyclopedia* in America (work on which began in earnest in 1898), demonstrate that they were not originally justified on the basis of the mass migration and have only limited initial connection to it. These were instead cultural and educational undertakings designed to promote Jewish learning on the part of native Jews, to promote America itself as a center of Jewish life, and to counter anti-Semitism.[8] Admittedly, some of these organizations subsequently changed their mission in response to the immigrant challenge. But we misunderstand a great deal if we assume, as so many today do, that immigration was the fountainhead from which all other turn-of-the-century developments flowed.

Finally, the immigrant interpretation is painfully insular. It assumes, quite wrongly, that American Jewish life in this period was largely shaped by Jewish events and that the impact of surrounding American cultural and religious developments was negligible. It also assumes, again wrongly, that the religious history of America's Jews was exclusively shaped by immigrating East Europeans. Instead of viewing American Jewish history in its broadest context, noting parallels to developments within American society and in Europe, the immigrant interpretation reflects and encourages a lamentable tunnel vision that clouds our understanding of what the period's history was really about.

A Jewish Renaissance in America

Contemporaries understood turn-of-the-century developments in American Jewish life quite differently. They used terms like "revival," "renaissance," and "awakening" to explain what was going on in their day, and they understood these terms in much the same way that contemporary Protestants did. The London *Jewish Chronicle* thus reported in 1887 that "a strong religious revival has apparently set in among the Jews in the United States." It was especially struck by the number of American synagogues looking for rabbis and by the comparatively high salaries that rabbinic candidates were then being offered.

Cyrus Adler, writing in the *American Hebrew* seven years later, described what he called an American Jewish "renaissance" and a "revival of Jewish learning." He listed a series of Jewish cultural and intellectual achievements in America dating back to 1879. By 1901, the lawyer and community leader Daniel P. Hays was persuaded that the previous decade had witnessed "a great awakening among our people—a realization that the Jew is not to become great by his material achievements, but by his contribution toward the higher ideals of life and by his endeavors toward the uplifting of the race." Edwin Wolf, in his presidential address to the Jewish Publication Society in 1904, carried the same theme into the future: "We are," he proclaimed, "laying the foundation for a Jewish renaissance in America."[9]

Historians of American Judaism have paid scant attention to these claims.[10] Terms such as "revival," "awakening," and "renaissance" play no part in the traditional religious vocabulary of Judaism, and in America they run counter to the standard assimilationist model that posits "linear descent," a movement over several generations of American Judaism from Orthodoxy to Reform to complete secularity.[11] Where historians of American Protestantism have long posited a cyclical pattern of revival and stagnation ("backsliding"), a model that Catholic historians have now borrowed, no such pattern has been discerned in the story of American Judaism—at least until we reach contemporary times.[12]

My argument here, however, is that the explanation offered by turn-of-the-century Jews to describe the developments of their day was essentially correct. Jews *were* experiencing a period of religious and cultural awakening, parallel but by no means identical to what Protestantism experienced during the same period.[13] This multifaceted awakening—its causes, manifestations, and implications—holds the key to understanding this critical period in American Jewish history, explaining much that the regnant "immigration synthesis" cannot adequately contain.

I shall argue that a "major cultural reorientation" began in the American Jewish community late in the 1870s and was subsequently augmented by mass immigration.[14] The critical developments that we associate with this period—the return to religion, the heightened sense of Jewish peoplehood and particularism, the far-reaching changes that opened up new opportunities and responsibilities for women, the renewed communitywide emphasis on education and culture, the "burst of organizational energy," and the growth of Conservative Judaism and Zionism—all reflect different efforts to resolve the "crisis of beliefs and values" that had developed during these decades.[15] By 1914, American Jewry had been transformed, and the awakening had run its course. The basic contours of the twentieth-century American Jewish community had by then fallen into place.

From Confidence to Crisis

The late 1860s and early 1870s were a period of confident optimism in American Jewish life. The Central European Jews who had immigrated two decades earlier had, by then, established themselves securely. The Jewish community had grown in wealth and power and now stood at about a quarter of a million strong, with close to three hundred synagogues from coast to coast. The community had created hospitals, orphanages, schools, newspapers, magazines, several fraternal organizations, a union of synagogues, and, in 1875, a rabbinical seminary. The nation was booming; liberal Jews and Protestants spoke warmly of universalism; and rabbis and ministers even occasionally traded pulpits.

Small wonder that Jews looked forward with anticipation to the onset of a glorious "new era" in history, described by one rabbi in an 1874 lecture delivered "in every important city east of the Mississippi River" as a time when "the whole human race shall be led to worship one Almighty God of rightousness and truth, goodness and love" and when Jews would stand in the forefront of those ushering in "the golden age of a true universal brotherhood."[16]

Beginning in the late 1870s, this hopeful scenario was undermined by a series of unanticipated crises that disrupted American Jewish life and called many of its guiding assumptions into question. "Anti-Semitism"—a word coined in Germany at the end of the 1870s to describe and justify ("scientifically") anti-Jewish propaganda and discrimination—explains part of what happened. The rise of racially based anti-Jewish hatred in Germany, a land that many American Jews had close ties to and had previously revered for its liberal spirit and cultural advancement, came as a shock. Here Jews had assumed that emancipation, enlightenment, and human progress would diminish residual prejudice directed toward them, and suddenly they saw it espoused in the highest intellectual circles, and by people in whom they had placed great faith. German anti-Semitism was widely reported upon in the United States, covered both in the Jewish and in the general press. "What American Jews were witnessing," Naomi W. Cohen explains, was nothing less than "the humiliation of their Jewish parents, a spectacle that could shake their faith in Judaism itself."[17]

What made this situation even worse was that anti-Semitism and particularly social discrimination soon spread to America's own shores. Anti-Jewish hatred was certainly not new to America, but Jews had previously considered it something of an anachronism, alien both to the modern temper and to American democracy. Like Jews in Germany, they optimistically assumed that prejudice against them would in time wither away. The two well-publicized incidents of the late 1870s— Judge Hilton's exclusion of the banker Joseph Seligman from the Grand Union Hotel (1877) and Austin Corbin's public announcement that "Jews as a class" would be unwelcome at Coney Island (1879)—proved so shocking precisely because they challenged this assumption.[18]

The questions posed by Hermann Baar, superintendent of the Hebrew Orphan Asylum, in his response to Corbin's outburst, were the questions that Jews in all walks of life suddenly had to ask of themselves:

> In what age and country do we live? Are we going to have the times of Philip II, of Spain, repeated, or do we really live in the year 1879, in that century of progress and improvement, of education and enlightenment? Do we really live in the year 1879, in that era of moral refinement and cultured tastes, of religious toleration and social intercourse? And if we really live in this era, can such an act of injustice and bigoted ostracism happen on American soil, in this land of the free and brave, in which the homeless finds a shelter and the persecuted a resting place, in which the peaceable citizen enjoys the blessings of his labor and the devout worshiper the full liberty of his religious conscience, and in which humanity teaches to other countries and nations the blessed code of right and justice?[19]

Calls for a "Christian America"

By brazenly defending and legitimating anti-Semitism on socioeconomic, racial, and legal grounds, incidents such as these paved the way for a depressing rise in anti-Semitic manifestations of all sorts, from social discrimination to anti-Semitic propaganda to efforts to stem the tide of Jewish immigrants. Over the next two decades, Jews experienced a substantial decline in their social status. "Gradually, but surely, we are being forced back into a physical and moral ghetto," the thirty-five-year-old professor Richard Gottheil, of Columbia University, complained, speaking in 1897 to a private meeting of the Judaeans, the cultural society of New York's Jewish elite. "Private schools are being closed against our children one by one; we are practically boycotted from all summer hotels—and our social lines run as far apart from those of our neighbors as they did in the worst days of our European degradation."[20]

Developments within American Protestantism added yet another dimension to the mood of uneasiness that I sense in the American Jewish community of this period. The spiritual crisis and internal divisions that plagued Protestant America during this era—one that confronted all American religious groups with the staggering implications of Darwinism and biblical criticism—drove evangelicals and liberals alike to renew their particularistic calls for a "Christian America." Visions of a liberal religious alliance and of close cooperation between Jews and Unitarians gradually evaporated. Although interfaith exchanges continued, Jews came to realize that many of their Christian friends continued to harbor hopes that one day Jews would "see the light." Much to the embarrassment of Jewish leaders, some Christian liberals looked to Felix Adler's de-Judaized Ethical Culture movement as a harbinger of Judaism's future course.[21]

On the Jewish side, this period witnessed a comparable crisis of the spirit. Alarmed at religious "indifference," Jewish ignorance, some well-publicized cases of intermarriage, and Felix Adler's success in attracting young Jews to his cause, many began to question prior assumptions regarding the direction in which American Judaism should move. Was Reform Judaism really the answer? Had the effort to modernize Judaism gone too far? Would assimilation triumph?

By the 1880s, the Reform movement was on the defensive, facing attacks from both left and right. Its uncertainty found expression in the 1885 conference of Reform rabbis that produced the Pittsburgh Platform. The question was also reflected in an 1884 letter to Rabbi Bernhard Felsenthal, a pioneer of American Reform, from a confused young rabbi named David Stern, who subsequently committed suicide. Stern remarked that the religious agenda of his day was "entirely different" from what it had been before. "Then the struggle was to remove the dross; to-day it is to conserve the pearl beneath."[22]

Mass East European Jewish immigration, coming on the heels of all of these developments, added a great deal of fuel to the crisis of confidence that Jews experienced in the 1880s. In Russia, as in Germany, liberalism had been tested and found wanting; reaction followed. The resulting mass exodus strained the Jewish community's resources, heightened fears of anti-Semitism, stimulated an array of Americanization and revitalization efforts, and threatened to change the whole character of the American Jewish community once East European Jews gained cultural hegemony.

So visible and long acting was the transformation wrought by East European Jewish immigration that it eventually overshadowed all other aspects of the late-nineteenth-century crisis. From the point of view of contemporaries, however, anti-Semitism at home and abroad, the specter of assimilation and intermarriage, and the changing religious and social environment of the United States were no less significant.

Faced with all of these unexpected problems at once, American Jews began to realize that their whole optimistic vision of the future had been built on false premises. Even the usually starry-eyed Reform Jewish leader Rabbi Isaac Mayer Wise, writing in 1881, felt his faith in the future slowly ebbing away:

> There is something wrong among us optimists and humanists, sad experience upsets our beautiful theories and we stand confounded before the angry eruptions of the treacherous volcano called humanity. There is a lie in its nature which has not been overcome. Will it ever be overcome? We hope and trust that it will. Till then, we poor optimists are sadly disappointed and made false prophets.[23]

Utopia, in short has proved more distant than expected. The universalistic prophecies of the 1860s and seventies had failed, the hoped-for "new era" had not materialized, and conditions for Jews in America and around the world had grown worse instead of better. This posed a cultural crisis of the highest order for American Jews and precipitated the cultural awakening that changed the face of American Jewish life.

A "Bottom-up" Revival

By far the most important group seeking to promote Jewish religious renewal in the last decades of the nineteenth century was centered in Philadelphia[24] and consisted largely of young single men. Mayer Sulzberger (1843–1923), the city's foremost Jewish citizen, was the "patriarch" of this group, and his associates (several of whom were also his relatives) included such future activists as Solomon Solis-Cohen (1857–1948), Cyrus Sulzberger (1858–1932), Joseph Fels (1854–1914), Samuel Fels (1860–1950), and Cyrus Adler (1863–1940). All were initially involved in the Young Men's Hebrew Association of Philadelphia, founded in 1875 to promote social as well as cultural activities of a Jewish nature, including lectures, literary discussions, formal Jewish classes, and the publication of a lively newsletter.

Of primary significance, for our purposes, was their campaign, carried out in association with the YMHA of New York (founded in 1874), for "the Grand Revival of the Jewish National Holiday of Chanucka," complete with appropriate pageants and publicity. This was an effort "to rescue this national festival from the oblivion into which it seemed rapidly falling" and was a direct challenge to Reform Judaism, which had renounced national aspects of Judaism as antithetical to the modern spirit; presumably, the campaign also sought to counteract the evident allure of Christmas. In 1879, the "revival" proved a triumphant success. "Every worker in the cause of a revived Judaism," one of the organizers wrote, "must have felt the inspiration exuded from the enthusiastic interest evinced by such a mass of Israel's people."[25]

A few months before this "revival," on October 5, 1879, several of the young people in this circle bound themselves together in a solemn covenant "for God and Judaism" that they called *Keyam Dishmaya* and in which they pledged all in their power to bring Jews back "to the ancient faith." On the first anniversary of this covenant, one of its leaders, Cyrus L. Sulzberger, spelled out the three cornerstones of the revival that he and his associates were trying to spawn. They sought, first, to revitalize and deepen the religious and spiritual lives of American Jews; second, to strengthen Jewish education; and, third, to promote the restoration of Jews as a people, including their ultimate restoration to the land of Israel.[26]

Together, these goals signified an inward turn among young American Jews. Their response to the cultural crisis of their day was to reject universalism, assimilationism, and the redefinition of Judaism along purely religious lines—themes heavily promoted by Reform Judaism at that time—in favor of a Judaism that was in their view more closely in tune with God and Jewish historical tradition.

The New Leaders

No movement for change can confine itself to secret societies and clandestine cells. For this reason, and in order to promote their lofty aims among the "movers and shakers" of the American Jewish community, these young Jewish revivalists established on November 21, 1879, a lively and important highbrow Jewish newspaper in New York entitled the *American Hebrew*. "Our work," they explained to the public in their first issue, "shall consist of untiring endeavors to stir up our brethren to pride in our time-honored faith." The newspaper's publisher, Philip Cowen, recalled half a century later that "we were fully convinced that not only New York Judaism, but American Judaism, awaited its journalistic redeemers!"[27]

The nine editors of the new newspaper, some Philadelphians, some New Yorkers, were all anonymous—understandably so, since their ages ranged from twenty-one to twenty-nine. They represented a new phenomenon on the American Jewish scene: most were American-born Jews who were at once "strong for traditional Judaism" (two of the nine were rabbis) yet at the same time eager to accommodate Judaism to American conditions.[28]

"Our proclivities . . . are toward 'reformed' Judaism and yet our disposition is toward orthodoxy," the editors admitted in their first issue. Years later, Max Cohen described his associates as having been "a group of young American Jews who, while not inordinately addicted to Orthodoxy as a rigid standardisation of thought and conduct, was yet opposed to the wholesale and reckless discarding of everything that was Jewish simply because it was inconvenient, oriental, or was not in conformity with Episcopalian customs."[29]

By the time he published this recollection, in 1920, Cohen and the other erstwhile members of his group had moved far beyond the *American Hebrew*. Led by the indefatigable Cyrus Adler, who had joined the editorial board of the paper in 1894, members of this cohort of New York and Philadelphia Jews established a wide range of cultural and religious institutions and involved themselves in an array of communal projects. Some were designed to strengthen what became known as Conservative Judaism, one of the most significant and far-reaching outcomes of this whole religious awakening.[30] And all were designed to extend the work of Jewish cultural and religious renewal in new directions.

In the space of a few decades they created, among other things, the Jewish

Theological Seminary (1886), the Jewish Publication Society (1888), the American Jewish Historical Society (1892), Gratz College (1893), and Dropsie College (1907). They were associated with the publication of the *Jewish Encyclopedia* (1901–1906); with the movement to bring the renowned Jewish scholar Solomon Schechter to America (he arrived in 1902); with the transfer to America's shores of the scholarly journal the *Jewish Quarterly Review* (1910); and with the establishment, by the Jewish Publication Society, of American Jewry's first high-quality Hebrew press (1921).

These highly ambitious and for the most part successful undertakings mirror the "organizing process" that Donald Mathews associated with the Protestant Second Great Awakening; they sought to provide "meaning and direction" to Jews suffering from the social and cultural strains of a transitional era.[31] Appropriately, the organizations intended to reach different audiences: some looked to scholars, some to rabbis and teachers, and some to the Jewish community at large and to non-Jews.

In the case of Cyrus Adler, Naomi W. Cohen describes this multitiered cultural agenda as a conscious creation:

> On one level, Adler envisioned the modern training of Jewish scholars, abetted by appropriate library and publication resources. On a second, he aimed for the education of American rabbis and teachers who would inculcate a loyalty to historical Judaism in consonance with acculturation to American surroundings. On still a third, he worked for a community knowledgeable about its heritage, that would appreciate the value of reading books of Jewish interest, of collecting Jewish artifacts, and of keeping alert to contemporary events that involved Jewry.[32]

All these levels sought to promote religious renewal, improved Jewish education, cultural revitalization, the professionalization of Jewish scholarship, a positive Jewish image to the Gentiles, and the elevation of American Jewry to a position of greater prominence, if not preeminence, among the Jews of the world.

Admittedly, the challenge posed by massive East European Jewish immigration led, for a time, to a greater rhetorical emphasis upon Americanization as a goal, but this should not be exaggerated. Promoters of Jewish renewal understood better than other Jewish leaders did that the real concern was not so much how to assimilate the East Europeans as how to ensure that all American Jews would not assimilate completely. It was this critical insight, coupled with a prescient sense that American Jewry needed to prepare itself to play a central role in the affairs of world Jewry, that prompted these Jews to participate in the creation of these great institutions and projects that shaped American-Jewish cultural and religious life into the late twentieth century.[33]

Although this remarkable cohort of Philadelphia and New York Jews—most of them young, male, and well-educated lay people, rather than rabbis[34]—formed the most visible leadership cadre of the late-nineteenth-century awakening, they were by no means its only source of energy. In fact, more than generally realized, the awakening marked a turning point both in the history of American Jewish women and in the history of the American Reform Movement.

The Role of Women

The role of women in American Judaism had been undergoing change since the early decades of the nineteenth century. Influenced by the Second Great Awakening, Rebecca Gratz, of Philadelphia, introduced Jewish women into the world of Jewish philanthropy, establishing in 1819 the Female Hebrew Benevolent Society, the progenitor of many similar benevolent organizations by and for Jewish women. Previously, Jewish philanthropy had been part of the synagogue's domain and governed by men.

The Jewish Sunday School movement, pioneered by Gratz in 1838, transformed the role of Jewish women still further by making them responsible for the religious education and spiritual guidance of the young. By the time Gratz died, in 1869, it can safely be estimated that the majority of American Jews who received any formal Jewish education at all learned most of what they knew from female teachers. These teachers, in turn, had to educate themselves in Judaism, which they did with the aid of new textbooks, some of them written by women, as well.[35]

By the end of the nineteenth century, thanks to a legacy left by Rebecca Gratz's brother, Hyman, women could received advanced training in Judaism at Gratz College, the first of a series of Hebrew teachers colleges across the United States that trained women on an equal basis with men.[36] In still another transformation, this one beginning in 1851 and confined to Reform temples, women achieved parity with their husbands in the realm of synagogue seating. No longer were they relegated to the balcony or separated from men by a physical barrier; instead, by the late 1870s, mixed seating was the rule throughout Reform congregations.[37] Now, building on these earlier developments, women experienced still more far-reaching changes as part of the late-nineteenth-century American Jewish awakening.

The first woman to achieve great prominence in the awakening was the poet Emma Lazarus (1849–1887), who was best known for her poem "The New Colossus," composed in 1883 to help raise funds for the pedestal on which the Statue of Liberty rests.[38] Born in New York to an aristocratic Jewish family of mixed Sephardic and Ashkenazic heritage, she had emerged at a young age as a sensitive poet (her first book was published when she was seventeen) but had never maintained close ties to the Jewish community; only a very small percentage of her early work bore on Jewish themes at all.

Anti-Semitism and the first wave of East European Jewish immigration shocked Lazarus. In 1882, in a burst of creative energy, she emerged as a staunch defender of Jewish rights, the poet laureate of the Jewish awakening, and as the foremost proponent of the "national-Jewish movement" aimed at "the establishment of a free Jewish State."[39] Her oft-quoted poem "The Banner of the Jew," composed in the spring of 1882, began with the words "Wake, Israel, wake!" and ended on a militant note:

> O deem not dead that martial fire.
>   Say not the mystic flame is spent!
> With Moses' law and David's lyre,
>   Your ancient strength remains unbent.

Let but an Ezra rise anew,
To lift the *Banner of the Jew!*
A rag, a mock at first—erelong
   When men have bled and women wept,
To guard its precious folds from wrong,
   Even they who shrunk, even they who slept,
Shall leap to bless it, and to save.
Strike! for the brave revere the brave![40]

Meanwhile, her essays, notably her *An Epistle to the Hebrews* (1882–1883), called for "a deepening and quickening of the sources of Jewish enthusiasm" in response to the " 'storm-centre' in our history" that Jews were passing through.[41]

Lazarus herself soon established close ties with the publisher of the *American Hebrew,* where much of her work now appeared, and she began studying the Hebrew language. Her interest, however, lay not in the religious revitalization of the Jews, as advocated by the members of *Keyam Dishmaya;* instead, she placed her emphasis on Jewish peoplehood, emphasizing the virtues of unity, discipline, and organization in the service of Jewish national renewal. Influenced by George Eliot's *Daniel Deronda,* Laurence Oliphant's *The Land of Gilead,* and Leon Pinsker's *Auto-Emancipation,* she abandoned her own skepticism concerning Jewish nationalism and became "one of the most devoted adherents to the new dogma." She embraced it as if it were a full-fledged religion, and in doing so she recognized that she was not alone:

> Under my own eyes I have seen equally rapid and thorough conversions to the same doctrine. In the minds of mature and thoughtful men, men of prudence and of earnest purpose, little apt to be swayed by the chance enthusiasm of a popular agitation, it has taken profound root, and in some cases overturned the theories and intellectual habits of a life-time.[42]

With her untimely death, of Hodgkins disease, at the age of thirty-eight, Lazarus became something of a saint to Jews caught up in the late-nineteenth-century awakening. A special issue of the *American Hebrew* memorialized her, with tributes "from the foremost literati of the age," and her *Epistle to the Hebrews,* published in pamphlet form in 1900, was kept in print for many years by the Federation of American Zionists.

Even as her memory was kept alive, however, her death came as a blow to the movement for Jewish renewal. It deprived it of its first truly significant convert to the cause, its most inspiring and cosmopolitan intellectual figure, and its foremost advocate (to that time) of what would shortly become known as American Zionism—the other great movement (along with Conservative Judaism) that the late-nineteenth-century American Jewish awakening did so much to spawn.[43]

Yet another dimension of the effervescence of late-nineteenth-century American Jewish religious life is suggested by the career of Ray Frank, known in her day as the "girl rabbi" and the "female messiah." While not of long-lasting significance, her brief stint as a charismatic woman Jewish revivalist demonstrates that the late-nineteenth-century American Jewish crisis of expectations and faith was not confined to the east coast, restricted to intellectual circles, or exclusively the preserve of traditionalists and proto-Zionists. It was, instead, a complex nationwide phenomenon that affected a wide range of Jews, men and women, in sometimes unpredictable ways.

Ray (Rachel) Frank (1861–1948),[44] born in San Francisco, was a schoolteacher, writer, and lecturer. Critical of the Judaism of her day, she published, in 1890, a stinging critique of the American rabbinate in response to a New York Jewish newspaper's call for articles on the question "What would you do if you were a rabbi?" What she "would not do," she emphasized, was to emulate the many abuses she considered characteristic of the pompously materialistic American rabbinate. She called on rabbis to don "the spiritual mantle of Elijah" and implied that women ("were the high office not denied us") might do the job better.[45]

Shortly after this article appeared, Ray Frank achieved momentary fame when she traveled to Spokane, Washington, and became "the one Jewish woman in the world, may be the first since the time of the prophets" to preach from a synagogue pulpit on the Jewish high holidays.[46] According to the story widely reported in her day and subsequently preserved by her husband:

> It happened to be on the eve of the High Holy Days and she made inquiries concerning the location of the synagogue as she wanted to attend services. When informed that there was no synagogue and there would be no services, she called on one of the wealthy Jews in town, to whom she had letters of introduction, and expressed surprise that a town containing many well-to-do Jews should be without a place of worship. The man, who knew Ray Frank by reputation, said, "If you will deliver a sermon we shall have services tonight." Ray acquiesced. At about five o'clock on that day special editions of Spokane Falls Gazette appeared on the streets announcing that a young lady would preach to the Jews that evening at the Opera House. The place was crowded. After the services were read, Ray spoke on the obligations of a Jew as a Jew and a citizen. In an impassioned appeal she asked her coreligionists to drop their dissensions with regard to ceremonials and join hands in a glorious cause, that of praying to the God of their fathers. She emphasized the fact that they shirked their duty if they did not form a permanent congregation and that by being without a place of worship and all that it stands for they were doing an incalculable harm to their children. After Ray finished her sermon, a "Christian gentleman" who was in the audience arose and said that he had been very much impressed by what he heard and if the Jews would undertake the building of a synagogue, he would present them with a site to be used for that purpose.[47]

Throughout the 1890s, Ray Frank delivered sermons and lectures, mostly in the West, and published articles extolling the virtues of Judaism, the Jewish family, and Jewish women. According to the memoir published by her husband after her death, people "flocked to listen" as she talked on "Heart Throbs of Israel," "Moses," "Music and Its Revelations," "Nature as a Supreme Teacher," and related topics.[48] In these lectures, she attacked divisions in Jewish life, called for peace in the pulpit, and promoted spirituality, simplicity, earnestness, and righteousness:

> Give us congregational singing which comes direct from the heart and ascends as a tribute to God. . . . Give us simplicity in our rabbi, sympathy with things which prac-

tically concern us, give us earnestness, and our synagogues will no longer mourn in their loneliness.[49]

On one occasion, she disclosed a mystical vision, a call from God in which she herself was cast in the role of Moses ("I know I hold in my hand the staff of Moses. I kneel and raise my hands in adoration of the Eternal. I pray that all knowledge be mine. . . . I go down. I will tell all I know to the world . . . I must wherever and whenever I can preach my message.")[50] For the most part, however, hers was a conservative message. She opposed women's suffrage, spoke of motherhood as the culmination of womanhood, and reminded women "how all-important the home and the family are."[51]

Much like a Protestant revivalist, Frank was described by those who heard her as a spellbinding preacher whose enthusiasm proved infectious. "Before she had finished," the *San Francisco Chronicle* wrote of one of her lectures, "her words were dropping like sparks into the souls of aroused people before her."[52] So well known had she become that, at the Jewish Women's Congress, held in Chicago in 1893, she was invited to deliver the opening prayer. Four years later, in 1897, seven thousand people reportedly turned out to hear her at the adult education Chautauqua at Gladstone Park in Portland, Oregon, on what was billed as "Ray Frank Day."[53]

In 1898, Ray Frank traveled to Europe, where she met and married an economist named Simon Litman. Her marriage and sojourn abroad (the couple did not return until 1902) effectively ended her public career.[54] The success that she demonstrated during her years on the lecture circuit, however, suggests that her message struck a meaningful chord.[55] On the one hand, she spoke to the spiritual concerns and traditional values of American Jews of her day; on the other hand, simply by virtue of her sex, she challenged Jews' religious and gender-based assumptions. In evoking, simultaneously, both new and old, she embodied, but in no way resolved, the cultural contradictions that underlay the religious ferment to which she herself contributed.

In raising the issue of women's role both in American society and in Judaism, Ray Frank had pointed to one of the central concerns of the late-nineteenth-century American Jewish awakening. In response to the manifold crises of the day; particularly assimilation and immigration, responsibility for "saving Judaism" came increasingly to rest upon the shoulders of women. Just as in Protestantism, so, too, in Judaism, religion had become "feminized." The home, the synagogue, and philanthropic social work came increasingly to be seen as part of women's domain, especially among Reform Jews. As a result, women became significant players in the campaign to revitalize Judaism to meet the needs of a new era.[56]

The National Council of Jewish Women, established in 1893, was the first national Jewish organization to take up this challenge. Created at the Jewish Women's Congress of the Columbian Exposition, its original goals explicitly addressed the responsibilities of Jewish women to strengthen Jewish life:

> Resolved, that the National Council of Jewish Women shall (1) seek to unite in closer relation women interested in the work of Religion, Philanthropy and Education and

shall consider practical means of solving problems in these fields; shall (2) organize and encourage the study of the underlying principles of Judaism; the history, literature and customs of the Jews, and their bearing on their own and the world's history; shall (3) apply knowledge gained in this study to the improvement of the Sabbath Schools, and in the work of social reform; shall (4) secure the interest and aid of influential persons in arousing general sentiment against religious persecutions, wherever, whenever and against whomever shown, and in finding means to prevent such persecutions.[57]

Faith Rogow, in her history of the Council, points out that "no one believed more strongly in woman's ability to save Judaism than did Council women themselves." Motherhood, the primacy of the home, the extension of motherhood into the synagogue—these were the values and goals that Council members proudly espoused. Indeed, "motherhood and its presumed opportunity to influence husbands and children" was touted "as the only possible savior of Jewish life in America."[58]

Through "sisterhoods of personal service," Jewish women extended the sphere of "motherhood" into new realms aimed at combating the social crisis within the Jewish community. Initiated at Temple Emanu-El of New York in 1887, sisterhoods offered Jewish women the opportunity to emulate, from within a synagogue setting, the same kind of philanthropically directed urban missionary work performed by New York's Protestant and Catholic women, as well as by the women of the Ethical Culture Society. Outdoor relief, home visits, religious schooling, industrial and domestic education, day nurseries, kindergartens, employment bureaus: these and related efforts devoted "to the care of the needy and the distressed" harnessed the energies of Jewish women in ways that synagogues never had before. By 1896, practically every major uptown synagogue in New York had established a sisterhood, and in 1896 the Federation of Sisterhoods was established, in cooperation with the United Hebrew Charities.

What distinguished these efforts from their more secular counterparts was their religious character. Indeed, Rabbi David de Sola Pool, recounting the activities undertaken by the Orthodox sisterhood established in 1896 at the venerable Shearith Israel Synagogue in New York, stressed its role in "the loyal conservation and transmission of Jewish religious values." Increasingly, in response to the perceived crisis of the day, women were fulfilling new roles within the Jewish community, expanding on those that they had formerly carried out almost exclusively within the home.[59]

All of these new themes—the cultural and educational work of young Jews in Philadelphia and New York, the Zionism of Emma Lazarus, the spirituality of Ray Frank, salvation through motherhood as preached by the National Council of Jewish Women, and the charity work of the Sisterhoods of Personal Service—eventually came together in what became, after our period, the largest and the strongest of the Jewish women's organizations created to revitalize American Jewish life: Hadassah, the Women's Zionist Organization of America.

Henrietta Szold (1860–1945), who played the dominant role in the establishment of Hadassah in 1912, had been involved in the work of Jewish renewal since she was a teenager, first as an essayist and educator, later as secretary of the Publication Committee (that is, editor) of the Jewish Publication Society, and still later, in addition to her other work, as a leader of the Federation of American Zionists. She served as a role model to her peers and was respected as one of the most learned and accomplished Jewish women of her day.[60] Now, in the wake of her first visit to Palestine (1909), she and a few like-minded Zionist women activists in the New York area met to form a new women's Zionist organization, which, at Szold's insistence, would have both a general and a highly specific purpose: "In America, to foster Jewish ideals and make Zionist propaganda; in Palestine, to establish a system of District Visiting Nursing."[61]

In many ways, the new organization did for Jewish women what foreign missions did for Protestant women: it provided them with an opportunity to participate in the "holy work" of "salvation through social, medical, and educational agencies."[62] As the historian of Hadassah's early years explains, Henrietta Szold firmly believed that women, unlike men, were interested in "specific practical projects of immediate emotional appeal to their maternal and Jewish religious instincts." Szold was convinced, therefore, that "we [American Jewish women] need Zionism as much as those Jews do who need a physical home." By working to strengthen Jewish life in the land of Israel, she hoped, women's own Judaism, and American Judaism generally, would be strengthened and renewed.[63]

A Paradigm Shift

The late-nineteenth-century American Jewish awakening outlined here was thus a broad-based and multifaceted movement of religious renewal, parallel to the awakening taking place at the same time within American Protestantism. Of course, many Jews remained unaffected by it—such is always the case with movements of religious revitalization. Those who did fall under its spell, however, included traditionalists and reformers, women as well as men, and Jews living in all regions of the country. There was no clear focus to this movement, no central leader, and no listing of agreed-upon principles. What did unite the various participants was a shared sense of cultural crisis and personal stress, a palpable loss of faith in the norms, institutions, authorities, and goals of an earlier era, and an optimistic belief, particularly on the part of young people, that through their personal efforts American Judaism as a whole could be saved.

As a consequence of the awakening, a massive long-term paradigm shift took place within the American Jewish community: a shift over time toward greater particularism as opposed to the earlier universalism; toward a heightened sense of Jewish peoplehood as opposed to the former stress on Judaism as a faith; toward a new emphasis on the spiritual and emotional aspects of Judaism as opposed to the former emphasis on rationalism; and toward the goal of a Jewish homeland opposed to the diaspora-glorifying ideology of mission that was formerly predominant.

The transformation of women's roles, the revival of Chanukah and other Jewish ceremonies, the shift back to traditional Jewish terminology, the new emphasis on Jewish education and culture, the rise of the Conservative movement, the Zionist movement, and the Social Justice movement, and, of course, many individual "conversions" of assimilated Jews back to their faith: all testify to the magnitude of the transformation that ultimately took place.

Meanwhile, massive East European Jewish immigration heightened the sense of urgency that underlay the work of revival and resulted in parallel efforts to revitalize the Judaism of the ghetto.[64] The result, discernible only in retrospect, was a new American Judaism—the Judaism of the twentieth century.

NOTES

An earlier version of this paper was delivered at the Conference on New Directions in American Religious History, held at Brown University, March 18–19, 1994. This article is an abridged version of "A Great Awakening: The Transformation That Shaped Twentieth Century American Judaism and Its Implications for Today," *CIJE Essay Series* (New York: Council for Initiatives in Jewish Education, 1995?). Another version of this article appeared as "The Late Nineteenth-Century American Jewish Awakening," in *Religious Diversity and American Religious History: Studies in Traditions and Cultures,* ed. Walter H. Conser Jr. and Sumner B. Twiss (Athens: University of Georgia Press, 1997). I am greatly indebted to Professors Ewa Morawska, Lance Sussman, and Ellen Umansky and to Nessa Rapport for their helpful and detailed comments on earlier drafts of this essay.

1. Leon Jick, *The Americanization of the Synagogue, 1820–1870* (Hanover, NH: University Press of New England, 1976), 193.

2. *American Hebrew* 88 (April 7, 1911), 667; on Schindler, see Arthur Mann, ed., *Growth and Achievement: Temple Israel 1854–1954* (Boston: Congregation Adath Israel, 1954), 45–62; Arthur Mann, *Yankee Reformers in the Urban Age: Social Reform in Boston, 1880–1900* (New York: Harper Torchbook, 1954), 52–72.

3. Nathan Glazer, *American Judaism* (Chicago: University of Chicago Press, 1972), 53, 60 (quoted); Henry Feingold, *Zion in America* (New York: Hippocrene Books, 1974), 112.

4. *The Jewish Advance* 79 (December 12, 1879), 4.

5. Max Cohen to Solomon Solis-Cohen (November 10, 1879), Solomon Solis-Cohen Papers, Collection of Helen Solis-Cohen Sax and Hays Solis-Cohen Jr., National Museum of American Jewish History, Philadelphia, PA. I am grateful to Helen Solis-Cohen Sax, Solomon Solis-Cohen's granddaughter, for granting me access to these papers. See also Philip Cowen, *Memories of an American Jew* (New York: International Press, 1932), 50.

6. See Jonathan D. Sarna, "The Making of an American Jewish Culture," in *When Philadelphia Was the Capital of Jewish America,* ed. Murray Friedman (Philadelphia: Balch Institute Press, 1993), 148–150.

7. Benjamin Rabinowitz, *The Young Men's Hebrew Associations* (1854–1913) (New York: National Jewish Welfare Board, 1948) [largely reprinted from *Publications of the American Jewish Historical Society* 37 (1947)]; Jonathan D. Sarna, *JPS: The Americanization of Jewish Culture* (Philadelphia: Jewish Publication Society, 1989), 15–16.

8. Sarna, *JPS,* 13–27; Nathan M. Kaganoff, "AJHS at 90: Reflections on the History of the Oldest Ethnic Historical Society in America," *American Jewish History* 71 (June 1982): 466–85; Mitchell E. Panzer, "Gratz College: A Community's Involvement in Jewish Education," *Gratz College Anniversary Volume,* ed. Isidore D. Passow and Samuel T. Lachs

(Philadelphia: Gratz College, 1971), 1–9; Peggy K. Pearlstein, "Understanding through Education: One Hundred Years of the Jewish Chautauqua Society, 1893–1993," Ph.D. diss., George Washington University, 1993, 1–68; Faith Rogow, *Gone to Another Meeting: The National Council of Jewish Women, 1893–1993* (Tuscaloosa: University of Alabama Press, 1993), 9–85; Shuly Rubin Schwartz, *The Emergence of Jewish Scholarship in America: The Publication of the Jewish Encyclopedia* (Cincinnati: Hebrew Union College Press, 1991), 1–36.

9. [London] *Jewish Chronicle* (March 11, 1887), 13; *American Hebrew* 56 (1894), 22, 181; *American Jewish Year Book* 3 (1901–2), 216; 6 (1904–5), 388; see also "What Renascence Means," *Maccabean* 4 (May 1903): 288.

10. Evyatar Friesel comes closest to the mark in his "The Age of Optimism in American Judaism, 1900–1920," in *A Bicentennial Festschrift for Jacob Rader Marcus*, ed. Bertram W. Korn (New York: Ktav, 1976), 131–55, but he sees the idea of "optimism" as the motivating force behind developments in this period, while to my mind this optimism is not a cause but a result.

11. For a review of recent research, see Steven M. Cohen, *American Assimilation or Jewish Revival* (Bloomington: Indiana University Press, 1988), 43–57. Cohen properly observes (43) that "generational change has long occupied a central place in research on Jewish identification in the United States." I have critiqued "generational determinism" in American Jewish historical writing elsewhere; see *Modern Judaism* 10 (October 1990): 353, and *Judaism* 34 (spring 1985): 246–47.

12. Glazer, writing in 1957, titled his final chapter in *American Judaism*, covering the period 1945–1956, "The Jewish Revival." For more recent developments, see, for example, M. Herbert Danzger, *Returning to Tradition: The Contemporary Revival of Orthodox Judaism* (New Haven: Yale University Press, 1989).

13. Compare William G. McLoughlin, *Revivals, Awakenings, and Reform* (University of Chicago, 1978), 2: "Until the present generation . . . periods of cultural readjustment have been associated almost wholly with the Protestant churches."

14. The quotation comes from William G. McLoughlin, "Timepieces and Butterflies: A Note on the Great-Awakening-Construct and Its Critics," *Sociological Analysis* 44 (1983): 108.

15. McLoughlin, *Revivals, Awakenings, and Reform*, xiii.

16. Isidor Kalisch, "Ancient and Modern Judaism," in *Studies in Ancient and Modern Judaism*, ed. Samuel Kalisch (New York: George Dobsevage, 1928), 61. For a statistical picture of Jews in this period, see *Statistics of the Jews of the United States* (Philadelphia: Union of American Hebrew Congregations, 1880). See also Benny Kraut, "Judaism Triumphant: Isaac Mayer Wise on Unitarianism and Liberal Christianity," *AJS Review* 7–8 (1982–83): 179–230.

17. Naomi W. Cohen, "American Jewish Reactions to Anti-Semitism in Western Europe, 1875–1900," *Proceedings of the American Academy of Jewish Research* 45 (1978): 29–65 (quotation is from p. 31); Michael A. Meyer, "German-Jewish Identity in Nineteenth-Century America," in *Toward Modernity: The European Jewish Model*, ed. Jacob Katz (New Brunswick, NJ: Transaction Books, 1987), 247–267; Michael A. Meyer, "The Great Debate on Antisemitism: Jewish Reactions to New Hostility in Germany, 1879–1881," *Leo Baeck Institute Year Book* 11 (1966): 137–70; Hans L. Trefousse, "The German-American Immigrants and the Newly Founded Reich," in *America and the Germans: An Assessment of a Three-Hundred-Year History*, ed. Frank Tommler and Joseph McVeigh (Philadelphia: University of Pennsylvania Press, 1985), 160–75.

18. Leonard Dinnerstein, *Antisemitism in America* (New York: Oxford University Press, 1994), 39–41; Stephen Birmingham, *Our Crowd* (New York: Dell, 1967), 169–180; *Coney Island and the Jews* (New York: G. W. Carleton, 1879).

19. Hermann Baar, *Addresses on Homely and Religious Subjects Delivered Before the Children of the Hebrew Orphan Asylum* (New York: H.O.A. Industrial School, 1880), 238.

20. *American Hebrew* 62 (December 10, 1897), 163. For developments in this period, see Naomi W. Cohen, "Anti-Semitism in the Gilded Age: The Jewish View," *Jewish Social Studies* 41 (1979): 187–210; and John Higham, *Send These to Me* (New York: Atheneum, 1975), 116–95.

21. Paul A. Carter, *The Spiritual Crisis of the Gilded Age* (DeKalb: Northern Illinois University Press, 1971); Naomi W. Cohen, "The Challenges of Darwinism and Biblical Criticism to American Judaism," *Modern Judaism* 4 (May 1984): 121–57; Kraut, "Judaism Triumphant," 202–25; Benny Kraut, "The Ambivalent Relations of American Reform Judaism with Unitarianism in the Last Third of the Nineteenth Century," *Journal of Ecumenical Studies* 23 (winter 1986): 58–68.

22. David Stern to Bernhard Felsenthal (April 24, 1884), Felsenthal Papers, AJHS.

23. *American Israelite* (May 1881) as quoted in Dena Wilansky, *Sinai to Cincinnati* (New York: Renaissance Book Company, 1937), 101. Although not noticed by recent biographers, a contemporary, Henry Illiowizi, believed that a "remarkable change" came over Wise in the 1880s; he became more conservative. See Henry Illiowizi, *Through Morocco to Minnesota: Sketches of Life in Three Continents* (n.p., 1888), 87.

24. The leadership role played by Philadelphia Jews during this critical period in American Jewish history was first pointed to by Maxwell Whiteman, "The Philadelphia Group," in *Jewish Life in Philadelphia, 1830–1940,* ed. Murray Friedman (Philadelphia: ISHI Publications, 1983), 163–78, and is further analyzed in Friedman, ed., *When Philadelphia Was the Capital of Jewish America.*

25. David G. Dalin, "The Patriarch: The Life and Legacy of Mayer Sulzberger," in *When Philadelphia Was the Capital of Jewish America,* ed. Murray Friedman, 58–74; Philip Rosen, "Dr. Solomon Solis-Cohen and the Philadelphia Group," in ibid., 106–25; Jonathan D. Sarna, "The Making of an American Jewish Culture," in ibid., 145–55; Jonathan D. Sarna, "Is Judaism Compatible with American Civil Religion? The Problem of Christmas and the 'National Faith,' " in *Religion and the Life of the Nation: American Recoveries,* ed. Rowland A. Sherrill (Urbana: University of Illinois Press, 1990), 162–63; Sarna, *JPS,* 14–15. The quotation is from a letter from Max Cohen to Solomon Solis-Cohen (December 22, 1879), Solomon Solis-Cohen Papers.

26. Cyrus L. Sulzberger to Solomon Solis-Cohen (October 5, 1880), Solomon Solis-Cohen Papers. The letter is signed with Cyrus's Hebrew name, "Yitzhak Aryeh."

27. *American Hebrew* (November 21, 1879), 3, reprinted in Philip Cowen, *Memories of an American Jew,* 55; see also 49, and Max Cohen to Solomon Solis-Cohen (November 10, 1879), Solomon Solis-Cohen Papers.

28. Cowen, *Memories of an American Jew,* 40–111, esp. 42, 50; Charles Wyszkowski, *A Community in Conflict: American Jewry during the Great European Immigration* (New York: University Press of America, 1991), xiii–xvii.

29. *American Hebrew* (November 21, 1879), 4, as quoted in Wyszkowski, *A Community in Conflict,* 101; Max Cohen, "Some Memories of Alexander Kohut," in Alexander Kohut, *The Ethics of the Fathers* (New York: privately printed, 1920), xcviii.

30. For a somewhat different analysis of the relationship between the "Historical School"

and Conservative Judaism, see Moshe Davis, *The Emergence of Conservative Judaism: The Historical School in Nineteenth Century America* (Philadelphia: Jewish Publication Society, 1965), 169–70.

31. Donald G. Mathews, "The Second Great Awakening as an Organizing Process," *American Quarterly* 21 (1969): 23–43. Some measure of the organizational revolution within the American Jewish community of that time may be discerned from the fact that thirteen of the nineteen national Jewish organizations listed in the first volume of the *American Jewish Year Book* (1899) were founded after 1879.

32. Naomi W. Cohen, "Introduction," in *Cyrus Adler: Selected Letters,* ed. Ira Robinson, (Philadelphia: Jewish Publication Society, 1985), I, xxx.

33. Cf. Sarna, *JPS,* 13–20, and Sarna, "The Making of an American Jewish Culture," 149–50, where portions of this argument first appeared.

34. On this point, see Sarna, "The Making of an American Jewish Culture," 151.

35. Dianne Ashton, "Rebecca Gratz and the Domestication of American Judaism," Ph.D. diss., Temple University, 1986; Evelyn Bodek, " 'Making Do': Jewish Women and Philanthropy," in *Jewish Life in Philadelphia,* ed. Murray Friedman 143–62.

36. Panzer, "Gratz College," 1–6. According to Panzer's footnote, three of the college's first four graduates were women (6, n. 12).

37. Jonathan D. Sarna, "The Debate over Mixed Seating in the American Synagogue," in *The American Synagogue: A Sanctuary Transformed,* ed. Jack Wertheimer (New York: Cambridge University Press, 1987), 366–79.

38. John Higham, "The Transformation of the Statue of Liberty," *Send These to Me: Immigrants in Urban America* (Baltimore: Johns Hopkins University Press, 1984), 71–80.

39. A large literature seeks to explain Lazarus's "conversion"; for an analysis of this literature see Joe Rooks Rapport, "The Lazarus Sisters: A Family Portrait," Ph.D. diss., Washington University, 1988, 12–108. Quotations are from the centennial edition of Emma Lazarus, *An Epistle to the Hebrews,* with an introduction and notes by Morris U. Schappes (New York: Jewish Historical Society of New York, 1987), 64, 73.

40. Emma Lazarus, *Selections from Her Poetry and Prose,* ed. Morris U. Schappes (New York: Emma Lazarus Federation of Jewish Women's Clubs, 1978), 35–37.

41. Lazarus, *Epistle to the Hebrews,* 8.

42. Lazarus, *Epistle to the Hebrews,* 34–35, 80; Arthur Zieger, "Emma Lazarus and Pre-Herzlian Zionism," in *Early History of Zionism in America,* ed. I. S. Meyer (New York: American Jewish Historical Society, 1958), 77–108. Emma's older sister, Josephine Lazarus (1846–1910), also came to adopt Zionism as her religion, although she sought a universal religion and dabbled with Unitarianism as well. Her *The Spirit of Judaism* (New York: Dodd, Mead, 1895) documents in part American Judaism's spiritual crisis. For her Zionism, see Josephine Lazarus, "Zionism," *American Hebrew* 62 (December 10, 1897), 159–62 [and revised in *New World* 8 (June 1899), 228–42]; and her "Zionism and American Ideals," *Maccabean* 8 (May 1905): 198–204. No full-length study of Josephine Lazarus exists, but useful information can be found in Rapport, "The Lazarus Sisters," 109–54.

43. Cowen, *Memories of an American Jew,* 344.

44. Ray Frank's year of birth is a matter of dispute. I follow Reva Clar and William M. Kramer, "The Girl Rabbi of the Golden West," *Western States Jewish History* 18 (January 1986): 99, who base their date on the 1870 United States census records. The standard date, supplied by her husband (who expressed some uncertainty about it) is 1864 or 1865; see Simon Litman, *Ray Frank Litman: A Memoir* (New York: American Jewish Historical Society, 1957), 4. Rogow in *Gone to Another Meeting,* 228, cites unnamed records dating

her birth to April 10, 1866. Might she have sought to conceal her date of birth when she married her much younger husband, Simon Litman, who was born in 1873?

45. *Jewish Messenger,* May 23, 1890. Reprinted in Jacob R. Marcus, *The American Jewish Woman: A Documentary History* (New York: Ktav, 1981), 380; see also Litman, *Ray Frank Litman: A Memoir,* 12–13. A month later, she replied to this question from *The Jewish Times and Observer:* "What would you do if you were a *rebbitzen* [rabbi's wife]?" Her reply is reprinted in Litman, 14.

46. Excerpts from her Yom Kippur sermon (1890), where this quotation appears, may be found reprinted in Ellen M. Umansky and Dianne Ashton, *Four Centuries of Jewish Women's Spirituality: A Sourcebook* (Boston: Beacon Press, 1992), 128–29.

47. Litman, *Ray Frank Litman,* 8–9; see also Clar and Kramer, "The Girl Rabbi of the Golden West," 104–5, 108.

48. Litman, *Ray Frank Litman,* 68.

49. Quoted in Litman, 15.

50. Ibid., 43–45.

51. Ibid., 55–57.

52. *San Francisco Chronicle* (August 18, 1895), quoted in ibid. 50.

53. *Papers of the Jewish Women's Congress* (Philadelphia: Jewish Publication Society of America, 1894), 8, cf. also 52–65; *Reform Advocate* (August 7, 1897), 412, cited in Clar and Kramer, "Girl Rabbi of the Golden West," 231.

54. For her subsequent career and her contributions to the founding of Hillel, see Clar and Kramer, "Girl Rabbi of the Golden West," 143–202; and Winton U. Solberg, "The Early Years of the Jewish Presence at the University of Illinois," *Religion and American Culture* 2 (summer 1992): 215–45.

55. Clar and Kramer, "Girl Rabbi of the Golden West," 345–51, discount Frank's religious motivations and credit her success to her agent, Samuel H. Friedlander, whom they believe both managed her affairs and kept her name before the press. It seems more likely that Frank hired Friedlander as a consequence of her success. Only *after* she demonstrated that she had something to promote did it make sense for her to have a promoter. Even Clar and Kramer agree that she was a woman of "multiple and formidable talents."

56. Rogow, *Gone to Another Meeting,* 43–78; Karla Goldman, "The Ambivalence of Reform Judaism: Kaufmann Kohler and the Ideal Jewish Woman," *American Jewish History* 79 (summer 1990): 477–99.

57. Rogow, *Gone to Another Meeting,* p. 23. Note that immigrant aid, later so important a part of the Council's work, went unmentioned in this resolution.

58. Ibid., 53, 76.

59. No full-scale history of synagogue sisterhoods has yet appeared. I base this sketch on Jenna Weissman Joselit, "The Special Sphere of the Middle-Class American Jewish Woman: The Synagogue Sisterhood, 1890–1940," *The American Synagogue,* ed. Jack Wertheimer, esp. 208–10; Richard Gottheil, *The Life of Gustav Gottheil* (Williamsport, PA: Bayard Press, 1936), 179–81; Hannah B. Einstein, "Sisterhoods of Personal Service," *Jewish Encyclopedia* (1906), 11:398; and David de Sola Pool, *An Old Faith in the New World* (New York: Columbia University Press, 1955), 369–70. In response to the demand for professional social workers, sisterhoods later transformed their activities and forgot their origins, as Gottheil and Joselit indicate. For the development of the National Federation of Temple Sisterhoods (1913), see Michael A. Meyer, *Response to Modernity: A History of the Reform Movement in Judaism* (New York: Oxford University Press, 1988), 285–86.

60. The most recent full-length biography is Joan Dash, *Summoned to Jerusalem: The*

Life of Henrietta Szold (New York: Harper and Row, 1979); for Szold's early life and work see Alexandra Lee Levin, *The Szolds of Lombard Street* (Philadelphia: Jewish Publication Society, 1960); and Sarna, *JPS*, 23–135.

61. *American Jewish Year Book* 16 (1914–15): 284.

62. William R. Hutchison, *Errand to the World: American Protestant Thought and Foreign Missions* (Chicago: University of Chicago Press, 1987), 111; cf. Patricia Hill, *The World Their Household* (Ann Arbor: University of Michigan Press, 1984).

63. Carol B. Kutscher, "Hadassah," in *Jewish American Voluntary Organizations,* ed. Michael N. Dobkowski (New York: Greenwood Press, 1986), 151–52; Michael N. Dobkowski, "The Early Years of Hadassah, 1912–1922," Ph.D. diss., Brandeis University, 1976; Henrietta Szold to Alice L. Seligsberg (October 10, 1913) in Marvin Lowenthal, *Henrietta Szold: Life and Letters* (New York: Viking Press, 1942), 82.

64. On various aspects of the Social Justice movement and its relationship to the Social Gospel, see Egal Feldman, "The Social Gospel and the Jews," *American Jewish Historical Quarterly* 8 (March 1969): 308–22; Leonard J. Mervis, "The Social Justice Movement and the American Reform Rabbi," *American Jewish Archives* 7 (1955): 171–230; Bernard Martin, "The Social Philosophy of Emil G. Hirsch," *American Jewish Archives* 6 (June 1954): 151–66; John F. Sutherland, "Rabbi Joseph Krauskopf of Philadelphia: The Urban Reformer Returns to the Land," *American Jewish History* 67 (June 1978): 342–62; and Jonathan D. Sarna, "Seating and the American Synagogue," in *Belief and Behavior: Essays in the New Religious History,* ed. Philip R. Vandermeer and Robert P. Swierenga (New Brunswick, NJ: Rutgers University Press, 1991), esp. 195–202.

Chapter Four

Gone to Another Meeting
The National Council of Jewish Women, 1893–1993

Faith Rogow

If hard work earned Hannah Greenebaum Solomon the honor of being named NCJW's first president, she became its founder by being in the right place at the right time. In 1890, Chicago's elites were excitedly beginning to plan various facets of the forthcoming World's Fair. The Fair was designed to provide an international showcase for American industrial leadership. Organized into congresses planned and run by appropriate experts, the Fair highlighted the best of America's technological and social advances. For practical reasons, residents of Chicago did much of the preparation for the Exhibition. Tasks were assigned to committees, and committees were divided by gender. The most important of the women's committees was the Board of Lady Managers of the Exposition, formed in 1891.[1]

The Board, headed by Bertha Honoré Palmer, was responsible for providing exhibit staff and for organizing much of the women's programming, both in and out of the proposed Woman's Building. Palmer quickly recruited friends from the elite Chicago Women's Club to aid in the planning, including Ellen M. Henrotin, whom she appointed vice president of the Board of Lady Managers. Henrotin's duties included chairing the women's branch of the General Committee on Religious Parliament. The responsibilities of this position required her to appoint chairs for the women's committees representing each major religious denomination. Thus, Henrotin came to consider possible candidates for the Jewish Women's Committee. Unable to find Jewish female clergy or nationally known Jewish suffragists, Henrotin turned to her friends in Chicago.

Thirty-three-year-old Hannah Solomon was an obvious choice. Fifteen years earlier, Solomon and her sister, Henrietta Frank, were the first Jews invited to join the prestigious Chicago Women's Club. Solomon's father was a prominent merchant, and her family members had been active in several civic organizations since the 1850s. As a Woman's Club member, Solomon had demonstrated she was "properly" cultured, as well as an ardent and effective social reformer. She was a self-proclaimed suffragist but disavowed radical tactics. She was also involved in Chicago's most prominent Jewish organizations. She belonged to the radical Reform Temple Sinai, but her relatives helped found all five of Chicago's original Reform synagogues, providing her with connections to several leading rabbis, as well as to a wide range of Chicago's Jewish community.[2] In short, Solomon was the perfect chair: a consummate clubwoman and a dedicated Jew from a respected family.

Ellen Henrotin invited her friend Hannah to convene the Jewish Women's Committee "under whatever division or divisions of the Exposition she thought best."[3] Solomon accepted with idealistic hopes that the Exposition would inspire international unity and that, for the first time in recorded history, it would give the Jewish community a showcase "on an equal footing with Christianity, not to defend itself but to tell the world what are its tenets and its deeds."[4]

Solomon viewed the Exposition as a golden opportunity for the Jewish community to prove its worth, and she assumed her role with a grave sense of responsibility and unbounded energy. Sources indicate that she did much of the early work alone.[5] Her first major decision was to organize the Jewish Woman's Congress under the auspices of the World Parliament of Religions, rather than as part of the events being housed at the Woman's Building, where programs were dominated by a women's rights agenda. Deborah Grand Golomb has explained this decision as choosing allegiance to Jews over allegiance to women, a choice she claims manifested itself in later NCJW policy.[6] Solomon, however, had no reason to view the two groups as mutually exclusive. Many prominent advocates of women's rights participated in the Parliament of Religions, including Elizabeth Cady Stanton and Frances Willard.[7] In fact, Solomon explained that she chose the Parliament because she "felt that in the Parliament of Religions, where women of all creeds were represented, the Jewish woman should have a place."[8]

Moreover, though Solomon generally favored positions of the women's rights activists planning the Woman's Building programs, she had reason to wonder whether Jewish women, as Jews, would be welcomed there. Particularly troubling was the feminist debate over the role of western religion in the subjection of women. Like much of the Jewish press, Solomon reacted negatively to the book around which much of that debate centered, Elizabeth Cady Stanton's *Woman's Bible*.[9] Stanton's critique of Christianity included the accusation that Judaism was ultimately at fault for women's oppression. She explained: "The dogmas incorporated in the religious creeds derived from Judaism, teaching that woman was an afterthought in creation, her sex a misfortune. . . . These dogmas are an insidious poison."[10] Solomon may have believed that this debate would be continued in any religious programming done through the Woman's Building, and, feeling uncomfortable with those women who backed Stanton's position, she chose to avoid them or at least to deny them a public forum that could have conceivably obscured Jewish women's contributions with anti-Jewish rhetoric.

More important, while Solomon was certain that Judaism promoted rather than precluded rights for women, she knew that Jewish women were not yet ready to substantiate that position. Unlike their Christian sisters, some of whom were ordained clergy, most of whom were well versed in the Bible, and all of whom had been debating these religious issues for at least forty years, most Jewish women barely possessed even elementary knowledge of the fine points of Jewish learning. Jewish tradition held that formal religious education was extraneous to women's duties in the home, and American religious schools were too few in number and too poor in material resources and teachers to provide a quality education, so few Jewish women had seriously studied the texts around which the feminist debate centered. Moreover, neither American culture nor Judaism approved of a public religious leadership role for women, so few Jewish women had experience speaking in public. At the time of the Exposition, there were no Jewish women's organizations anywhere in the world that publicly discussed religious issues. Solomon even commented that many of the women who spoke at the Jewish Women's Congress were speaking in public for the first time in their lives.[11] Finally, Jewish women were relatively new to America. Most had been in the United States for a generation or less, and, as immigrants fighting for acceptance, Jewish women were reluctant to enter any public debate, especially one that had so aroused emotions nationwide.

Solomon did not want to avoid the debate completely. In fact, she believed that defending Judaism was a primary responsibility of every Jew, especially those in the public eye, as those who spoke at the Congress would surely be. As the first Jew in the Chicago Woman's Club, Solomon was familiar with the role of being the representative Jew in a non-Jewish context. She knew that many of her co-members based their opinion of Jews on their opinion of her. She was naturally concerned that these women know enough of Judaism to understand why it differed from Christianity without resorting to that difference as a basis for discrimination. She expressed her concern in 1892 by daring to break an unspoken Club ban on formal discussions of religion.[12] The paper she delivered, "Our Debt to Judaism," was an attempt to demonstrate that the Christian society of the clubwomen sprang from Jewish roots. One of Solomon's major hopes for the Congress was to publicize this positive view of Judaism by providing the groundwork for Jewish women's entrance into the discussion of religion's role in women's lives. Later, that hope would be expressed in her insistence that a large portion of NCJW's energy be directed toward educating Jewish women about Judaism. In Solomon's mind, the only way to ensure that this discussion could begin in a nonthreatening environment was to place it in the Jewish context of the Parliament of Religions' Jewish Congress, rather than the feminist environment in the Woman's Building.

Solomon also knew that, in many of the Congresses, particularly those planned by Woman's Building organizers, women and men were preparing to square off as enemies. Solomon believed that Jewish men and women could bring their reputed cooperation in the home to the public sphere as a shining example to the women's movement that cooperation was more effective in advancing women's rights than setting men up as opponents.[13]

Solomon recruited a planning committee sympathetic with this view that, "on an occasion when men and women of all creeds are realizing that the ties that bind us are stronger than the differences that separate, that when the world is giving to Israel the liberty, long withheld, of taking its place among all religions to teach the truths it holds for the benefit of man and the glory of the Creator, the place of the Jewish woman would not be vacant."[14] The likeminded committee Solomon secured was carefully selected from a pool of Jewish women with whom Solomon had already worked, including members of the Chicago Women's Aid Society, the South Side Sewing Society, Chicago's Reform synagogues, and her own family.[15]

According to Solomon, "At the first meeting of the Jewish Women's Committee, it was decided to work along the lines adopted by other committees. The committee also decided to collect and publish the traditional melodies of the Jews as a souvenir of the occasion." To sell the hymnbook and to advertise the Congress, the committee issued notices "to all Jewish publications, inviting the cooperation of all persons interested."[16] The committee naturally wanted to prepare the souvenir with the expertise befitting the occasion, and, knowing of no capable women, they arranged for the Reverend William Sparger and Cantor Alois Kaiser to write the text and Dr. Cyrus Adler the introduction. They found a willing publisher in Mr. T. Rubovits, and the committee's first task was quickly completed.

In addition to publicizing the Congress in Jewish publications, the committee began to correspond with the few Jewish women authors and clubwomen they knew in other cities, seeking potential speakers for the occasion. They also wrote to rabbis asking for suggestions of names to include in the program.[17] Solomon alone wrote ninety letters by hand.

Early in this process the committee happened upon two important discoveries. First, the correspondence indicated that "dozens of Jewesses disclaim affiliation" and "hundreds proclaim indifference and confess absolute ignorance of Jewish history and literature."[18] Second, it was difficult to track down those women who were still committed to Judaism and might be qualified to speak or be interested in attending.[19] These two discoveries were the seeds from which NCJW sprang.

The committee was deeply committed to the survival of Judaism in the United States and adhered to the traditional notion that religious practice in the home was the key to such survival. Custom also held that women were responsible for such religious observance. If Jewish women were too ignorant or too apathetic to keep a Jewish home, then the committee could only conclude that the next generation would be lost and Judaism in the United States would succumb to assimilation. These women had grown up in an age that embraced the Enlightenment (and popular women's club) idea that education would be the great equalizer and that public education would produce a country of responsible citizens who would solve the nation's problems with their new-found knowledge. The committee members had found that many of the women they contacted were almost Jewishly illiterate, so they idealistically concluded that they could save Judaism simply by informing Jewish women of their religious duties. This notion would become a cornerstone of NCJW policy.

The decision to work toward this goal by creating a formal organization had its source in more practical considerations. Solomon explained, "The difficulty we experienced in reaching Jewish women for organized effort made it apparent that a national organization was necessary to obviate such difficulties in the future."[20] The committee recognized that, as a much publicized national gathering, the Jewish Women's Congress was an ideal place to reach potential members, and the founding of a national Jewish women's organization became "an integral part of the plan of the Congress . . . at one of [the committee's] earliest meetings. . . ."[21]

Commenting on her busy schedule, the turn-of-the-century Chicago Council member Sara Hart quipped that, if she were writing her own epitaph, her tombstone would read, "Gone to Another Meeting."[22] Her joke reflected the lifestyle of most early National Council of Jewish Women members. Like Hart, who served on more than twenty-five committees in a variety of Progressive social reform organizations, Council women considered volunteer work their special vocation. Council founder Hannah G. Solomon declared, "I was born a clubwoman, just as I was born . . . a Jew."[23] The pride inherent in this remark exposes the faultiness of common depictions of club "ladies" as incompetent, flighty, and shallow. To the contrary, clubwomen recognized their power to influence their communities through their organizations and consequently took their work quite seriously. Though outwardly they may have promoted themselves as genteel ladies, Council Board members were important community leaders.

Modeled after secular women's clubs, NCJW grew out of an organizational heritage that was a combination of nineteenth-century women's clubs and Progressive social reform efforts. In some arenas, such as the fight against the white slave trade, the development of settlement houses, and the aid of female immigrants, NCJW served as the Jewish component of a broader effort. As such, Council supplied both a Jewish voice in the world of women's clubs and a way to Americanize without sacrificing Jewish identity. NCJW was popular with Hart, Solomon, and their peers largely because it provided this point of intersection for otherwise scattered (and sometimes conflicting) facets of their identities as women, as Americans, and as Jews. The organization succeeded primarily because it was able to furnish its members a means by which to acculturate without losing ethnic identity or challenging the limited definitions of gender roles dominant in the United States.

An exemplary though not ideologically innovative Progressive social reform organization, Council made a distinctive contribution, which came as much from its ability to transfer social reform ideology to the Jewish community as from its role as the Jewish component of a broad American movement. Likewise, though NCJW enabled its members to bring their Jewish identity into the world of women's clubs, Council also provided a means by which Jewish women could adapt women's clubs' ideology of gender to the Jewish community. Founded in 1893, NCJW was the offspring of the economic and social success achieved by German Jewish immigrants in the United States. As this community of German Jews matured and stabilized, it faced the same challenge to gender role definitions that had accompanied Jacksonian democracy half a century earlier. That is, in light of their reverence for popular democracy and its promise of equal rights for every individual, how could the community justify continuing a double standard that granted men rights not given to women?[24]

The popular American answer to that dilemma was to define male and female natures (and therefore needs) as intrinsically different. Victorian notions of womanhood prevailed, limiting woman's arena to her home and her emotions. To men fell the public worlds of work and politics, as well as the tools of intellectual pursuit that would advance those areas. This division of gender roles left middle- and upper-class American women in an ironic position. On one hand, they enjoyed the prosperity brought by their husbands' labor, they believed in American democracy as the best guarantor of that prosperity, and they saw America's continued technological and commercial progress ease the burdens of caring for home and children. On the other hand, women found themselves excluded from any direct exercise of power in American society and prevented by social convention and law from taking advantage of the growing opportunities available to men.

By the mid-nineteenth century, many of these women had solved their conflict by transforming themselves from dutiful helpmates to domestic scientists and club-women. Participation in clubs took women beyond the confines of the home into the community, giving them what the historian Theodora Penny Martin has termed a "semi-public" voice.[25] That is, women's clubs never seriously competed with men for public power, but they provided women with a piece of the "male" public pie by fostering self-education, public socializing, and charity work.

Council's role in American debates over attempts to modernize Jewish practice exemplified this "semi-public" club experience. Coming from communities to which they believed they could never return, German Jews had developed a uniquely American form of Reform Judaism as a way of adapting to American life without losing their religious identity. Reform's emphasis on modernization and acceptance of pragmatic changes in ritual would be an important precondition for NCJW's expansion of the traditional boundaries of Jewish womanhood, but it also invited late-nineteenth-century challenges from traditionalists upset by Reform's apparent devaluation of Jewish law and custom. By 1893, movements promoting radical Reform and those insisting on a more moderate approach had coalesced. As these groups of predominantly German Jews battled for hegemony over the American Jewish community, their positions began to solidify. Prior to Council, women largely had been excluded from this debate. NCJW provided Study Circles where women could familiarize themselves with the texts and issues under discussion. Its conventions and publications, as well as invitations its leaders received from other Jewish groups to represent Jewish women, provided forums through which women could enter the deliberations. As the *American Hebrew* recognized, unlike the scattered or fraternal Jewish women's organizations that had preceded it, Council was "a potent factor" in the Jewish community with which people of this generation (1895) "must seriously reckon when [they] consider the elements that make up the religious condition of Israel in America."[26] Most important, as a women's club, NCJW allowed its members to enter religious debates without breaking "proper" gender roles, thus providing a means through which Jewish women could publicly influence the future of their community without confronting such difficult and potentially divisive issues as acceptance of women as rabbis or scholars.

In fact, though NCJW's success in finding a way to express American gender roles in a Jewish context contributed decisively to creating a unique American Jewish womanhood, Council would in no way initiate radical change in the Jewish community. Like other clubwomen faced with the need to justify public activities in light of their adherence to the precepts of "True Womanhood," Council members adopted what scholars have dubbed "domestic feminism." In her study of the General Federation of Women's Clubs, an umbrella organization with which NCJW eventually affiliated, Karen Blair explains that clubs were successful because they used accepted notions of womanhood to justify their activities.[27] The term "domestic feminism" was coined by the historian Daniel Scott Smith, who theorized about how nineteenth-century women asserted power in the home. His research documented a declining American birthrate in an era when birth control was not widely available. He concluded that women used prevailing notions of womanhood, which depicted proper ladies as pure and chaste, to justify limiting sexual contact with their husbands.[28] Blair notes that this pattern of justification went well beyond the bedroom. For example, clubwomen insisted that social welfare work was simply an extension of motherhood, thus justifying an expansion of woman's sphere beyond the home by using the very ideology that seemingly confined her to the hearth. This pattern of justification was the core of "domestic feminism." Rather than redefining the "ideal lady," as Blair has suggested, domestic feminism simply recast women's tasks. In Hannah G. Solomon's words, "Through it all women have not changed, but their opportunities have."[29] Council, especially, placed motherhood at the core of its definition of what it meant to be a Jewish woman, even as it demanded service outside the home from its members.

Council's pattern of conservatism was not unique to the Jewish community. As Ann Douglas has demonstrated, because women's clubs were created as a way for women to "fit in" to the male scheme of things rather than challenge society's sexist ideology, they tended to foster the preservation of the status quo.[30] Douglas cites the glorification of motherhood as one example of this conservative influence. She argues that, as production moved out of the home while women remained confined behind its thresholds, women in mid-nineteenth-century America lost their ability to be productive. America tried to compensate by "establishing a perpetual Mother's Day."[31] Thus, Council's glorification of motherhood reflected popular American sentiment as well as traditional Jewish notions of the "Eyshet Hayil" (Woman of Valor—a passage from Proverbs that extols the virtues of an ideal wife). This fusion of American and Jewish notions of womanhood was NCJW's primary raison d'être.

Council's ability to alter significantly women's position in the Jewish community was limited, not enhanced, by its acceptance of the notion of complementary gender roles and the resulting equation of womanhood with motherhood. NCJW argued that gender roles had been divinely designed to remain separate and that women's oppression came not from the denial of rights but from the withholding of respect. In this spirit, NCJW did not support the ordination of women as rabbis until the 1970s, viewing such ordination as an infringement of the divine order. Instead, it elevated woman's traditional role as mother to the status previously reserved for the most respected scholars. Thus, while NCJW insisted that women's opinions be accorded the attention due a dignitary, they provided women with no direct means to gain power in the Jewish community.

Furthermore, although it developed an elaborate social and philanthropic network based on women's unique experience of life in America, the separation of gender roles which created that unique perspective resulted from male constructions of womanhood. That is, Jewish women's culture, though distinctly different from the world as experienced by Jewish men, was not created in a vacuum. It was the result of the fusion of American values and Jewish tradition, both defined almost exclusively by men. NCJW's womanhood thus reaffirmed men's power rather than challenged it. Thus, though Council seemed to carve substantial inroads to equal representation for women in Jewish communal institutions, those gains were temporary. By the 1950s almost no women held major positions in synagogues or (nonwomen's) Jewish communal institutions. Not until the rise of modern feminism in the 1970s would Jewish women again protest their exclusion from these positions. Despite their efforts and the groundwork laid by organizations like NCJW, parity has not yet been achieved.

Still, Council women certainly believed that their work advanced the interests of women, and NCJW indisputably opened up new paths to Jewish women. The great diversity among Council Sections and shifts in its ideology of womanhood since the 1960s make NCJW difficult to place neatly in the scheme of American feminism or the development of the women's movement. If one accepts the historian Nancy Cott's general threefold definition of feminism as opposition to a hierarchy that posits one sex as superior to the other, the perception of women as a social as well as biological grouping, and the recognition that woman's condition is socially but not divinely constructed, then NCJW was only partially feminist.[32] It adopted Cott's first two conditions but steadfastly clung to the primacy of motherhood as woman's divinely assigned role.

Writing about the General Federation of Women's Clubs, the historian Karen Blair has argued that, despite adherence to such traditional conceptions of womanhood, the public activities of clubwomen "rendered obsolete the notion that 'woman's place is in the home,' and thereby made a significant contribution to women's struggle for autonomy."[33] In fact, Blair has argued that domestic feminism's moderate approach to effecting change in women's roles was more successful than was the militant feminism of many suffragists because it was able to attract more adherents and because it brought real change while appearing to be nonthreatening.[34] Council member and Barnard founder Annie Nathan Meyer expressed a similar idea when, commenting on turn-of-the-century struggles for women's rights, she wrote, "to put any radical scheme across, it must be done in the most conservative manner possible."[35] Council's role in the Jewish community contradicts both Nathan and Blair.

Though Council's expression of Jewish womanhood would not bring radical change to the Jewish community, it did contribute a distinctive voice. The fact that Council worked from a specifically female perspective resulted in the development of programs that were often different from those implemented by comparable male-run organizations. Among other things, this female perspective provided the impetus for NCJW's instrumental role in carving out a Jewish niche in the social reform movement.

Yet, Council was not founded because Jewish women were excluded from non-Jewish social reform efforts. Most Council members felt quite comfortable in the world of women's clubs and social reform organizations, as is attested by their tendency to affiliate with such organizations even while committed to NCJW.

Though Council founders occasionally encountered some prejudice in these groups, they prided themselves on their successful acculturation to life in America, and class interests shared with club sisters outweighed ethnic divisions. More detailed comparative studies must be done to ascertain whether Gentile clubwomen shared this attitude or whether Council women romanticized their acceptance into women's clubs because to do otherwise would have been to admit that either their efforts to acculturate had failed or the United States was not the panacea for Jews they believed it to be. In any case, Council founders never named anti-Semitism[36] as a justification for creating their own organization. They formed NCJW to give Jewish women a stronger voice in the women's world, not to back away from participation in an anti-Semitic environment.

In many ways, NCJW represents the intersection of several crossroads within the American Jewish community. Though NCJW was founded and dominated by German Jews, Council's philanthropic work would immerse its members in the newer Eastern European immigrant Jewish community. Engaged in a religious revival, the organization would be caught in the power struggle between the Reform movement and more traditional interpretations of Judaism. Immersed in the debates of the turn-of-the-century women's movement, Council would come to represent both the modernization of and the renewal of Jewish womanhood. Council's uniqueness lay in its ability to make a cloth of these varied threads. Its intricate weave of American and Jewish cultures, as well as its longevity, make it an ideal starting point for the study of the development of modern Jewish womanhood.

This study of NCJW will remain incomplete, however, until scholars have examined all facets of the development of American Jewish womanhood. Though Council provides an example of how American definitions of religion as feminine influenced the Jewish community to alter its vision of womanhood, the resulting religious character attributed to Jewish women is here reported only through Council eyes. Before we can claim to understand American Jewish womanhood, we must trace the influence of America's connection of womanhood and religion on all facets of the Jewish community. The absence of such studies makes this examination of NCJW a starting point. Its gaps are an invitation to include gender analysis in future studies of the American Jewish experience.

NOTES

1. For details of the Women's Building and women's programing at the Chicago World Columbian Exposition, see Jane Madeline Weimann, *The Fair Women* (Chicago: Academy Chicago, 1981).

2. Hannah G. Solomon, *Fabric of My Life* (New York: Bloch, 1946).

3. Ibid., 80.

4. *Reform Advocate* (July 22, 1893), 442.

5. Mrs. Henry [Hannah] Solomon, *Jews of Illinois in Story and Tableaux* (Chicago: Chicago Section-Council of Jewish Women, 1919), 11.

6. Deborah Grand Golomb, "The 1893 Congress of Jewish Women: Evolution or Revolution in American Jewish Women's History?" *American Jewish History* 70 (September 1980): 52–67.

7. Though Solomon was not among them, even Chicago's militant suffragists opposed a separate women's building and argued that any woman who was worthy of inclusion should be given space in the appropriate general exhibition, so Solomon's position was, in fact, in accordance with her community's most visible feminists. Weimann, *Fair Women*, 39.

8. Hannah Greenebaum Solomon, *A Sheaf of Leaves* (privately printed, 1911), 50.

9. *Papers of the Jewish Women's Congress, 1893* (Philadelphia: Jewish Publication Society, 1894), 171–72; "The New Woman," *American Israelite* (December 1895), 4–5.

10. Quoted in Donna A. Behnke, *Religious Issues in Nineteenth Century Feminism* (Troy, NY: Whitston, 1982), 189.

11. "Council of Jewish Women," *Reform Advocate* (October 24, 1896), 151.

12. Solomon, *Fabric*, 43.

13. Ellen Sue Levi Elwell, "The Founding and Early Programs of the National Council of Jewish Women: Study and Practice as Jewish Women's Religious Expression," Ph.D. diss., Indiana University, 1982, 64.

14. Solomon, *Sheaf*, 50.

15. The original committee of sixteen included Vice-Chair Lillian (Mrs. I. S.) Moses, secretary Fanny (Mrs. Henry) Adler, Mary (Mrs. Charles) Greenebaum Haas, Julia Felsenthal, Carrie (Mrs. L. J.) Wolf, Etta Rosenbaum, Mrs. Charles Stettauer, Bertha Loeb, Sadie (Mrs. Max) Leopold, Flora Nusbaum, Lena (Mrs. Martin) Emmerich, Esther (Etta) Witkowski, Babette (Mrs. Emanuel) Mandel, Lena (Mrs. August) Frank, and Sadie American. Marital status and husband's names are included to aid in identification and because that is how the women addressed each other in print. The first name of Mrs. Charles Stettauer was not indicated in any Council sources.

16. Solomon, *Sheaf*, 48. For the actual notice, see *Reform Advocate*, July 22, 1893, 442.

17. Rose Wolf, Hortense Wolf, and Ruth C. Feibel, *History of the Council (Cincinnati Section), 1895–1965* (Cincinnati: Cincinnati Section, NCJW, 1965), 1. Unfortunately, records do not indicate who received the letters or how recipients were chosen.

18. Solomon, *Sheaf*, 71.

19. Mrs. Hannah G. Solomon, "Report of the National Council of Jewish Women," *American Jewess* (April 1895), 27.

20. Ibid.

21. Mrs. Henry [Hannah] Solomon, "Beginnings of the Council of Jewish Women," *American Hebrew* (April 12, 1912), 725.

22. Sara L. Hart, *The Pleasure is Mine: An Autobiography* (Chicago: Valentine-Newman, 1947), 263.

23. Ibid. Also, Hannah Solomon Scrapbook, Box X-172, American Jewish Archives; Rebekah Kohut, *More Yesterdays* (New York: Bloch, 1950), 36.

24. Kathryn Kish Sklar, *Catharine Beecher, A Study in American Domesticity* (New York: Norton, 1976), 156.

25. Theodora Penny Martin, *The Sound of Our Own Voices: Women's Study Clubs, 1860–1910* (Boston: Beacon, 1987), 18.

26. *American Hebrew* (May 31, 1895), 86.

27. Karen Blair, *The Clubwoman as Feminist: True Womanhood Redefined, 1868–1914* (New York: Holmes and Meier, 1980), 3.

28. Daniel Scott Smith, "Family Limitation, Sexual Control, and Domestic Feminism in

Victorian America," in *Clio's Consciousness Raised,* ed. Mary Hartman and Lois W. Banner (New York: Harper and Row, 1974), 119–36.

29. *Chicago Herald and Examiner,* (January 11, 1938), clipping in the Hannah Solomon Scrapbook, Box X-172, American Jewish Archives.

30. Ann Douglas, *The Feminization of American Culture* (New York: Knopf, 1977), 8–9.

31. Ibid., 6, 74.

32. Nancy Cott, *The Grounding of Modern Feminism* (New Haven: Yale University Press, 1987), 4.

33. Blair, *Clubwoman as Feminist,* 119.

34. Ibid., 41.

35. Annie Nathan Meyer, *It's Been Fun* (New York: Henry Schuman, 1951), 4–5.

36. Using the term "anti-Semitism" to mean "anti-Jew" is problematic because it obscures the existence of other Semitic peoples, especially Arabs. However, in an effort to reflect accurately NCJW's language and understanding (rather than current usage standards), this study will follow Council's pattern and use the term "anti-Semitism" to mean "anti-Jew."

Part II

Worlds of Difference

Between 1881 and 1924, millions of Europeans—Italians, Greeks, Russians, Poles, and some two million East European Jews—streamed to America. Propelled by grinding poverty, violent pogroms, and the dislocations of revolutionary turmoil and war, immigrants believed, as did the writer Anzia Yezierska, that "America was a land of living hope, woven of dreams, aflame with longing and desire." But they discovered, as she wrote in her classic story, "America and I," "[b]etween my soul and the American soul were worlds of difference."[1] East European Jewish immigrant women strove—as did Yezierska in her stories, novels, and films[2]—to bridge that difference, to claim their places in America.

The East European Jewish migration utterly transformed American Jewry. By 1930, the 4.4 million American Jews made up almost 3.6 percent of the U.S. population, nearly a third of world Jewry.[3] The extraordinary numbers brought with them enormous diversity. Immigrant Jewish women and men discovered that, in America, freedom empowered them to choose different paths for adjusting, adapting, and reinterpreting Judaism and for reshaping their Jewish identities as they became Americans.

It is perhaps not surprising, then, that many of the new women's historians who studied American Jewish women turned first to these immigrants.[4] Moreover, the bulk of the subsequent scholarship in the field has analyzed how they, their daughters, and their granddaughters encountered America.[5]

The chapters that follow reveal "worlds of difference," not only between immigrants and Americans but also among Jews. Gender, geography, class, and politics deeply affected Jewish women's paths to influence and their revisioning of their Jewish and emerging American identities. Moreover, since poverty was an overwhelming (if, for many, transient) characteristic of the immigrant experience, several of the essays examine how gender, work, and politics intersected, demonstrating that the contours of Jewish women's immigrant lives indeed differed both from those of Jewish men and from those of other female immigrants.

Shelly Tenenbaum's "Borrowers or Lenders Be" shows how, with the help of local Jewish credit associations, poor women whose husbands couldn't or wouldn't give them extra money and those who had fallen upon hard times, like the newly widowed, managed to survive. Most borrowed for personal needs—to buy clothes for the baby, to pay the doctor and the grocer. But a significant number borrowed for business—to buy cloth to sew and coal to heat the bathhouse. In the years when married women all over America could rarely borrow money without their husband's signature, the ladies' Hebrew free loan associations offered borrowers a financial cushion, even as they allowed the lenders to move "outside of the private sphere and into the public world of communal service and credit."[6]

Poverty compelled Jewish immigrant women to work. Among immigrants in New York and Boston, Philadelphia and Chicago, the garment industry dominated the world of women's work. But, in " 'We Dug More Rocks,' " Linda Mack Schloff considers the immigrant women of the Upper Midwest and finds that here the "economy and geography of the region dictated that Jewish women's work would diversify in ways few immigrants dreaming of America could have imagined."[7] While some immigrants indeed labored in the needle trades like their sisters in the big cities, Schloff finds Jewish women becoming farm wives on the plains and "helping out" in family stores on Main Street. However, their daughters, who had the benefit of an American education, had new opportunities. They became clerks and bookkeepers, even teachers and social workers, but, as they moved into the middle class, and well into the 1970s, marriage and especially the birth of their children marked the end of their labor outside the home.

While among midwestern immigrant Jewish women union activity "was muted," the garment unions and their quest to better the lives of workers form a central theme of the immigrant Jewish experience. And Jewish women's unionism provides a unique dimension of this history. In "Organizing the Unorganizable," Alice Kessler-Harris reveals the "persistent conflict" of female union organizers torn "between their experiences as women and their tasks as union officers . . . offer[ing] insight into the ways women tried to adapt familiar cultural tradition to the needs of a new world." Pauline Newman, Fannia Cohn, and Rose Pesotta started out as operators in the dress and waist industry, a trade that employed great numbers of Jewish women. Low wages, poor working conditions, and frequent layoffs pushed the girls whose bleeding fingers ached to join the International Ladies Garment Workers Union and walk the picket lines. Kessler-Harris shows that gender meant that men and women had very different union experiences. She also sheds light on an important theme of early-twentieth-century American women's history, namely feminism and what it meant to these Jewish working women.[8]

But political activity was not restricted to working women. In "Immigrant Women and Consumer Protest," Paula E. Hyman shows a "modern and sophisticated political mentality emerging in a rapidly changing community" among immigrant housewives. In 1902, after the price of kosher meat soared from twelve to eighteen cents a pound, mothers with children in immigrant neighborhoods all over New York City staged "a successful three-week boycott of kosher meat shops." As they broke into butcher shops, setting meat afire, and canvassed house-to-house, compelling their neighbors to honor the boycott, the "strikers" unleashed "their power as consumers and domestic managers."

But the radical politics of boycotts and strikes meant to improve their own lives and those of their families and neighbors were not the only signs of Jewish women's public activism in these years. Hadassah, the Women's Zionist Organization of America, founded in 1912, harnessed "the talents and efficiency of thousands" of middle-class Jewish women, including acculturating immigrants and their American-born daughters. In "Zion in Our Hearts," Joyce Antler surveys the life and career of its founder, the "exceptional" Henrietta Szold (1860–1945), and the unfolding of her mission "to educate women in Judaism." Drawn to the fledgling Zionist movement, which set out to resettle Jews in their historic homeland, Szold directed Hadassah into a practical program of providing health care for the women and children of Palestine (after 1948, the State of Israel). As a result, "Hadassah came to offer American Jewish women a meaningful route to Jewish female identity," through the "restored Zion in your own hearts."[9]

NOTES

1. Anzia Yezierska, "America and I," in *America and I: Short Stories by American Jewish Women Writers,* ed. Joyce Antler (Boston: Beacon, 1990), 72–82, quotations 72, 81. The story was originally published in 1922.

2. Among her best-known works are Anzia Yezierska, *Bread Givers* (1925; rpt., New York: Persea Books, 1975), and the silent film based on her short story "Hungry Hearts" (1922; repr., videocassette, National Center for Jewish Film, 1993).

3. Jonathan D. Sarna, ed., *The American Jewish Experience,* (1986; 2d ed., New York: Holmes and Meier, 1997), 359.

4. Alice Kessler-Harris's "Organizing the Unorganizable" was first published in 1976. Paula E. Hyman's "Immigrant Women and Consumer Protest" was first published in 1980. See also Sydney Stahl Weinberg, *The World of Our Mothers* (New York: Schocken Books, 1988); Susan A. Glenn, *Daughters of the Shtetl: Life and Labor in the Immigrant Generation* (Ithaca: Cornell University Press, 1990).

5. An important exception is Karla Goldman, *Beyond the Synagogue Gallery: Finding a Place for Women in American Judaism* (Cambridge, MA: Harvard University Press, 2000).

6. This new essay is based on Shelly Tenenbaum, *A Credit to Their Community: Jewish Loan Societies in the United States, 1880–1945* (Detroit: Wayne State University Press, 1993).

7. For another evaluation of how economy and geography intersected with gender in the Jewish community, see William Toll, *Women, Men, and Ethnicity: Essays on the Structure and Thought of American Jewry* (Lanham, MD: University Press of America, 1991), esp. 45–84.

8. See, among others, Nancy F. Cott, *The Grounding of Modern Feminism* (New Haven: Yale University Press, 1987); Linda Gordon Kuzmack, *Woman's Cause: The Jewish Woman's Movement in England and the United States, 1881–1933* (Columbus: Ohio State University Press, 1990).

9. At the beginning of the twenty-first century, Szold remains a deeply revered icon of American Jewish womanhood, and a large scholarship reflects this. See, among others, Joan Dash, *Summoned to Jerusalem: The Life of Henrietta Szold* (New York: Harper and Row, 1979); Baila Round Shargel, *Lost Love: The Untold Story of Henrietta Szold, Unpublished Diary and Letters* (Philadelphia: Jewish Publication Society, 1997).

Chapter Five

Borrowers or Lenders Be
Jewish Immigrant Women's Credit Networks

Shelly Tenenbaum

Eva Bernstein, a widow with six children, needed a loan to buy chickens for her poultry business. Ida Bender, a gasoline attendant who had three children, sought one hundred dollars to pay personal bills. May Berman, separated from her husband and a mother of five, needed funds to purchase merchandise for her electrical supplies store.[1] Each of these Jewish women applied for loans during the Depression, and each was successful in her quest for credit. With the help of local Jewish credit associations, they, and scores of women like them, managed to survive through hard times. They had access to traditional Hebrew free loan societies and to modern credit unions. Organized around biblical and Talmudic proscriptions against charging interest, Hebrew free loan societies provided borrowers with interest-free loans. Credit unions, in contrast, used a cooperative model that charged interest on their loans.[2]

Beginning in the 1880s, East European Jewish immigrants transported Hebrew free loan societies from Europe to America. These philanthropic organizations raised capital from supporters' contributions and then loaned the funds without interest to borrowers who furnished the names of appropriate endorsers. The endorser system, predicated on mutual trust, proved so effective that most societies experienced an annual default rate of less than 1 percent. By 1927, more than five hundred Hebrew free loan societies existed in communities as diverse as Des Moines, Nashville, San Francisco, and New York.[3]

Ethnic culture and religious tradition, however, did not limit the parameters of immigrant loan activity. In addition to traditional free loan societies, American Jews organized modern credit cooperatives that charged interest on loans and therefore had no basis within Jewish law. Unlike the philanthropic Hebrew free loan societies that had two distinct classes of people—contributors who provided the loan capital and borrowers who made use of the funds—cooperative credit unions generated their loan capital from the borrowers themselves. German Jews—most notably Edward A. Filene, the Boston department store owner—provided the leadership for the credit union movement, and in the Northeast, at least, East European Jews were disproportionately active as rank-and-file members. For example, in 1916, Jews operated half of all urban credit unions in New York State, and, by the early years of the Depression, three-quarters of the state's 117 credit unions had a predominately Jewish membership.[4] In neighboring Massachusetts, Jews made up, most of the members of more than half of the state's 311 credit unions in 1930. In 1927, of Boston's 139 credit unions, three-quarters had either explicitly Jewish names like Arbeiter Ring, Tifereth Jacob, Jewish Women, Love of Peace, Zion, Palestine, and King Solomon or boards of directors that were at least two-thirds Jewish. Massachusetts credit union organizers recognized the potential for recruiting members from the Jewish community when, in 1914, they hired a Yiddish-speaking credit union organizer who had been affiliated with the Roxbury Credit Union.[5]

Why Women Borrowed

While researching these ethnic loan facilities, I found that women appeared regularly in the records, although less frequently than men, as lenders, as well as borrowers. In the Dorchester district of Boston, women made up one-third of the membership of the Blue Hill Neighborhood Credit Union during the mid-1920s.[6] On the West Coast, women made up 11 percent of San Francisco Hebrew Free Loan Association (HFLA) borrowers and 10 percent of the people who received money from the Los Angeles Jewish Loan Fund during the 1930s. The Jewish Loan Fund was an unusual organization, however. Until 1948, when the Jewish Loan Fund and the local HFLA combined their resources to become the Jewish Free Loan Association, it granted small free loans, as well as larger business loans, with interest. Female Jewish Loan Fund borrowers received free loans four times as often as they received interest loans, suggesting that women borrowed more often for consumption than for business purposes.[7]

By setting its loan maximum at twenty-five dollars during the early 1930s, leaders of the Providence Ladies' HFLA, an organization that limited its services to women, catered to a population that needed extra money for household and personal expenses. Although the low maximum amount rendered the organization inadequate for entrepreneurial purposes, it was beneficial to housewives who otherwise were totally dependent on their husbands for money. By not requiring husbands' signatures or permission, the Providence Ladies' HFLA provided Jewish women with at least some degree of autonomy.

For many American women, pleading and even stealing from their husbands were their only options when they needed more than their husbands allowed them. Letters to the editor of women's magazines portray the financial struggles that many early-twentieth-century women faced. Margaret, for example, wrote to *Good Housekeeping* about how her husband, John, would get very angry when she needed more than her fifty-dollar monthly allowance to run the house, pay all bills, and buy clothes for herself and a baby. If Theresa Marabella, a forty-year-old homemaker, had had access to an institution like the Providence Ladies' HFLA, she might not have stolen ten dollars from her husband's trousers for a trip to New

York. For her misdeed, according to a 1921 *New York Times* article, Marabella was sentenced to four months in a county jail.[8]

Credit organizations that catered to the needs of housewives were not unique to the Jewish community. Based on models that had existed in their country of origin, turn-of-the-century Japanese-American women organized rotating credit associations, known as *ko* or *tanamoshi-ko,* through their social clubs, religious institutions, and educational organizations. In groups of about twenty, Japanese women generated their own loan funds by pooling money earned through sewing and domestic work. Each woman made a monthly contribution of between five and twenty dollars; every month, a different woman borrowed the combined funds. After each woman had a borrowing turn, the *ko* disbanded. According to the sociologist Evelyn Nakano Glenn, the *ko* "was a serious savings device that enabled women to accumulate a large lump sum of money for special expenses, such as a winter coat, a trip to Japan, or school clothes for children."[9] Japanese women, like Jewish women, borrowed primarily for consumption and personal purposes.

In Pittsburgh, women made up one of every nine Hebrew Free Loan borrowers. Unlike male borrowers, however, most women did not request loans for business pursuits. Sixty percent of the women borrowed only for private needs, while the majority of men, some 70 percent, applied for business loans. Women requested money mainly to pay for rent, household expenses, medical bills, insurance, home repairs, education for themselves and their children, moving expenses, holiday necessities, and divorce costs. Ida Bender and Clara Appelbaum provide typical portraits of female Pittsburgh HFLA borrowers. Ida, the gasoline attendant who had received one hundred dollars during the Depression to pay personal bills, borrowed an additional one hundred dollars for dental work and sixty dollars for coal in the early 1940s. Clara, a single woman and property owner, worked for the Department of Public Works. In 1941, she received two loans in order to pay taxes. The Pittsburgh data suggest a second important difference between male and female applicants. Women were far more likely to be single when they received a loan. Twenty-seven percent of women borrowers in Pittsburgh were widowed, and an additional 21 percent were divorced, separated, or never married. In contrast, almost all the male applicants were married.[10]

While Ida Bender and Clara Appelbaum represent the majority of female Pittsburgh borrowers, the fact that 40 percent of the women borrowed for their businesses requires further consideration.[11] Examples of individual Pittsburgh borrowers illustrate the relationship between free loans and women's business development. Esther Berger, married to a Hebrew teacher, borrowed two hundred dollars in 1937 to purchase machines for her gym and bathhouse. Over a five-year period, Clara Cohen, married with three children, borrowed five hundred dollars for her peddling trade. Mary Ackerman, a widow with two children, took out two loans in 1939 for a total of $170 to help her in her dressmaking business. Rose Dorman, a widow and mother of four children, peddled dresses to support her family and received five fifty dollars loans between 1933 and 1936 for stock money.

Given early-twentieth-century gender roles, it is not surprising that more men than women sought funds for their businesses. At the same time, however, it is very likely that more Jewish businesswomen benefited from free loans than these data suggest. When women operated businesses jointly with their spouses, a relatively common occurrence, the husbands would have been the ones most likely to apply for loans. The records of a special émigré free loan fund administered by the Los Angeles Jewish Loan Fund during the early 1940s provide some helpful detail for exploring this issue. Between December 1940 and November 1942, the secretary listed sixty-seven loan applications in the minutes. The records make it absolutely clear that at least seven of the loans listed solely under male names were for businesses run jointly by husbands and wives. For example, Adolph Mintz received money for a dry cleaning store run by him and his wife. Although a loan was listed under Peter Olinsky's name, the organization approved the money for a guest home administered by Mr. and Mrs. Olinsky. There was also one additional case of a husband, an immigrant from Hungary, who took out a ninety-dollar loan to be used solely by his wife, who was a masseuse. She needed to buy a car to transport heavy equipment.[12] In general, statistics regarding business ownership often disguise the actual role women played. The absence of women's names from official documents, such as deeds, tax forms, and loan applications, does not necessarily prove that women were not working as partners within family businesses or even as managers of their own businesses. Census data also underestimate women's enterprising roles. When census takers collected occupational data, husbands and wives often failed to report women's work in family-owned businesses because they both viewed women as helpers, rather than owners, managers, or even workers. The historical role played by women in small businesses was, in the words of the historical sociologists Lenore Davidoff and Catherine Hall, a "hidden investment."[13]

Jewish Women As Lenders

Women not only borrowed from free loan funds but also loaned money through women's credit organizations.[14] As indicated by the existence of the Providence Ladies' HFLA, women administered their own institutions. Ladies' free loan associations existed in many communities, such as Baltimore, Boston, Chicago, Cleveland, Columbus, Hartford, Jersey City (New Jersey), Lawrence (Massachusetts), Los Angeles, New York, Omaha, Philadelphia, Providence, Rochester, Salem (Massachusetts), Scranton, Seattle, South Bend, and Springfield (Massachusetts). While Jewish women created and directed ladies' free loan societies, they typically loaned money to members of both sexes.

In 1897, the Chicago Woman's Loan Association, one of the earliest Jewish women's credit organizations, gave out its first loan. Mrs. I. J. Robin, the head of the loan committee, granted it from her drugstore. Beginning with eighty-seven dollars in its treasury, by 1918 the society had disbursed as much as thirty-three thousand dollars per year, with minimal losses of approximately 1 percent of the total amount borrowed. Ten women constituted the loan committee, which met weekly to review the applications. The administrators limited the membership to fifty, composed "entirely of Russian women," and kept expenses to a minimum since, with the exception of a paid investigator, they relied on volunteer workers.[15]

Originally members of a local relief organization, the founders of the Woman's Loan Association started this new organization after attending an 1896 lecture on scientific methods of philanthropy. Scientific philanthropy, the dominant philanthropic ideology of the mid-nineteenth to the early twentieth centuries, emphasized organizational efficiency and the importance of encouraging the poor to rely on their own initiative, rather than on handouts. The leaders of the Woman's Loan Association felt strongly about the advantages of loans over conventional almsgiving. Loans preserved recipients' dignity, while monetary gifts were humiliating. Minnie Low, one of the founders, represented her organization's view:

> Loan a small amount to a man struggling for existence, let him invest it in a legitimate occupation, let him by thrift manage to keep body and soul together; let him at the same time repay the loan in small installments, without flinching, and without shirking his responsibility, and what greater proof do we require that undaunted courage, ambition, honor, and manliness are virtues of the poor? Not to annihilate but rather to preserve these sterling qualities is the mission of the loan organizations.[16]

The influence of scientific philanthropy was apparent not only in the organization's rhetoric but also in its practices. The Woman's Loan Association was one of the few free loan societies that insisted on the merits of investigating borrowers in order to maximize the benefits of any given loan. Loan committee members approved only loans they deemed to be for a worthy purpose. In contrast, most free loan associations deliberately did not investigate their clients because they did not want to probe into their lives by asking personal and potentially embarrassing questions. The officers of the Woman's Loan Association, however, feared that a lack of information about the borrowers would lead to fraud and to inappropriate loans for luxury items.

An ardent supporter of women's rights, Low was proud that women administered this Chicago loan facility. At a 1914 national meeting on Jewish philanthropy, not long after the state of Illinois voted in favor of women's suffrage, she boldly asserted,

> No man has ever had an active voice in the affairs of this [Woman's Loan] Association. As contributing members, men have been granted the courtesy of affixing their names to the subscription list, otherwise all privileges have been denied them. What bearing woman's emancipation in our state will have in extending the privilege of the vote to the sterner sex, the future alone will tell. At the present time the sentiment is still against the open door policy.[17]

Low, known as the "Jane Addams of the Jews," was thirty years old when she helped found the Woman's Loan Association. Despite a history of poor health (she dropped out of high school in her first year because of illness), she was very active within Chicago's social service agencies, such as the Maxwell Street Settlement, the Juvenile Protective League, and the Central Bureau of Jewish Charities. Low

achieved national recognition for her abilities when her colleagues elected her president of the National Conference of Jewish Charities in 1914.[18]

Providing capital for entrepreneurial purposes was an explicit goal of the
Woman's Loan Association, as it was for most free loan societies.[19] Low attributed
Jewish immigrant business development in Chicago to the existence of local loan
societies. "In the Chicago Ghetto, along the Jefferson Street market, as well as
throughout the district, there are comparatively few of the peddlers, vendors, and
keepers of small stands and shops, who have not been given a start in life or helped
over rugged places by loans from local organizations."[20]

Since banks did not provide funds for early-twentieth-century small entrepreneurs, organizations like the Woman's Loan Association played a critical role for
Jewish immigrant enterprises. Before 1925, only one bank in all of New England
and only one among the Middle Atlantic states operated personal loan departments.
An estimated 85 percent of the population was "beyond the pale of bank credit";
only those who furnished tangible security could obtain bank loans. Because of a
pattern of poor management and investment strategies, attempts to form ethnic
banks proved largely unsuccessful.[21] Unlicensed lenders were always willing to lend
money, but their excessive interest rate militated against this source's offering an
adequate answer to the immigrants' credit needs. Rates of 400 percent per year
were not uncommon.[22] Therefore, in order to raise business capital, East European
Jewish immigrants created hundreds of ethnic loan societies, such as the Woman's
Loan Association, the Blue Hill Neighborhood Credit Union, the Los Angeles Jewish Loan Fund, and the New York Hebrew Free Loan Society (HFLS), throughout
the United States.

West of Chicago, women organized a free loan society in Seattle. According to a
brief history complied by an organization member, the Seattle Hebrew Ladies' Free
Loan Society began in 1909, when a group of women from a local synagogue,
Congregation Bikur Cholim, organized a whist and sewing club with dues of
twenty-five cents a month. By 1913, they had accumulated sixty-four dollars in
their treasury and began making small loans to Jewish residents of Seattle. However,
when the women approached their rabbi to offer to buy something for the synagogue, he refused their donation because of its ties to gambling activities. As a
result, the women appropriated the money entirely for free loans.[23]

The Seattle Hebrew Ladies' Free Loan Society and the Chicago Woman's Loan
Association were typical of most women's free loan organizations; women ran the
agencies but disbursed loans to female and male clients. In contrast, women
founded the Providence Ladies' HFLA in 1931 with the explicit goal of providing
funds for women only. Providence women formed this organization because the
local free loan society denied women loans without their husbands' signatures.[24]

Other free loan societies also discriminated against women. In Canada, the
Montreal HFLA rejected "applicants not of age, women married or endorsers
unsatisfactory." The Seattle HFLA (administered by men and different from the
Seattle Hebrew Ladies' Free Loan Society) began accepting women members only
in 1955. A differential dues structure based on gender was in place as recently as
1982. Although the constitution of the Lafayette Orthodox HFLA, in Indiana, had

stipulated that any Jewish resident of the greater Lafayette area was eligible for membership, it denied membership to women as late as the early 1970s. When Lillian Kaplan, a crusader for women's equality within the Lafayette Orthodox HFLA, was nominated for a board position in 1973, one male director tried to bar her election. He claimed that only men could be on the board since the organization's constitution referred to a director with the pronoun "he." The legal counsel present at the meeting, however, refuted this argument. Kaplan won the election, making her the first woman board director of the Lafayette Orthodox HFLA.[25]

Gender discrimination, however, was not unique to Jewish loan societies. Until the passage of the Equal Opportunity Credit Act in 1974, banks and other credit organizations routinely denied women consumer credit, home mortgages, and business loans. Testimony before the National Commission on Consumer Finance, whose 1972 report was central for raising public awareness about credit inequities, highlighted the institutionalized discrimination within the credit industry:

> It was determined that single women had more trouble obtaining credit than single men; creditors generally required a woman upon marriage to reapply for credit, usually in her husband's name (whereas similar reapplication was not demanded of men when they married); creditors were often unwilling to extend credit to a married woman in her own name, or to count the wife's income when a married couple applied for credit; and women who were divorced or widowed had trouble reestablishing personal credit.[26]

Since gender discrimination was normative practice for credit organizations, that Hebrew free loan societies often refused loans to married women without their husbands' signatures is not surprising. What is unusual, however, is that not all of the male-dominated free loan societies practiced such overt forms of sex discrimination. Although women borrowed less often than men did, women's names appear regularly on loan listings with endorsers who are not their husbands. Women sometimes even served as cosigners, as illustrated by a 1901 loan given by the New York HFLS to a man on his wife's endorsement and by a 1938 loan granted by the Cleveland HFLA to a man on the endorsement of his two employed daughters. Clara Appelbaum, the Pittsburgh woman who owned property and borrowed for tax purposes in the early 1940s, endorsed her father's two-hundred-dollar loan for a truck license and stock money. In 1935, Rebecca Bernstein endorsed loans for both her mother and her brother through the Pittsburgh HFLA. During the 1930s, the Los Angeles HFLA implemented a policy requiring wives' signatures before it would approve loans to their husbands.[27]

A few of the male organizations allowed some degree of women's participation on an administrative level. With twenty-five other Hebrew free loan activists, Leah Goldstein, Jennie Gordon, and Celia Grosberg, members of the North End Loan Association, attended the first meeting of the Boston HFLS in 1912. The participants appointed all three women to a seven-person committee responsible for drafting bylaws for the new organization and voted to list the women on the organization's charter, but only under the condition that the "North End Loan Association will hand over their funds to our society." In the mid-1930s, also by way of a financial merger, Rose Schwartz became the first woman director of the New York HFLS after Daughters of Peace, a free loan society in which both she and her mother had been very active, relinquished its twenty-five-thousand-dollar treasury. In at least one case, a woman was elected as an officer of a nonwoman's organization. Pauline Perlmutter Steinem (grandmother of the noted feminist Gloria Steinem), born in Poland and educated in Germany, became president of the Jewish Free Loan Society in Toledo, Ohio, in 1908. A suffragist who spoke before the United States Senate, she was a prominent citizen who became the first woman elected to public office in Toledo.[28] Steinem was an anomaly, however, within free loan history. For the most part, women could ascend to high leadership roles only within the context of women's institutions. The ability to control their own organizations motivated Jewish women, just like other American women, to establish "parallel power structures" with access to "ongoing sources of recruitment, socialization, training, and advancement into public roles."[29]

Just as women administered their own free loan societies, they also founded their own credit cooperatives. In a 1932 discussion on Jewish credit unions in Massachusetts, Michael Freund, of the Bureau of Jewish Social Research, commented on the "establishment of credit unions in connection with various women's organizations."[30] Of the 104 Jewish credit unions in Boston in 1927, women administered eleven (10.5 percent) organizations. These included the Jewish Women's, the Mother's, the Roxbury Ladies', and the Sisters Social Credit Unions. In contrast, there were no non-Jewish cooperatives in which women made up all of the officers and directors and only one—the Industrial Credit Union, a relatively large facility created by the Women's Educational and Industrial Union in 1910—had a majority of female board members. According to a longtime activist familiar with Boston's credit unions, women formed separate credit unions, just as women had formed the Providence Ladies' HFLA, because of their difficulty securing loans without their husbands' signatures in the male-dominated facilities. Since the federal government did not legislate against gender discrimination within the credit industry until 1974, he argued that the early-twentieth-century women's credit union was "the forerunner of Women's Liberation."[31]

The Boston Jewish women's credit cooperatives, however, were small compared with those run by their male counterparts.[32] While the largest of the women's institutions, the Hill Credit Union in Roxbury, had one hundred members and assets totaling close to fifteen thousand dollars, the largest male-run organization, the Blue Hill Neighborhood Credit Union, in Dorchester, had more than twenty-five hundred members and assets of $430,000. The assets of the average men's organization were five times larger than those of the average women's credit facility.

Since there are no extant records of the borrowers of women's credit unions, we cannot make general conclusions about why they applied for money. However, homemakers who resided within the same neighborhood organized at least some of the women's credit unions for consumption purposes. In his talk before the 1914 National Conference of Jewish Charities, Jacob de Haas, of the Massachusetts Credit Union, spoke briefly about women's cooperative credit:

I am enthusiastic on the formation of neighborhood housewives' credit unions. Let a decent woman buy a $5.00 share by small installments and you put her in the position of borrowing at 6 per cent for her winter's coal, the family insurance or that doctor's bill, which is inevitable in the multiplication of the family. This credit thrift will save her 100 per cent on these particular domestic bills.[33]

Although Jewish loan societies provided many borrowers with a financial cushion during the Great Depression, the first signs of their decline appeared during the economic crisis. While this declining trend continued into the post–World War II era, with many organizations closing their doors, a small number still exist in the contemporary United States. Thirty-four Hebrew free loan societies across the United States are members of the International Association of Hebrew Free Loans.[34] Women, however, run none of the surviving institutions. As far back as 1953, members of the Seattle Hebrew Ladies' Free Loan Society considered donating their organizational funds to various charities because of a concern that their facility had "outlived its usefulness and that the days of small free loans had passed." After consulting with an attorney who advised them against appropriating loan funds for outright gifts because "[e]xisting funds of the Society and income therefrom must continue to be used for the object and purpose as now provided by the Constitution and By-Laws," the officers did not close their organization's doors at that time. In 1973, however, the Seattle Hebrew Ladies' Free Loan Society merged with the Jewish Family and Child Service.[35] During the 1940s, the Chicago Woman's Loan Association lost its autonomy when it turned over its funds to the Jewish Social Service Bureau. After donating five thousand dollars to the Building Fund for the Aged of Rhode Island in 1953, the Providence Ladies' HFLA conducted little business. In 1965, the board of directors held its last meeting and contributed the remaining capital to Jewish charities.[36]

Through modern credit cooperatives and traditional Hebrew free loan societies, early-twentieth-century Jewish women had access to capital. They could borrow funds to start or maintain a business or to tide them over a difficult period when medical bills or rent checks were due. Like their non-Jewish counterparts, married Jewish women often had to provide a husband's signature in order to obtain credit through their ethnic institutions. Some women's loan societies, such as the Providence Ladies' HFLA, however, defied the discriminatory norm and provided funds to women without male permission or even knowledge. Decades before the U.S. Congress passed the Equal Opportunity Act in 1974, Jewish women acted to rectify inequities within the credit industry through their autonomous loan associations. Furthermore, by establishing separate institutions with their own ladders of achievement, leaders of women's free loan associations and credit unions secured some degree of power and status. As founders and officers of economic institutions, Jewish women moved outside the private sphere and into the public world of communal service and credit.

NOTES

I thank Pamela Nadell for her helpful comments on an earlier draft of this essay.

1. Throughout this article, I have changed the names of borrowers to protect their anonymity.

2. For a detailed discussion of immigrant Jewish credit associations, see Shelly Tenenbaum, *A Credit to Their Community: Jewish Loan Societies in the United States, 1880–1945* (Detroit: Wayne State University Press), 1993.

3. Harry Linfield, *The Communal Organization of the Jews in the United States, 1927* (New York: American Jewish Committee, 1930), 92.

4. Michael Freund, "The New York Hebrew Free Loan Society and Available Small Loan Facilities in New York City," unpublished paper prepared for the Bureau of Jewish Social Research, November 1932, Microfilm No. 304.818, Harvard University, Widener Library, 50.

5. Freund, "New York HFLS," 57; Massachusetts Commissioner of Banks, *Annual Report on Credit Unions, 1927*; Massachusetts Credit Union, minutes of the Board of Directors, November 24, 1914, and December 27, 1914, Credit Union National Association Archives, Madison, WI.

6. Mildred John, "Why Workers Borrow: A Study of Four Thousand Credit Union Loans," *Monthly Labor Review* 25 (July 1927): 8.

7. San Francisco HFLA, Annual Report, January 1, 1932; Los Angeles Jewish Loan Fund, monthly reports, May 1936–May 1937; Los Angeles Jewish Loan Fund, minutes of the Board of Directors, April 6, 1936.

8. Viviana A. Zelizer, "The Social Meaning of Money: 'Special Monies,'" *American Journal of Sociology* 95, no. 2 (September 1989): 358–59.

9. Evelyn Nakano Glenn, *Issei, Nisei, War Bride: Three Generations of Japanese American Women in Domestic Service* (Philadelphia: Temple University Press, 1986), 39. For detailed discussions of non-Jewish immigrant credit associations in the United States, see Ivan Light, *Ethnic Enterprise in America: Business and Welfare among Chinese, Japanese, and Blacks* (Berkeley: University of California Press, 1972); Ivan Light, Im-jung Kwuon, and Deng Zhong, "Korean Rotating Credit Associations in Los Angeles," *Amerasia Journal* 16, no. 2 (1990): 35–54; G. Carlos Velez-Ibanez, *Bonds of Mutual Trust: The Cultural Systems of Rotating Credit Associations among Urban Mexicans and Chicanos* (New Brunswick, NJ: Rutgers University Press, 1983); and Aubrey Bonnett, *Institutional Adaptation of West Indian Immigrants to America: An Analysis of Rotating Credit Associations* (Washington, DC: University Press of America, 1981).

10. Pittsburgh Hebrew Free Loan Association, Application Cards, 1924–1950.

11. For a broad discussion of gender, ethnicity, and business, see Sally Westwood and Parminder Bhachu, eds., *Enterprising Women: Ethnicity, Economy, and Gender Relations* (London: Routledge, 1988).

12. Business Advisory Committee of the Los Angeles Jewish Loan Fund, minutes, December 1940–November 1942.

13. Lenore Davidoff and Catherine Hall, *Family Fortunes: Men and Women of the English Middle Class, 1780–1850* (London: Hutchinson, 1987) 272–315; Sidney Stahl Weinberg, *The World of Our Mothers,* (New York: Schocken Books, 1988), 134–137, 284, n. 42; Charlotte Baum, "What Made Yetta Work? The Economic Role of Eastern European Jewish Women in the Family," *Response* 7, no. 2 (1973): 32–38; and Judith Smith, *Family Connections: A History of Italian and Jewish Immigrant Lives in Providence, Rhode Island, 1900–1940* (Albany: State University of New York Press, 1985), 44–52.

14. While women's loan societies began in modern times, Jewish women have a long history as private creditors that dates back to medieval Europe. According to one estimate, about half of all European Jews who loaned money at interest to Christians were women. See William Chester Jordan, "Jews on Top: Women and the Availability of Consumption Loans in Northern France in the Mid-Thirteenth Century," *Journal of Jewish Studies* 29, no. 1 (spring 1978): 39–56.

15. *The Chicago Jewish Community Blue Book* (Chicago: Sentinel Company, [ca. 1918]), 16; National Conference of Jewish Charities, *Proceedings of the Second National Conference,* Detroit, NCJC, 1902, 62.

16. Charles Bernheimer, *The Russian Jew in the United States* (Philadelphia: John C. Winston, 1905), 97.

17. National Conference of Jewish Charities, *Proceedings of the Eighth Biennial Session,* Memphis, NCJC, 1914, 14.

18. For a short biography of Minnie Low see Shelly Tenenbaum, "Minnie Low," in *Jewish Women in America: An Historical Encyclopedia,* ed. Paula E. Hyman and Deborah Dash Moore (New York: Routledge, 1997).

19. Tenenbaum, *A Credit to Their Community,* 48–68.

20. Bernheimer, *Russian Jews,* 97.

21. Lizabeth Cohen, *Making a New Deal: Industrial Workers in Chicago, 1919–1939* (Cambridge: Cambridge University Press, 1990), 75–76; U.S. Congress, Senate, *Reports on Immigrant Banks,* 61st Cong., 3d sess., 1911, S.Doc. 19; "Opening the Door to the New World," *Jewish Exponent* (July 13, 1984), 85–87; Joseph Giovinco, "Democracy in Banking: The Bank of Italy and California's Italians," *California Historical Quarterly* 47, no. 3 (September 1968): 197; Irving Howe with Kenneth Libo, *World of Our Fathers* (New York: Harcourt, Brace, Jovanovich, 1976), 137; "To Protect Depositors in East Side Banks," *American Hebrew* 95, no. 16 (August 14, 1914), 407.

22. John C. Chapman, *Commercial Banks and Consumer Installment Credit* (New York: National Bureau of Economic Research, 1940), 28; Evan Clark, *Financing the Consumer,* (New York: Harper and Brothers, 1930), 5; "The Loan Shark Campaign," *New York Evening Post,* April 11, 1914, reprinted by the Division of Remedial Loans, Russell Sage Foundation, 5–6, Louis N. Robinson and Rolf Nugent, *Regulation of the Small Loan Business* (New York: Russell Sage Foundation, 1936).

23. "Hebrew Ladies' Free Loan Society Merger with JFCS," *Jewish Transcript* (December 20, 1973), 3; Grace Rubin, "History of the Seattle Hebrew Ladies' Free Loan Society," University of Washington Library, 1965.

24. Eleanor Horvitz, "The Jewish Woman Liberated: A History of the Ladies' Hebrew Free Loan Association," *Rhode Island Jewish Historical Notes* 7 (November 1978): 501–13.

25. Montreal HFLA, Seventh Annual Report, May 1, 1918; "Aid, Rather than Alms, Goal of Hebrew Free Loan Association," *Jewish Transcript* (December 22, 1983), 16; Martin Light, "A Brief History of the Lafayette Orthodox Hebrew Free Loan Association, Part 2: 1960–1980," *Indiana Jewish Historical Society Publication* 18 (1984): 50–54.

26. Joyce Gelb and Marian Lief Palley, *Women and Public Policies: Reassessing Gender Politics* (Charlottesville: University Press of Virginia, 1996), 67. Also see Sheila Tobias, *Faces of Feminism: An Activist's Reflections on the Women's Movement* (Boulder: Westview Press, 1997), 106–8; Ruth Rosen, *The World Split Open: How the Modern Women's Movement Changed America* (New York: Viking, 2000), xxiv.

27. New York HFLS, Application Cards, 1892–1906; Cleveland HFLS, minutes of the

Board of Directors, September 27, 1938; Los Angeles HFLA, minutes of the Board of Directors, June 9, 1931.

28. Boston HFLS, minutes, October 6 and 13, 1912; New York HFLS, minutes of the Board of Directors, December 7, 1936, and January 28, 1937; David Alexander, "History of the Jews of Toledo," *Reform Advocate* (June 20, 1908), 17.

29. Kathleen D. McCarthy, "Parallel Power Structures: Women and the Voluntary Sphere," in *Lady Bountiful Revisited,* ed. Kathleen D. McCarthy (New Brunswick, NJ: Rutgers University Press, 1990), 23. Also see Kathleen D. McCarthy, *Noblese Oblige: Charity and Cultural Philanthropy in Chicago, 1849–1929* (Chicago: University of Chicago Press, 1982), Lori D. Ginzberg, *Women and the Work of Benevolence: Morality, Politics, and Class in the Nineteenth-Century United States* (New Haven: Yale University Press, 1990).

30. Freund, "New York HFLS," 58.

31. Massachusetts Commissioner of Banks, *Annual Report on Credit Unions,* 1927; Meyer Finkel interview by Shelly Tenenbaum, February 3, 1984.

32. Freund, "New York HFLS," 58.

33. *Jewish Charities* 5, no. 1 (August 1914): 19; see also Freund, "New York HFLS," 58.

34. International Association of Hebrew Free Loans, 1999 Membership Directory. For an analysis of the decline, see Tenenbaum, *A Credit to Their Community,* 155–62.

35. Rubin, "History of the Seattle HLFLS," 6; Edward Dobrin to Mrs. E.E. Lescher, October 12, 1963, Seattle Hebrew Ladies' Free Loan Collection, University of Washington Library; "Hebrew Ladies' Free Loan Society Merger with JFCS," *Jewish Transcript* (December 20, 1973), 3.

36. Hyman Kaplan, "Memorandum Regarding 'A Study of the Woman's Loan Association of Chicago,' by Esther Beckenstein for the Jewish Charities of Chicago, March 1943," June 3, 1949, Federation of Jewish Charities of San Francisco Collection, Box 76, Western Jewish History Center; and Horvitz, "Jewish Woman Liberated," 509–512.

Chapter Six

"We Dug More Rocks"
Women and Work

Linda Mack Schloff

It was a tremendous transition for mother. She was a very fine seamstress and had worked in Bialystock making shirts for the army. . . . Here she was out in the bleak North Dakota prairie, living in a shack, no running water, no inside bathroom, cold in the winter, hot in the summer, and what they were doing was pulling the stones away so they could plow the land.

Laura Rapaport Borsten's mother's transition from an urban sewing room to the rough Upper Midwestern prairie in the early 1900s is typical of the adjustment many immigrant Jewish women made to the region's labor climate. She, like an estimated 70 percent of young Jewish females registered as artisans in the Pale of Settlement, had worked in the needle trades. Once transplanted to the Upper Midwest, though, they typically found themselves in settings, both rural and urban, where these skills were not in great demand. The economy and geography of the region dictated that Jewish women's work would diversify in ways few immigrants dreaming of America could have imagined.

Employment opportunities for these women contrasted sharply not only with the ones they had known in Europe but also with those prevailing in large American cities such as New York and Chicago, where the burgeoning ready-made clothing industry employed vast numbers of Jewish immigrants. But, in the cities of the Upper Midwest, that industry was small and centered in shops that typically employed fewer than half a dozen people each.

The economic well-being of the Upper Midwest was founded on agriculture, mining, grain milling, and forestry. Few Jews ever worked in the latter three areas. However, they experimented with farming, and they filled a traditional niche by providing commercial services to miners, millers, lumberjacks, and farmers. Farming, for a brief period, provided Jewish immigrants with what was long considered the quintessential American work experience—that of the independent yeoman farmer. With greater or lesser enthusiasm, Jewish women learned to be farm wives. And, as spouses of Main Street merchants all over the Upper Midwest, they balanced their Old World role as contributors to the family economy with the New World middle-class expectation that wives should be removed from the hurly-burly of the business world.

Daughters of Jewish immigrants commonly pursued white-collar jobs as bookkeepers and clerks, positions in which regional particularities did not figure. Those who could afford additional schooling characteristically chose teaching. Unlike East Coast Jewish women, who typically taught in large urban areas, many Upper Midwestern women who entered this field performed stints in small-town or rural settings.

The notion of farming as a livelihood was both politically improbable and emotionally alluring to Jews in czarist Russia. The czarist regimes would not allow Jews to own land, but the populist cultural nationalism of the times held that a life on the land was worthier than one spent in commercial ventures. Impelled by the ideology, Jews on three continents commenced farming in the late 1800s. By the early 1900s Zionists had established kibbutzim (collective farms) in Palestine, Jewish gauchos were riding the pampas in Argentina, and Jews were farming and ranching on the Dakota plains of the United States.

During the greater part of the massive Eastern European Jewish immigration to America that took place between 1880 and 1924, homestead land was plentiful in the Dakotas. As noted earlier homesteading was an affordable option for those with little money and plenty of hope and fortitude. The first Jewish farming colonies in the region, founded in the early 1880s, were Painted Woods and Devils Lake in present-day North Dakota and Bethlehem Yehudah and Cremieux in what is now South Dakota. They were all short lived, lasting on average less than five years. However, the news of free land printed in the Yiddish press in Russia and the eastern United States, combined with letters from friends, continued to draw Jewish would-be farmers to the plains. After the colonies had failed, Jews generally farmed in informal clusters, from roughly 1895 to 1910. The isolated Jewish farm was a rarity.

Many Jewish farmers received help in the form of loans from congregations. Rabbi Judah Wechsler, who led the Mount Zion Hebrew Congregation in St. Paul, was an ardent advocate of the Painted Woods colony, while the Devils Lake colonists were first aided by congregants of Minneapolis's Shaari Tof (Temple Israel). Sustained aid came from philanthropic societies such as the Jewish Agriculturalists Aid Society and the Jewish Agricultural Society, based in Chicago and New York City, respectively. Both organizations provided loans for land purchase and start-up capital and sent out representatives to determine results. According to figures collected by the sociologist J. Sanford Rikoon, 460 farmers in Minnesota and the Dakotas took out loans between 1888 and 1933. Beginning in 1908, the New York society also published a Yiddish-English magazine, *The Jewish Farmer,* which offered technical and agricultural advice.

The number of Jews who took out homestead deeds in the period from 1880 to

1910 is hard to pin down. The sociologist William Sherman estimated that, in those years, at least eight hundred Jews filed for deeds in North Dakota. Among these, several dozen were women—widows and other unmarried females.

The wives of these undercapitalized novice farmers often worked alongside their husbands to prepare the land and harvest the crops. "She worked in the fields digging rocks, pulling mustard, hauling hay, and shocking grain," recalled Samuel Dolf of his mother, Cecelia, who toiled on their Morton County, North Dakota, farm in 1903. The dust and heat at harvest time added to women's exhaustion. They also had children to contend with, "one child on the way, one cradled in her free arm, and another holding on to her skirt," recalled Craney Goldman Bellin, whose parents broke the sod in McKenzie County, North Dakota, around 1906.

When farmers could afford men to help out, women traded field work for that of feeding the harvest crews. In order to satisfy them, Jewish women learned to prepare American foods. Many, like Sarah Thal, who immigrated from Germany to what is now North Dakota in the early 1880s, kept gardens, preserved fruits and vegetables, made cottage cheese and butter, gathered eggs, and sewed for the whole family. Women also worked in groups. Rose Rapaport Schwartz, for example, remembered her mother joining other Jewish farm women to pick and prepare rose petals and cherries for jams and cordials near their Ashley, North Dakota, farm in the early 1900s. The work went more quickly as they reminisced about life in the Old Country, exchanged recipes, worried about this year's crops, and shared hopes for the future. While Jewish farm women contributed to the family coffers through their domestic production, they helped in still other ways, selling butter and eggs in town and contracting to provide meals for local road crews.

These farm wives were not the only Jewish women milking cows and raising chickens. They were joined by women living in small towns and even in cities. St. Paul, where one Jewish-immigrant neighborhood was situated on a sparsely developed flood plain of the Mississippi, was a prime example. There, cows grazed and chickens scratched until after World War II. Edith Milavetz remembered her mother's work as an urban chicken farmer in St. Paul in the period around World War I. After the *shochet* killed the chickens, she recalled, the whole family would help pluck the feathers and deliver the birds to the buyers, using a child's wagon. The family also sold milk, butter, sour cream, and cottage cheese, and matzoh at Passover.

Farmers' daughters had numerous tasks, as well. Tending the garden and helping with washing, ironing, and canning were customary chores. They did other work as the need or opportunity arose. For example, Lillian, Frieda, Jennie, and Nellie Brody drove their family's cows to pasture on their way to school, near Regan, North Dakota, in the 1910s. During the same period, young Sophie Turnoy, near Wilton, North Dakota, harvested wheat and received the same wages as men because, as her employer said, she "had . . . accomplished as much as any of the men."

The Jewish farming experience lasted from the early 1880s to about 1920. Although not long lived, the episode was an important one. For most Eastern

European Jewish farmers, the very fact of owning land was a considerable accomplishment. They appreciated the personal freedom farming offered. Many families used their farms to establish an economic foothold, staying long enough to "prove them up" and sell them, which provided a resource for entry into another occupation. More often than not, such a move was necessary because farming on the arid plains was a risky enterprise. The homestead allotment of 160 acres was small, the climate was harsh, natural disasters were frequent, and crop prices were subject to violent fluctuations. In addition, Jewish parents with an eye to their children's education knew that rural schools ended at the eighth grade. Finally, they understood that the prospects of finding other Jews to marry in rural society were slim; the prospect of wedding a non-Jew was generally unacceptable. Farm unions like the weddings of Eva and Rose Kremenetsky to Joe and Charles Losk and Henry Kremenetsky to Dora Weinberg, all three of which occurred near Wilton, North Dakota, about 1910, were exceptions to the rule. By the 1920s, most Jewish farmers had moved to the West Coast, to the Twin Cities, to regional centers such as Sioux Falls or Minot, or to nearby small towns that served the farming population. Nearly all who moved to towns opened stores.

Their establishments were of several varieties. Those on the plains were general stores that sold clothing, boots, lanterns, saddles, canned goods, blankets, and hundreds of other items farmers and ranchers needed. The proprietors of such operations generally were the only Jewish families in town. Other stores were located in the larger railroad hubs, in mining and market towns, and in the cities. In these places, Eastern European Jews joined countrymen who had started as peddlers and become minor merchants and scrap dealers and German Jews who were well-established merchants. Virtually all the stores sold clothing, although a few specialized in meat or groceries.

Women worked in all these varied locales. Wives generally served by acting as salesclerks or bookkeepers or, less frequently, by actually running the stores. Their involvement was crucial to the success of the family enterprise, although as "helpers" they are invisible in the census, a prime source of statistical data for the period of major immigration. (Censuses counted women as having no occupation unless they earned wages.) Even if their employment went unlisted, however, it is certain that many women worked in family-owned businesses. For example, a study of the roughly sixty Jewish families living in the Mesabi Iron Range town of Virginia between 1920 and 1940 indicated that about twenty of the wives worked, the majority in their husbands' stores. The many accounts and the numerous photos of husbands and wives behind the counters of their stores further attest to a joint effort.

There were many benefits to "helping out." Women could help earn a living for their families while not violating a long-held Jewish distaste for wives being supervised by other men. Helping out also gave married women a great deal of flexibility, for they could schedule their store hours around housework and child rearing. The utmost flexibility was achieved when the family lived behind or above the store, as was common. Women who had clerked in city stores or had done sales work prior to marriage often welcomed such labor as a respite from minding children and keeping house. Finally, helping out was a way to befriend the customers and offer better service, particularly to farm wives. Jewish wives might note the growth of customers' children, pull out the new bolts of fabric attractive for clothing, and exchange recipes or household hints. Store work also provided Jewish women with some measure of social intercourse, sorely lacking for them in small towns dominated by church activities.

Some women were freely recognized as partners. Emma Herbst helped out as her husband established a large department store in Fargo. After his death in 1910, she was "the guiding light" of the store until her son became old enough to take control. Similarly, Lena Oreckovsky and Fannie Goldfine were vital partners in their husbands' businesses in Duluth. Oreckovsky worked in the family department stores, named Oreck's, from the 1890s until 1927. Her last title was president. Goldfine took care of bookkeeping and financing and was a one-woman consumer-relations department in the family's cattle-buying and feed businesses and furniture stores from the time of her marriage in the 1920s until the 1960s.

Other women had rather loose business partnerships with their husbands. Rose Levy Overbach's mother ran the family grocery store in St. Cloud, Minnesota, while her husband peddled fruit. In Lael Singer-Miller's family account, *Rachel* (1980), each evening during the early decades of the century, the mother, Rachel, cut cloth into five-yard pieces. These were sold to peddlers from the front room of her Duluth house. Her husband worked as a peddler.

Women also supplanted their spouses as heads of business, particularly if their husbands had difficulty learning English or were not able to make the transition from Talmudic study to American entrepreneurship. Other wives simply possessed a better business sense. Theodore Shuirman said that his mother "could add up four column numbers on sight" and was "the driving force" in the family's Keewatin, Minnesota, store, which opened in 1905, while his father "made up Yiddish stories for the kids."

Women also owned businesses in their own names. These ranged from peddling to large enterprises. For example, in the 1910 United States manuscript census, seven women on St. Paul's West Side were listed as storeowners. One had a second-hand store, two were grocers, three had confectionery stores, and one was a peddler. All were listed as heads of households and so presumably were widows. Products aimed at the female market served as a niche for entrepreneurial women. Mary T. Goldman owned a large hair-products company bearing her name in St. Paul in the 1920s. Lena Kopelman created wigs and ran a beauty salon in Fargo in the early decades of the twentieth century. She also had a business agreement with the Fargo Hebrew Congregation to run the *mikvah,* which was located in the basement of her store.

Boarding was a form of helping out common in large cities; however, it was also practiced in smaller towns. It was a culturally acceptable economic activity, for it allowed married women to earn money without being supervised by strangers. The boarders and lodgers were often family members who had just arrived or *landsleit* (people from the same town or *shtetl*). One or two boarders was the average number per household. Jewish wives took in boarders when their children were young, generally stopped as children became teenagers, and resumed again, but to a lesser degree, later in life. One explanation for this pattern is that they boarded only when their children could not contribute to the family coffers, that is, when they were either too young or had moved out.

Twin Cities Jewish families may not have been so needy as those in New York City, however, for there were major differences between the numbers of those who took in boarders in the two locales. In 1910, the percentage of immigrant Jewish women in the Twin Cities who took in boarders was about half that of their counterparts in New York—27 percent versus 56 percent. There were differences as well between Italian and Jewish boarding patterns in St. Paul that reflected family need, demand, and potential for boarding and lodging. On St. Paul's West Side, the housing stock consisted of small houses and duplexes, whereas the Upper Town area, with its aging mansions, allowed Italian women to lodge great numbers of their compatriots who were employed as seasonal railroad laborers.

If mothers boarded and worked in family businesses, daughters, too, were expected to help. According to the 1910 United States manuscript census, the vast majority of Jewish girls in three Twin Cities immigrant neighborhoods—87 percent—stayed in school until age fifteen, although some worked after school. At age sixteen, roughly that same percentage went to work. While it may be shocking to learn that only 13 percent of Jewish girls were able to stay in high school, this percentage was twice as high as comparable figures gathered from East Coast cities and cited in the 1911 Immigration Commission report. The statistic is evidence that life was not quite so harsh for immigrant Jews in the Upper Midwest as in the East.

Upon leaving school, girls generally chose one of two paths, based on their educational plans, family financial resources, and acculturation. Those who had not been in America for long and who lacked English-language skills found factory work sewing garments, furs, or mattresses, making hats, or rolling cigars. The variety of factory jobs young Jewish women held reflects the fact that neither Minneapolis nor St. Paul was a garment-industry power house like New York City.

Beginning in the 1860s, New York was the acknowledged center of the ready-made garment industry. By 1909, 40 percent of men's clothing in the country was manufactured there. Tens of thousand of women were employed making men's garments and, by the early twentieth century, even more labored in the burgeoning women's and children's clothing industry. Various sources centering on the year 1900 list between 40 and 77 percent of New York's Russian Jewish females as garment workers.[1]

By contrast, in 1910, 23 percent of young Jewish women on St. Paul's West Side sewed in the nineteen clothing factories then situated in that city. Only 9 percent worked as seamstresses in Minneapolis's seven clothing factories. In 1910 fewer than a handful toiled at the Munsingwear Knitting Mills, which employed about two thousand workers—this despite the fact that the factory was contiguous to the heavily Jewish North Side. Munsingwear's very low number of Jewish workers may reflect anti-Semitism. But it may also simply be an indication that, as was often the case, an already-established ethnic group had made it a practice to secure all available jobs for their own compatriots.[2]

Although the comparison made here is between New York Jewish garment workers in 1900 and those in the Twin Cities in 1910, the differences are important. In 1910 New York's immigrant Jewish women were predominantly employed in garment factories whose payrolls included anywhere from twenty to more than one thousand workers. In the Twin Cities, significant numbers of Jewish women found needlework employment, but in far smaller establishments. Eleven percent of the North Side's young immigrant Jewish women and 15 percent of St. Paul's worked in small tailoring shops, each of which had fewer than a half-dozen employees.

It is probably because so many Twin Cities Jewish women labored in small shops that union activity among them was muted. Few appear to have been involved in Local Number 171 of the United Garment Workers of America, established in the Twin Cities around 1909. Ten years later, when the first Twin Cities local of the Amalgamated Clothing Workers Union (ACWU) was established, its ranks included a fair number of Jewish women. However, the 1920 roll of union members striking Guiterman Brothers, a St. Paul clothing factory, lists only nine of 258 female strikers who can be identified as Jewish. This is one sign that, by the time the unions were a strong force locally, young immigrant Jewish women had begun moving into white-collar work. Further evidence of the low level of union activity by this contingent comes from several other sources. In his 1949 study of Minneapolis Jewry from its beginnings to the 1930s, Rabbi Albert I. Gordon found only fifty Jewish women who were members of the ACWU in the 1930s. Finally, no Jewish women appear to have been involved in the bitter 1936 strike at Minneapolis's Strutwear Knitting Company.

The contrast between employment patterns among young immigrant Jewish women—who were well represented in the needle trades and almost absent from domestic service—and jobs held, for example, by Scandinavian women is striking. In 1910, fewer than 1 percent of Twin Cities immigrant Jewish women worked as domestics. By contrast, almost 63 percent of immigrant Swedish women were domestics during the same period. They found independence, good pay, and generally satisfactory working conditions in domestic service and greatly preferred it to the grueling farm labor they had left behind.

By about 1910, white-collar jobs began to be available to Jewish women who could speak English. The critical factor was not American birth but American education. Three or four years of schooling equipped young women for after-school work as cash girls and wrapping clerks. In 1910, 15 percent of Twin Cities immigrant Jewish daughters were employed in low white-collar work. Almost the same number, 14.3 percent, became saleswomen in department stores or trained to become stenographers or bookkeepers—then considered the acme of white-collar work. They generally gained such employment after attending business school, although some learned on the job. These figures correspond to national trends of the time.

The 1910 United States manuscript census provides a clear glimpse into the work patterns of a cohort of largely foreign-born mothers and daughters then living in the Twin Cities. The evidence available for the 1910s through the 1930s is sketchier, although the outlines are clear. Young unmarried women continued to seek white-collar work. As the general level of affluence among Jews rose, however, families began sending daughters to normal school or college. Daughters who worked in small-town family stores followed this pattern as well—as they did the unconcealed dictate that they were to find Jewish husbands. Some came back home and married storeowners, following in their mothers' footsteps. Others returned to their home-towns to teach. A multiyear teaching stint in a small town was commonplace. "It was a good experience," pronounced Sara Bashefkin Ryder, of St. Paul, about her sojourn in Nemadji, Minnesota, in 1929. "I wouldn't sell it for a million dollars, and I wouldn't wish to repeat it for a million dollars." Social work was another common career. A list of graduates of the University of Minnesota School of Social Work from 1931 to 1993 contains roughly 140 Jewish women, or 7 percent of the graduates—more than twice as high as their percentage in the general population.

Diplomas, however, were no guarantee of jobs. Anti-Semitism between the end of World War I and World War II dashed the hopes of many young Jewish women. A report in a 1922 issue of the Twin Cities newspaper *American Jewish World* pointed to the fact that there were no Jewish teachers in any Minneapolis high schools.[3] Blanche Halpern Goldberg recalled that a mentor at the University of Minnesota in the late 1920s urged her to have her photographs, which would be shown to school superintendents who were hiring teachers, reshot. "She said to me," Blanche related, 'You ought to take them over again so you don't look so Jewish. Your hair is too curly.' "

The Depression made a bad situation worse. By 1931, an employment service was formed in Minneapolis to help Jewish women and men find work. While it was somewhat effective, the service could not address the root assumptions that led to prejudicial hiring. As late as 1939, the head of the division of dental hygiene at the University of Minnesota informed three Jewish students that they had less chance of being hired than gentiles. The underlying assumption that Jewish women had to endure such job discrimination became increasingly intolerable. However, it was not until 1948, when the Minneapolis Mayor's Council on Human Relations pub-licized the endemic prejudice in the city, that jobs in banking, insurance, teaching, and dental hygiene became available to Jewish women.

Jewish women of the region worked in factories during World War II, while more than one hundred entered all branches of the armed forces. Like most middle-class women, they voluntarily stopped working, or were forced to, following de-mobilization. They rarely reentered the workforce once they had children, and then only as part-timers. This pattern of retirement after the birth of children persisted in the region's Jewish communities until the 1970s. Only 1 percent of Minneapolis Jewish mothers worked outside the home in 1971, but nationally more than 50 percent of mothers held jobs that year. The effects of the women's liberation movement that began in the early 1970s, combined with the need for two salaries in order to support a middle-class lifestyle, led many women once again to expect to work for most of their lives. Family-owned businesses were much rarer in the 1990s than earlier in the century, but the spectrum of job options had widened considerably. As a group, Jewish women had higher educational achievements than the general population. Many chose professions such as medicine, law, accounting, and communications. Others were artists, caterers, and travel agents, while social work and teaching still attracted significant numbers. The heavy Russian immigration that commenced in the early 1970s added a number of engineers, computer programmers, musicians, and teachers to the regional work force.

The career of Blanche Colman is emblematic both of the possibilities open to Jewish working women in the Upper Midwest and of the limitations the region has often placed on Jewish life. Her immigrant father arrived in Deadwood in 1877, soon opened store, and became active in politics. In 1911, she was the first female admitted to the South Dakota Bar. She spent most of her working life as an attorney for the Homestake Mining Company. Blanche spoke excellent Yiddish and observed many Jewish rituals and customs. Although able to make the leap from immigrant daughter to professional woman, she saw her own Jewish community disappear. She died in 1978 and was buried in the Jewish section of the Deadwood cemetery— probably the last burial that section will receive.

NOTES

1. Irving Howe, *World of Our Fathers* (New York: Harcourt Brace Jovanovich 1976), 154, cites a "census" figure of 40 percent. Isaac M. Rubinow, "Economic and Industrial Condition: New York," in *The Russian Jew in the United States,* ed. Charles S. Bernheimer (1905; repr., New York: Jerome S. Ozer, 1971), 112, writes that 77 percent of female Russian-Jewish workers were employed in the needle industries.

2. The factory's employee roster for 1920 contains a preponderance of Scandinavian and Finnish names. This is a reflection of Minneapolis's large Scandinavian population and of the fact that the city's main Finnish neighborhood abutted the factory. Fewer than five Jewish names are on the roster.

3. However, W. Gunther Plaut, *The Jews in Minnesota: The First Seventy-five Years* (New York: American Jewish Historical Society, 1959), 274, footnote reports that there were two Jewish high school teachers in Minneapolis that time.

Chapter Seven

Organizing the Unorganizable
Three Jewish Women and Their Union

Alice Kessler-Harris

Women who were actively engaged in the labor struggles of the first part of this century faced a continual dilemma. They were caught between a trade union movement hostile to women in the workforce and a women's movement whose participants did not work for wages. To improve working conditions for the increasing numbers of women entering the paid labor force, organizers painstakingly solicited support from labor unions that should have been their natural allies. At the same time, they got sympathetic aid from well-intentioned women with whom they otherwise had little in common. The wage-earning women who undertook the difficult task of organizing their coworkers also faced yet another problem: they had to reconcile active involvement in labor unionism with community traditions that often discouraged worldly roles.

Understanding how women who were union organizers experienced these tensions tells us much about the relationships of men and women within unions and throws into relief some of the central problems unionization posed for many working women. It also reveals something of what feminism meant for immigrant women. Evidence of conscious experience, frequently hard to come by, exists in the papers of three women who organized for the International Ladies Garment Workers Union, (ILGWV) Pauline Newman, Fannia Cohn, and Rose Pesotta. All were Jews working for a predominately Jewish organization. Their careers span the first half of the twentieth century. Taken together, their lives reveal a persistent conflict between their experiences as women and their tasks as union officers. Their shared Jewish heritage offers insight into the ways women tried to adapt familiar cultural tradition to the needs of a new world.

Like most of the women they represented, Newman, Cohn and Pesotta were born in Eastern Europe. Cohn and Newman emigrated as children before the turn of the century, Pesotta as a teenager in 1913. In the United States, poverty drove them to the East Side's garment shops. There they worked in the dress and waist industry, a rapidly expanding trade in which Jewish workers predominated until the 1930s, and in which women made up the bulk of the work force.[1]

Their experience was in many ways typical. Among immigrant Jews in New

York, Philadelphia, Boston, and other large cities, only the exceptional unmarried woman did not operate a sewing machine in a garment factory for part of her young adult life.[2] In the old country, where jobs were scarce, daughters were married off as fast as possible. In America, they were expected to work, for the family counted on their contributions. Many young girls emigrated as teenagers to go to an uncle or older sister who would help them to find a job so that a part of their wages could be sent back to Europe.[3] The wages of others helped to pay the rent, to buy food and clothing, to bring relatives to America, and to keep brothers in school. An eldest daughter's first job might mean a larger apartment for the family—"a dream of heaven itself accomplished."[4] When they married, young women normally stopped working in the garment shops. As in the old country, they were still expected to contribute to family income. Married women often took in boarders, helped in their husbands' businesses, or ran small shops.

A combination of factory work before marriage and the expectation of different kind of paid labor afterward presented problems for Jewish women, who, like Newman, Cohn, and Pesotta, wanted to take advantage the new world's possibilities. Women who earned wages could dream of self-sufficiency.[5] Adolescents hoped that the transition to America could bring about a previously unknown independence and offer them new and different roles. Rose Pesotta (the name had been changed from Peisoty) arrived in America in 1913, age seventeen. She had left Russia, she said, because she could "see no future for [herself] except to marry some young man . . . and be a housewife. That [was] not enough. . . . In America a decent middle class girl [could] work without disgrace."[6]

Expectations of independent self-assertion were frustrated when marriage intervened and women were confined to more restricted roles. But aspirations toward upward mobility may have provided the death blow. The legendary rapidity of Jewish economic success perhaps did women a disservice by encouraging husbands to deprive their wives of the limited economic roles marriage permitted—contributing, incidentally, to the American version of the "Jewish mother." Yet the hard physical labor required of women who worked for wages at the turn of the century led them to escape from the workforce as soon as possible. A folk song reportedly first sung in Eastern Europe at the turn of the century and later heard in New York's sweatshops records one woman's wish for a husband:

> Day the same as night, night the same as day.
> And all I do is sew and sew and sew
> May God help me and my love come soon
> That I may leave this work and go.[7]

Women who hoped they would soon marry and leave the shops joined trade unions only reluctantly, and male union leaders thought them poor candidates for membership.[8]

To choose a militant and active future among a people who valued marriage and the family as much as most Eastern European Jews did must have been extraordinarily difficult.[9] Women who chose to be continuously active in the labor movement knew consciously or unconsciously that they were rejecting traditional marriage. In her autobiography, Rose Schneiderman, just beginning a career in the Women's Trade Union League, recalls her mother warning her she'd never get married because she was so busy.[10] One woman organizer, who did marry, made the following verbatim comment to an interviewer who asked her about children: "I wouldn't know what to do with them. First of all I never . . . we were very active, both of us, and then the unions. I don't think I . . . there were always meetings . . . so we had no time to have children. I am sorry now."[11] Even after so many years, her discomfort at talking about her unusual choice was apparent. Despite difficulties, many in the first generation of immigrants, Newman and Cohn among them, did not marry, and there are numerous examples of women whose marriages did not survive the urge to independence. Rose Pesotta divorced two husbands and the anarchist Emma Goldman and the novelist Anzia Yezierska one each before they sought satisfying lives outside marriage.

These women were not entirely outside the pale, for while on the one hand American-Jewish culture urged women into marriage, that culture's injunction to self-sufficiency encouraged extraordinary militancy. In this respect, Jewish women may have been luckier than most. They came from a class-conscious background in which competitive individualism and the desire to make it in America was only one facet. A well-developed ethic of social justice was equally important and played its part in producing perhaps the most politically aware of all immigrant groups. Socialist newspapers predominated in the Yiddish-speaking Lower East Side. Jews were well represented in the Socialist Party at the turn of the century and were among the best organized of semiskilled immigrants.[12] On the Lower East Side, as in Europe, women absorbed much of their community's concern for social justice.[13] A popular lullaby provides a clue to the extent to which women experienced a prevailing class consciousness:

> Sleep my child sleep,
> I'll sing you a lullabye
> When my little baby's grown
> He'll know the difference and why
>
> When my little baby's grown
> You'll soon see which is which
> Like the rest of us, you'll know
> The difference between poor and rich.
>
> The largest mansions, finest homes
> The poor man builds them on the hill
> But do you know who'll live in them?
> Why of course the rich man will!
>
> The poor man lives in a cellar
> The walls are wet with damp
> He gets pain in his arms and legs
> And a rheumatic cramp.[14]

There is no way of knowing whether Cohn, Newman, or Pesotta knew that song, but it is likely that they sang the following tune:

No sooner in my bed
Than I must up again
To drag my weary limbs
Off to work again

To God will I cry
With a great outcry!
Why was I born
To be a seamstress, why?

Should I once come late
'Tis a long way
They dock me straight off
A full half-day!

The machines are old
The needles they break
My bleeding fingers—
Oh, how they ache!

I've nothing to eat
I'm hungry all the day
They tell me: forget it
When I ask for pay![15]

Like the women who sang them, the songs had traveled to America steerage class. In the garment shops of the Lower East Side, they could sometimes be heard over the noise of the machines, reflecting always the conscious desire of working women not only to get out of the shops but to make life in them better.

Faced with the exploitative working conditions characteristic of the early-twentieth-century United States, many women turned naturally to unionism. The ILG, founded and nurtured by socialist Jews from New York's Lower East Side, offered an appropriate organizing agency, and early expressions of enthusiasm indicate something of its romantic appeal. "I think the union is like a mother and father to its children. I'd give my whole life for the union," said one young woman in 1913.[16] Half a century after she joined the union in 1908, an eighty-year-old woman wrote to David Dubinsky, the ILG's president, "And I still have my membership book of that year. And I will keep it with reverence until the end of my days."[17] Another recalled her experience on the picket line: "I felt as if I were in a holy fight when I ran after a scab."[18]

It could be said of the early 1900s that Jewish women courted the unions that should have been courting them. Rose Schneiderman solicited the signatures of twenty-five capmakers before the union would acknowledge them or provide aid.[19] Her friend Pauline Newman recalled that when she and her friends "organized a group, we immediately called the union . . . so that they could take the members in and naturally treat them as they would treat any member who joined the union. Our job was to attract women which men were not willing . . . to do."[20] But unions did not treat women evenhandedly. During a capmakers strike, for example, when married men got strike benefits amounting to six dollars per week, women, even those who supported widowed mothers and young siblings, got nothing.[21]

Women who had had to struggle to create and enter trade unions, who were baited, beaten, and arrested on picket lines, and who had already rejected traditional roles sought help from other women, identifying their problems as different from those of male workers. Large numbers indicated their need for organization by participating in spontaneous strikes. Workers on women's clothing (largely female) tended to strike without union support more than half again as many times as workers on men's clothing (largely male).[22] In the early years of organizing, attacks against other women often elicited support from coworkers. Clara Lemlich, whose proposal to strike sparked the 1909 uprising of twenty thousand in the dress and waist trade, had been badly beaten by thugs. A woman who had participated in the Chicago garment strike of 1911 recalled that violent attacks against other female strikers had persuaded her not to return to work until the strike was won. As she and her fellow workers were negotiating with their employer to call a halt to the strike, they heard a terrific noise. "We all rushed to the windows, and there we [saw] the police beating the strikers—clubbing them on our account and when we saw that we went out."[23] A sense of female solidarity joined the oppressed together. A 1913 striker who said she was "in good" at her job refused to work without a union "for the sake of those that didn't have it good."[24] In jail women strikers passively resisted when their captors tried to separate them.[25]

Yet solidarity among women was limited by ethnic and class antagonisms that persistently interfered with the best efforts of organizers and of which the organizers themselves were often guilty. Organizers repeatedly complained that their work was hampered by ethnic conflict among women. Jewish women thought they were superior unionists. They treated non-Jews in the garment shops suspiciously, complaining, for example, that Polish women would listen to their speeches quietly and then report them to the boss.[26] Italian women were felt to be unreliable allies, and fear that they would not join in a strike sometimes hindered other garment workers from going out.[27] In the 1909 uprising, Italian and Jewish women, divided by language barriers, met separately. The ILG, without an Italian-speaking organizer, selected women to harangue that Italians in English daily until the Italians agreed not to desert the strike.[28] Julia Poyntz, the ILG's first educational director, used the pages of *Justice,* its official journal, to argue in 1919 that "our Italian sisters who are still suffering from the age long seclusion of women in the home need a long and serious education to enable them to function intelligently as members of the working class in the shop and in the political field."[29]

"American" women, as the organizers persistently called them, were hardest of all for Jewish women to unionize. It was a necessary assignment in order to prevent some shops from undercutting the wages of others, enabling them to charge lower prices for finished goods. But it was dreaded by Jewish organizers who saw "shickses" as at best indifferent to unionism, and more often as strike breakers and scabs.[30] Success at organizing "Americans" evoked unconcealed glee. Pauline Newman wrote to Rose Schneiderman from Massachusetts that they had "at last succeeded in organizing an English-speaking branch of the waist makers union. And my dear not with ten or eleven members—but with a good sturdy membership of forty. Now what will you say to that!"[31] Long after most Jewish women were comfortable within unions, Rose Pesotta complained that she was having a "hell of a job" with the Seattle workers she had been sent to organize. They were, she said, the "100 percent American white daughters of the sturdy pioneers. They are all members of bridge clubs, card clubs, lodges, etc. Class consciousness is as remote from their thoughts as any idea that smacks with radicalism."[32] Women from such an ethnic background could severely inhibit the success of an organization drive. Pesotta complained that she could not call a strike as women would not picket. "No one will stand in front of the shop . . . as they will be ashamed. Not even the promise of getting regular strike benefits moved them."[33]

Isolated from the mainstream of the labor movement and divided from other working women who came from less class-conscious backgrounds, Jewish women gratefully accepted help from middle-class groups like the Women's Trade Union League (WTUL). But the financial and moral support of the WTUL came at a price. Jewish women had been nurtured in the cradle of socialism, and, for them, alliances with other women were largely ways of achieving a more just society. Many middle-class members of the WTUL, in contrast, held that political, social, and biological oppression of women was the major problem. They saw labor organization among women as a way of transcending class lines in the service of feminist interests.

Contemporary testimony and filtered memory agree that the WTUL provided enormously valuable organizing help.[34] Yet the tensions were not easily suppressed. Rose Schneiderman, working for the WTUL in 1911, needed reassurance from a friend: "You need not chide yourself for not being able to be more active in the Socialist Party. You are doing a much needed and splendid work."[35] And it was always clear to those who continued to work for the union that the women of the WTUL had only limited access to and limited understanding of the Jewish labor movement. "Remember Rose," wrote Pauline, "that no matter how much you are with the Jewish people, you are still more with the people of the League."[36] And, again, Pauline comforted her friend: "They don't understand the difference between the Jewish girl and the gentile girl."[37]

Neither the trade union nor solidarity from other women offered adequate support to the exceptional women who devoted themselves to organizing. How did they choose between the two? And at what cost? They worked in a lonely and isolated world, weighing the elements of their success against the conflict and tension of their lives. They were not typical of rank-and-file union women, nor symbolic of others' lives. The three female ILG organizers I have selected each chose not to conform to traditional patterns and to pursue what for women was an extraordinary lifestyle. Their particular struggles crystallize the tensions other women faced and more easily resolved in the service of a familiar destiny. As their relationship to the union is filled with conflict, so their attitudes toward women reflect the way feminism is experienced by working women. Their lives illustrate a continuing uncertainty over the sources of their oppression.

Pauline Newman became the ILG's first female organizer in the aftermath of the "Great Uprising" of 1909. She had a stormy relationship with the union until she settled down in 1913 to work for the Joint Board of Sanitary Control—a combined trade union and manufacturers unit designed to establish standards for maintaining sanitary conditions in the shops. Fannia Cohn worked for the union from 1919 to the end of her life. For most of that time she was educational director, though she also served as an executive secretary and briefly as a vice president. Rose Pesotta (some ten years younger than the other two) became a full-time organizer in 1933 and a vice president of the union in 1934. She remained active until 1944, when she returned to work in the shops.

Their lifestyles varied. Pauline Newman, warm, open, and impulsive, had a successful long-term relationship with a woman with whom she adopted a baby in 1923. Fannia Cohn lived alone—a sensitive, slightly irritable woman, concerned with her ability to make and retain friends. Rose Pesotta married twice and afterward fell in love with first one married man and then another. Cohn and Newman called themselves socialists. Pesotta was an anarchist. No easy generalization captures their positions on women or their relationships to the union. But all felt some conflict surrounding the two issues.

From 1909 to 1912, just before she went to work for the Joint Board, Newman vacillated between the union and the middle-class women of the WTUL. Frequently unhappy with a union that often treated her shabbily, she nevertheless continued to work for them throughout her life. "I cannot leave them," she wrote in 1911, "as long as they don't want to accept my resignation." "Besides," she rationalized a few months later, "they are beginning to realize . . . women can do more effective work than men, especially where girls are involved."[38] Yet later that year she angrily severed her connection with the ILG, for which she had been organizing in Cleveland. "They wanted me to work for *less* than the other organizers get," she wrote angrily to her friend Rose Schneiderman, "and while it was not a question of the few dol[lars] a week with me, I felt that I would lower myself before the others were I to go out on the price offered to me." Her anger increased as the letter continued to describe the women selected by John Dyche, the union's executive secretary, to replace her: "Well they too are not bad looking, and one is rather liberal with her body. That is more than enough for Dyche."[39] Two months later, she was still angry. "The International does not give a hang whether a local lives or dies," she wrote to Rose.[40] And several weeks after that: "I for one would not advise you to work for any Jewish organization."[41] But within a few months she was back at work again for the ILG.

She had little choice. Though she disliked the union's attitude toward women, she had equal difficulty relating to the middle class women who were potential nonunion allies. Not that she disagreed with them on the women's issues: she was more than sympathetic. An ardent supporter of the ballot for women, she could not, she said later, recall any woman (save for Mother Jones) "in any of our organizations who was not in favor of getting the vote." Like her friends, she was convinced that the ballot would "add greatly to our effectiveness for lobbying or sponsoring labor legislation."[42] Moreover, she not only willingly accepted aid and support from women who were not workers but she actively solicited it, even quoting Christ in order to induce church women to help garment workers.[43] To gather support for striking corset workers in Kalamazoo, Michigan, in 1912, she visited women's clubs. When local officials and the mayor had been unable to help resolve the strike, she "decided that the best thing to do would be to ask the ladies who wear corsets not to buy that particular brand."[44]

Yet the task of reconciling class and feminist interests exhausted her. "My work is horrible," she complained from Detroit a few months before the Kalamazoo strike. "The keeping sweet all the time and pleading for aid from the 'dear ladies' and the ministers is simply sickening."[45] Her greatest praise went to the St. Louis, Missouri, WTUL. It was, she said, "a strictly working class organization in spirit as well as in action." When she sent off an article praising it to the WTUL journal, *Life and Labor,* Margaret Dreier Robbins suppressed it.[46] Newman, in a remarkable letter to Rose Schneiderman, written in 1911, explored her feelings about the effect of the WTUL on women workers. Mrs. Robbins, she noted, "has made all the girls of the League think her way and as a consequence they do not use their own mind and do not act the way they feel but the way Mrs. R. wants them to." She frowned at the League's Saturday afternoon teas (which served "a glass Russian Tea") and disapproved of giving the girls folk dancing lessons. "It is of course very nice of her," conceded Newman, "but that is the instinct of charity rather than of unionism."[47]

Her disagreements were not simply matters of style. She was more than willing to give way when she thought a well-spoken woman could influence a stubborn manufacturer. But she thought it bad strategy to raise issues of morality when they threatened to interfere with negotiations over wages and hours. It may have been true, she argued, that a factory owner's son and his superintendent had taken liberties with female employees: "There is not a factory today where the same immoral conditions [do] not exist. . . . This to my mind can be done away with by educating the girls instead of attacking the company."[48]

Caught between the union and middle-class allies, Newman called for help—a pattern repeated by other women involved in the labor movement. Her letters to Schneiderman are filled with longing: "all evening I kept saying if only Rose were here," and with loneliness: "No matter how good the people are to me, they do not know me as yet."[49] At times one can only guess at the toll her job took. She wrote repeatedly of trying to "get away from the blues" and complained, "I am just thrown like a wave from one city to another. When will it end?"[50] Respite came at last in the form of the Joint Board of Sanitary Control. With the struggles to organize behind her, she could spend her energies improving working conditions for women in the factories.

Feelings of displacement and the need for support may have preceded the drive by women members of ILG's Local 25 to create first an educational department and then a vacation retreat. The men in the union had no patience with the demands at first. One active woman recalled the men's snickers: "What do the girls know— instead of a union they want to dance."[51] But the women persisted, insisting that the union would be better if the members danced with each other. The women proved to be right. By 1919 Unity House, as the vacation home was called, had moved to quarters capable of sleeping nine hundred people, and two years later Local 25 turned it over to a grateful International.

Unity House may have symbolized a growing solidarity among working-class Jewish women. In any event, the feminism of ILG members seems to have become a problem, for just at the peak of its success, *Justice,* the Union's official journal, began to attack middle-class women. Could it have been that some union leaders feared that working women were seeking alliances with others of their sex and would eventually cease to identify their interests with those of working men? "Women who work," an editorial intoned early in 1919, are not like "that type of woman, who to her shame be it said, is less a person than a thing."[52] Increasingly *Justice's* writers insisted that working women had it in their own power to defend themselves. When female pickets faced attacks by gangsters, *Justice* insisted that the solution was in the hands of the strikers themselves. It urged women to "take a little trip down to City Hall and get the vote that will put these fellows out of business."[53] Julia Poyntz, *Justice's* writer on women's affairs, was adamant that middle-class women no longer interfere with their sisters. "The interests of the women of the working classes are diametrically opposed to those of the middle classes."[54] A month later, she attacked a Women's International League for Peace and Freedom conference for virtually excluding working women and their problems.[55] Although the journal continued to solicit support for the WTUL and the ILG continued to send women to the Bryn Mawr Summer School, attacks did not cease. A 1923 article protested the absence of working women at a conference on women in industry: "The ladies who employ domestics came to Washington to speak about higher wages, shorter hours, and better working conditions for their help. The domestics, of course, or their representatives were not invited."[56]

It was just in this period that Fannia Cohn climbed to a position of authority in the ILGWU. In many ways she was fully aware of women's issues. In 1919, in the aftermath of a successful shirtwaist strike, she pleaded for tolerance from male union members. Recalling the militancy of the young female strikers, she wrote: "Our brother workers in the past regarded with suspicion the masses of women who were entering the trades. They did everything to halt the 'hostile army' whose competition they feared."[57] Wasn't it time, she asked, finally to accept fully the women strikers who had so often been jailed and beaten. An ardent supporter of the Bryn Mawr Summer School and a regular contributor to the WTUL, Cohn had friendly relations with many of its officers.[58] In 1926, she protested the absence of women's names on a list of antiwar petition signatures, and later she was to fire off a rapid telegram insisting that Anne Muste be included in a tribute offered to her husband.[59] Her experiences strike familiar chords. She complained of the difficulty of holding independent views from the men she worked with but noted, "It is still more painful to have women, too, assume a similar attitude toward their sex."[60] She laughed with a friend whose husband was called by his wife's surname ("let men have the sensation of changing their lifelong name for a new one") and supported Mary Beard's proposed world center to preserve a record of women's achievements.[61]

Cohn's strong empathy for women's feelings surely derived from her own un-comfortable experiences in the ILG. Theresa Wolfson, later to become a well-known economist and an expert on the problem of working women, glimpsed this suffering in 1923. "Never have I realized with such poignancy of feeling," she wrote to her, "what it means to be a woman among men in a fighting organization as last Monday when I heard your outcry and realized the stress under which you were working."[62] In a letter she hesitated at first to mail, Cohn shared some of her angry frustration with a woman who taught at Brookwood Labor College. Cohn had urgently requested the college's faculty to make two studies of union women for her. The faculty had repeatedly postponed the request. "I wonder whether they would treat in the same manner, a 'man' who would find himself in a similar position." She wrote, "The labor movement is guilty of not realizing the importance of placing the interest of women on the same basis as of men and until they will accept this, I am afraid the movement will be much hampered in its progress."[63]

Despite the anguish caused by her male colleagues and her strong sympathy with women's causes, Cohn came down on the side of the labor movement when a choice had to be made. She rejected a request to segregate men and women workers in evening classes: "I am a great believer that men and women working together in the labor movement or in the classroom have much to gain from each other."[64] In 1925, she appealed to William Green, the AFL's president, "not as an officer speaking for her organization [but as] a woman trade unionist" protesting confer-ences called by ladies. "When the deplorable conditions of the unorganized working woman are to be considered," she objected, "a conference is called by many ladies' organization who have no connection with the labor movement and they are the ones to decide 'how to improve the conditions of the poor working woman.' "[65] A year and a half later, she regretfully refused an invitation to attend a WTUL conference on working women, cautioning the delegates to "bear in mind that it is very difficult nowadays to even organize men and they should remember that in proportion there are not enough men organized in our country as yet."[66] On the question of protective legislation for women, Cohn only reluctantly sided with the middle-class reformers who favored it: "I did not think the problem of working women could be solved in any other way than the problem of working men and that is through trade union organization, but considering that very few women are as yet organized into trade unions, it would be folly to agitate against protective legislation."[67]

These contradictory positions were not taken without inner struggle. Cohn knew well the sacrifice she was making to stay in the labor movement. "Did you ever think of the inner pain, worry and spiritual humiliation?" she lamented in 1922.[68] Her remedy, like Newman's, was close friendship. "You know that I . . . must be in constant touch with my friends," she wrote. "If I can't have personal contact then the medium of letters can be employed."[69] Or again, "To satisfy my own inner self, I must be surrounded by true friends . . . [who] never for a moment doubt my motives and always understand me thoroughly."[70] Cohn found refuge in the edu-cation department of the ILG, where she could continue the battle and yet remain sheltered from the worst of the storm.

Rose Pesotta took no shelter and asked no quarter. By 1933, when she began full-time organizing for the ILG, it had become clear to many that women, married and unmarried, were in the workforce to stay, and the ILG willingly committed both money and resources to organizing them.[71] Membership campaigns no longer focused on the East Coast cities. In the garment centers of the Far West and in places like Buffalo and Montreal, Jews took second place to Mexican, Italian, and "American" women. But Pesotta was a Russian Jew who worked for a still Jewish union, and, like her predecessors, she suffered the turmoil of being a woman in ambivalent territory. Sent by the ILG to Los Angeles in 1933, she moved from there to organize women in San Francisco, Seattle, Portland, Puerto Rico, Buffalo, and Montreal before she became involved with war mobilization.

None could question her awareness of women's particular problems. Persuaded by the argument that there were no women on the union's General Executive Board, she accepted a much-dreaded nomination for vice president. "I feel as if I lost my independence," she confided to her diary.[72] She often berated the union leadership for its neglect of women "our union, due to the fact that it has a WOMAN leader is supposed to do everything, organizing, speechmaking, etc., etc."[73] She was not shy about asking for courtesies that men might have had trouble obtaining. Women who earned meager wages could not be expected to pay even modest union initiation fees, she urged at one point. At another, she demanded that ILG pay not only the expenses but make up the lost income of a Spanish woman elected to attend the biennial ILG convention.[74] And she knew the advantages of solidarity among women, making personal sacrifices to "win the support of the ladies who might some day be of great help to the girls."[75]

Repeatedly, however, Pesotta and her fellow West Coast organizers sacrificed the feminist issues in the interests of generating an enthusiastic and loyal membership. To keep striking women happy, they agreed to double strike benefits before Easter Sunday "for the girls to buy something."[76] When newly organized women brought their husbands to discussion meetings, the men were made welcome.[77] In 1933, Pesotta compromised to the extent of abandoning the negotiating process to men and confining her own activities to organizing women because "our late President Schlesinger once told your humble servant to stop this kind of business and go home and get married. I hate to hear that from an employer."[78] Her perspectives were not always those of other women. While WTUL officials were praising the NRA codes, Rose Pesotta condemned them. Organizing in Seattle and witness to how badly the codes were abused, she complained "the women are satisfied that the N.R.A. gave them 35 hours and better wages, why pay dues to a union that does nothing for the workers?"[79]

Pesotta carried the scars of the woman organizer. "A flitting happy little whirlwind," her friends called her. It was an image that did not fit. "Nobody knows how many cheerless, sleepless nights I have spent crying in my loneliness," she confided to her diary.[80] Unlike Newman and Cohn, she sought solace in men, and depriving herself of close women friends exacerbated her isolation. Tormented by the gossip of her female colleagues, she struggled with her self-image. Occasionally she confessed, "I feel so futile," or sorrowed, "everybody has a private life. I have none."[81]

In an effort to avoid entangling herself with a married man, she exiled herself to Montreal in 1936. It was no use. She wrote from there to her lover: "Why must I find happiness always slipping out of my hand . . . I'm sinking now and who knows where I will land."[82] For ten years, Rose Pesotta battled against police alongside her union colleagues. Then she returned to the comparative peace of the garment shop from which she had come.

By the middle 1930s, with unionism apparently secure and the ILG's membership expanding rapidly, it looked as though women might at last begin to raise issues peculiar to them within the confines of the union. Fannia Cohn wrote a play in 1935 which raised critical issues. Intended for presentation at union meetings, it described a husband and his "intellectually superior" wife. Both worked, but, because the wife had to devote her evenings to caring for the home, the husband rapidly developed more interests and became increasingly discontented with his spouse. The wife, wrote Cohn, brought with her the resentment and "the protest of a woman worker, wife, and mother against an economic condition that compels her to work days in the shop and evenings at home."[83] Chivalry, Rose Schneiderman had said, "is thrown away" when a girl enters the factory or store: "Women have to work and then are thrown on the dust heap the same as working men."[84] Working men were by no means chivalrous in 1935, but enough women had been organized in the ILG so that the union, no longer afraid of imminent disintegration and collapse, could lend an ear to the women's issues. Perhaps in consequence, the solidarity of women within the unions diminished.

Those who came before walked an uneasy tightrope—slipping first to one side and then to the other. Tempted sometimes by the money and support of middle-class women, at others by the militance of a changing labor union leadership, alternately repelled by "ladies" and repeatedly hurt by their union's male leadership, women who tried to organize their sisters were in a precarious position. They were not feminist—they did not put the social and political rights of women before all else. They did draw strength and support from the solidarity of women inside unions and outside them. Their lives illustrate the critical importance of "female bonding" and of female friendship networks. Newman and Cohn, who had particularly strong relationships with women and who managed to find relatively passive roles within the union, maintained their relationship with the ILG far longer than Pesotta, who relied on men for support and who stayed in the front lines of battle. All were class conscious, insisting that the class struggle was preeminent. When their class consciousness and their identification as women conflicted, they bowed to tradition and threw in their lot with the working class.

NOTES

This paper is a revised draft of one presented at the Conference on Class and Ethnicity in Women's History, SUNY, Binghamton, Sept 21–22, 1974. The author gratefully acknowledges the generous support of the Louis H Rabinowitz foundation.

1. In 1913, 56.56 percent of the workers in the industry were Jews, and 34.35 percent were Italian. Seventy percent or more were women. See Hyman Berman, "Era of the

Protocol: A Chapter in the History of the International Ladies Garment Workers Union, 1910–1916," unpublished Ph.D. diss., Columbia University, 1956, 22, 24. Jewish women were much more likely to be working inside a garment shop than were Italian women, who often preferred to take work home; 53.6 percent of all employed Jewish women were in the garment industry in 1900. Nathan Goldberg, *Occupational Patterns of American Jewry* (New York: J.T.S.P. University Press, 1947), 21. The relative proportion of women in the garment industry declined between 1900 and 1930. In addition to dresses and waists, women were heavily employed on kimonos, housedresses, underwear, children's clothing, and neckwear. Melvyn Dubovsky, *When Workers Organize: New York City in the Progressive Era* (Amherst: University of Massachusetts Press, 1968), 73 ff, has a good description of conditions in the garment industry.

2. The industry was characterized by the rapid turnover of its employees. In 1910, about 50 percent of the dress and waist makers were under twenty years old. The best estimate is that less than 10 percent of the women working on dresses and waists were married. See U.S. Senate, 61st Congress, 2nd Session. *Abstracts of the Report of the Immigration Commission,* Doc. #747, 1911, vol. II, 336; Berman, "Era of the Protocol," 23.

3. The proportion of women in the Jewish immigration between 1899 and 1910 was higher than in any other immigrant group except the Irish. See Samuel Joseph, *Jewish Immigration to the U.S. 1881–1910* (New York: Columbia University, 1914), 179. This can be accounted for in part by the high proportion of family emigration, and in part by the numbers of young women who came to America without their parents, to work. Rose Pesotta, Rose Cohn, Emma Goldman fall into this category.

4. Unpublished autobiography #92, YIVO archives. See also #160, p. 8; Etta Byer, *Transplanted People* (Chicago: M.J. Aron, 1905), 28.

5. Flora Weiss, interview in Amerikaner Yiddishe Geschichte Bel-Pe, YIVO archives, June 15, 1964, 4. See also Anzia Yezierska, *Bread Givers* (Garden City, New York: Doubleday, Page, 1925), 28.

6. Rose Pesotta, *Bread upon the Waters* (New York: Dodd, Mead, 1944), 4. The novels of Anzia Yezierska, who arrived in America from Russian Poland in 1901, beautifully express these aspirations. See also *Bread Givers; All I Could Never Be* (New York: Brewer, Warren, and Putnam, 1932); *Arrogant Beggar* (Garden City, New York: Doubleday, Page, 1927); and her semifictional autobiography *Red Ribbon on a White Horse* (New York: Scribner, 1950).

7. Ruth Rubin, *A Treasury of Jewish Folksong* (New York: Schocken, 1950), 43, 97.

8. See for example, Rose Schneiderman as quoted in, "Finds Hard Job Unionizing Girls Whose Aim is to Wed," New York *Telegram,* June 18, 1924; Julia Stuart Poyntz, "Marriage and Motherhood," *Justice,* March 18, 1919, 5; Matilda Robbins, "My Story," unpublished manuscript, Matilda Robbins collection, Wayne State University Archives of Labor History, 38. Mechanics of organizing women are illustrated in Alice Kessler-Harris, "Where Are All the Women Unionists?" *Feminist Studies* 3 (fall 1975): 92–110.

9. Although the same tensions existed for women of other cultural backgrounds, one does not always get the impression that non-Jewish women were quite so torn. Mary Kenney, for example, continued to be active after she married John O'Sullivan. The most prominent Jewish women who remained active after marriage married outside their ethnic group. Anna Strunsky Walling and Rose Pastor Stokes are two examples. In some ways, Emma Goldman's life acted out the protest many women must have felt but expressed in more limited ways. See Blanche Wiesen Cook, "Emma Goldman and Crystal Eastman," unpublished paper delivered at the Organization of American Historians meeting, April 1973.

10. Rose Schneiderman with Lucy Goldthwaite, *All for One* (New York: P.S. Erickson 1967), 50.

11. Interview with Pearl Halpern in Irving Howe collection, YIVO (undated), 8.

12. Report of the Immigration Commission, vol. 11, 317, indicates that, in 1910, 23.9 percent of Jewish men belonged to trade unions, as opposed to 14 percent of Italian men.

13. See for example unpublished autobiography, #160, YIVO, 8, 12.

14. Rubin, *A Treasury of Jewish Folksong,* 23.

15. Ibid., 97. These songs, with their hope of escape, should be compared with the hopeless and agonized verse of Morris Rosenfeld. See *The Teardrop Millionaire and Other Poems* (New York: Manhattan Emma Lazarus Clubs, 1955), 14, 19.

16. "Manhattan's Young Factory Girls," New York *World,* March 2, 1913.

17. Lillian Mallach to David Dubinsky, December 18, 1964, Glicksberg mss., YIVO.

18. Weiss, YIVO, 11. The same woman recorded the influence the legend of Mother Jones had had on her, 20.

19. Schneiderman, *All for One,* 49. Officially, ILGWU policy was to organize whoever was in the shop, regardless of sex. It was easier in practice to discriminate against women since they were often employed in sex-segregated jobs.

20. Pauline Newman, Interview, Amenkaner Yiddishe Geshichte Bel-Pe, June 26, 1965, YIVO, 19.

21. Schneiderman, *All for One,* 61.

22. Isaac Hourwich, *Immigration and Labor: The Economic Aspects of European Immigration to the United States* (New York: B. W. Huebsch, 1922), 373. These figures are for the period 1880–1905.

23. *Life and Labor,* February 1911, 52.

24. "Manhattan's Young Factory Girls," New York *World,* March 2, 1913.

25. Weiss, YIVO, 28.

26. Faigele Shapiro, Interview, Amerikaner Yiddishe Geshichte Bel-Pe, August 6, 1964, YIVO, 9.

27. Constant D. Leupp, "Shirtwaist Makers Strike," in *Selected Articles on the Employment of Women,* ed. Edna Bullock (Minneapolis: H. W. Wilson 1919), 126.

28. Louis Lorwin, *The Women's Garment Workers: A History of the International Ladies Garment Workers Union* (New York: B. W. Huebsch, 1924), 156.

29. Julia Stuart Poyntz, "What Do You Do with Leisure," *Justice,* February 22, 1919, 13.

30. Unpublished autobiography, #160, YIVO, p. 13.

31. Pauline Newman to Rose Schneiderman, September 20, 1910, Rose Schneiderman Collection, Tamiment, Box A94. Hereinafter referred to as P.N. and R.S., respectively.

32. Rose Pesotta to David Dubinsky, February 6, 1935, Rose Pesotta Collection, New York Public Library, General Correspondence. Hereinafter referred to as R.P.

33. Jennie Matyas to R.P., February 25, 1935.

34. See Weiss, YIVO, 32, for one encomium. For the WTUL side of the story, see Nancy Schrom Dye, "Creating A Feminist Alliance: Sisterhood and Class Conflict in the New York Women's Trade Union League, 1903–1914," paper presented at the Conference on Class and Ethnicity in Women's History, SUNY, Binghamton, September 22, 1974; and Robin Miller Jacoby, "The Women's Trade Union League and American Feminism," *Feminist Studies,* 3 (fall 1975): 126–40.

35. "Joe" to R.S., November 8, 1911, R.S., A94.

36. P.N. to R.S., April 17, 1911, R.S., A94.

37. P.N. to R.S., February 9, 1912, R.S., A94.

38. P.N. to R.S., April 17, 1911, and P.N. to R.S., August 9, 1911, R.S., A94.

39. P.N. to R.S., November 14, 1911, R.S., A94. Three months later, the ILG fired the new organizers, and Pauline crowed, "I tell you, Rose, it feels fine when you can say to a secretary of an International to 'go to hell with your job together' and after have the same man beg you to work for them again!" P.N. to R.S., February 22, 1912, R.S., A94.

40. P.N. to R.S., January 17, 1912, R.S., A94.

41. P.N. to R.S., February 9, 1912, R.S., A94.

42. Newman interview, YIVO, 21, 22. See also P.N. to R.S., May 17, 1911, R.S., A94, where Newman expresses sadness at not being able to attend a conference to discuss the "woman problem." "You must tell me about it in your next letter."

43. P.N. to R.S., April 11, 1910, R.S., A94.

44. Newman interview, YIVO, 2.

45. P.N. to R.S., March 5, 1912, R.S., A94.

46. P.N. to R.S., November 7, 1911, R.S., A94. Newman had already had a similar experience with the *Ladies Garment Worker (Justice's* predecessor), which mutilated an article on the League she had written for them.

47. P.N. to R.S., December 1, 1911, R.S., A94.

48. P.N. to R.S., July 11, 1912, R.S., A94.

49. P.N. to R.S., October 19, 1910, and April 11, 1910, R.S., A94.

50. P.N. to R.S., October 29, 1911, and November 7, 1911, R.S., A94.

51. Shapiro interview, YIVO, 17.

52. "On Lightheaded Women," *Justice,* March 8, 1919.

53. Julia Poyntz, "The Unity Corner," *Justice,* March 29, 1919, 3.

54. "The Problem of Life for the Working Girl," *Justice,* February 1, 1919, 3.

55. *Justice,* March 15, 1919, 5.

56. B. Maiman, "Conference on Women in Industry," *Justice,* January 19, 1923, 4.

57. Fannia Cohn, "With the Strikers," *Justice,* February 22, 1919.

58. Fannia Cohn (hereinafter referred to as F.C.) to R.S., January 24, 1929, Fannia Cohn papers, New York Public Library, Box 4, see also E. Christman to F.C., October 2, 1915, F.C., Bx. 1.

59. James Shotwell to F.C., December 31, 1926, F.C., Bx. 1; F.C. to James Maurer, March 6, 1931 F.C., Bx. 5.

60. F.C. to Helen Norton, February 9, 1932, F.C., Bx. 5. The rest of the letter reads in part: "It hurt me also to know that while 'men' frequently come to each others' assistance in an emergency 'women' frequently remain indifferent when one of their own sex is confronted with a similar emergency. Of course, a woman is expected to assist a man in his accomplishments, but she (the woman) is forced in her aspirations—in social and economic field—to struggle along. She is compelled to depend upon her own resources, whether this be material, moral intellectual."

61 F.C., to Dorothea Heinrich, February 3, 1937, F.C., Bx. 5; F.C. to Mary Beard, January 23, 1940, F.C., Bx. 5.

62. Theresa Wolfson to F.C., November 19, 1923, F.C., Bx. 1.

63. F.C. to Helen Norton, February 9, 1932, F.C., Bx. 5.

64. F.C. to Evelyn Preston, September 21, 1923, F.C. Bx. 4.

65. F.C. to William Green, March 6, 1925, F.C., Bx. 4.

66. F.C. to R.S., October 5, 1926, F.C., Bx. 4.

67. F.C. to Dr. Marion Phillips, September 13, 1927, F.C., Bx. 4.

68. F.C. to Theresa Wolfson, May 15, 1922, F.C., Bx. 4.

69. F.C. to Evelyn Preston, September 9, 1922, F.C., Bx. 4; see also F.C to E.P., February 19, 1924.

70. F.C. to Theresa Wolfson, May 15, 1922, F.C., Bx. 4.

71. Fannia Cohn, "A New Era Opens for Labor Education," *Justice,* October 1, 1933, 9. The article may be more hopeful than real. Cohn said in part "the women strikers, many of whom were married and their younger sisters, too, increasingly realized that no longer do they want a strong union as a temporary protection for themselves but as a permanent safeguard for their present and future families." There is no question, however, that the industry's workers were increasingly drawn from married women and older women.

72. R.P., diary, June 9, 1934, Rose Pesotta Collection, New York Public Library. In her autobiography, *Bread upon the Waters,* 101, Pesotta wrote that "the voice of a solitary woman on the General Executive Board would be a voice lost in the wilderness."

73. R.P. to Rae Brandstein, April 9, 1934.

74. R.P. to David Dubinsky, April 26, 1934.

75. R.P. to David Dubinsky, March 3, 1934. Pesotta on this occasion stayed in a YMCA because it was "respectable."

76. R.P. to Jennie Matyas, April 16, 1935.

77. R.P. to Paul Berg, February 15, 1934.

78. R.P. to David Dubinsky, September 30, 1933. Pesotta's snippy attitude comes through in the rest of that letter. "Now, my dear President, you will have to come across with the help we need namely; financial, moral and the representative for a week or two. After we'll pull this through you will come to visit these whores and I am confident that you will see with your own eyes that enthusiasm is not such a bad thing after all."

79. Rose Schneiderman called the codes "the Magna Charta of the working woman" and characterized them as "the most thrilling thing that has happened in my lifetime." New York Evening *Journal,* October 24, 1933, 15 (clipping in R.S., A97); R.P. to David Dubinsky, February 1, 1935.

80. R.P., diary, November 3, 1931.

81. R.P., diary, February 24, 1934, March 12, 1934, August 9, 1934.

82. R.P. to Powers Hapgood, February 21, 1937.

83. F.C. to Jess Ogden, June 25, 1935, F.C. A second play described how two sisters, both of whom worked, nevertheless waited on their brother at home because they had to atone for earning less than he did.

84. Quoted in a clipping entitled "Says Chivalry Stops at Door of Workshop," from an unidentified newspaper, 1912, R.S., A97.

Chapter Eight

Immigrant Women and Consumer Protest
The New York City Kosher Meat Boycott of 1902

Paula E. Hyman

Women have always participated in politics. Despite their eclipse in the conventional seats of political power, women in preindustrial societies frequently engaged in popular protest, particularly when the price, or availability, of basic foodstuffs was at issue. As one English historian of the working class and of popular culture has pointed out regarding eighteenth-century food riots, women were "those most involved in face-to-face marketing [and hence] most sensitive to price significancies...." In fact, he adds, "it is probable that the women most frequently precipitated the spontaneous actions."[1] In the popular ferment of the early days of the French Revolution, women were also conspicuous by their presence. The image of grim-faced market women on the march to Versailles to bring the royal family back to Paris has been sharply etched in the mind of every student of history or enthusiast of historical dramas.[2] Even before the emergence of modern political movements committed to the recruitment of women into the political process, the "crowd" was an important means of expression for women's economic and political interests.

Immigrant Jewish women, too, took to the streets in spontaneous food riots on several occasions.[3] Like their British and French forerunners more than a century before, they were reacting to the sharp rise in the price of food. Most noted and flamboyant of these incidents were the 1902 kosher meat riots in New York City. Erupting in mid-May, they precipitated political activity which continued for almost a month, attracting considerable attention both within the Jewish community and the larger urban society. Indeed, in a fierce and vitriolic editorial of May 24, 1902, the *New York Times* called for a speedy and determined police repression of this "dangerous class ... especially the women [who] are very ignorant [and] ... mostly speak a foreign language.... It will not do," the editorial continued, "to have a swarm of ignorant and infuriated women going about any part of this city with petroleum destroying goods and trying to set fire to the shops of those against whom they are angry."[4]

What impelled immigrant Jewish housewives to take to the streets (of Williamsburg, in this case) with bottles of kerosene in their hands? Was this simply an act of spontaneous rage, a corroboration of the English writer Robert Southey's comment that "women are more disposed to be mutinous [than men]"?[5] Are the kosher meat riots a late manifestation, as Herbert Gutman has suggested, of a preindustrial sensibility that focused upon the illegitimacy of violating a fair price for food?[6] Finally, and most importantly, what can we learn of the self-perceptions, political consciousness, and sense of community of immigrant Jewish women by examining their role in this incident?

Despite their superficial similarity to earlier food riots, the kosher meat riots of 1902 give evidence of a modern and sophisticated political mentality emerging in a rapidly changing community. With this issue of the high price of food, immigrant housewives found a vehicle for political organization. They articulated a rudimentary grasp of their power as consumers and domestic managers. And, combining both traditional and modern tactics, they temporarily turned their status as housewives to good advantage and used the neighborhood network to stage a successful three-week boycott of kosher meat shops throughout the Lower East Side, parts of upper Manhattan and the Bronx, and Brooklyn. The dynamics of the kosher meat boycott suggest that, by focusing almost exclusively upon organized political activity in the labor movement and the socialist parties, historians have overlooked the role of women. Although for a great part of their lives absent from the wage-earning market, immigrant Jewish women were not apolitical. They simply expressed their political concerns in a different, less historically accessible arena—the neighborhood—where they pioneered in local community organizing.[7]

In early May 1902, the retail price of kosher meat had soared from twelve cents to eighteen cents a pound. Small retail butchers, concerned that their customers would not be able to afford their produce, refused to sell meat for a week to pressure the wholesalers (commonly referred to as the Meat Trust) to lower their prices.[8] When their May fourteenth settlement with the wholesalers brought no reduction in the retail price of meat, Lower East Side housewives, milling in the street, began to call for a strike against the butchers. As one activist, Mrs. Levy, the wife of a cloakmaker, shouted, "This is their strike? Look at the good it has brought! Now, if *we women* make a strike, then it will be a strike." Gathering support on the block—Monroe Street and Pike Street—Mrs. Levy and Sarah Edelson, owner of a small restaurant, called a mass meeting to spread the word of the planned boycott.[9]

The next day, after a neighborhood canvas staged by the organizing committee, thousands of women streamed through the streets of the Lower East Side, breaking into butcher shops, flinging meat into the streets, and declaring a boycott. "Women were the ringleaders at all hours,"[10] noted the *New York Herald*. Customers who tried to carry their purchased meat from the butcher shops were forced to drop it. One woman emerging from a butcher store with meat for her sick husband was vociferously chided by an elderly woman wearing the traditional *sheitel* that "a sick man can eat tref meat."[11] Within half an hour, the *Forward* reported, the strike had spread from one block through the entire area. Twenty thousand people were reported to have massed in front of the New Irving Hall. "Women were pushed and hustled about [by the police], thrown to the pavement . . . and trampled upon," wrote the *Herald*. One policeman, trying to rescue those buying meat, had "an unpleasant moist piece of liver slapped in his face."[12] Patrol wagons filled the streets, hauling women, some bleeding from their encounters with the police, into court. About seventy women and fifteen men were arrested on charges of disorderly conduct.[13]

After the first day of street rioting, a mass meeting to rally support and map strategy was held at the initiative of the women activists, who had formed a committee. Two of their number addressed the crowd, as did the popular figure Joseph Barondess and the Zionist leader Rabbi Zeft. The next day, May 16, Lower East Side women again went from house to house to strengthen the boycott. Individuals were urged not to enter butcher shops or purchase meat. Pickets were appointed to stand in front of each butcher shop. On each block, funds were collected to pay the fines of those arrested and to reimburse those customers whose meat had been confiscated in the first day of rioting. The *Tribune* reported that "an excitable and aroused crowd roamed the streets. . . . As was the case on the previous day, the main disturbance was caused by the women. Armed with sticks, vocabularies and well-sharpened nails, they made life miserable for the policemen." On the second day of rioting, another hundred people were arrested.[14] The boycott also spread, under local leadership, to the Bronx and to Harlem, where a mass meeting was held at Central Hall.[15]

On Saturday, May 17, the women leaders of the boycott continued their efforts, going from synagogue to synagogue to agitate on behalf of the boycott. Using the traditional communal tactic of interrupting the Torah reading when a matter of justice was at stake, they called on the men in each congregation to encourage their wives not to buy meat and sought rabbinic endorsement of their efforts. For once, urged a boycott leader, citing a biblical passage, let the men use the power of "And he shall rule over her" to the good—by seeing to it that their wives refrain from purchasing meat.[16]

By Sunday, May 18, most butcher shops on the Lower East Side bowed to reality and closed their doors. And the boycott had spread to Brooklyn, where the store windows of open butcher shops had been broken and meat burned. That night, the women held another meeting, attended by more than five hundred persons, to consolidate their organization, now named the Ladies' Anti-Beef Trust Association. Under the presidency of Mrs. Caroline Schatzburg, it proposed to continue house-to-house patrols, keep watch over butcher stores, and begin agitating for similar action among Christian women. Circulars bearing a skull and crossbones and the slogan "Eat no meat while the Trust is taking meat from the bones of your women and children" were distributed throughout the Jewish quarters of the city. The Association established six similar committees to consolidate the boycott in Brownsville, East New York, and the Bronx. Other committees were set up to visit the labor and benevolent societies, labor union meetings, and lodges and to plan the establishment of cooperative stores.[17] The Association also sent a delegation to the mayor's office to seek permission for an open-air rally. Local groups of women continued to enforce the boycott in their neighborhoods. In Brooklyn, four hundred women signed up to patrol neighborhood butcher stores. Buyers of meat continued to be assaulted and butcher shop windows smashed. In Harlem, two women were arrested when they lay down on the elevated tracks to prevent a local butcher from heading downtown with meat for sale. Throughout the city's Jewish neighborhoods, restaurants had ceased serving meat.[18]

However, competition between Sarah Edelson, one of the founders of the boycott, and Caroline Schatzburg, the president of the Ladies' Anti-Beef Trust Association, erupted by May 18 into open quarrels between their followers at meetings. Taking advantage of this rivalry and winning the support of Edelson and her backers, on May 21st male communal leaders, with David Blaustein of the Educational Alliance presiding, held a conference of three hundred representatives of synagogues, *hevras, landsmanshaften,* and unions "to bring order to the great struggle for cheap meat."[19] In his remarks at the conference meeting, Joseph Barondess made explicit that a new leadership was asserting itself. Urging the women to be quiet and leave the fighting to the men, he noted that otherwise the women would be held responsible in the event of the boycott's defeat.[20] Calling themselves the Allied Conference for Cheap Kosher Meat, the male conference leaders appointed a ten-person steering committee, among whom were only three women. (Women continued, however, to engage in propaganda activities and sporadic rioting in their neighborhoods.) The Allied Conference published a circular in both Yiddish and English, noting that "brave and honest men [were] now aiding the women" and declaring that the conference had "decided to help those butchers who [would] sell cheap kosher meat under the supervision of the rabbis and the conference." "The people feel very justly," continued the statement, "that they are being ground down, not only by the Beef Trust of the country, but also by the Jewish Beef Trust of the City."[21]

On May 22, the Retail Butchers Association succumbed and affiliated itself with the boycott against the Trust. On May 27, Orthodox leaders, who had hesitated to express formal endorsement of the boycott, joined the fray. By June 5, the strike was concluded. The wholesale price of kosher meat was rolled back to nine cents a pound so that the retail price would be pegged at fourteen cents a pound. Kosher meat cooperatives, which were established during the strike in both Brooklyn and Harlem, continued in existence. While meat prices began to rise inexorably again in the period following the conclusion of the boycott, the movement can still be considered a qualified success.[22]

The leaders of the boycott were not typical of other women political activists of the period. Unlike the majority of women organized in the nascent garment unions, they were not young. Unlike the female union leaders, they were housewives with children.[23] The mean age of those boycott leaders who could be traced in the 1905 New York state manuscript census was thirty-nine. They ranged from Mamie Ghilman, the thirty-two-year-old Russian-born wife of a tailor, to Mrs. L. Finkelstein, a fifty-four-year-old member of the Women's Committee. All but two were more than thirty-five years of age at the time of the boycott.[24] These women were mothers of large families, averaging 4.3 children apiece living at home. Fannie Levy, who initiated the call for the strike, was the mother of six children, all below the age of thirteen. None had fewer than three children. While only two women were United States citizens, the strike leaders were not, for the most part, recent arrivals to America. They had been living in New York City from three to twenty-seven years, with a median residence of eleven years. Having had sufficient time to accommodate themselves to the American scene, they were not simply expressing traditional forms of cultural resistance to industrial society imported from the Old Country.[25]

In socioeconomic terms, the women initiators of the boycott appear representative of the larger immigrant Jewish community of the Lower East Side. Their husbands were, by and large, employed as artisans in the garment industry, though three were self-employed small businessmen. The husband of Annie Block, a member of the Women's Committee, was a tailor, as were three other husbands. Fannie Levy's husband was a cloakmaker and Bessie Norkin's a carpenter, while J. Jaffe's husband, Meyer, and Annie Levine's husband, Morris, topped the occupational scale as a real estate agent and a storekeeper, respectively. With one exception, all of their children above the age of sixteen were working—two-thirds of them in artisan trades and the remainder as clerks or low-level business employees (e.g., salesladies). Only the eighteen-year-old son of the real estate agent was still in school (though his older brothers were employed as garment industry operators). Thus, the women formed not an elite in their community but a true grass-roots leadership.[26]

It is clear from their statements and their activity that the women who led the boycott had a distinct economic objective in mind and a clear political strategy for achieving their goal. Unlike traditional food rioters, the Lower East Side housewives were not demanding the imposition of a just and popular price on retailers. Nor were they forcibly appropriating meat for purchase at a popularly determined fair price, though they did retain a traditional sense of a moral economy in which food should be available at prices which the working classes could afford. Rather, recognizing that prices were set by the operation of the laws of supply and demand, as modified, in this case, by the concentration of the wholesale meat industry, they hit upon a boycott of meat as the most effective way to dramatically curtail demand. They referred to themselves as strikers; those who did not comply with the boycott were called "scabs." When they were harassed in the street by police, they complained that denial by police of their right to assemble was an attack on their freedom of speech. Thus, Lower East Side women were familiar with the political rhetoric of their day, with the workings of the market economy, and with the potential of consumers to affect the market.[27]

While the impulse for the boycott originated in spontaneous outrage of women consumers at the price of kosher meat and their sense that they had been manipulated (or swindled, as they put it) by the retail butchers, who had sold out their customers in their agreement with the wholesalers, this incident was not simply an explosion of rage. It was a sustained, though limited, movement, whose success lay in its careful organization. As the *New York Herald* rightly commented, "These women were in earnest. For days they had been considering the situation, and when they decided on action, they perfected an organization, elected officers, . . . and even went so far as to take coins from their slender purses until there was an expense fund of eighty dollars with which to carry on the fight."[28]

In fact, the neighborhood focus of the boycott organization proved to be its source of strength. The initial boycott committee, composed of nineteen women, numbered nine neighbors from Monroe Street, four from Cherry Street, and six from adjacent blocks.[29] This was not the anonymous city so often portrayed by antiurban polemicists and historians but a neighborhood community whose residents maintained close ties. The first show of strength on May 15th was preceded by an early morning house-to-house canvas of housewives in the heart of the boycott area. A similar canvas occurred the next day in Harlem under the aegis of local women. Rooted in the neighborhood, where many activities were quasi-public rather than strictly private, housewives were able to exert moral (as well as physical) suasion upon the women whom they saw on a daily basis. They assumed the existence of collective goals and the right to demand shared sacrifices. Individual desires for the consumption of meat were to be subordinated to the larger public good. As one boycott enthusiast stated while grabbing meat from a girl leaving a butcher store, "If we can't eat meat, the customers can't eat meat."[30] Shouting similar sentiments in another incident, striking women attempted to remove the meat from cholent pots which their neighbors had brought to a local bakery on a Friday afternoon.[31] Participants in the boycott picketed local butchers and also resolved not to speak to the "scabs" in their midst.[32] The constant presence in the neighborhood of the housewife leaders of the boycott made it difficult for individuals to evade their surveillance. The neighborhood, a form of female network, thus provided the locus of community for the boycott: all were giving up meat together, celebrating dairy *shabbosim* together, and contributing together to the boycott fund.

The women who organized and led the boycott considered themselves the natural leaders of such an enterprise. As consumers and housewives, they saw their task as complementary to that of their wage-earning spouses: "Our husbands work hard," stated one of the leaders at the initial planning meeting. "They try their best to bring a few cents into the house. We must manage to spend as little as possible. We will not give away our last few cents to the butcher and let our children go barefoot." In response, the women shouted, "We will not be silent; we will overturn the world."[33] Describing themselves as soldiers, they determined to circulate leaflets calling upon all women to "join the great women's war."[34] An appeal to their "worthy sisters," published by the Ladies' Anti-Beef Trust in the *Forward*, expressed similar sentiments, calling for "help . . . in the name of humanity in this great struggle which we have undertaken out of need."[35]

Sharper formulations of class resentment mingled with pride in their own talents in some of the women's shouts in the street demonstrations. One woman was heard lamenting to another, "Your children must go to work, and the millionaires snatch the last bit from our mouths." Another called out, "My husband brings me eight dollars a week. Should I give it away to the butcher? What would the landlord say?" Still another screamed, "They think women aren't people, that they can bluff us; we'll show them that we are more people than the fat millionaires who suck our blood." When the son of the Chief Rabbi, who supervised the *kashrut* of the meat, passed through the area, he was met with shouts of "Trust—Kosher

Korobke," a reference to the kosher meat tax, much despised by the poor in Czarist Russia.[36]

The ringleaders who were arrested and charged with disorderly conduct defined their behavior in political terms and considered it both just and appropriate to their status as housewives. "Did you throw meat on the street?" Rosa Peskin was asked. "Certainly," she replied. "I should have looked it in the teeth?" When the judge condescendingly commented, "What do you know of a trust? It's no business of yours," she responded, "Whose business is it, then, that our pockets are empty?" "What do you have against a woman who has bought meat?" the judge persisted. "I have nothing against her," retorted Peskin. "It doesn't matter to me what others want to do. But it's because of others that we must suffer." Rebecca Ablowitz also presented the boycotters' rationale to the judge: "We're not rioting. Only see how thin our children are, our husbands have no more strength to work harder. . . . If we stay home and cry, what good will that do us?"[37]

Of similar conviction and eloquence was Mrs. Silver, one of the most articulate spokeswomen of the boycott, who headed the campaign to interrupt services in the synagogues. When one irate opponent roared that her speaking thus from the *bima* was an effrontery (*chutzpa*) and a desecration of God's name (*chillul ha-Shem*), Mrs. Silver coolly responded that the Torah would pardon her.[38]

The climate of the immigrant Jewish community facilitated the resolute behavior of the women. While a few rabbis, particularly those with close ties to the meat industry, were hostile to the boycott enterprise, they were the exception. Support for the boycott was widespread within the community. Friendly crowds packed the courtroom to cheer the arrested women. In every one of the synagogues on the Lower East Side, it was reported, "the uprising of the Hebrew women was referred to by the rabbis."[39] Most synagogue members warmly greeted the women who brought their cause to the congregation. When police were brought in to arrest Mrs. Silver after a disturbance erupted in one synagogue, a congregant rose to compare the woman to the prophet Zachariah, "who preached truly and whose blood demanded vengeance." So persuasive was he that Mrs. Silver was released.[40] Feeling that they could count upon the support of the traditionally observant community, the Ladies' Anti-Beef Trust Association, in an appeal printed by the *Forward,* called for communal ostracism of the one prominent rabbi, Dr. Adolph N. Radin of the People's Synagogue, who had not only refused to approve the boycott but had treated representatives of the Association rudely in his synagogue. He should be removed from his position as chaplain to Jewish prisoners, urged the women, for if this "half-German" could refer publicly to the boycotting women as "beasts" and receive them so coarsely in front of his congregation, how must he treat the unfortunate Jewish inmates he sees within the confines of the prison?[41]

Both the socialist *Forward* and the Orthodox *Yiddishes Tageblat* portrayed the initial disturbances as well as the later movement in a sympathetic manner and were offended by the rough treatment meted out to the women and their families by the police, as well as by the unsympathetic attitude of much of the English-language press. Jewish socialists, in particular, stood squarely behind the protest. The *Forward* heralded the boycott with the banner headline, "Bravo, bravo, bravo, Jewish women!"[42] To the *Forward,* the boycott provided an opportunity not only to support a grass roots protest action but also to level an attack upon the collusion of the rabbis with the German Jewish meat trust. There was little reason for the differential between kosher and nonkosher meat to stand at five to six cents a pound, proclaimed the newspaper's editorial. Those who raised the prices "are Yahudim with gilded beards, who never eat kosher. Why are they suddenly so *frum* (pious)? Since when is there a partnership between those who give rabbinic endorsements in the Chief Rabbi's name and those Yahudi meat handlers? . . . The Chief Rabbi's son is merely a salesman for the Trust," continued the editorial. "He goes about in carriages collecting money in the name of his unfortunate father's endorsement. . . . Whether the strike of the good Jewish women brings down the prices or not," concluded the *Forward,* "one thing remains certain, the bond between the Trust and the rabbis must end. If they are truly pious, let them serve their religion and not the Trust in whose pay they are in."[43] In Russian Poland, noted the paper the next day, the meat tax was seven cents a pound, but at least there the *korobke* supported all *kehilla* (communal) activities. Here, on the other hand, it went only to the Trust.[44]

While the *Forward* conducted its pro-boycott campaign, the labor movement as a whole extended monetary donations and aid to the boycott; two men active in the Ladies' Garment Workers' Union were appointed as vice president and secretary of the Ladies' Anti-Beef Trust Association, while the posts of president and treasurer remained in women's hands.[45] In Harlem, it was the Women's Branch No. Two of the Workmen's Circle, with the support of the parent organization, that coordinated local boycott activity.[46]

Communal support was not, however, without its limits. Jewish communal leaders were clearly upset by the initiative assumed by the women activists. The sight of Jewish women engaged in picketing and in the physical coercion of butcher shop customers, as well as of their arrest at the hands of a none too gentle police force, aroused concern. "Don't give the Trust and the police an opportunity to break heads," cautioned the *Forward.* "More can be accomplished lawfully than not. . . . Agitate quietly in your homes."[47] Moreover, when the boycott was recognized as a force to be reckoned with, men tried to wrest control of the movement from its female leaders. However, the women were never entirely displaced, and the Yiddish language media continued, if somewhat ambivalently, to view the success of the boycott as a legitimate example of the "power of women."[48] (On the other hand, the *American Hebrew,* the organ of the Uptown Jews, studiously ignored the kosher meat riots.)[49]

In a larger sense, the immigrant Jewish community was quite supportive of women's political activity. East European Jewish immigrants were highly politicized; just how highly can be seen in the meat boycott, whose participants were sufficiently traditional to buy kosher meat and to use the synagogues and *hevras* as areas for potential recruitment. Indeed, the development of the boycott suggests that the compartmentalization of the immigrant community by historians into Orthodox, socialist and anarchist, and Zionist sectors does not do justice to the interplay among the groups. Boundary lines were fluid, and socialist rhetoric tripped easily from the tongues of women who still cared about kosher meat, could cite biblical passages in Hebrew, and felt at ease in the synagogue. Moreover, the boycotters consciously addressed themselves to several different constituencies— synagogues, *landsmanshaften,* the labor movement, and socialist groups.

Even within the traditional community, women had never been banned from the *secular* public sphere. In developing cadres of female activists, both the Jewish labor and the Zionist movements in Russia built upon the relative freedom of public activity accorded women within the Jewish community. As Mary Van Kleeck, of the Russell Sage Foundation, commented in her study of one Lower East Side trade which employed Jewish women, "The Jewish girl . . . has a distinct sense of her social responsibility and often displays an eager zest for discussion of labor problems. . . . Her attitude is likely to be that of an agitator. Nevertheless, she has the foundation of that admirable trait, 'public spirit,' and a sense of relationship to a community larger than the family or the personal group of which she happens to be a member."[50] Sufficient toleration existed within the family circle to enable Jewish women to express their "public spirit," to permit wives and mothers to attend evening meetings and to demonstrate in the streets. As the *Yiddishes Tageblat* put it, somewhat condescendingly, at the beginning of the boycott, "The women this time let the men play at home with the children while they went to attend the meeting."[51] While this was clearly a situation worthy of comment, it was not a violation of communal values.

If the immigrant Jewish community helped to sustain the meat boycott, the English-language socialist press was far more ambivalent in its attitude to this form of political activity. Indeed, it saw the only appropriate weapon for workers in the struggle against capitalism in the organization of producers, rather than consumers. As *The Worker* commented,

> The Meat Trust does not care two cents for such opposition as this, no matter how sincere the boycotters may be. . . . [A boycott] is so orderly and law-abiding, so free from all taint of socialism or confiscation or class hatred, so truly individualistic, and, above all, so perfectly harmless—to all except the poor workingmen. . . . We cannot oppose the aggression of twentieth-century capitalism with weapons fitted to the petty conflicts of eighteenth-century small producers.[52]

Added the *Daily People,* organ of the Socialist Labor Party, "It does not make the capitalist hungry if the workingman goes without food."[53] Such an attitude overlooked the potential of community organization outside the workplace. It precluded reaching out to the neighborhood as a possible secondary locus of political activism and incidentally resulted in an inability on the part of the socialists to tap the ranks of the politically conscious housewife.

The difference in attitudes between the Yiddish-speaking and the English-language socialists is also of broader interest. While the Jewish socialists were often seen as assimilationist, they remained closer to the shared value of their own immigrant community than to the perhaps ideologically purer stance of the American radicals.

*

The boycott movement enables us to look at the potential for political organization among Lower East Side women, the majority of whom were housewives unaffiliated in any formal sense with the trade union movement. But it also raises questions for which there are no readily available answers.

Was there any precedent for this type of direct action among married women in Eastern Europe? One can find a tenuous connection to the Eastern European scene in reference to the *korobke,* the meat tax, which in the nineteenth century constituted as much as one-third of the budget of some Jewish communities and was passionately resented. Some Hasidic rebbes in the first half of the last century urged passive resistance against the tax, even including a boycott on the purchase of meat.[54] Clearly, the ability to draw an analogy, as both the women activists and the *Forward* editorials did, between the *korobke* and the high price of kosher meat caused by collusion between the meat trust and rabbis selling their *hechsher* (certification of kashrut) was an appealing propaganda device. It linked the 1902 boycott to the longstanding disaffection of the poor with the authorities of the Eastern European *kehilla.* However, the boycott's leaders do not refer to earlier Eastern European examples of reaction against the *korobke,* nor is there any other evidence of direct influence from the Eastern European to the American scene.

As interesting as the boycott is as a vehicle for examining the political sensibilities and assessing the political potential of Jewish housewives on the Lower East Side, the fading away of the Ladies' Anti-Beef Trust Association is as significant as its sudden appearance. If the neighborhood network was so effective a means to reach women and mobilize them, why was it not sustained to deal with other social problems? True, the 1904 and 1907–08 rent strikes on the Lower East Side espoused similar tactics and hailed the meat boycott as their model. Beginning with a house-to-house canvas initiated by women, strike leaders promoted neighborhood solidarity by collecting written pledges of refusal to pay rent. In 1908, women also lent their support to retail butchers protesting the rising cost in wholesale meat prices.[55] These further incidents of local activism confirm the growing consumer consciousness of Lower East Side women. However, there appears to be no overlap in leadership between these several expressions of female popular protest.[56] Were women coopted into already established fraternal and political organizations, or did the politics of crisis bring with it inertia once the crisis had passed?

Because its leaders faded into obscurity with the conclusion of the boycott, because of the very nature of a short-lived grass roots movement, it is impossible to assess the impact of the movement upon its participants. However, it is likely that the political awareness expressed by the boycotters was no isolated phenomenon but was communicated effectively, if quietly and informally, to their younger sisters and daughters. The boycott alerted the immigrant community as a whole and the labor movement in particular to the political potential of women. Moreover, the communal support of the boycott could only have encouraged women themselves to further activity. As Alice Kessler-Harris notes of Jewish women in the garment trades, whose numbers in the unions exceeded their proportion in the industry as a whole, they "unionized at their own initiative" and were "responsible for at least one quarter of the increased number of unionized women [in America] in the second decade of the twentieth century."[57] In that sense, the kosher meat boycott should be seen not as an isolated incident but as a prelude to the explosion of women activists in the great garment industry strikes at the end of the decade.[58]

NOTES

1. E.P. Thompson, "The Moral Economy of the English Crowd in the Eighteenth Century," *Past and Present* 50 (February, 1971); 116.

2. George Rudé, *The Crowd in History* (New York: Wiley, 1964), 220; Rudé, *The Crowd in the French Revolution* (Oxford: Clarendon, 1959), 73–76.

3. The 1902 incident had repercussions in Boston. There were also food riots in Patterson, New Jersey and in Philadelphia in 1907 and more extensive riots in New York City in 1917. *New York Times,* May 23, 1902; June 26, 1907, November 13, 14, 15, 1907. On the 1917 riots, see Zosa Szajkowski, *Jews, Wars, and Communism* (New York: Ktav, 1972), vol. I, 111–15.

4. *New York Times,* May 24, 1902.

5. Thompson, "The Moral Economy of the English Crowd," 116.

6. For a discussion of the popular consensus underlying preindustrial food riots, see ibid., 77–79. Herbert Gutman interprets the kosher meat riots in this fashion, noting a demand by the women for rabbis to determine the just price for the meat. (It is worth noting that such a demand appears in none of the Yiddish sources, though rabbinic endorsement of the *kashrut* of the meat was assumed by strike leaders.) See Herbert Gutman, "Work, Culture, and Society in Industrializing America, 1815–1919," *American Historical Review* 78, no. 3 (June 1973): 576–77. In reprinting the *New York Times* description of the food riots, Rosalyn Baxandall et al. also define the purpose of the rioters as "to mete out justice and punishment," in *America's Working Women: A Documentary History 1600 to the Present* (New York: W. W. Norton, 1976), 184.

7. For a similar critique, see Daphne Kis, "The Political Role of Women in Community: New York's Lower East Side, 1900–1910" (Division Three paper, Hampshire College, 1976).

8. Harold P. Gastwirt, *Fraud, Corruption, and Holiness: The Controversy over the Supervision of the Jewish Dietary Practice in New York* (Port Washington: Kennikat Press, 1974), 39.

9. *Jewish Daily Forward,* May 14, 1902, 1.

10. *New York Herald,* May 16, 1902, 4.

11. *Forward,* May 15, 1902.

12. *New York Herald,* May 16, 1902; *Forward,* May 15, 1902; *New York Daily Tribune,* May 16, 1902, 1.

13. *Forward,* May 15, 1902.

14. *New York Daily Tribune,* May 17, 1902, 1; *Forward,* May 16, 1902.

15. *Forward,* May 16, 1902, May 17, 1902; *Yiddishes Tageblat,* May 16, 1902. On the boycott in Harlem, see Jeffrey Gurock, *When Harlem was Jewish* (New York: Columbia University Press, 1979), 69–70.

16. *Forward,* May 18, 1902.

17. Ibid.; *New York Herald,* May 18, 1902, 9; *New York Daily Tribune,* May 19, 1902, p. 4.

18. *Forward,* May 19, May 20, 1902; *New York Herald,* May 20, 1902, 7; May 24, 1902, 4; *New York Daily Tribune,* May 20, 1902, 16.

19. *Yiddishes Tageblat,* May 22, 1902; *New York Herald,* May 18, 1902, 4; May 20, 1902, 7; May 21, 1902, p. 6.

20. *New York Times,* May 22, 1902.

21. *New York Herald,* May 26, 1902, p. 6.

22. *Forward,* May 20, June 4, June 5, 1902; *Yiddishes Tageblat,* May 21, May 22, May, 28, May 30, June 5, 1902; *New York Herald,* May 22, 1902, 6.

23. Alice Kessler-Harris, "Where Are the Organized Women Workers?" *Feminist Studies* 3, nos. 1, 2 (fall 1975): 92–93.

24. Nine boycott activists mentioned by name and address in the Yiddish press could be traced in the 1905 New York state manuscript census and two others in the 1902 New York City directory. While their number is regrettably small, their socioeconomic characteristics are so similar as to suggest that they are typical of the entire leadership.

25. New York state manuscript census, 1905.

26. Ibid.

27. *Forward; New York Herald,* May 26, 1902, 6.

28. Ibid., May 16, 1902, 4.

29. *Forward,* May 15, 1902.

30. Ibid.

31. *Yiddishes Tageblat,* May 18, 1902.

32. *Forward,* May 18, 1902.

33. *Yiddishes Tageblat,* May 15, 1902.

34. Ibid.

35. *Forward,* May 19, 1902.

36. Ibid., May 15, 1902.

37. Ibid.

38. Ibid., May 18, 1902.

39. *New York Herald,* May 18, 1902, 4.

40. *Forward,* May 18, 1902.

41. Ibid., May 19, 1902, 2; *New York Herald,* May 18, 1902, 4; May 19, 1902, 3. Communal pressure forced Radin to offer a public apology to the women whom he had insulted.

42. *Forward,* May 18, 1902.

43. Ibid., May 17, 1902.

44. Ibid., May 18, 1902.

45. Ibid.

46. Ibid., May 17, 1902.

47. Ibid., May 18, 1902.

48. See cartoon of women holding key to locked kosher meat trust, *Forward,* May 24, 1902.

49. *American Hebrew,* May 2–June 7, 1902.

50. Mary van Kleeck, *Artificial Flower Makers* (New York: Survey Associates, 1913), 34–35.

51. *Yiddishes Tageblat,* May 15, 1902.

52. *The Worker,* May 18, 1902, 2.

53. *Daily People,* May 21, 1902, 2.

54. Raphael Mahler, *ha-Hasidut veha-Haskalah* (Merhavia: Sifriat Po'alim, 1961), 33–

34. On the growing tension between the *kehilla* leadership and the masses, see Isaac Levitats, *The Jewish Community in Russia, 1772–1844* (New York: Columbia University Press, 1943).

55. Daphne Kis, "Political Role of Women in Community," 58–80.

56. Personal communication from Jenna Weissman Joselit.

57. Kessler-Harris, "Where Are the Organized Women Workers?" 102.

58. Louis Levine, *The Women's Garment Workers: A History of the International Ladies' Garment Workers' Union* (New York, B. W. Huebsch, 1924).

Chapter Nine

Zion in Our Hearts
Henrietta Szold and the
American Jewish Women's Movement

Joyce Antler

Guiding spirit and founder of Hadassah and political leader in pre-statehood Palestine, Henrietta Szold embodied in her life and career a truly revolutionary transformation in traditional notions of Jewish women's roles. Yet so singular was her temperament and so unique her achievements that even her closest allies failed to appreciate the extent of the innovations she had wrought. Brilliantly forging Hadassah into an effective fundraising and social welfare organization in support of a Jewish homeland, Szold helped create a Jewish women's movement that called upon the talents and efficiency of thousands. In this endeavor and in her own pathbreaking service as educator, administrator, and government official, she enlarged the boundaries of women's sphere while never formally abandoning the familial, domestic ideal of *Aishes Chayil* [Woman of Valor]. Combining flexibility and openness to risks with steely determination, she pursued new paths, one after the other, where no women had gone before. Her high visibility and devotion to duty created a model of female public service which a great many American women would emulate.

A superb organizer, administrator, and leader, Szold was a rationalist to the extreme, a woman who devoted her entire life to the call of duty. The daughter of a distinguished Baltimore rabbi, Szold had been educated by her father for a life of Jewish scholarship. In the 1880s, however, she became interested in the plight of the Jewish immigrants who had started arriving at the port of Baltimore after fleeing from pogroms in Russia. Within a few years she had started a night school for Russian Jewish immigrants, one of the first in America. Out of her contact with these Russians came her interest in Zionism and her charter membership in the Baltimore Zion Association, one of the first Zionist organizations in America.

It was not this organization but Hadassah, the Women's Zionist Organization, which Szold established in 1912, that catapulted Henrietta Szold to national and international renown. From this time until her death in 1945, Szold stood for most Americans—particularly women—as the living symbol of the Zionist dream. Capitalizing on Szold's image and the clearly defined mission she imparted to Hadassah, the organization grew by leaps and bounds, numbering over one hundred thousand at the time of Szold's death. Two decades later, with a membership three and a half times that number, it had become one of the largest voluntary women's organizations in the world.

While the public Henrietta Szold which Hadassah created allowed the organization to consolidate its mission, the group's adulation and "myth-worship," as Szold saw it, caused her endless pain.[1] Driven by the needs of Hadassah and Zionism, she felt that she had forever lost the opportunity to exercise the truly creative aspects of her womanhood, to explore and express her private self. While the establishment of a popular woman's movement in support of the creation of a Jewish homeland compensated in large part for this loss, Szold acknowledged to her closest confidantes that she had failed to live an expressive, personally fulfilling life. She envied friends like Jessie Sampter, a younger American Zionist writer, who made *aliyah* to Palestine. As a founding member of the kibbutz Givat Brenner, Sampter seemed to satisfy both her own spiritual and creative needs and those of the struggling Jewish homeland.

Yet through Hadassah, Szold had established a remarkably successful mechanism for American women to support Zionism without actually living in Palestine. Szold herself would spend the greater part of twenty-five years in the country, although she never considered her stay to be permanent and thought of herself as an American temporarily pursuing Zionist projects in Palestine.

Mediating Between the Worlds of Women and Men: The Origins and Transformation of Szold's Spiritual Mission

Szold was born in 1860, a birth date she shared with Jane Addams and Charlotte Perkins Gilman, pioneering American feminists whose theory and practice also pointed to new directions for women. All three reached adulthood during an era which had just begun to entertain new educational and vocational opportunities for women. Szold, for example, never went to college. Though she secretly longed to attend Vassar, which had opened a few years after her birth, leaving home was out of the question, and there were no colleges in Baltimore which admitted women. In fact, an unsigned article Szold wrote in 1883 in *Education* calling for the endowment of a college for women in the city attracted the attention of M. Carey Thomas, another Baltimorean—who had gone to Cornell for her B.A. and then to Zurich for a Ph.D. The two women became friends on the basis of their shared interest in establishing women's right to a higher education.[2]

Unlike Thomas, who would become president of Bryn Mawr College and a leading champion of women's professional and educational opportunities, Szold would not leave Baltimore to fulfill her own intellectual aspirations. Her father relied on her as his literary secretary, and her mother and sisters needed her too much.[3] But Szold did do some writing as Baltimore correspondent for the *Jewish Messenger,* signing herself as "Sulamith," eventually commenting not only on community events but on national and international affairs and on Jewish culture and character. When a critic once wrote that "Sulamith" had no authority to assert opinions on political and intellectual topics since she, a woman, was merely a "pot and pan scourer," the eighteen-year-old columnist responded by defending not her own authority as writer but the "peculiar privilege" of women's domesticity. The *Messenger*'s publisher, nervous over the controversy, urged "Sulamith" to write on less controversial topics, suggesting a handbook for girls on moral topics. "Sulamith" refused.[4]

Yet, at this stage of her life, Szold was ambivalent in her championship of women's rights. First of all, she was too much under the thrall of her father's benign but controlling influence to assert her own interests. Second, her own painful shyness, which translated into an awkward stiffness with men, left her longing for romantic attachments. While she did not imagine a future for herself outside the conventional bounds of Jewish domesticity, her intellectual ability, religious commitments, and penchant for teaching (which she considered an avocation, never a steady career) found ready outlets in a series of instructional and club activities she pursued in Baltimore.

When she was twenty, her father took Henrietta to Europe to visit relatives. Her keenest memory of the trip came from the Alt-Neu Shul in Prague, the oldest synagogue in Europe, where she had observed women congregants physically locked away from services. At a small window which opened into the hidden women's gallery above—a window too dark to let in more than a small beam of light—stood one woman who was acting as minister to the others, relaying to them what was going on in the men's synagogue below. Here Henrietta had an epiphany: this was what she could do with the rest of her life, serve as a teacher to Jewish women, as an intermediary between the male-oriented worlds to which she had access and women's space. After all, had not Miriam, Moses' sister, led women into the Promised Land with song and prayer?[5]

The vision Szold saw of herself ministering to women's spiritual needs would crystallize only slowly as its two preconditions—immersion in each of the gender-segregated worlds of women and men—matured. A few years after her return from her European trip, Szold began to volunteer her services for the newly founded Jewish Publication Society, an organization dedicated to the promotion of Jewish literature. Szold's work for the JPS was a commitment undertaken to further the scholarly interests she shared with her father; it did little to advance the mission of educating Jewish women. Nonetheless, at the JPS, where she was the only woman, Szold translated many significant books on Jewish history and religion and wrote over a dozen articles of her own. She served as editorial secretary of the Society for twenty-three years, editing most of its books and overseeing its publication schedule. Although Szold thus played a pioneering role in creating Jewish literary culture in the United States, later in life she confessed that she believed the JPS had been "too academic," "pedantic," and "afraid of life." Because it did not use "all its possibilities"—with hindsight, perhaps because it had failed to reach the vast majority of women who had little Jewish education—the JPS model of achievement fell short.[6]

At the time, however, Szold continued to espouse conventional ideals. In a reply to a questionnaire on "Woman in the Synagogue" from a Jewish newspaper in the mid-nineties, Szold advanced a traditional concept of women's roles.

> I believe that woman can best serve the interests of the synagogue by devoting herself to her home; by filling any administrative position for which her executive ability is admittedly greater than that of any available man—"Where there are no men, be thou a man" is addressed to both sexes—and by occupying the pulpit only when her knowledge of the law, history and literature of Judaism is masterful, and her natural gift so extraordinary as to forbid hesitation. . . . Religion being sexless, no necessity exists for Jewish women's organizations, whose interference in religious affairs I should therefore deprecate.[7]

While making exceptions for "masterful" women, Szold thus found no special "necessity" for a public religious role for Jewish women as a group. She would continue to lead her own scholarly life as an exceptional woman for some time further.

After her father's death in 1902, Szold applied to the Jewish Theological Seminary in New York to acquire the knowledge she hoped would assist her in publishing her father's manuscripts. Because of her sex, Szold's application for admission was controversial, and she was accepted only after she assured the trustees that she would not pursue a rabbinic diploma. In New York, Szold also continued her work for the JPS, putting in fifteen-hour days to complete the *American Jewish Yearbook,* whose editorship she now took on as well.

As the only female at the JTS, Szold refused to attend the formal dinners the Seminary held for students, no doubt considering her private relationships with the Seminary circle of a different order than more public sociability between the sexes. She also hesitated to take a Talmud class given by one of the Seminary's most impressive scholars, Dr. Louis Ginzberg, because Ginzberg had apparently once told her that women were not fit to study "Mother Torah." Szold joined the class after Ginzberg invited her to enroll, yet due to her presence he refrained from discussing what Szold called "awkward passage[s]"—regarding marriage, divorce, and sexual relations in the Talmud.[8]

Szold was not a delicate youngster at the time; in her mid-forties, she had gained a well-deserved reputation as a learned woman. A few years earlier, after she had spoken before the National Council of Jewish Women, a Jewish weekly had commented that her address was "almost too profound for an American woman."[9] Yet Szold was hesitant about asserting either her womanhood or her rights as a woman too boldly. At the Seminary, she began to translate and edit Ginzberg's writings, just as she had done for her father. It was not long before she fell in love. Ginzberg, thirteen years her junior, welcomed her friendship, but it was doubtful whether his attraction to Henrietta was ever more than intellectual and comradely. The two spent many hours together, with Szold translating and editing several volumes of his masterful work, *The Legends of the Jews.* When Solomon Schechter, president of the JTS, asked Szold to write an English prayerbook for women, she refused, preferring to assist Ginzberg.[10]

Yet Szold's life during this time was marked by increasingly close associations with women. Her mother, who had moved to New York with her and kept house for the two of them, was a constant support, helping Szold adapt to her grueling schedule. Szold also began making important female friends, especially Alice Seligsberg, thirteen years younger than Henrietta, the daughter of a well-to-do New York German Jewish family and one of Barnard College's first graduates. Though their families were acquainted, Seligsberg and Szold did not become personal friends until the fall of 1908, shortly after Szold suffered a severe emotional crisis when Louis Ginzberg rejected her for a younger woman. Over the next few months, Alice played an important role in helping Henrietta through what the latter called the "shock" of her life.[11] By the summer of 1909, one month before Henrietta set sail with her mother for a much-needed six-month vacation to Europe and Palestine, Alice had become a precious confidante, in Szold's words, and more: she was an "equal friend," an intellectual companion.[12]

By 1907, Szold had also become associated with a group of women—some of them daughters or wives of her Seminary colleagues—engaged in the study of Zionism. At that time, several small women's Zionist study groups existed in the city. According to Lotta Levensohn, one of the founders of Hadassah, it was Judah Magnes who suggested asking Szold to join her own study group. Levensohn was "so dumbfounded at the idea of asking so renowned a scholar and editor to study Zionism with young girls far inferior to her in knowledge" that Magnes had to extend the invitation. Szold agreed to join, but as a "working," not an "honorary," member. Although Szold refused to be president, "wherever she sat and led the discussion," Levensohn recalled, "there was the head of the table."[13] Under Szold's guidance, the organization developed a program of study which included Zionism, Jewish current events, and Jewish history. Zionist men at the time considered the group merely as "organizers of Strawberry festivals," no more.[14] Szold herself felt the study groups, and the entire Zionist movement, lacked direction. Nonetheless, the groups provided a vehicle with which to channel Szold's still potent desire to educate women in Judaism.

The opportunity came after her return from her first visit to Palestine. The trip changed her life, causing the painful rejection by Ginzberg to recede. More important, in taking her to Palestine, the journey engaged her connection to Zionism in an immediate, urgent fashion. Contrary to her friends' expectation that exposure to the primitive living conditions and political rivalries of Palestine would unmake her Zionism, Szold returned "more than ever convinced that our only salvation lies that way," as she wrote to her young friend Jessie Sampter, whose Zionist education Szold had fostered.[15] Especially significant was Szold's visit to the Girls' School in Jaffa, where she and her mother saw "a most horrible sight—children playing with sand, with a wreath of flies around their eyes." Horrified, Szold's mother suggested to her that "this is what your group ought to do. What is the use of reading papers . . . ? You should do practical work in Palestine . . ."[16]

The trip to Palestine became the occasion of Szold's second epiphany, not cancelling but redirecting the vision she had when she traveled with her father to Prague and glimpsed Jewish women's separation from the mainstream of religious devotion. Guided by her mother's influence and supported by her friendships with

Zionist women, Szold would transform American women's Zionist activity into a practical program of philanthropy that not only aided the desperate plight of women and children in Palestine but provided educational and spiritual nurturance to American women in the Diaspora. Through Szold's moral and intellectual leadership, Hadassah came to offer American Jewish women a meaningful route to Jewish female identity. Though Szold herself would take on consecutive positions of leadership within Palestine's male governing elites, her association with the women's world of American Zionism and her special female friends supported her political efforts and sustained her spirituality.

Late in her life, in one of the few autobiographical interviews she permitted, Szold acknowledged that her main intellectual make-up came not from her father but her mother, Sophie Szold. Like her mother, Henrietta considered herself "practical [with a] strong sense of duty." In this, the fundamental aspect of her nature, she felt that she was "exactly" like her mother, although her father's influence had shaped her mode of thinking. Rabbi Szold's contribution was not so much the content of her Jewishness or her love of learning but the very notion of a central idea, which he insisted should guide her life. "Adopt some central idea; never depart from it, but relate everything to that central idea," her father advised her.[17] Zionism became this determining influence, but it was her mother's concreteness, her practical idealism, as Szold described it, that provided an arena for the expression of the idea. Szold's genius would be to combine the modes of action and thought which her parents represented into a model which could be replicated by thousands of other Jewish women. In each of her activities, as an intermediary between the social spaces of the sexes, she successfully negotiated greater opportunities for women's influence and achievement.

The Settlement Model, Zionism, and the Founding and Nurturing of Hadassah

After her return from Palestine, Szold, together with Sophia Berger, Emma Gottheil, Lotta Levensohn, Mathilde Schechter, Gertrude Goldsmith, and Rosalia Phillips, issued a call to New York City women to come together to build a large organization of women Zionists for two purposes: the propagation of Zionism in America and the establishment of health and welfare for women and children in Palestine.[18] Ten days later, on February 23, 1912, thirty-eight women met in the vestry rooms of Temple Emanu-El. The group took the name of Hadassah for its chapter, absorbing the original study group of that name, and Israel Friedlaender supplied the motto, "The Healing of the Daughter of My People" (Arukhat Bat-Ammi). It was Szold's idea that the group should devote itself to the practical purposes of healing that her trip to Palestine had revealed as essential to the well-being of women and children. Although several ideas were discussed in addition to nursing—the establishment of a day nursery, maternity hospital, or vocational training; employing girls in lace-making or the pearl industry; supervising midwives—the nursing idea immediately took hold. After funding was secured from Nathan and Lina Straus, Szold went to Lillian Wald, founder of the Nurses' Settlement (later known as Henry Street) on New York's Lower East Side, to ask her to recommend Jewish nurses willing to go to the slums of Palestine. Wald was skeptical—"you don't think you will find Jewish girls who would do that sort of work," she replied to Szold—but an advertisement turned up many applicants.[19] Rose Kaplan from New York and Rachel Landy from Cleveland became Hadassah's first nurses in Palestine. There, according to a contemporary report, they "rented a simple home, placed the sign, 'Hadassah Chapter, Daughters of Zion' above the door, and invited the needy to come for free advice and help."[20] Notwithstanding early suspicions that the nurses were missionaries (despite their Yiddish language and the Hebrew sign), their unstinting efforts to provide maternity, infant care, and school health services soon won them the gratitude of the populace. During the first year alone, they had treated some five-thousand patients.

Hadassah's nursing project was largely based on the American settlement model of a community of residents living among the poor and working to prevent the social as well as physical causes of illness. As Hadassah put it, the goal was "not so much to bring relief to individual cases of illness as to organize a thorough system of district-nursing throughout the towns and colonies of Palestine, beginning with Jerusalem."[21] "Our nurses must be community nurses," Szold explained, "able to minister to all wants of the community"—pre- and postnatal care, school health, tuberculosis work, infant welfare, and preventive education.[22] Szold no doubt had in mind the model pioneered by Lillian Wald; she urged Hadassah nurses to spend time observing Wald's program before coming to Palestine. Szold was also influenced by Jane Addams, founder of Chicago's Hull House and leader of the American settlement movement. Addams, in fact, visited the Nurses' Settlement in Palestine shortly after it began operations.[23] Yet Szold never imagined a permanent body of nursing residents from the United States or a health system administered by Americans; from the very beginning she emphasized that, while Hadassah might create a Nurses' Training School and develop community health services, responsibility for training and implementation should be transferred as soon as possible to the people of Palestine. Like Addams and Wald, who had come to recognize the value of extending settlement work into the political sphere and connecting women residents' neighborhood involvements with larger systems of government, Szold would also work on a broader political canvas. Her own career with the Zionist Executive and, later, with the *Vaad Leumi* [Palestine General Council] reflected this direction.

At about the time that Hadassah's nurses began their pioneering health work in Palestine, Daughters of Zion chapters were organized in other cities, each affiliated to the Federation of American Zionists and the World Zionist Organization.[24] At the time of the first annual convention of the Daughters of Zion, eight such chapters—in New York, Baltimore, Chicago, Cleveland, Newark, Boston, Philadelphia, and St. Paul—had been formed; Szold was elected president. At their second annual convention, in Rochester, in 1914, the Daughters of Zion adopted

"Hadassah" as a generic name for the organization in the belief that the word "Hadassah" had already come to signify "trained nurse" throughout Palestine and was widely respected.[25]

Szold and the founders of Hadassah believed that their association could provide a special home for women which did not exist for them in general Zionist organizations. Szold admitted that the Zionist Organization of America had never been hospitable to women or recognized their contributions; she wanted to remedy the deficiency of preexisting women's Zionist organizations, which were little more than auxiliaries to male members. While this pattern predominated in the world of the Jewish communal organization (with such exceptions as the gender-based National Council of Jewish Women), Hadassah argued that it made sense to organize a separate women's Zionist society, since the very basis of Zionism was the social group. Hadassah would provide an arena for practical service and, equally important, a "natural social grouping of friends" which could attract Jewish women who were unaffiliated with Zionism or who were unhappy with other mixed-group Jewish organizations.[26] Such a society would appeal to women occupied with traditional domestic concerns who sought broader outlets, English-speaking, middle-class women as well as Eastern European immigrants, who were most familiar with Zionism. Anticipating that Zionist men might oppose the new organization, Hadassah leaders argued that a women's Zionist group would not prevent Jewish women from working "side by side" with men: "We have not taken anything from the men's organization. Adam's lost rib leaves no gap, and in its place there was found a full grown woman and helpmate."[27]

While Hadassah would be devoted to the practical "healing of the daughter of my people" in Palestine, Szold always remarked that its members would find "spiritual healing for themselves" in America through Zionism. For Szold, Zionism meant the establishment of a Jewish homeland where Jews could "govern themselves in a Jewish way." It was the only "positive, constructive movement among Jews," vital not only to Palestine but to the Diaspora, since it countered assimilation, which Szold felt had "annihilat[ed] the Jews." "We need Zionism as much as those Jews do who need a physical home," she told friends. It was not a question of Reform or Orthodozy, but of Judaism or non-Judaism. Zionism was "the only anchor in sight."[28]

For Szold, to live and work for Zionism meant living the prophetic values of Judaism, not in some future sacred time but in the confused and ungodly present. In Palestine, through the routines of daily living, the Zionist dream, based in Jewish law and faith, could become reality: Judaism would be "changed back from creed to a way of life." Zionism, said Szold, was "Jewish messianism in a practical form. It is Jewish hope, aspiration, dream, prayer made practical."[29]

Before she left for Palestine, Szold had explained to Jessie Sampter that it was the opportunity to change Jewish law—the basis of all Jewish values—that made Zionism so important:

> Most of [Jewish] laws seem to me good, wise and beautiful. But some do not. Shall I break those? For me the answer lies in Zionism, in Palestine. We are a democratic

people that has kept its identity for two thousand years through the preservation of its laws; but in recent centuries our developing law has stood still; it needs revisions. I cannot revise it. For an individual to revise the law is anarchy. Nor can a small group revise it. The whole people must revise it . . . This I believe must happen in Palestine, when we shall have a nation there.[30]

While the "right road to Zion" was thus necessarily the road east to Palestine, Szold believed that Zionism was also an internal, organic, spiritual turning—the "restored Zion in your own hearts," as she told Hadassah members.[31] At the same time that Jewish women promoted righteous, healthful living in the new Zion of Palestine, Hadassah's dream would be fulfilled as American Jewish womanhood kindled a rebirth of Judaic values at home. Earlier, Szold had taken issue with a leader's assertion that the National Council of Jewish Women was a "religious organization," a declaration which Szold believed had been made for the "propaganda purposes" of Jewish revival.[32] Yet, while Szold believed that religion was a "personal, individual matter, not subject to organization," she did not doubt that true spirituality could be a byproduct of Zionist women's practical idealism. As she reminded Hadassah: "We are an organization of Jewish women who believe in the 'healing of the daughter of the people,' in the healing of the soul of the Jewish people as well as its body."[33]

The identification of practical with spiritual healing which lay at the core of Szold's utopianism became central to Hadassah's program. "It is a mistake to think that the practical and ideal conflict," Hadassah acknowledged in its early mission statements. In Hadassah's formulations, women's "imagination and insight," the creation of a broad "national vision and the big national way of doing things," became characteristic female traits given practical scope through Zionist work: through Zionism, Hadassah proclaimed, the "principles of womanliness [were] translated into public service."[34] Thus, Szold's theme of practical idealism became the rallying cry of Hadassah's gender-based Zionism. Though Szold had once considered religion "sexless" and a Jewish women's organization superfluous, her prophetic vision of the necessity of women's work in Palestine gave women a public role, and a public Jewish identity, in Zionism.[35] Szold took heart in Hadassah's unusually broad appeal; its early success exemplified the spiritual need of American women which Zionism could satisfy. "Isn't it curious how the Hadassah idea has taken hold of women?" she wrote to Alice Seligsberg. "It is necessary to invent, actually invent, a specific Hadassah task to satisfy them. What we are doing is a makeshift—it doesn't meet their heart hunger."[36] According to Seligsberg, Szold herself had become the symbol of spiritual purpose that guided Hadassah's astonishing growth. Seligsberg recalled that in the beginning, the National Council of Jewish Women had much greater prestige.

The Council of Jewish Women had a popular philosophy of American Jewish life. It was Americanized. It made fewer demands upon its members, and made no concessions to Yiddish speaking women. Miss Szold, on the other hand, from the outset, was insistent upon drawing together the women who were not Americanized and those others who were far removed in time from their immigrant forbears. We were not permitted to have more than one chapter in a city, and that chapter had to include rich and poor, Americanized socially elite and foreign born.[37]

All one had to do to become a member of Hadassah was to become a "conscious Zionist," subscribing to the notion that Palestine ought to be declared the legal Jewish homeland. But it was not the theory of Zionism that brought American Jewish women, rich and poor, American-born and immigrants, housewives and college-educated girls, flocking to Hadassah. It was, said Seligsberg, "what every cause needs:—a living example."[38]

Despite the admiration Jewish women felt for Szold, she was not accorded her due from male leaders. In 1910, the Federation of American Zionists pleaded with Szold to untangle the financial chaos into which the organization had fallen, and Szold reluctantly complied even though it meant staying up every night till after the work for the Jewish Publication Society was done. After the Federation had become the Zionist Organization of America, incorporating Hadassah as a constituent group, Szold was the only woman chosen to head one of its departments. Yet, according to Jessie Sampter, the Zionist men "withheld their appreciation of her personally, never gave her place she deserved in their councils." "Had only the Zionist men appreciated her as we women did!" Sampter complained. "She stood above them all in organizing ability, judgment, leadership. Her democratic organization of Hadassah, which now had thousands of members and covered a network of cities, was afterward made the model of American Zionist organization."[39] But Zionist men did not take the women's organization seriously. They "always made fun of Hadassah," Szold recalled.[40] "For all that Hadassah was called the Woman's Zionist Organization of America," she acknowledged, there had been "no warm feeling" for the women in the general organization. Instead there was "constant criticism because it was not political enough, or . . . it was too political—either it didn't think or it thought too independently." One male associate affirmed that Szold was "very bitter . . . very openly" about her treatment by Zionist men.[41]

Despite her treatment by Zionist men, Szold remained faithful to the cause of Zionist organization. Judah Magnes believed that, even though she disapproved of the ZOA's policies and leadership, she "slaved for it all the harder," convinced that she could help it find the "right way." Her conscience must have been that of an "ascetic" or a "flagellant," Magnes acknowledged.[42]

Szold's accommodations, which may have seemed at the time like unnecessary compromise, in fact revealed a goal-oriented vision of Hadassah as the central American women's Zionist organization, pursuing its independent fundraising and practical philanthropy. Though she never ruled out a strategy of integration with male Zionists on common issues and sanctioned the rule that Hadassah, as a ZOA constituent agency, would pay a portion of its dues to that organization, she continuously exerted her moral force to urge Hadassah to conduct its own affairs. At the same time, she insisted that Hadassah women could play a vital role in framing central Zionist policies: "Let no one tell you that it is womanly not to exercise the right, not to fulfill th[at] duty."[43]

Szold in Palestine: Circles of Female Friendship and an Unwanted Political Career

In 1921, when the American Zionist Medical Unit (AZMU) which Hadassah had organized became bogged down in seemingly intractable administrative and political difficulties, Szold accepted a call to direct the unit. With a hiatus of three years in the mid-twenties when she returned to the United States to assume the presidency of Hadassah and several short visits, she would remain in Palestine until her death in 1945, although she never acknowledged, even to herself, that her residency had become permanent; she still called the United States "home." Despite her many achievements in Palestine, the separation from friends and family remained painful, and she endured it only through the bonds of friendship and sisterhood she shared with her family and with Hadassah women. Biographers have ignored the circle of friendship that existed among Szold and these women, though they have mentioned, usually in passing, that a few intimate friends played a role in Szold's life and in Sampter's. Irving Fineman mentions Alice Seligsberg and Jessie Sampter as, for example, "friends who, like [Szold] herself, had failed to find mates."[44] Joan Dash notes that Seligsberg was an early, sweet, and gentle confidante of Szold, observing that, like Alice, most of Szold's friends were "unmarried and high minded and middle-aged like herself."[45]

Yet the considerable correspondence among these women proves that the bonds between them stretched far beyond the similarity of marital circumstance. Friendship played a central, not an ancillary, role in the lives of American Zionist women. At a time of great turmoil and challenge in their personal lives and to Zionism generally, the ties they formed with each other were emotionally sustaining, intellectually challenging, and politically enabling. Supporting each other's goals, testing ideas and strategies regarding religion, politics, and social reform, each helped make it possible for the others to innovate in both public and private spheres, to lead lives that strayed beyond the conventional.

To live and work in colonial Palestine was a bold venture not only because of the difficult physical, social, and political conditions of the prestatehood period but, as these women's letters poignantly reveal, because of an intense personal and spiritual loneliness. Often separated for long periods of time from their families and Hadassah colleagues, they attempted to fashion, out of whole cloth, solutions to the vexing social, medical, and political problems of a needy population. For all their efforts, they frequently confronted hostility, disparagement, and a decided lack of cooperation from male coworkers and authorities. Even in the United States, as they struggled to build Hadassah into a vital political organization and to maintain its integrity and independence, they had to swim against strong currents of indifference and antagonism within the male-controlled American Zionist movement. Divisions within Hadassah and competition from other Zionist women's groups both in the United States and abroad complicated a complex political situation. Religious life proved equally fractious and unfulfilling, despite Szold's efforts to create her own worship services.

In the face of these challenges and the disruptions to personal life that resulted from their Zionist mission, the friendship between these women became life sustaining. Though each of them had other companions with whom they shared their lives and work, the network they created became an intellectual alliance which allowed for the molding of a distinct brand of Zionism, one that was both religious and woman-centered.

After Seligsberg's death in 1937, Szold revealed how profound her friend's influence had been.

> Alice was unique, and the relation that existed between us . . . was a unique passage in my life. When I came in close contact with her, I was already on my own intellectually and spiritually. I was no longer malleable—so I thought. She made me think otherwise. No meeting with her, no conversation with her, left me as I had been before. There was always some addition to my spiritual store, always a stimulus to think through a problem to the point of clarity, or at least greater clarity than I had attained before . . . Under her influence, my conscience was kept awake . . . In all the twenty years during which I have been deprived of close association with her, she has been at my side whenever a momentous decision was to be made. How [w]ould Alice approach this question?—I ask myself without cease. Even in our long separation she was monitor and guide to me.[46]

Just a year after Seligsberg's death, Jessie Sampter passed away. At Sampter's funeral, Szold's longtime Hadassah friends saw their iron-willed leader weep for the first time. "A part of myself which was of the best" had gone from her, she wrote to another friend, "one of my teachers had gone from me."[47] Though Szold had mentioned the younger woman, Sampter's lifelong "search for the truth" and her intellectual mastery of Zionism (reflected in Sampter's publications and her early School for Zionism, established at Szold's urging) made Sampter a treasured "teacher," as well as friend.[48]

The friendship between Szold, Sampter, and Seligsberg was unique even among an extended group of women Zionists because of its common intellectual vision. Each of these women recognized in the others a Zionist soul-mate with whom she shared religious and social ideals as well as a personal history of sacrifice. Even when they did not see eye-to-eye on specific matters, the fundamental principle was not in doubt: Zionism offered to Jews (both in Palestine and the Diaspora) the fulfillment of the prophetic ideals of Judaism, both spiritually and socially. It would enable Jews to embody their religion not only as a creed but as a total way of life. Undergirding this principle was the shared assumption that women's practical skills and devotion to service were essential if these ideals were to be realized and that, as a corollary, women needed to be full partners in the Zionist enterprise.

While devoted to their cause, Szold and her friends did not consider themselves zealots or missionaries; in an interview late in her life, Szold distanced herself from Lillian Wald, founder of the Henry Street Settlement and the Visiting Nurse movement in the United States. "I never had a missionary spirit," Szold insisted; "I always see the other person's point of view." She felt that the missionary, like Wald, who "grasped every opportunity offered her," did not.[49] Szold, Sampter, and Seligsberg shared not the certainty of mission but a common experimentation with modes of thought and action which would fit their emerging understandings. Their friendship allowed them to venture, to explore, and to probe.

In one respect, however, this circle of Zionist friends fits the American settlement model quite comfortably. The historian Kathryn Kish Sklar has described Hull House, for example, as a "community of women [which] provided its members with a lifelong substitute for family life." In that sense, "it resembled a religious order, supplying women with a radical degree of independence from the claims of family life and inviting them to commit their energies elsewhere."[50] As Alice Seligsberg remarked to Henrietta Szold, they could be annoyed at each other precisely because they were, indeed, "family."[51] Despite the fact that Szold and Sampter had sisters to whom they were emotionally close and with whom they corresponded regularly (Seligsberg had a cousin who held a similar place), they did not share a core belief with their blood relatives in a prophetic, feminist Zionism. Yet, Szold and Sampter were deeply attached to their sisters, despaired of their separations from them, and felt responsible for the grief they caused their sisters because of their distance from family concerns.[52]

In the face of these feelings regarding their own sisters, the intellectual companionship of a circle of Zionist women helped sustain Szold and her friends in their dedication to the Zionist dream. Friendship made it possible for them to free themselves from the "family claim," a claim which was as difficult for them to renounce as it had been for Hull House women a generation earlier. Friendship gave them independence, as well as a substitute "family," as it did for the Hull House women. Set free, however, these Zionist pioneers found themselves face to face with loneliness, political conflict, and social calamity, and often, as Szold put it in one letter to Jessie Sampter, stark "terror." Time and time again, they were forced to recognize, as Szold wrote in one letter to Sampter, that "our overnight transformation of Palestine into the utopia of the Zionist dreamer" was a "foolish expectation."[53] In these circumstances, what was needed most of all was what Szold called an "equal friend" who could offer not only intellectual and spiritual comfort but an alter ego, a mirror for the self. After one especially long letter which Szold wrote to Seligsberg discussing the pros and cons of accepting a lifetime annuity offered to her by a Zionist woman friend, an offer which she feared might compromise her independence, Szold told her friend, "You realize do you not? that I am thinking aloud with you. You need not reply to this letter . . . you have helped me greatly. . . . Do not reply to any of my torturing—and torturous? self-questionings."[54] To Sampter she had written, characteristically: "I write all this to you to unburden myself."[55]

Letters among Szold, Seligsberg, and Sampter were thus written not only to the addressee but sometimes also to the self. At the same time, they could be passed on to mutual friends, enlarging the circle of allies and partners and embedding the self even further in a responsive, interacting group—a group which served, in many respects, as a new family of spiritual and intellectual sisters. In this way the letters of women Zionists both strengthened the individual and created a community, bringing its members even closer to the "New Zion" that stirred their hopes and dreams. Providing outlets for emotional and spiritual growth, friendship also of-fered a release from despair in darker moments, an anchor to ground shaky struc-tures of self.

The darker moments appear regularly in Szold's correspondence with her friends. No sooner had she arrived in Palestine to head the AZMU, for example, than she found herself in the midst of incredible "ferment, disagreements, and misunder-standings," all the worse since everyone had awaited her arrival as a "prophet and a soothsayer."[56] Jessie Sampter, who had arrived the year before, saw Szold's hair grow white as she became "the butt for hundreds of complaints and reproaches." Nonetheless, it was not long before Szold's management and political skills soon won her, according to Sampter, what few in Palestine ever attained, "the undivided respect, admiration, and affection of a hypercritical community."[57] Her sixtieth birthday was celebrated with great fanfare by much of Jerusalem's Jewish commu-nity; Szold herself danced through the night. In the even more difficult years ahead, she would never lose the respect of that community.

While Szold continued to believe that women had special domestic interests and a common sensibility which united mothers of all races and religions, she had come to believe strongly in the necessity of guaranteeing them equal rights with men. In Palestine, she began working to increase women's social, health, and economic opportunities. On her very first trip to Palestine, she had commented in a travel diary that "the women are too patient; they sit and rock from early morning until late at night. If they had only risen up in arms and demanded better sanitation and better conditions. That is what should be aroused in them by the women from the West."[58] Concerned that Jewish women not lag behind Christian and even Moslem women in terms of legal rights, Szold helped organize a Society of Jewish Women [*Histadrut Nashim Ibriot*] to provide prenatal and educational services for women and to promote equal rights in politics and religion. Hadassah's championship of women's rights in Palestine attracted the support of leading American feminists.[59]

Szold returned to the United States in 1923, accepting another term as president of Hadassah in order to help heal a rift in the organization that had developed during her absence. But she found that working for the organization in the United States lacked the excitement of living in Zion; it was "drudgery without a redeeming feature."[60] To Sampter, who had already returned to Palestine, she voiced another, rather typical, complaint, about the burden of Zionist administrative duties:

> My life is made up of so many, many routine, confused details that there is no pattern to it. Occasionally there arises from the swirling mass of "categorical imperatives" that keep me submerged spiritually, a momentary, blue electric shaft, in the light of which I see my plans for myself made oh! so many years ago. The plans were for something so different from that which has come about, and they were so much finer than this incessant wrestling with projects, organizational details, and defensive tactics.[61]

In 1927, Szold returned to Palestine when the World Zionist Organization elected her to its three-member Palestine Executive Committee with the porfolio of Health and Education, a position she held until 1930. The only candidate on whom all factions could agree, Szold accepted the post with great reluctance. A letter to Sampter, one of many, reveals a mood of deep anxiety, disappointment, and self-pity.

> I was screamed at that my Zionist duty lay this way or that. . . . I planned for a return to domestic life. I longed to release my library from the bondage of seven years in a storage house; I dreamed of living in a flat, not a large one, but at least larger than the three trunks I have been living in for seven years, larger than the steamer cabins that have been my chief habitation for four years. And see what happened at Basle! [the Zionist Congress which she was "forced" into attending] The most disconcerting feature is that, at this critical juncture, the great Zionist movement had none other to turn to but a worn out, tired old woman of 67.

Not only was she sure that Zionism had robbed her of her "last chance to live," but she also feared that the sacrifice would be unavailing.[62] She was full of "terror" for what lay ahead.[63] "More than ever my life is devoid of spiritual content and cultivation," she wrote to Sampter. "It is made up of details without end, many depressing details, of much despair and not a little personal heartache. I don't see how I can survive two such years."[64]

Yet survive Szold did. For three years she did yeoman's service, then finally yielded to her yearning to go "home" to her sisters. She had begun to make a new life in the United States when the *Vaad Leumi* elected her to its executive board, asking her organize a transfer of health and education services from the Zionist organization to the people of Palestine, a goal she had long championed. In the face of considerable opposition and without adequate resources, Szold succeeded in establishing the Central Social Services Bureau, a modern and remarkably progressive system of services, including family welfare, immigrant aid, vocational schooling, child care services, and the rehabilitation of juvenile delinquents.[65] When she assumed office in 1932, there was no established system of relief in Palestine and no organized social services for destitute families, new immigrants, or children with special needs. Over the years she headed the department, model services in family welfare, immigrant aid, and child care sprang into existence.

Szold credited women's practical bent for implementing these programs. Yet, because "social service is the concern of men as well as of women," she urged women to win support for the social legislation needed to sustain their efforts.[66] Szold knew then what contemporary feminists have recognized only belatedly: programs to support women, children, and families would not succeed unless embraced by all people.

Szold as Leader and Legend

While Szold had left the practical administration of Hadassah to take responsibility for one branch of Zionist work after another, she continued to exert moral and intellectual leadership of the American Zionist women's movement. The unromantic attention to detail and duty for which she castigated herself so severely, as her letters to her women friends reveal, seemed to others a model of cooperative service.

At times, Szold herself acknowledged that her own acceptance of duty, however onerous, reflected the fundamental necessity of feminine idealism. In greeting the Women's International Zionist Organization in Palestine in 1935, she acknowledged the "greatest of all lessons" which she, as a Jewish woman, wanted to pass on to other Jewish women: "the subordination of the individual will and desire to the common need."[67] Zionist women, like Zionist men, were never able to achieve the level of selflessness that Szold personified in her own career, but many came to Palestine, following Szold's lead to work on projects she had initiated.

The thousands of Hadassah women who never journeyed to Palestine found meaning in raising funds for its many projects and in supporting the cultural programs that Szold had from the first insisted become a component of the organization. "We formed our study circles not for the sake of studying Jewish history and literature . . . but in order to plunge ourselves into the Jewish past and rediscover our own self," reported one Hadassah leader. In no time at all, it was this educational work that had become the organization's "élan vital . . . its living impetus," making Hadassah the true "symbol of Jewish spiritual life."[68]

Through her practical philanthropy, her mother's idea, Szold in fact had fulfilled the vision she had with her father at the Prague shul of leading Jewish women to a deeper spirituality. According to its leaders, the Hadassah woman was one "who lives the Jewish life in its entirety. . . . Together with creating a land, she recreates herself. She is the *Chalutza* of her own soul." Whether or not Hadassah members visited Palestine was immaterial, since the group's vital spirit would be infused into the country through Henrietta Szold; "through her presence in Palestine [she] will carry its life to us and ours to it."[69] As leader, symbol, and model, Szold became the medium through which American Jewish women expressed the "Zion in [their] own hearts."

Szold's contribution to Hadassah members was as utilitarian as it was spiritual. Her belief that all women could contribute something of value, whether they were volunteers or professionals, housewives or public servants, fostered a spirit of creativity, self-development, and teamwork. Under her guidance, Zionist women became public speakers, fiscal experts, administrators, technicians, and officials.[70]

Thus, while Szold's sense of duty, fairness, and justice had served Palestine well, in America, too, Hadassah benefited enormously. Under Szold's direction, though she was reluctant to accept her singular role, Hadassah's initial aim—"the healing of the daughter of my people"—had been successfully carried out and, in 1935, with the inauguration of Youth Aliyah, extended to the rescue of children. Szold herself was the living embodiment of the link between Palestine and the United States, between women's spiritual healing and their practical accomplishments. No other Jewish women's group was so completely identified with its founder, as Hadassah was (and remains today) identified with Henrietta Szold.

Yet Szold accepted her role as Hadassah icon with great reluctance. So modest that as a child she had refused to stand in the center of a family photograph, she hated Hadassah's "mawkish" publicity and the elaborate birthday celebrations it staged for its own "propaganda purposes." The result was that she then had to answer "an avalanche of letters" and put up with all kinds of "sentimental lubrication" poured on her by American tourists.[71]

It was not only her own sanity that was at stake. Because the myth of Henrietta Szold had come to stand in the stead of true Zionist purpose, the "moral and spiritual integrity of the Hadassah movement" was imperiled. Szold felt that her existence had become a "disservice" to the cause. The "plague" of publicity obstructed the performance of legitimate Zionist work, to be sure. It offended her modesty as well, but, more important, it came perilously close to challenging Judaism's fundamental opposition to idolatry.[72]

Szold's own religiosity never faltered. One of her sisters wrote that, more than any of Szold's other virtues, it was Szold's spirituality—the "steady blue flame, the holy eternal light" within her—that cast a spell on all who came into contact with her.[73] Szold's long-time secretary, Emma Ehrlich, believed that, on entering Szold's room, many had the sensation of "entering a cathedral," a "holy place." They sensed that the frail, delicate woman possessed within her the "strength of armies"; many experienced moments of "revelation" in her presence.[74]

Despite her image as a dogged, meticulous worker, a bureaucrat's bureaucrat, Szold was a "superbly aesthetic" creature, Ehrlich pointed out, with a lifelong love of art, dance, and music, as well as nature. She prided herself on her strength and personal fitness, spending the early hours of every morning in gymnastics and grooming her long, silken hair. For Ehrlich, Szold's concern with her appearance was without vanity, a simple reflection of the fact that a public woman had to guard her appearance and that, for Szold, beauty of self and surroundings were synonymous. "For her, beauty begins with order," Ehrlich comments, "and it is her aesthetic sense, perhaps, which makes her so systematic. Everything around her is perfectly arranged; she can put her hand on any of her belongings in the dark. The same system and order which are an integral part of her public work are also part of her personal program, each item having its assigned time and place. The careful ordering of her life in mechanical things, she thinks, saves her time, keeps her in good condition, and leaves her mind free for the important problems of the day."[75]

Yet Szold's spiritual and aesthetic satisfactions, even the tremendous gratification she received from Youth Aliyah, the most rewarding of all her Zionist services, did not substitute for the lack of personal fulfillment. According to Ehrlich, the person closest to her on a daily basis for the last quarter of her life, Szold paid a high price for her years of grinding, ceaseless work. Outside of the small pleasures of her daily routine, "she had no home, no family, no personal life."[76] Her weekly letters to her sister connected her to her family, but she despaired constantly of her separation from them, longing to make a home near them. Her loneliness grew more poignant after the deaths of Sampter and Seligsberg and two of her beloved sisters. While the devoted Emma Ehrlich, much her junior, provided comfort, Ehrlich's relationship to Szold was as adoring disciple rather than as frank comrade, as her older friends had been. After her sister Adele's death especially, she felt that no one knew her; she was all alone.

In her sisters' view, Szold always suffered "from a sense of being orphaned, of moving among aliens," never able to recreate the warmth and security of her childhood home.[77] But, after all, Szold chose to remain in Palestine and to serve Zionism and Hadassah at every point when a choice was possible. Serving the public interest, denying her private self, became the motif of her life; she could not escape the call of service. Once, early in her stay, she wrote to Adele that "Palestine to me connotes wretchedness of spirit and the deepest despair I have ever known; and you know, I went deep enough down the two years before I left America. . . . But sadness or joy I know [Palestine] means duty."[78] For Szold, the call of service to the Jewish people—not on a local or a national basis but the Jewish people as a unit, the people of the past and future as well as of the present—spoke loudest. To such a call the response was clear, even if meant stilling her own womanly voice.

On Szold's desk in Jerusalem at the time of her death lay two yellowed clippings which indicate the continuing power of that call and the sacrifice she made in answering it. One was a copy of Emma Lazarus's "The New Colossus," the welcoming poem now engraved on the Statue of Liberty. Perhaps this verse, so well known today, was the centerpiece of the first public speech that Szold gave, very reluctantly, in an early address to the Hebrew Literary Society of Baltimore. The second was a cartoon from the Baltimore *Evening Sun* of March 30, 1936, showing a woman struggling with mountains of letters. The attached clipping tells the story: it is about Selma Lagerlöf, who won the Nobel Prize for Literature in 1909 and was five years later elected to the Swedish Academy. This notable woman was sent such a *deluge of birthday mail* [italics Szold's] that a *special railway car* was needed to deliver it, and her secretaries were *busy* for many months answering the congratulatory messages.[79]

So Szold's Zionist work and the celebrity it brought her had deluged her life. Yet her model of public service, chiseled out at so high a personal cost, inspired other American Jewish women to contribute to Jewish continuity. Even if she did not acknowledge her contribution, Szold had created a powerful vision of Jewish womanhood that would outlast her most concrete administrative accomplishments. Although Szold always denied that she possessed originality, in many ways this vision was her most "creative" as well as her most practical achievement.

NOTES

I would like to thank Ira Daly of the Hadassah Archives in New York and the staffs of the Schlesinger Library at Radcliffe College, Cambridge, and the Central Zionist Archives in Jerusalem for their assistance.

1. Henrietta Szold to Alice Seligsberg, January 7, 1938, Central Zionist Archives, Jerusalem (hereafter CZA).

2. Alexandra Lee Levin, *The Szolds of Lombard Street: A Baltimore Family, 1859–1909* (Philadelphia: Jewish Publication Society of America, 1960), 153–55.

3. Joan Dash, *Summoned to Jerusalem: The Life of Henrietta Szold* (New York: Harper and Row, 1979), 14.

4. Irving Fineman, *Woman of Valor: The Life of Henrietta Szold, 1860–1945* (New York: Simon and Schuster, 1961), 47.

5. Fineman, *Woman of Valor*, 57–58.

6. Marvin Lowenthal, Interview with Henrietta Szold, December 29, 1935, 42–43, Hadassah Archives, New York (hereafter HA).

7. Cited in Fineman, *Woman of Valor*, 95.

8. Fineman, *Woman of Valor*, 124–26; Dash, *Summoned to Jerusalem*, 54.

9. Marvin Lowenthal, *Henrietta Szold: Life and Letters* (New York: Viking Press, 1942), 54.

10. Fineman, *Woman of Valor*, 128.

11. Henrietta Szold to Alice Seligsberg, January 1, 1909, CZA.

12. Henrietta Szold to Alice Seligsberg, July 23, 1909, CZA.

13. Lotta Levensohn, "Recollections Concerning the Origin and Activities of the Hadassah Women's Study Group of New York," HA.

14. Lowenthal, Interview with Szold, 8.

15. Henrietta Szold to Alice Seligsberg, December 12, 1909, CZA.

16. Lowenthal, Interview with Szold, 9.

17. Lowenthal, Interview with Szold, 19. Also see Bertha Levin, "Rooms in Our House," *Hadassah News Letter*, December 1935, 16.

18. Invitation Sent for the Formation of Hadassah, February 14, 1924, HA; Lowenthal, Interview with Szold, 9.

19. Lowenthal, Interview with Szold, 11.

20. Sarah Kussy, "Hadassah—How It Came Into Being," 2–3, HA.

21. Ibid., 3. After a visit by Szold in 1914, Rebecca Schatz of the Henry Street settlement noted that many of the principles which Hadassah used in Palestine were those that had "secured success" at Henry Street. See Alice Seligsberg, "Chronicle of Hadassah: 1912–1914, Part I," HA; printed in *Hadassah News Letter*, May 1927, 9.

22. Henrietta Szold, Address at Hotel Astor, New York, November 26, 1923, HA.

23. Seligsberg, "Chronicle of Hadassah," 6, 39, 125.

24. Kussy, "Hadassah—How It Came Into Being."

25. Report of the Proceedings of the First Annual Convention of the Daughters of Zion of America, June 29–30, 1914, New York, HA; Seligsberg, "Chronicles of Hadassah," 9.

26. Ibid. On the founding of Hadassah, see Carol Bosworth Kutscher, "The Early Years of Hadassah, 1912–1921," Ph.D. diss., Brandeis University, 1976.

27. "Our Reason for Being" and "The Group and the Individual," *Maccabaean* 30 February 1917): 146.

28. Henrietta Szold at the Laying of the Cornerstone of Hadassah University Hospital on Mount Scopus, October 16, 1934, CZA; Szold to Junior Hadassah, September 20, 1932, HA; Szold, "Zionism: A Progressive and Democratic Movement," Speech at People's Institute, Cooper's Union, New York, February 13, 1916, Szold Papers, Schlesinger Library, Radcliffe College; Szold to Alice Seligsberg, October 10, 1913, in Lowenthal, *Henrietta Szold: Life and Letters*, 82; Szold to Elvira Solis, January 18, 1918, Schlesinger Library. Also see Szold's letter to the editor, "The Promised Land," *The Nation*, August 13, 1914.

29. Henrietta Szold, Notes on Talk at Wilkes-Barre, December 11, 1917, Schlesinger Library. Also see Henrietta Szold, Letter to Hadassah, June 27, 1928, HA.

30. Jessie Sampter, *The Speaking Heart*, MS, CZA.

31. Henrietta Szold to Hadassah, June 6, 1928, HA.

32. Henrietta Szold to Sadie American, March 27, 1900, Schlesinger Library.

33. Henrietta Szold, Address at Hotel Astor, New York, November 26, 1923 HA. On women's psychology and idealism called practical, see Henrietta Szold, "The Future of Women's Work for Palestine," Jerusalem, May 1930, CZA.

34. "The Woman in Zionism," *Maccabaean* 30 (February 1917): 148.

35. See Henrietta Szold, "The Future of Women's Work for Palestine," Jerusalem, May 1930, CZA.

36. Henrietta Szold to Alice Seligsberg, January 7, 1920, CZA.

37. Alice Seligsberg, "Follow On," *Hadassah News Letter,* December 1935, 12.

38. Ibid.

39. Jessie Sampter, *The Speaking Heart.*

40. Lowenthal, Interview with Szold, 12.

41. Henrietta Szold to Hadassah, June 27, 1928, HA. Szold's sister, Adele Seltzer, wrote of "the hatred of the men for Hadassah"; see her January 25, 1928, letter to Szold, CZA. Alexander Dushkin cited in Dash, *Summoned to Jerusalem,* 129.

42. Judah L. Magnes, "The Symbol of Hope," *Hadassah News Letter*, February 1936, 2.

43. Henrietta Szold to Hadassah, June 27, 1928, HA.

44. Fineman, *Woman of Valor,* 260.

45. Dash, *Summoned to Jerusalem,* 109, 127.

46. Henrietta Szold to Elsa, October 29, 1940, CZA.

47. Julia A. Dushkin, "Farewell to Jessie Sampter," *Hadassah Newsletter,* January 1939, Henrietta Szold to Mrs. Wackenheim, December 10, 1938, CZA.

48. See, for example, Jessie Sampter, *Guide to Zionism* (New York: Zionist Organization of America, 1920).

49. Lowenthal, Interview with Szold, 5.

50. Kathryn Kish Sklar, "Hull House in the 1890s: A Community of Women Reformers," *Signs* 10 (summer 1985): 660.

51. Alice Seligsberg to Henrietta Szold, April 5, 1921, CZA.

52. Bertha Szold Levin, Adele Szold Seltzer, and Benjamin Hartogensis, "MS Notes on the Early Life of Henrietta Szold," n.d., HA.

53. Henrietta Szold to Jessie Sampter, July 29, 1922, CZA.

54. Henrietta Szold to Alice Seligsberg, August 30, 1915, CZA.

55. Henrietta Szold to Jessie Sampter, March 3, 1916, CZA.

56. Sampter, *The Speaking Heart,* 341–42.

57. Jessie Sampter, typescript, December 1920, CZA.

58. Levin et al., "MS Notes on HS."

59. See, for example, Alice Stone Blackwell to editor of *Maccabaean,* 31 (February 1918): 44.

60. Henrietta Szold to Jessie Sampter, June 13, 1924, CZA.

61. Henrietta Szold to Jessie Sampter, August 24, 1924, CZA.

62. Henrietta Szold to Jessie Sampter, October 3, 1927, CZA.

63. Henrietta Szold to Jessie Sampter, November 1, 1927, CZA.

64. Henrietta Szold to Jessie Sampter, February 20, 1928, CZA.

65. Szold, Women's Day Address, May 31, 1934, CZA; also see Dash, *Summoned to Jerusalem,* 225.

66. Szold, Woman's Day Address, May 31, 1934, CZA.

67. Henrietta Szold, Speech to WIZO, 1935, CZA.

68. Report of Cultural Committee to Mid-Winter Conference of Hadassah, December 28, 1927, CZA.

69. Ibid.

70. Lotta Levensohn, typescript, "Miss Szold as a Leader of Women," 1930, HA.

71. Levin et al., "MS Notes on HS"; Henrietta Szold to Rose Jacobs, July 28, 1937, CZA.

72. Henrietta Szold to Rose Jacobs, July 28, 1937; Szold to Mrs. Joshua Kohn, January 30, 1939, CZA.

73. Levin et al., "MS Notes on HS."

74. Emma Ehrlich, typescript, "Notes and Impressions," March 1941, CZA.

75. Ibid.

76. Ibid.

77. Levin et al., "MS Notes on HS."

78. Henrietta Szold to Adele S. Seltzer, April 14, 1919, CZA.

79. Emma Ehrlich collection, Szold Papers, CZA.

Part III

A Wider World

In the years between World War I and World War II, Jews found themselves increasingly at home in "a wider world."[1] For nearly a third of American Jewish women, that world was New York City.[2]

"Out of the second generation's encounter with the city," the historian Deborah Dash Moore writes, "emerged a new American Jew, one whose Jewishness was shaped by the city's peculiar dynamic." The travel writer Kate Simon explained: "We were also tearing away from the restraints of who we thought we were to the freedoms of who we thought we wanted to be."[3] As they did, American Jewish women and men, Moore concludes, "recast available institutions into instruments of self-perpetuation,"[4] forging a new synthesis of American and Jewish identities. Yet, these remained decidedly gendered.

Framing American Jewish identity as religion, as so many did, Jewish women revisioned the synagogue. As Jenna Weissman Joselit shows in "The Jewish Priestess and Ritual," a new generation of American-born Jewish women compelled the Orthodox community to make "Orthodox life more appealing to the modern woman." Seeking to sustain "a highly motivated observant American Jewish woman, a 'faithful Jewess,' " Orthodox women embraced the synagogue sisterhood (originally invented by Reform Jewish women),[5] public worship (which was not customary for traditional Jewish women), and new avenues of education where they learned that an Orthodox lifestyle was utterly "consonant with middle-class life."

But diversity had long characterized American Judaism. Already, in these years, some Reform Jews presumed that America would allow for the emergence of a very different intersection of gender and religion, the ordination of women as rabbis. "The Women Who Would be Rabbis" demonstrates that the American woman's movement compelled Jews to consider whether its demand for equal access to the professions applied to Judaism. Even as the movement for women's ordination belongs to the histories of women's "entry into the male-dominated professions," it reveals the limits of American Jewry's revisioning of gender in the interwar years, when "Jewish women, gifted with knowledge and education and skilled in leadership, were to serve American Jewry . . . as 'professional' volunteers." Half a century would pass before an American woman could call herself rabbi.[6]

In the 1930s, "Depression was the country we lived in," Kate Simon recalled.[7] Beth S. Wenger defines this as "a transitional moment for American Jews."[8] Her analysis of Jewish wives and mothers echoes the immigrant women's survival strategies already iterated. With their husbands out of work, Jewish wives returned to the wage-labor force, shopped for bargains to stretch their budgets, and, remembering their mothers' neighborhood politics, staged rent strikes. For their American-born daughters, family income and birth order, as well as gender expectations, determined who went out to work, who stayed in school, and when these women would marry. And, when they did marry, they postponed childbearing and ultimately had fewer children, thus setting "patterns that continue to define American Jewish families to the present day."[9]

The wider world of New York, the cultural capital of America, beckoned American Jews in these years, as Julia L. Foulkes shows in "Angels 'Rewolt!'." New York Jewish women in the 1930s "shaped the foundations of modern dance." As students, teachers, performers, choreographers, critics, and the audience, Jewish women, engaging in the radical politics of the interwar years, "promoted modern dance as a political art form open to the masses." As they "battled anti-Semitism and politicized dance," these women created another place for themselves in the wider world of American culture.[10]

NOTES

1. Kate Simon, *A Wider World: Portraits in an Adolescence* (New York: Harper and Row, 1986).

2. Of the 4.8 million Jews in the United States in 1940, 1.95 million lived in New York City. Sources: Jonathan D. Sarna, ed., *The American Jewish Experience* (1986; 2d ed., New York: Holmes and Meier, 1997), 359; Deborah Dash Moore, *At Home in America: Second Generation New York Jews* (New York: Columbia University Press, 1981), 21. That all the chapters in this section are set in New York City reflects the weight of the scholarship in this field, a result, in part, of this demographic pattern.

3. Simon, *A Wider World*, 19–20.

4. Moore, *At Home in America*, quotations 4, 9.

5. On Reform synagogue sisterhoods, see Pamela S. Nadell and Rita J. Simon, "Ladies of the Sisterhood: Women in the American Reform Synagogue, 1900–1930," in *Active Voices: Women in Jewish Culture*, ed. Maurie Sacks (Urbana: University of Illinois Press, 1995), 63–75; Karla Goldman, "The Public Religious Lives of Cincinnati's Jewish Women," in *Women and American Judaism: Historical Perspectives*, ed. Pamela S. Nadell and Jonathan D. Sarna (Hanover, NH: Brandeis University Press/University Press of New England, 2001), 107–27, especially 118–24.

6. For a full discussion of this, see Pamela S. Nadell, *Women Who Would Be Rabbis: A History of Women's Ordination, 1889–1985* (Boston: Beacon Press, 1998).

7. Simon, *A Wider World*, 109–10.

8. Note that in these years the majority of American Jews became native born; Lloyd P. Gartner, "The Midpassage of American Jewry," in *The American Jewish Experience*, ed. Jonathan D. Sarna (1986; 2d ed., New York: Holmes and Meier, 1997), 258–67, 264.

9. This new article is based on Beth S. Wenger, *New York Jews and the Great Depression: Uncertain Promise* (New Haven: Yale University Press, 1996).

10. On images of Jewish women in popular culture, see Joyce Antler, ed., *Talking Back; Images of Jewish Women in American Popular Culture* (Hanover, NH: Brandeis University Press/University Press of New England 1998).

Chapter Ten

The Jewish Priestess and Ritual
The Sacred Life of American Orthodox Women

Jenna Weissman Joselit

"Priestess of the Jewish ideal, Prophetess of Purity and Refinement," the American Jewish woman of the interwar years, it was widely believed, was a quintessential religious being.[1] Seen by the vast majority of American Jews of all denominations as the guardian of Jewish life, the safeguard of its future, it was she who upheld its standards and promoted Jewish ritual while seeing to the religious education of the children. And yet, it was not as a rarefied priestess or prophetess that the Jewish woman was most commonly esteemed and idealized; rather, it was in her capacity as mother and homemaker, as "queen of the home."[2] "The Jewish ideal of womanhood," one of its admiring students wrote, "is not the entrancing beauty of the queen of a knightly tournament nor the ascetic life of a virgin saint but wifehood and motherhood."[3] It followed, then, that the American Jewish woman most fully realized herself within her home, the staging ground for her "essential work."[4] Using language derived from the sanctuary, both male and female observers compared the housework of Jewish women to "service at the altar" and enjoined the American Jewish woman to "make of her home a miniature Temple" by consecrating it to religion.[5] The home, explained one popular Jewish text, "is the grandest of all institutions . . . and woman its presiding genius."[6]

Despite this widely shared belief in the religious distinctiveness of the Jewish woman and in the centrality of the Jewish home, notions that would remain intact well into the 1960s, challenges to its hegemony began to appear during the interwar years, first among Reform and Conservative women and then, belatedly, among Orthodox women, as well. With their newly acquired middle-class incomes and heightened secular awareness, affluent Jewish women of the interwar years began increasingly and more vociferously to articulate a need for broader "separate spheres" of communal involvement. "Conditions among Jewish women of culture have grown to be alarming," observed Mathilde Schechter, the founder of the Women's League and wife of the Jewish Theological Seminary's chancellor. She found her counterparts in 1918 turning aside from Jewish tradition to "the opera, movies, the theater, and society" for cultural fulfillment.[7] "The former queen of the home," complained an Orthodox observer, "has voluntarily reduced her rank and the Jewish home, the erstwhile temple in miniature is breaking down."[8] The etiology of this disaffection, or what several commentators labeled the "current spiritual unrest," was clear: it was not that modern Jewish women rejected the community's characterization of themselves as keenly spiritual personalities, for they did not; nor did they reject the community's characterization of the home as their primary "religious domain." Rather, they sought, in their designated capacity as spiritual and religious entities, to exercise their talents and capabilities in new and expanded directions: to involve themselves with a wider number of institutions and causes and to extend their influence beyond the home into the community at large. "The solution for much of the present domestic unrest," counseled Irene Wolff, an Orthodox Jewish writer, "is not to take women out of the home but to enlarge the concept of the home so as to bring into the home a widened interest."[9] Or, as one Reform advocate put it, the way to retain the interest and commitment of Jewish women was to put "Jewish womanhood on the road of highest usefulness to the cause of American Israel."[10]

Making use of the talents of modern Jewish womanhood by "enlarging the concept of the home" was yet another way of talking about the integration of the American Jewish woman into the larger Jewish community. A complicated process and one bound up with the modernization of the American synagogue, it entailed a gradual tempering and rethinking of the community's attitude toward women. "While the Jewish woman was honored as the priestess of the family hearth and the mistress of her home, her range of initiative ended there," remarked one observer.[11] But the modern American Jewish woman, the "new type of American Jewess," required a broader venue for her talents and one that was "beyond the shadow of her hearth."[12] Where some spoke of integration and others of the emergence of a new American Jewish woman, still others likened the would-be expanded communal involvement of the Jewish woman to a kind of coming of age of American Jewry and dubbed the process, somewhat fancifully perhaps, "deorientalization." The emancipation of the traditional Jewish woman from some of Judaism's allegedly "oriental inhibitions and constraints," deorientalization assumed a number of concrete manifestations: the abolition of the separate women's gallery and its replacement with mixed pews or family seating was one example, while the granting to women of full rights of congregational membership, and sometimes even inclusion within the synagogue's board, was another.[13] "Woman has at last found her niche in religious life well as in civic and political work," observed one "new type of American Jewess" in 1924. "We do not find her today relegated to the gallery of the synagogue docilely watching the men of the congregation. Her voice is heard on the Temple Board, her advice is asked in the direction of affairs of the Sabbath School, she is in fact a force in the religious community."[14]

By far the most common example of "deorientalization" was the establishment of a synagogue sisterhood. Greatly expanding the "range of initiatives" available to the interested Jewish woman, the women's auxiliary harnessed her religious inclinations and organizational talents to the synagogue, providing a permanent and enduring outlet for communal affairs. Essentially a religious organization, the sisterhood of the interwar years pressed for greater ritual observance among its members even as it helped to render the American synagogue a warm, friendly, and accessible institution. Holding luncheons, equipping the synagogue kitchen, conducting Bible classes, decorating the sanctuary and the *succah,* raising funds, and publishing manuals on how best to administer a sisterhood and to have a "Jewish Home Beautiful," the American synagogue sisterhood sought to promote Jewish ritual observance both within and without the home.[15] An ally of the rabbi, perhaps even his "best friend," the synagogue sisterhood became an integral aspect of American synagogue life and, as such, marked "the ascendancy of women in the synagogue."[16] By World War II, hundreds of American synagogues of all persuasions maintained women's auxiliaries; in fact, no self-consciously modern and proudly American congregation was without one. Referring to the synagogue sisterhood, one writer on contemporary American Jewish affairs remarked as early as 1925 that as an institution the sisterhood "was not singular nor unique. It is a transcript of the zeitgeist."[17] Putting it somewhat differently and less poetically, the Orthodox rabbi Joseph Lookstein observed a decade later that "we cannot but be impressed by the invasion of all institutions and movements in Jewish life by the ever increasing numbers of women."[18]

Admittedly, this "invasion" was far more pronounced and widespread in Reform and even Conservative circles than it was in Orthodox ones. And yet, all throughout the 1920s and 1930s, the Orthodox community, abetted by several Orthodox clergymen and sustained by the grass-roots encouragement of well-educated and cultured Orthodox Jewish women, also began to take more and more notice of its women and their spiritual needs. In editorials with titles like "A New Deal for the Forgotten Jewish Woman," Jewish women were encouraged to attend synagogue, to establish sisterhoods, to acquire a firm Jewish education, and to practice Jewish rituals like *kashrut* and family-purity laws with interest and commitment.[19] Sensing growing disaffection among Orthodox Jewish women and determined to arrest it, the Orthodox community sought to integrate its women more fully within its boundaries. While the home remained the unquestioned lodestar of the Orthodox Jewish woman's spiritual and existential condition, Orthodox Jews become increasingly aware of the need to supplement the home with complementary alternatives and thus, in their own way, to "deorientalize" the Orthodox Jewish woman.

No doubt influenced, in part, by developments within the larger Jewish community and determined, as always, to keep abreast of them, Orthodox Jewry was beginning to realize that the traditional Jewish home was no longer immune to the blandishments of secular society. Insisting, as they had for centuries, on the primacy of the home, Orthodox Jews had not only failed to provide the observant Jewish woman with other communal and educational opportunities—preferring instead, as one rabbi put it, "to invest in manhood"—but they had also overestimated the home's durability.[20] "Formerly, the Jewish woman received her spiritual inspiration from the piety and religious fervor of her home. But in this age of scientific inquiry, children will not follow blindly in the footsteps and practices of their parents. Frequently do they question and even challenge the necessity for observing certain ceremonies."[21] Though such laments are a constant refrain in the Jewish historical experience, as each generation bemoans anew the failings of its successor, the frequency, passion, and gender specificity of these interwar complaints appears to reflect an altered set of circumstances: the emergence of a new generation of American-born women from observant families who were not only basically unlettered but also without the kind of nostalgic and atavistic attachment to ritual that had characterized their mothers. In the eyes of many communal leaders, the much-vaunted ideal of the ritually scrupulous and knowledgeable Jewish housewife and mother was fast becoming more of an ideal than a reality, a prescription of Orthodox behavior rather than a widespread social norm. "Do we wonder, then," asked Mrs. Rebecca Goldstein, the wife of one of Orthodoxy's leading young rabbis and herself a Barnard graduate, "that so many homes of today are un-Jewish? Why should a Jewish girl maintain a kosher home after she marries when she has never been taught the meaning of the dietary laws? Why kindle the Sabbath lights . . . ? Why observe the issue of Family Purity?"[22]

As the limits of the home became increasingly apparent, Orthodox leaders began to reevaluate that institution and, like Jewish leaders elsewhere, to redress its imbalances by providing suitable alternatives. Seeking to make more room within Orthodoxy for its women and, in effect, to develop (and ensure) a constituency of observant women, the community launched what in retrospect appears to have been a concerted effort to win their institutional loyalty. Its leaders addressed themselves to both the public and private spheres of the American Jewish woman's sacred or ritual life and in the areas of synagogue participation and ritual performance made determined overtures to her.

"Cultivating the synagogue attendance habit," as one Orthodox rabbi put it, was the most frequent, and easily attended to, feature of the community's efforts to render Orthodox life more appealing to the modern woman.[23] From the pulpit and the printed page, women were urged to make attendance at Sabbath services a regular and accustomed part of their religious ritual. Such encouragement was sorely needed, for the notion of an Orthodox female worshiper was somewhat of a novelty. Widespread in American Christian communities, female attendance at services was generally rare in traditional Jewish circles. For centuries, the American churchgoing public was largely female; as such, the church became the "property of the ladies" and church membership a "woman's activity."[24] But, among America's Jews, especially those Orthodox in denomination, the attendance of women was occasional, limited to the High Holidays and those ritual moments on which *Yizkor,* the memorial prayer, was said. Despite the widely received notion that Jewish women were inherently spiritual, women simply did not attend services.

The absence of Jewish women from the traditional synagogue service was itself a kind of tradition. In the Old World, as in the New, women simply did not make synagogue attendance a part of their sacred lives. This is not to suggest that Jewish women did not pray—only that the context for their devotions was more private than public. The existence of *thines* (supplications), a rich Yiddish penitential literature designed almost exclusively for a female audience, suggests the multiplicity of occasions for female prayer. Women would routinely offer up a *thine,* often phrasing it in the first-person singular and inserting the personal names of loved ones, when they lit the Sabbath candles, buried the dead, gave birth, immersed in a *mikvah* (ritual bath), prepared holiday foods, and even when they cleaned house! In fact, the recitation of a *thine* tended to transform a routine and mundane event into more of a sacred moment. Suggestively enough, few *thines* were designed for recitation in the synagogue; most were recited in the intimate setting of the home.[25]

A striking departure, then, from established social convention, the presence of women in the Orthodox sanctuary had become, by the war years, a familiar and perhaps even normative practice, so much so that Orthodox girls who had come of age during the fifties could scarcely remember a time when they and their mothers were absent from the Sabbath service.[26] "The synagogue finds in woman not only a most generous supporter," commented Rabbi Lookstein, "but also a far more frequent worshiper than it finds in man."[27] At the urging and encouragement of their husbands, clergy, and peers, women went to synagogue more and more frequently, and, for many observant women of the interwar years, attending services became an indispensable part of their ritual life, one they cultivated meticulously. "Going to services," recalled an Orthodox woman who grew up during the interwar years, "was a big deal."[28] Some, undoubtedly, simply "went along," attending services out of deference to their husbands' wishes.[29] Others, however, found synagogue attendance to their liking, not simply a marital obligation. Like their middle-class non-Jewish counterparts, for whom churchgoing was an approved and highly valued social convention, middle-class observant Jewish women construed synagogue attendance as a reflection and affirmation of their middle-class status, as well as the "thing to do."[30]

Arriving between 10:30 and 11:00, toward the latter part of the service, women worshipers sat among friends or family members, exchanged news of the week, chatted about who was in attendance and who was not, and eyed one another's clothing. Dressing up, "getting *faputzt*," was an essential aspect of the ritual and one that attested concretely to the social significance of shul-going.[31] Almost as important a ritual as worship itself, dressing up afforded women the opportunity to display their finery and with it their financial status within a sacred context; it thus legitimated dress in a way that more secular venues like the theater or the opera could not. On an "ordinary Sabbath," women would don suits, gloves, hats, and "important jewelry," or, as one frequent Sabbath service attendee put it, look *"balebatish"*; young girls, generally those over the age of three, would be clad in hat, gloves, and a "good dress." Not surprisingly, synagogue attire developed into a complex ritual of its own with different requirements for different occasions: a regular Sabbath mandated one kind of uniform, while a *yontef* (holiday) called for slightly more fancy attire. The coup de grace, sartorially speaking, was Erev Yom Kippur, when women donned their very best. Fancy evening wear was customary: "cocktail dress was de rigueur," reported one contemporary, as was lavish jewelry and, if the weather permitted, even furs.[32] Reflecting the importance attached to dressing for these public ritual occasions, the purchase of new clothes often coincided with the Jewish calendar: it was customary to buy one's "fall" wardrobe in time for the Jewish New Year and one's "spring" wardrobe in time for Passover.

The sanctuary was not merely the setting for displaying one's finery; it was, after all, a venue for prayer. Despite the hum of gossip and the distraction of the beautifully clad, women worshipers did attend to their prayers. The architectural ambience of the modernized Orthodox synagogue sanctuary helped to focus their attention on the service. Historically, Orthodox synagogues (both in the Old World and in the New) were not known to give much thought, let alone much space, to their admittedly small female audience. Almost an afterthought, the women's section of the traditional New York synagogue was a "little shut-in stuffy gallery," barely more than an alcove.[33] Poorly ventilated, the "woman's precinct" was designed for a handful of visitors but expanded to "forty when necessary."[34] By the World War I years, however, the American Orthodox synagogue, now a dignified and often monumental structure, had begun to provide ample and capacious seating for its women. "Women have much to be thankful for in this new type of synagogue," one female eyewitness related. "To be sure, they still are not counted toward a quorum but they are not hidden behind a curtain. They have plenty of elbow-room."[35] The characteristically modernized Orthodox sanctuary accommodated its women worshipers, granting them ample "elbow room" in one of two ways: either by providing a spacious upstairs gallery with clear sight lines or by situating the women on the main floor of the sanctuary and separating them from the men by a *mechitzah*, or partition. These architectural alterations or improvements made women worshipers feel more welcome than they had been when relegated to a little nook of the sanctuary. Including them within the architecture of the sanctuary gave them sense, though perhaps one that remained unarticulated, that they were no mere appendages or occasional intruders but an integral or entirely welcome part of the ritual drama. No longer hidden behind a homemade curtain or grille, the female worshiper was able to observe the service firsthand, directly, and thus have a keener and clearer sense of the proceedings.

While it is sorely tempting to see in these altered spatial configurations of the interwar years, particularly in the *mechitzah* per se, evidence of a heightened sensitivity to the needs of the Orthodox American Jewish woman, corroborative evidence is hard to come by. Among Reform and Conservative Jews, seating patterns were often intertwined with questions of sexual equality. "Jews came to view the debate over the synagogue seating of women," observes the historian Jonathan Sarna, "as a debate over the synagogue status of women."[36] But this was not the case among the Orthodox of the interwar years; nowhere do they associate a *mechitzah* or, for that matter, ample seating room with modernity or its corollary of deorientalization. The connection between the two apparently escaped them— or, if they did think in such terms, the link remained unarticulated. Unlike their Reform and Conservative counterparts, the Orthodox Jewish rabbinate simply did not view seating patterns as an avowedly women's issue and, in turn, as an index to their own modernity. Despite ample opportunity to make a case for the modernity of the Orthodox sanctuary, Orthodox synagogues during this period repeatedly failed to do so. Take, for example, the dedication, in 1918, of the Jewish Center, a showpiece of New York's Americanized Orthodox community, whose sanctuary employed a *mechitzah* on its main floor, in lieu of the more customary gallery, to segregate the sexes. Dedication exercises provided a tailor-made opportunity for trumpeting that congregation's modernity and parallel concern for its female members. And yet, neither the press, which generally seized on instances of nonconformity, nor Mordecai M. Kaplan, at whose behest and direction the sanctuary was designed, had anything to say on its novelty; the Center's somewhat unusual seating configuration—what Kaplan called a "kind of false gallery"—was a source of neither praise nor criticism. That it figures not at all in contemporary Orthodox records or even in the collective memory of Jewish Center congregants—folkloristic accounts of the intramural tensions that frequently accompany the construction of a synagogue have not been handed down—suggests, by indirection, that during the interwar years, Orthodox Jews themselves did not link synagogue seating patterns with their denomination's attitude toward women.[37] The most one can say with certainty is that a women's section with "more elbow room" was more an incidental feature of the newly grandiose and monumental American Orthodox sanctuary of the interwar years than it was a direct consequence of modernity or conscious deorientalization. While the net result of these architectural alterations fed directly into and sustained Orthodoxy's experiment with deorientalization, the *mechitzah* per se was not a conscious part of that process.

It was only during the years following World War II, when the *mechitzah* became the yardstick by which American Jews distinguished an Orthodox from a Conservative synagogue—and the subject of increasingly vituperative debates between the two denominations—that Orthodox clergy picked up on the connection between seating patterns and attitudes toward women. Seeking to counter the claims of their more liberal coreligionists that Orthodoxy was inconsistent with modernity or, as one observer put it, to illustrate that segregated seating was "erroneously interpreted as a slur upon emancipated womanhood," Orthodox leaders raised the women's issue but only to refute it passionately.[38] The "foolish accusation hurled at the Orthodox synagogue, that its separate seating implies an acceptance of women's inequality," was dismantled, layer by layer, by Orthodox apologists.[39] Some drew on biblical and talmudic literature, while others invoked anthropology to demonstrate the high regard in which Jewish tradition held its women. "It is simply untrue that separate seating in a synagogue, or elsewhere, *has anything at all to do with quality or inequality,*" insisted Rabbi Norman Lamm, one of the postwar era's most eloquent rabbis.[40] The modern-oriented Orthodox clergy remained adamant on that point and energetically campaigned in the postwar period to maintain the practice of segregated seating, thus keeping their ideological boundaries intact and inviolate.

Whether consciously intended or not, the welcoming environment of the interwar American Orthodox synagogue provided the physical context in which women's attendance at the synagogue grew and developed. Within that context the nature of the aestheticized Orthodox prayer service hastened the process still further. The introduction of decorum into the Orthodox sanctuary had the effect of rendering the service even more accessible to the female worshiper than it had once been. Many of the new features of the Kehilath Jeshurun service, noted that synagogue's bulletin, had been instituted "in response to numerous requests coming especially from women who want to participate in the services in an intelligent manner."[41] As a byproduct of the decorous service, the female audience was now better able to follow the Orthodox ritual and to participate more directly in it. Once English replaced Yiddish as the prevailing and public language of the service, the language in which announcements were made, sermons preached, and occasional prayers enunciated, the service was no longer foreign or mysterious; those without Yiddish or the requisite prayer skills—skills that native-born American Jewish women generally lacked—had no reason to feel ill at ease. Devotees of English responsive readings and of the rabbi's sermon, women had become, willy-nilly, more adept at following the rhythms of the service. Were they temporarily lost, the frequent announcement of pages in English helped them to reorient themselves; failing that, there were always one or two women congregants, *mishers* or page turners, who, approximating informally the Eastern European *zugerin* or *zugerke,* knew the ins and outs of that text. Congregational use of a common prayer book with English translations and transliterations also facilitated the woman worshiper's dexterity and familiarity with the prayer service, enabling her to feel at home within its pages.[42]

The transformation of the service from a wholly performance-oriented one, in which the cantor held complete sway as the congregation listened in silence, to a service in which congregants sang along at selected key moments also occasioned a greater sense of participation. "Teaching the congregation to join in, nay, even to maintain the service," was one way to enliven the proceedings and to banish apathy.[43] "The traditional melodies," Rabbi David De Sola Pool observed, "are all simple and of small range so that the least musical congregant may sing to them."[44] The Young Israel movement, one of the first organized religious expressions of modern Orthodoxy, took great pains to introduce congregational singing, then a novelty, into its pre–World War I service; its concerted effort to get women to join in the singing was even perceived, at the time, as somewhat "revolutionary" and radical. More established congregations like the 85th Street Shul and the Jewish Center also actively promoted congregational singing, even going so far as to sponsor coeducational classes in Jewish music or to institute a choral group to familiarize worshipers with the new tunes. "We must ask the support of women in the choral circles," Rabbi De Sola Pool explained, "so that they also may swell the melodious cadence of prayer in the synagogue."[45]

As they lifted their voices in song, listened attentively to the sermon, keenly participated in the responsive readings, and managed the prayer ritual, female worshipers became an integral and expected fixture of the Orthodox synagogue. Ultimately, what brought women into the synagogue and then kept them there was its transformation from an exclusively prayer-oriented and male-centered institution into an active social center geared toward the entire family. Once the Orthodox synagogue sought determinedly to become a hub of community life, a center for extradevotional activities like classes, sports activities, teas, and luncheons, women felt increasingly more comfortable within its sacred precincts. By more broadly defining its role within the community, the Orthodox synagogue enabled the American Orthodox woman to feel that the synagogue was as much her institution as it was her husband's or her son's.

In large measure, the sisterhood was the agent of this transformation. Assigned the "inner life, the housewivery" of the synagogue, sisterhood women applied their domestic sensibilities to the task, making of the synagogue a miniature home.[46] Much as she cultivated a spirit of warmth and hospitality within her private life, the sisterhood woman was expected to cultivate a spirit of good feeling and hospitality within the synagogue. As the "backbone" of the congregation's social spirit, the sisterhood institutionalized the natural impulse toward confraternity and, in that way, helped to build a community or, as Rabbi Lookstein liked to say, "weld[ed] [the] congregation into a happy family unit."[47] In the characteristic premodern Orthodox synagogue, there was little sense of a community whose interests extended beyond that of prayer; whatever fraternizing existed was informal and largely outside (both literally and figuratively) of the shul. The proudly modern Orthodox congregation, however, transformed socializing into one of its integral functions, an essential ingredient in its modern makeup. Through a continual round of social events—teas, dances, luncheons—the sisterhood kept alive and nourished the healthy social spirit that developed into the hallmark of the American Orthodox synagogue. "Serv[ing] in large measure as *the* cultural and social arm of the congregation," sisterhood women were made to feel not only welcome in but important to the success and vitality of their local synagogue.[48]

As more and more Orthodox women took to the synagogue during the interwar years, making the sisterhood their "fortunate cause"[49] and emerging as active participants in American Orthodox synagogue life, the Union of Orthodox Jewish Congregations of America (UOJCA), American Orthodox Jewry's umbrella organization, began to take note of them and their efforts. Alerted to the potential of this increasingly numerous and articulate element in the community and eager to tap its resources, the UOJCA in 1923 developed a women's division, known succinctly as the Women's Branch, much as Reform and Conservative Jews had established comparable organizations years before. Coordinating and overseeing the activities of the local synagogue sisterhoods, the Women's Branch unified these discrete entities into one centralized unit, and in that way provided Jewish women with an organizational framework in which they could pursue their interests as observant Jews. With the backing of dozens of local New York Orthodox sisterhoods and hundreds nationally. Women's Branch grew to represent an Orthodox female constituency and one, moreover, that sought to define the Orthodox Jewish experience from a woman's perspective.[50]

On the simplest level, Women's Branch assisted the local synagogue sisterhood with its administrative and cultural programming. After all, most Orthodox women of that time were newcomers to organizational ventures like the sisterhood and keenly in need of advice on how best to administer their organization and keep it afloat. As a clearinghouse of information on the workings of an Orthodox sisterhood, Women's Branch provided direction to the sisterhood movement and systematized its efforts from the top on down. Dispensing detailed, generous advice, the Women's Branch helped fledgling sisterhoods to get off the ground, even going so far as to provide them with a model constitution, complete with preamble and articles of incorporation. It also published a series of "how to" pamphlets and manuals, like the popular *Manual for Sisterhoods,* in its attempt to develop "an efficient sisterhood."[51] Women's Branch was the place to turn with questions on cultural and social activities; here the organization lent its expertise and collective wisdom in cultural and social programming and provided step-by-step or, more precisely, month-by-month advice. December, explained the *Manual,* might be an appropriate time to celebrate the rededication of the family to the synagogue with a "dutch supper," while a February tea on the theme of American patriotism might be worthwhile; May, the *Manual* noted, was a promising time for an extended discussion on women's place in Judaism.[52]

Not everything associated with the local sisterhood was frivolous or lighthearted. The members of the Women's Branch took themselves seriously and were most sensitive to the importance of developing not only a committed but also a knowledgeable female Orthodox population. "To make orthodox women convincingly articulate in discussing Jewish tradition," Women's Branch encouraged them to attend classes in Hebrew, Bible, religious ceremonies, literature ("The Jewish Classics"), sociology, family problems, and housewivery"—the latter an in-depth course in kashrut and cooking.[53] Where no classes existed, the Women's Branch created them and provided instructors, syllabi, and recommended reading lists as well as speakers for special lectures. But the fashioning of an articulate and well-read Women's Branch member was only part of that organization's overall agenda. Even more to the point was the creation of a highly motivated *observant* American Jewish woman, a "faithful Jewess." "An awakened observance of Jewish tradition," an editorial on the Women's Page related, "would result from a revival of Jewish learning."[54]

Women's Branch did everything it could to awaken Jewish ritual observance among its members. As a vehicle for the promotion of greater and better-informed religious practice, Women's Branch worked in concert with local sisterhoods to encourage the Jewish woman's performance of her ritual obligations. Like Reform and Conservative national sisterhood organizations, it too defined itself in religious terms, as an institution making for enhanced religious observance or, as one spokeswoman would have it, as "a force for Jewishness."[55] In its efforts "to nurture spiritually the adolescent and grown-up tradition-true daughter of the American Jewish home," Women's Branch campaigned energetically for synagogue attendance and holiday observance; published a series of slender volumes with such titles as "Marriage and the Home: A Jewish Guide for Marital Happiness," and "Yes, I Keep Kosher," an "attractive one page leaflet on the Woman's View of Kashruth" that touted the benefits of Orthodox ritual; and, increasingly, toward the end of the thirties and in the early forties, crusaded for Jewish education for girls and women.[56] "There are over a million Jewish women in this country," observed the founder and president of Women's Branch, Mrs. Herbert S. Goldstein, in 1925. "Do all of them attend divine services on the Sabbath? Does each woman see to it that her children are raised strong in the faith of our fathers? Does each woman observe all the ceremonials of her religion? . . . Till this can be answered in the affirmative," Mrs. Goldstein firmly concluded, "we must concentrate all our efforts."[57]

In an attempt to reach the unobservant Jewish woman, Women's Branch published and widely disseminated guidebooks or, more accurately, primers in Jewish ritual observance. Keenly aware, perhaps from personal experience, that most American Jewish women of that period were somewhat deficient in their ritual knowledge, Women's Branch sought to reacquaint them with their tradition through the publication of what one contemporary labeled "an abridged *shulkan aruch* for women."[58] Lucidly written, texts like *Symbols and Ceremonies of the Jewish Home* took the reader by the hand and guided her, point by point, step by step, through the basics of Jewish ritual observance: *Shabbos, yomtovim, kashrut, mikvah*.[59] Grounding the reader in the particularities of Jewish ritual observance, these guidebooks made explicit and clear what, in all probability, had been implicit, widely shared assumptions of the Jewish homemaker of an earlier generation.

At its heart, this emphasis on the ritual education of Women's Branch members reflected the sorry state of Jewish educational opportunities then available for women. Though a few afternoon Talmud Torahs for girls could be found through-out the city—Williamsburg, for example, was home to the Brooklyn National Hebrew School, while the Herzliah Hebrew High School was located in Manhattan—most Jewish girls received a minimal and spotty Jewish education, schooled at home by a parent or a tutor. "Reading Hebrew," related Mrs. Elizabeth Gilbert, herself the daughter of a rabbi, "was considered enough."[60] "What have most American-born observant Jewish women been taught?" asked one writer on the topic of the religious training of the adolescent girl. "The reading of a few prayers? A few biblical stories? Some superstitions of an East European ghetto?"[61] Once an unquestioned norm, this informal and superficial kind of Jewish education became the subject of increasing criticism during the inter war years, which culmi-nated, some years later, in the formation of coeducational Jewish day or parochial schools. "In the past," observed Rabbi Lookstein, "the primary concern of Jewish education has been the Jewish boy. . . . His Jewish sister had to be content with a few private lessons at home and with rudimentary instruction in the religious duties of Jewish wifehood and motherhood. The inevitable result was generation upon generation of righteous women, but not of learned women."[62]

The creation of a new modern generation of "learned women" became the mandate of the Women's Branch as it sought "to get off the educational double standard and offer to women the educational advantages that hitherto seemed to be only man's prerogative."[63] Beginning in the 1930s and gaining momentum in the years following World War II, as the Jewish parochial or day school came into its own, girls were increasingly offered these educational advantages. In the interim, "hundreds" of American Jewish girls "of fine families" attended the Hebrew Teach-ers Training School, a Women's Branch enterprise that prepared college-age women for careers as Hebrew teachers.[64] For their mothers, however, it was too late to do anything more than apply stopgap, remedial measures to make up for their educa-tional deficiencies. For the older generation, guide-books and supplementary adult education were the sole avenues by which to acquire the "necessary tools" for being observant Jews.[65]

The need to define both the practice and the rationale of selected religious rituals was most clearly demonstrated when it came to the observance of *kashrut*. Respon-sibility for adhering to the dietary laws evolved organically from the Jewish woman's role as homemaker and consumer; Jewish tradition also viewed it as one of her specific ritual obligations, "the mandate of the Jewish woman . . . a duty that falls naturally and almost exclusively within the women's sphere."[66] Given the primacy of *kashrut* in the sacred life of the traditional Jewish woman, it was not surprising that Women's Branch focused on its promotion. Keeping kosher became a test case of the inherent adaptability and relevance of ancient Jewish ritual to modern urban America. Repeatedly, Women's Branch leaders urged their constituent sisterhoods to press for the observance of *kashrut* likening its promotion to a "sacred rite."[67] Under its aegis, classes were held on the divine origins of the dietary laws, instruction in kosher cooking sponsored, and the publication of sisterhood kosher cookbooks widely encouraged. "The dietary laws," explained *Jewish Home Beautiful,* a widely published ritual guide and a household staple, "must find their first expression in the home and the Jewish woman must be their exponent."[68]

In the attempt to convince the modern Jewish woman to be the "exponent" of the dietary laws, the rationale for *kashrut* observance was thoroughly recast and, in a very real sense, reinvented. Neither halakhic nor biblical precedents for the observance of *kashrut* were invoked, for these explanations, *kashrut* advocates knew, were likely to be of limited appeal. Instead, arguments in favor of *kashrut* were couched in terms believed to be of interest to the modern, middle-class American woman. Keeping and cooking kosher, according to the new interpretations proferred by their interwar exponents, were symbols of refinement and civility, of high moral tone and character. "On the whole," one authority noted, "nothing has refined the Jewish character as much as the dietary laws."[69] "Abstinence from foods permitted to others," it explained, "develop[s] and strengthen[s] self mastery and control."[70] Helping to build moral Jews, keeping *kashrut* also helped to build healthy Jewish bodies, for *kashrut,* its adherents boasted, induced greater immunity from disease and promoted longevity. But of all the explanations for keeping kosher, the one most favored held that *kashrut* was nothing less than an artistic opportunity, an occasion to demonstrate the aesthetic sensibility of the modern ritually observant Jewish woman. "A fine art," cooking kosher challenged the artistry inherent in the Jewish woman.[71] "Living as [a] Jewess is more than a matter of faith, knowledge, or observance," stated one popular ritual text. "To live as a Jewess, a woman must have something of the artist in her."[72] *Kashrut,* then, was the instrument by which that talent and artistry could be revealed.

In their new idiom, these arguments for keeping kosher sought unmistakably to make the point that observance of the dietary laws was as consonant with middle-class life as handsomely appointed apartments or visits to the opera. The terms and conditions, as well as the language, of bourgeois life were now freely extended even to traditional Jewish rituals. "Increased substance and status has found expression, among the Orthodox, as often in elegance of cuisine and dining ritual as in the greater modishness of matters pertaining to the synagogue," observed the author of a *Commentary* article on the success of Barton's, the kosher candy manufacturer. "It is perhaps not inconceivable," he noted somewhat glibly, "that a 'Jewish' taste, which had to satisfy itself until recently with such things as kosher delicatessen, has now found an additional source of satiety in Continental candies."[73] And, this author might have added, in Continental cuisine. From the kinds of questions kosher consumers put to experts on such matters in the pages of the *Orthodox Union,* one sees evidence not only of a sophisticated palate but also of interest in "eating American." Is caviar kosher? Housewives from Brooklyn, the Bronx, Long Island, and Manhattan wanted to know. What about capers? Sturgeon? Is smoked fish permissible? Anchovies? Nestlés chocolates? Ovaltine? Or Aunt Jemima pancakes? (In most of the instances cited, the Union affirmed the *kashrut* of the product in question. But when it came to the reliability of Nestlés and Hershey's chocolates, they responded: "We are investigating and will let you know as soon as possible.")[74]

Advertising campaigns for kosher food products reinforced the message that *kashrut* married well with urbane America. Bold and contemporary in their graphics, there was nothing hesitant or diffident about the promotion of matzoh, shortening, or baked goods. Displaying young, cheerful, and trim cooks as they made use of kosher canned goods or desserts, the ads affirmed the notion that, in modern America, the dietary laws were no obstacle to full gastronomic enjoyment. Thus, a 1936 advertisement for Spry, whose copy read "Orthodox Women Hail New White Kosher Shortening," noted that the kosher consumer's affinity for the product made perfect culinary sense: "No wonder! For now you can use a beautiful White shortening and *still* keep the Dietary laws."[75] The promotion of ritually supervised Sheffield Farms dairy products had this to say: "Keep in Shape with Sheffield: Women like to be busy. But women don't like to be tired. A wife does a thousand things to make her house a home. But she doesn't mind—if she's fit. Milk is her helper." Thus fitness, shapeliness, and *kashrut* were subtly linked all together in one product.[76] Purveyors of kosher services like restaurateurs and caterers similarly capitalized on the newly heralded modernity of *kashrut* by explicitly connecting matters of taste with the kind of ritual services they made available. The logo of Max Braun, a Harlem caterer, affirmed "Catering with a taste to families of taste and refinement," while those of the other kosher caterers, with such elegant-sounding and decidedly subtle names as Patrician and Carlton, boasted of their access to New York's best hotels, once again tying kosher food to sophistication and elegance.[77] Describing the "social life" of New York's Orthodox community, the *Jewish Forum* in 1927 noted the existence of kosher restaurants (and hotels) that not only served kosher food "but . . . effect[ed] a refined home-like atmosphere." Such establishments, the paper explained, "encourage not only the aesthetic but also the vitally religious needs in Jewish life."[78]

The kosher cookbook, often a sisterhood project, delivered this message even more graphically and concretely.[79] Though concerned explicitly with food and its preparation, these cookbooks can be read as social statements that reflected and sometimes even created a set of attitudes toward the observance of the dietary laws. Through the medium of a recipe, the inherent suitability and adaptability of *kashrut* to modern times was directly conveyed. After dispensing with a few general comments about the laws of *kashrut,* the kosher cookbook provided dozens, sometimes even hundreds, of recipes divided by type: appetizers, main dishes, desserts, condiments. In the vast majority of instances, the recipes cited were examples not of Ashkenazic, representative Jewish food but rather of basic American middle-class culinary fare: corn fritters, oatmeal cookies, stews, steamed puddings, marshmallow salads, creamed soups. Only the subtle, barely perceptible, substitution of almond milk for the real thing or vegetable oil for lard indicates that these dishes were inherently unkosher.[80]

Explicitly familiar, Jewish foods were set aside, relegated to a different section of the cookbook where they were associated with ceremonial and distinctive occasions: Jewish food, it seemed, was special fare to be consumed on the Sabbath and holidays but not on Tuesdays. In fact, foods associated with the Sabbath and the holidays were frequently hailed, in lavish, often emotional prose, as distinctive. Items like *charoset* and *russel,* one text observed, urging their consumption on wary readers, "acquire a dignity, bordering upon sanctity which elevate them to the status of religious traditions."[81] Among other religious culinary traditions were borscht, "an ambrosial dish," and blintzes, customarily prepared for Shavuot. In the latter instance, serious cooks were urged to arrange the blintzes "like the two Tablets of the Law"; by sprinkling cinnamon on their surface in two parallel lines, the text advised, one could even "suggest the Ten Commandments themselves."[82]

Though many of the specifically Jewish recipes and the circumstances under which their preparation was detailed may strike a slightly silly note, the sisterhood cookbook or its extension, the kosher cookbook, was a high-minded endeavor. An attempt to create, if only culinarily, a traditional Jewish community with shared norms and values, the kosher cookbook promoted the exchange—and consumption—of recipes and in that respect bound together its readers and practitioners into a community with a shared culinary preference and, even more to the point, a shared ritual.

Whether in the form of an advertisement or of a recipe, the implicit and subtle message in this marriage of the contemporary and the hoary was their inherent compatibility. Keeping kosher, it seemed, was not inconsistent with modernity; the two could be comfortably accommodated to each other. *Kashrut* posed no barrier to participation in the wider world. Through actual physical substitutes, on the one hand, and intellectual reinterpretations, on the other, it was made part of that world. "In a Jewish home, a perfectly prepared meal, daintily served is not enough," Jewish housewives were told. "It may satisfy the physical desires and the esthetic sense, but, *to be perfect,* it must be kosher."[83]

Concern for rendering *kashrut* compatible with modernity took observant women out of the kitchen and into the marketplace. Bringing to bear their sensibility as astute consumers and assiduous homemakers even as they fulfilled one of the most fundamental of their ritual obligations, Orthodox women of the Women's Branch not only encouraged the observance of *kashrut* but also sought to make it more viable by expanding the range of available kosher food products. "We have within our power to give these kosher products nationwide sanction and publicity," explained Women's Branch members as they exerted concerted pressure on food manufacturers to produce kosher food products.[84]

No doubt tired of a limited number of kosher canned and processed goods and perhaps even more weary of having constantly to tell their children what they could not eat, Women's Branch explored the possibility of having a wider array of kosher foodstuffs at their disposal and on their table. Women's Branch groups visited factories and manufacturing plants, defrayed the costs of expensive laboratory analyses, and ultimately secured a broad number of kosher food products by convincing manufacturers of the financial benefits likely to accrue from the kosher market. Thanks to their labors, the UOJCA became increasingly known for its sophisticated approach to ritual supervision; its discrete seal, OU, inconspicuously situated on the base of a food item, emerged during these years as a synonym for careful and reliable *hasgacha* (ritual supervision). "The women," related a former Women's Branch president, "made the OU," referring to the barely noticeable seal, while "the OU," explained one kosher Upper West Side hostess, "made Passover and *kashrut*."[85]

Kashrut observers eagerly awaited the addition of a new American foodstuff to the list of ritually sanctioned items and avidly followed the often complex negotiations that attended the process. Widely publicized in the Orthodox press, the news that one or another American food manufacturer had agreed to ritual supervision of his products was an occasion for excitement and hyperbole. When, in 1935, the manufacturer of Loft's ice creams and candy agreed to cooperate with the OU, one periodical hailed the news as "an historic event for the Jews of America."[86] A symbolic as well as a gastronomic success believed to represent the coming of age of the kosher market, the kasherization of one of America's most popular ice cream and candy manufacturers was formally marked by a celebration dinner at the Hotel Biltmore. Loft's gentile president was the guest of honor at this occasion, singled out by the OU for his role in seeking ritual supervision. Congratulating the food executive for his "broad and humane vision," the OU officials extolled "his foresight in anticipating the tremendous goodwill which will redound to the benefit of his already well-known company as a result of his cordial cooperation with the OU in this enterprise."[87] By the late thirties, the number of American food manufacturers that "cooperated cordially" with the OU by submitting to the ritual supervision of their products was substantial. As a result, the kosher consumer had a wide array of products from which to choose: breads, dairy products, cereals, candies, desserts, mayonnaise, mustards, oils, shortening, noodles, and soups. The OU's "Kashruth Directory," a list of ritually sanctioned items, took up a full single-spaced page in the *Orthodox Union* and included a who's who of American food manufacturers, among them Pepsi-Cola, Wrigley's, Dugan's, and Heinz Good Foods, of whose fifty-seven varieties, the *Union* noted solemnly, "twenty-six were kosher."[88]

Orthodox women of the interwar years by no means exhausted their organizational energies and talents in pursuit of the efficient sisterhood or exemplary kosher recipe. Throughout the 1920s and 1930s, the cause of Zionism or, to be more precise, that of religious Zionism, increasingly engaged them, as well. The Mizrachi Zionist Movement, also known to some as "clerical Zionism," fused the political pragmatism of secular Zionists with the religious ideology of observant Jews and as such formally represented the interests of religious Zionists within the world Zionist movement.[89] Established in Europe in 1902, Mizrachi was launched in America in 1913 by its president, Rabbi Meyer Berlin, who had traveled to the New World in search of funds. When stranded by the outbreak of the Great War, Berlin turned his attentions to the creation of an American branch of the world Mizrachi movement.

The involvement of Orthodox women in the affairs of the American Mizrachi did not get under way for another decade. Organized in 1925, the Mizrachi Women's Organization of America grew quickly and, despite its late start, encompassed close to fifty chapters nationally by the mid-thirties; by 1950, it boasted of fifty thousand members in thirty-eight states throughout the country. On the local level, virtually every Orthodox community in Brooklyn, Manhattan, and the Bronx contained a Mizrachi chapter whose whirl of luncheons, inventively named "Tikvah Teas," bazaars, and cultural "Palestinian Evenings" contributed much-needed moral and financial support to the *Yishuv,* the Jewish settlement of Palestine.

Like the sisterhood, members of American Mizrachi Women applied their special feminine qualities as mothers and homemakers to the upbuilding of Palestine. "We realized that the home has always been the logical starting place for the carrying out of ideas," explained Mrs. Jesse Ginsberg, the organization's president, echoing a common refrain as she reflected on its history. "We realized that it is the mother who makes the home what it is. It is not surprising, therefore," she concluded, "that we decided to concentrate our efforts on the adolescent girl, who is the Jewish mother of the future."[90] Accordingly, American Mizrachi Women built a series of academic, agricultural, and vocational institutions throughout Palestine to house and instruct young girls in such fields as child care, education, farming, gardening, dressmaking, and dietetics, all typically female enterprises.[91] Later, the organization broadened its base to include recently arrived émigrés from Hitler's Europe, smoothing their course of adjustment to life in the Middle East. Male Zionist circles did not always understand the exclusively domestic focus of American Mizrachi Women, finding its Judaic version of *Kinder und Kuchen* difficult to take seriously. Those of an antireligious bent were even more pronounced in their criticism. "I have heard very often from other organizations," reported a Mizrachi representative stationed in Jerusalem, "of how they have tried to paraphrase the work of the Mizrachi Women as kosher kitchens. Kosher kitchens!" she exclaimed, taking umbrage at the description.[92] "Mizrachi," retorted another of its devotees, "is not just an interest in kosher meat."[93]

To some, participation in a Mizrachi chapter was an expression of support for the Zionist experiment; for others, it afforded yet another opportunity, one beyond that of the sisterhood or Women's Branch, to assert their affiliation with American Orthodox causes. The Mizrachi Women's Organization, insisted one of its charter members, "is the very organization in which [Jewish women] may reveal and confirm their orthodoxy."[94] Whatever the rationale for membership, the association of Orthodox women with Zionist affairs helped to render Zionism a socially acceptable enterprise in middle-class circles and, as an institutional outlet, a close second to the sisterhood. Admittedly, the Mizrachi Women's Organization never quite achieved the kind of social cachet and prominence that the Hadassah Women's Organization, established in 1912, had already attained. Rivals for the affections and dollars (or, in this case, the *shekels*) of the middle-class American Jewish woman, the two organizations maintained cordial, if cool, relations with each other. Publicly, they stressed the extent to which they worked in tandem, "through common channels and . . . along a common path."[95] Privately, though, the Mizrachi Women's Organization bridled at the notion that it was a poor cousin to the older and more established Hadassah. "Whereas it is fashionable and respectable to be a Zionist or to belong to a Hadassah," one contemporary observed, "it is queer and quaint to belong to Mizrachi. It is associated with old people and old interests and old methods."[96] American Mizrachi Women sought, however, to overturn that widely prevalent view of their organization and, like so much else associated with the interwar Orthodox experience, to recast even religious Zionism in acceptable, bourgeois terms. American Mizrachi Women, explained a member in 1937, "is our answer to the question of how orthodox Jewesses take care of their own."[97] . . .

For the American Jewish woman of the interwar years, modernity brought with it considerable opportunities for an expanded religious life: Orthodox Jewish women were now actively encouraged to attend synagogue regularly, to form sisterhoods, to exert pressure on the marketplace, and to have a voice and a presence in Orthodox communal affairs. And yet, if a boon in some instances, in others modernity carried with it considerable challenges. As the interwar history of American Orthodox Women makes clear, modernity posed a serious threat to the hegemony of tradition and often entailed a reinterpretation, and at times the abandonment, of selected ritual behaviors, even among those who considered themselves Orthodox.

Through it all, "a new personage" had emerged eager to avail herself of modernity's challenges and complexities. "As there is a new woman," noted the author of a 1925 text on American Judaism, "there is also a new Jewess. . . . They are finding themselves . . . glorifying in their birthright."[98] Experimenting with a new and often perplexing ritual identity and with emerging forms of communal involvement, the interwar generation of Orthodox women was as involved with defining the limits and possibilities of their own sacred lives as their daughters and granddaughters have been, most recently, with theirs.

NOTES

1. Emil Hirsch, "The Modern Jewess," *The American Jewess* 1, no. 1 (April 1895): 11; Betty F. Goldstein, "The Women's Branch of the UOJCA," in *The Jewish Library,* Third Series (New York: Jewish Library Publishing, 1934), 108.

2. See, for example, "Save the Sabbath," *The American Jewess* 7, no. 2 (May 1898): 97.

3. David Philipson, "Woman and the Congregation," in *Proceedings, National Federation of Temple Sisterhoods* (1913), 22.

4. Irene Wolff, "The Jewish Woman in the Home, in *The Jewish Library,* 100, 103.

5. See, for example, Betty Greenberg and Althea O. Silverman, *The Jewish Home Beautiful* (New York: Women's League of the United Synagogue of America, 1941), 17; David Philipson, "The Ideal Jewess," *The American Jewess* 4, no. 6 (March 1897): 257; David Goldberg. "Woman's Part in Religion's Decline," *Jewish Forum* (hereinafter referred to as *JF*) 4, no. 4 (May 1921): 871.

6. Wolff, "The Jewish Woman," 93–94.

7. Mathilde (Mrs. Solomon) Schechter, "Aims and Ideals of the Women's League," typescript address, May 1918, 1, 4, Women's League Archives.

8. Goldberg, "Woman's Part in Religion's Decline," 874.

9. Wolff, "The Jewish Woman," 103.

10. Mrs. Abram Simon, "The President's Message," in *Proceedings of the National Federation of Temple Sisterhoods* (1915), 46.

11. Joseph Leiser, *American Judaism* (New York: Bloch, 1925), 180.

12. Ibid., 179, 198.

13. Ibid., 198.

14. Mrs. Stella Freiberg, "Report of the President," in *Proceedings of the National Federation of Temple Sisterhoods,* January 4, 1924, 14.

15. Jenna Weissman Joselit, "The Special Sphere of the Middle-Class American Jewish Woman: The Synagogue Sisterhood, 1890–1940," in *The American Synagogue: A Sanctuary Transformed,* ed. Jack Wertheimer (New York: Cambridge University Press, 1987), 206–30.

16. *American Hebrew,* January 6, 1928; Leiser, *American Judaism,* 191.

17. Leiser, *American Judaism,* 193.

18. Joseph H. Lookstein, "The Jewish Woman," *Orthodox Union* (hereinafter referred to as *OU*) 2, no. II (August 1935): 3.

19. See, for example, Joseph H. Lookstein, "A New Deal for the Forgotten Jewish Woman," *OU* 5, no. 7 (April–May 1938): 2.

20. Ibid.

21. Mrs. Herbert S. Goldstein, "A Rosh Hashonah Message," *OU* 3, no. I (September 1935): 2. See also Mrs. Moses Hyamson, "The Rabbi's Wife," *JF* 8, no. 10 (December 1925): 584.

22. Goldstein, "Rosh Hashonah Message," 2.

23. *Kehilath Jeshurun* (hereinafter referred to as *KJ Bulletin,* October 28, 1938; Minutes of the Jewish Center, May 10, 1923, 2, Jewish Center Archives; "New Features in Sabbath Services," *KJ Bulletin,* November 18, 1938; "Mrs. Freedman Again Heads Women's Branch of UOJCA," *OU* 12, no. 2 (December 1944): 24; Ina Israelite, "The Woman and Her Part in Young Israel," *JF* 9, no. 10 (December 1926): 547.

24. Barbara Welter, "The Feminization of American Religion: 1800–1860," in *Clio's Consciousness Raised,* ed. Mary Hartman and Lois Banner (New York: Octagon Books, 1973), 138; Richard Stiels, "The Feminization of American Congregationalism, 1730–1835," *American Quarterly* 33, no. 1 (spring 1981): 52.

25. Chava Weissler, "Issues in the Study of Women's Religion: An Eighteenth-Century Example," paper, 1986. Quoted with permission of the author.

26. The presence of a significant number of attentive, well-clad, and eager women worshipers occasioned considerable comment. Somewhat tongue in cheek, Israel Zangwill allegedly remarked that "when women in the gallery were admitted to the main floor of the synagogue, the men disappeared from the services," while another observer, somewhat less humorously, noted that women were the most frequent and "enthusiastic" of worshipers. While this may have been the case in Reform and Conservative circles, where the men often

worked on the Sabbath, the proportion of women in the Orthodox sanctuary never exceeded that of the men. At KJ, for example, it has been estimated that, during the forties, women worshipers numbered approximately one hundred and male worshipers 150. (Israel Zangwill, quoted in *Proceedings of the First Convention of the National Federation of Temple Sisterhoods* [1913], 27.) See also Alter Landesman, "Synagogue Attendance: A Statistical Survey," *Proceedings of the Rabbinical Assembly* 1928), vol. 2, 50; Benjamin Kline Hunnicutt, "The Jewish Sabbath Movement in the Early 20th Century," *American Jewish History* 69, no. 2 (December 1979): 196–215; Rabbi Lookstein's handwritten comments on the Sabbath service, KJ Archives; interview with Rabbi Haskel Lookstein, August 4, 1981.

27. Lookstein, "The Jewish Woman."

28. Interview with Mrs. Gertrude Engelberg, December 21, 1986.

29. Interviews with Mrs. Gertrude Lookstein and Dr. Nathalie Friedman, August 17, 1987.

30. Interview with Mrs. Elizabeth Gilbert, August 18, 1987.

31. Interview with Mrs. Gertrude Lookstein, August 17, 1987. In virtually every interview conducted with modern Orthodox women of this period, the importance of dressing up for services was stressed.

32. Interviews with Mrs. Sylvia Kramer, December 25, 1986; Mrs. Sadie Wohl and Mrs. Selma Roeder, September 1, 1987.

33. Ray Stannard Baker, *The Spiritual Unrest* (New York, 1909), 115.

34. Sarah Schack, "O'Leary's Shul—and Others," *Menorah Journal* 16, no. 5 (May 1929): 463.

35. Ibid., 464.

36. Jonathan Sarna, "The Debate over Mixed Seating in the American Synagogue," in Wertheimer, *American Synagogue,* 369.

37. Personal communication with Rabbi Jacob J. Schacter, September 7, 1987.

38. "Solutions and Resolutions," *OU* 1, no. 8 (April 1934): 2.

39. Rabbi Norman Lamm, "Separate Pews in the Synagogue: A Social and Psychological Approach," in *The Sanctity of the Synagogue,* ed. Baruch Litvin (New York: Spero Foundation, 1962), 323.

40. Ibid., 318. See also Morris Max, "Mixed Pews," *OU* 17, no. 1 (October 1949): 16–24.

41. *KJ Bulletin,* November 18, 1938.

42. In fact, women congregants were often among the first to protest the introduction of a new prayer book. Even if they did not fully understand every prayer or interpolation, women worshipers were accustomed to the text and knew their way around it. The introduction of a new and different version of the *siddur* confused and dislocated them; the comfort of the familiar, even if somewhat outdated, was much preferred.

43. David de Sola Pool, "Congregational Singing," *Hebrew Standard,* November 18, 1910, 1.

44. Ibid. See also Israel Goldfarb, "Congregational Singing," *United Synagogue Recorder* 1, no. 1 (January 1921): 12, 13.

45. De Sola Pool, "Congregational Singing," 1.

46. *Reform Advocate* 13, no. 1 (February) 1897: 17, and 13, no. 4 (March 1897): 60.

47. *KJ Yearbook,* 1945, 12.

48. *KJ Yearbook,* 1948–49, n.p.

49. Quoted in Joselit, "Special Sphere," 211.

50. Material in this section is derived from interviews with former Women's Branch presidents, most notably Mrs. Elizabeth Gilbert, and from the *Orthodox Union,* which carried news of the organization's activities. See especially Selma Freedman, "The Women's Branch—Twenty-five Years of Achievement," *Jewish Life* 15, no. 5 (June 1948): 51–56; and Goldstein, "The Women's Branch," 107–11.

51. "The Efficient Sisterhood," Women's Page, *OU* 12, no. 4 (April 1945): 12, Stella Burstein, *Manual for Sisterhoods* (New York: Woman's Branch of the Union of Orthodox Jewish Congregations of America, 1947).

52. Burstein, *Manual,* 19.

53. "Women's Branch Calls for the Study of Jewish History," *OU* 3, no. 8 (May 1936): 7.

54. Ibid.

55. Mrs. Herbert S. Goldstein, "The Jewish Woman—A Force for Jewishness," *JF* 8, no. 10 (December 1925): 571–73. On the religious nature of pre–World War II sisterhoods, see Joselit, "Special Sphere," passim.

56. "UOJCA Publications," *Jewish Life* 21, no. 1 (September/October 1953): 85.

57. Goldstein, "The Jewish Woman," 572.

58. *OU* 12, no. 2 (December 1944): 17.

59. Eva Schechter, *Symbols and Ceremonies of the Jewish Home* (New York: Bloch, 1930).

60. Interview with Mrs. Elizabeth Gilbert.

61. Beatrice S. Genn, "The Religious Training of the Adolescent Girl," *JF* 9, no. 10 (December 1926): 543. See also "The Wall of Difference," *JF* 8, no. 5 (June 1925): 234, in which Bernard Revel was taken to task for failing to provide Jewish education for American-born Orthodox girls.

62. Lookstein, "A New Deal," 2.

63. Ibid.

64. "Hebrew Teachers Training School for Girls," *OU* 1, no. 2 (September 1933): 6; "The American Orthodox Scene: Torah-Training for Women," *OU* 4, no. 9 (June 1937): 3; interviews with Mrs. Elizabeth Gilbert and Mrs. Gertrude Lookstein.

65. Lookstein, "A New Deal"; "Mrs. Freedman," 24.

66. Wolff, "The Jewish Woman," 100.

67. "Women's Branch Holds Successful Convention," Women's Page, *OU* 5, no. 8 (June 1938): 12.

68. Greenberg and Silverman, *Jewish Home Beautiful,* 40–41. An extremely popular guide to Jewish observance, as well as a compilation of recipes, *The Jewish Home Beautiful,* in its own words, "offered a few suggestions . . . [to] inspire Jewish women to a deeper search of their own treasure house." It attempted to wean middle-class Jewish women away from "the attractive settings offered by our large department stores and women's magazines for Valentine's Day, Halloween, Christmas, and other non-Jewish festive days" (14) and direct them toward the richness of Jewish tradition.

69. Deborah Melamed, *The Three Pillars of Wisdom: A Book for Jewish Women* (New York: Women's League of the United Synagogue of America, 1927), 40. See also "Yes, I Keep Kosher," *Jewish Life* 21, no. 1 (September/October 1953): 85.

70. Melamed, *Three Pillars,* 39.

71. "Cookery, *Jewish Encyclopedia,* 1903, 254.

72. Greenberg and Silverman, *Jewish Home Beautiful,* 13.

73. Morris Freedman, "Orthodox Sweets for Heterodox New York: The Story of Barton's," *Commentary,* May 1952, 478.

74. The *Orthodox Union* inaugurated a *"Kashrut* Column" in August 1933 to respond to inquiries of this sort. See, for example, *OU* 1, no. 1 (August 1933): 5; 1, no. 6 (January/February 1934): 7; 2, no. 5 (March 1935): 4; 4, no. 3 (December 1936): 7.

75. *OU* 3, no. 11 (July/August 1936): 7 (my emphasis).

76. *OU* 1, no. 3 (October 1933): 7.

77. *JF* 10, no. 3 (March 1927): 167. The advertisements of kosher caterers can be found in the pages of the *Orthodox Union* and in synagogue bulletins like that of Manhattan's Jewish Center.

78. "The Social Life of the Orthodox Jew," *JF* 10, no. 12 (December 1927): 596. See also advertisement for "Gottleib's Kosher Restaurant—Eating Place of Refinement," *OU* 3, no. 3 (November 1935): 4.

79. The following section is derived from an examination of dozens of kosher cookbooks, some of them printed publications and others informal, mimeographed texts, and from personal communications with the anthropologist and folklorist Barbara Kirshenblatt-Gimblett. For a survey of the Jewish cookbook as a literary genre, see Barbara Kirshenblatt-Gimblett, "The Kosher Gourmet in the Nineteenth-Century Kitchen: Three Jewish Cookbooks in Historical Perspective," *Journal of Gastronomy* 2, no. 4 (1986/7): 51–89, and Barbara Kirshenblatt-Gimblett, "Jewish Charity Cookbooks in the United States and Canada: A Bibliography of 201 Recent Publications," *Jewish Folklore and Ethnology Review* 9, no. 1 (1987): 13–18.

80. One of the most popular and representative kosher cookbooks was Florence K. Greenbaum's *Jewish Cookbook* (New York: Bloch, 1918). By the time of its twelfth printing in 1938, it was said to have sold more than one hundred thousand copies. Interestingly enough, the publishers of this volume touted the author's scientific credentials as a way of highlighting the modernity of the dietary laws. Mrs. Greenbaum, Bloch Publishers noted in a "Publisher's Note" to the 1931 edition, "is a household efficiency woman, an expert Jewish cook, and thoroughly understands the scientific combining of foods."

81. Greenberg and Silverman, *Jewish Home Beautiful,* 88.

82. Ibid., 72.

83. Ibid., 40.

84. Goldstein, "The Jewish Woman," 571.

85. Interviews with Mrs. Elizabeth Gilbert and Mrs. Sylvia Kramer. See also Gella Block, "Passover Meals—For Today," *Jewish Life* 17, no. 4 (April 1950): 65–79.

86. Full-page advertisement in the *Orthodox Union,* 3, no. 4 (December 1935). See also "Dinner Celebrates Endorsement of Loft Candies," *OU* 3, no. 5 (January 1936): 2.

87. "Dinner Celebrates."

88. "Kashruth Directory," *OU* 4, no. 10 (July/August 1937): 10; *OU* 3, no. 3 (November 1935): last page.

89. Henry Keller, "Mizrachism—The Cornerstone of Zionism," in *Mizrachi, Jubilee Publication of the Mizrachi Organization of America (1011–36),* ed. Pinchos Churgin and Leon Gellman (New York: n.p., 1936), 11.

90. "Presidential Message at Convention Delivered by Acting President Mrs. Jesse Ginsberg," *Mizrachi Women's News* 5, no. 2 (Convention Issue 1937): 4.

91. See, for example, *Mizrachi Women's News* 5, no. 1 (spring 1937): 4.

92. "Mrs. Simcha Rabinowitz: Excerpts from an Address," *The Mizrachi Woman* 20, no. 2 (December 1947): 4.

93. Rabbi Manuel Laderman, "American Orthodoxy and Mizrachi," in Churgin and Gellman, *Jubilee Volume,* p. 28.

94. Mrs. Abraham Shapiro, "Message to the Mizrachi Woman," *Mizrachi Women's News* 4, no. 2 (fall 1936): 2.

95. "Our President, Mrs. Abraham Shapiro, Brought Greetings to Hadassah's Recent Convention in Atlantic City," *Mizrachi Women's News* 5, no. 4 (fall 1937): 2.

96. Laderman, "American Orthodoxy," p. 28.

97. Quoted in *Mizrachi Women's News* 5, no. 1 (spring 1937): 1.

98. Leiser, *American Judaism,* 178.

Chapter Eleven

The Women Who Would Be Rabbis

Pamela S. Nadell

In 1977, Mary Roth Walsh wrote, in the preface to *Doctors Wanted: No Women Need Apply,* that historians had by and large neglected the study of the entry of women into the male-dominated professions.[1] Since then, however, a number of fine books have documented the history of women's efforts to become physicians, lawyers, scholars, and scientists; the institutional, social, and psychological barriers they faced in their struggles; and the various strategies they employed to cope with the roadblocks they encountered as they pursued their careers.[2] The histories of American Protestant women's efforts to join the clergy became part of this new interest in American women's entrance into the male-dominated professions.[3] What these works collectively uncovered was a largely forgotten record of the struggles of individual women over the course of the nineteenth and twentieth centuries to enter the "brotherhoods" of the male-dominated professions.[4]

Toward the end of the eighteenth century, as Carl Degler has shown, some women (in Europe represented by Mary Wollstonecraft) began to espouse the idea of individualism, assuming that "women, like men, had interests and lives that were separate and different in purpose from those of other members of a family."[5] As significant numbers of women embraced this idea, it augured dramatic changes in their lives and helped launch the women's rights movement. For some, one goal of that movement was entrance into the professions. Inspired by the joint ideals of individualism and feminism, small numbers of American women gradually won entry into the male-dominated professions, first in medicine and the ministry, and then in law and the academy.[6] In some cases, these pioneers were successful in opening the doors, however marginally, for others to follow. In other cases, such as the women who failed to achieve ordination in certain Protestant denominations and those denied admission to Harvard University Medical School before 1945 and its law school before 1950, they kept the issue of women's access alive.[7]

In the late 1960s and 1970s, unprecedented numbers of college-educated American middle-class women flocked to the seminaries and medical, law, and graduate schools that would launch them into careers in the professions. They sensed, as Anna Quindlen has written of those years, "that all over America and indeed the world women were beginning to feel this same way, beginning to feel the great blessing and the horrible curse of enormous possibility."[8] Although these women were by and large unaware of those who had gone before them to open the gates to the professions, their efforts proved to be, as these histories have shown, but the latest stage in a long struggle for women to enter and to advance in the professions.

The movement for women's rabbinical ordination rightly belongs within this developing historiography of women in the professions. By the time Sally Priesand was on the verge of becoming the first woman to be ordained a rabbi in America, she had learned that she was not the first woman to try to enter the rabbinate. In her 1972 rabbinical thesis, written in the same year of her ordination, she wrote briefly about a handful of women who had preceded her in the attempt to achieve rabbinical ordination, including Regina Jonas, who was privately ordained in Germany in 1935.[9] Since then, Ellen Umansky has illuminated some of the names of the women who tried for and failed to become rabbis.[10] But if the histories of women's entrance into the other professions are paradigmatic, the history of the emergence of female rabbis merits a fuller analysis.

The subject raises a number of significant questions and suggests three approaches. The first is to explore, as I have begun to do elsewhere, in what ways women's roles in the American synagogue changed over the course of the late nineteenth and twentieth centuries, paving the way for women to assume new leadership roles in their congregations. In particular, this requires an examination of the emergence of synagogue sisterhoods and how they afforded women opportunities for new roles in their congregations.[11] It also requires examining women who may be considered the "functional equivalents" of rabbis; that is, those who led services in the small-town congregations that could not afford regular rabbis, those who served as synagogue presidents before that position opened to women in the wake of feminist challenges to circumscribed female roles within the synagogue, those whose careers as educators afforded them opportunities to fulfill roles typically associated with rabbis, and those who filled in for their rabbinical husbands when they were ill and after their death.[12] The second approach is to examine the elite institutions that have granted women's ordination (the Hebrew Union College-Jewish Institute of Religion, Reconstructionist Rabbinical College, and Jewish Theological Seminary of America) and their rabbinical alumni associations to consider what internal changes and external forces propelled their leaders to break with the tradition of male ordination. And the third is to explore the pioneers, to study the handful of women who by enrolling in courses in the rabbinical schools raised in real, not in abstract, terms the question of female rabbinical students and the issue of women's ordination.

This last approach, the focus of this essay, which in the short space allotted here can but touch upon the subject, raises a number of additional questions. Who were these women? Where and how did they manage to become students in the various rabbinical programs? What were their aspirations? What happened to sidetrack their ambitions away from the rabbinate or to stop them from achieving their goal? What then did they do with their lives? In what ways did the choices they made in terms of family and careers reflect on their initial aspirations for Jewish leadership and draw on the educations they received? To what extent did they remain advocates for the expansion of women's roles in the synagogue and for women's ordination?

Prior to the early 1970s, the chief arena for women attempting to pioneer women's ordination lay within the institutions associated with Reform Judaism: Cincinnati's Hebrew Union College and New York's Jewish Institute of Religion. Yet the more traditional institutions of American Judaism were by no means entirely isolated from the debate. One of the first women to study in rabbinical school, albeit with no intention of seeking ordination, was Henrietta Szold. From 1903 to 1906, she attended the Jewish Theological Seminary, Conservative Judaism's rabbinical school. And she reported with glee the consternation this aroused in the Yiddish press that assumed she would use her training to adjudicate questions of Jewish law.[13] After 1909, the Seminary channeled women who wished advanced Jewish educations to its Teachers Institute. In 1941, when Zionah Maximon found that its courses would not give her the education in Talmud and Midrash she wanted, Seminary faculty granted her special permission to attend classes in the rabbinical program with the caveat that she receive no credit of any kind or be listed as a special student.[14] Later, in 1957, Seminary Chancellor Louis Finkelstein replied to Gladys Citrin's request to study for the rabbinate: "Perhaps you would come to our Teachers Institute and become a teacher."[15] Although these examples suggest an awareness of the issue of women's ordination that went well beyond the Reform movement, the pioneers who attempted, albeit unsuccessfully before 1972, to challenge the male hegemony over the rabbinate by and large turned to Reform settings.

The extent to which they were aware of Reform's commitment to liberalism and its long history of statements supporting women's equality within Judaism and steps taken to ameliorate women's status within Jewish law is unclear.[16] Nevertheless, women interested in the rabbinate entered Reform institutions. From the 1890s forward, in almost every decade, there were one or more women studying for the rabbinate at these schools. Some of their names are familiar; others are not. At Hebrew Union College in Cincinnati, they included Ray Frank, Martha Neumark, Avis Shulman, and a number of the female students at the University of Cincinnati who took advantage of the undergraduate program launched by Hebrew Union College in 1957. In New York at the Jewish Institute of Religion, their ranks included Irma Lindheim, Dora Askowith, and Helen Levinthal. While Reform leaders in the Central Conference of American Rabbis and synagogue sisterhood members united in the National Federation of Temple Sisterhoods would from time to time raise the question of women's ordination in the abstract, these women, like those who pioneered in the professions in the nineteenth century, attempted on their own and unsuccessfully to push the question from the "bottom up."[17]

When Isaac Mayer Wise opened Hebrew Union College in 1875, one of the approximately dozen students in what was then really "little more than an intensive religious school" was eleven-year-old Julia Ettlinger.[18] Although Ray Frank, the "girl rabbi of the West," apparently studied there in 1893, and some young women completed the College's Preparatory Department, earning Bachelor of Hebrew Letters degrees while they finished high school, the debate over women's ordination erupted within Reform Judaism in the early 1920s.[19] In 1921, seventeen-year old Martha Neumark, a student in the Preparatory Department and daughter of its professor David Neumark, launched a two-year-long debate among the College faculty, its rabbinical graduates, and its Board of Governors over whether or not the College would ordain women as rabbis. As the deliberation over Neumark's efforts to become a rabbi was reaching its negative conclusion,[20] Irma Lindheim began raising the question, this time in New York City at the Jewish Institute of Religion.

The Jewish Institute of Religion had been founded by Rabbi Stephen Wise, the noted orator and Zionist, in 1922. Wise, after deciding against matriculation at Hebrew Union College, had been privately ordained by Adolf Jellinek, the liberal rabbi of Vienna. When his negotiations with New York's premier Reform synagogue, Temple Emanu-El, broke down over its lay leaders efforts to muzzle his freedom of speech in the pulpit, he founded the Free Synagogue, which joined Reform's Union of American Hebrew Congregations. Increasingly dissatisfied with the quality of Hebrew Union College and especially with its anti-Zionist stance, Wise, who was unquestionably associated with Reform or what is elsewhere called liberal Judaism, determined to act on a dream to found his own school. With the aid of the Free Synagogue, the Jewish Institute of Religion opened in 1922. The nontraditional nature of the seminary and its dedication to the free expression of all forms of Judaism marked the school as liberal while avoiding the label Reform.[21] Just as its was registering its first class, a chance meeting with Stephen Wise brought Irma Levy Lindheim to its doors.[22]

Born in New York City in 1886, Irma Levy was the daughter of well-to-do German Jewish immigrants. In 1907, she defied her father's wishes to arrange a suitable marriage and wed Norvin Lindheim, who was socially her peer but whose career as a fledgling attorney was deemed unsuitable by her father. Together the Lindheims raised five children and made their New York City home a center "for a mixture of important people from the worlds of business, diplomacy, finance, and the arts," many of them Germans her husband had met in his growing international law practice.[23]

Yet raising a family and the life of hostess were not enough to absorb Irma Lindheim, a woman of apparently remarkable energy and talent. Her fourth child was but five weeks old when she enlisted for active service in the Motor Corps of America, an organization established when the United States went to war with Germany to recruit female volunteers to drive and do odd jobs for the military. Quickly she rose to first lieutenant, the only Jewish woman to become one of its high officers. In the midst of her service, Lindheim became increasingly aware of "the disgrace of [her] basic ignorance as a Jew." While on weekend leave from the Motor Corps, she visited Baltimore, spending an evening at the home of the ardent Zionist Harry Friedenwald. Returning on the train to New York, she had what she later described as a "conversion," the moment when her life mystically changed, and she determined to use her vast energies on behalf of Zionism. She met Henrietta Szold and began to work for Hadassah. She became Chairperson of the Seventh

District of the Zionist Organization of America and used her monies (her father's death in 1914 had left her independently wealthy) to buy a brownstone on 74th Street in which to establish its educational and cultural center. Her involvement in Zionist work helped distract her from what came to be a family tragedy—her husband's wrongful conviction of conspiracy in making a false report concerning the registration of German property in America during World War I.

Her Zionist work made Lindheim increasingly aware of her woefully inadequate knowledge of Jewish history, tradition, and culture. Although as a child she had attended religious services with her grandmother and Sunday School, she recognized how little she knew of Judaism and all things Jewish. Not only did the Lindheims not celebrate Jewish holidays—they crafted their first Chanukah celebration in 1918—when told that she had to serve her dinner guest, the Zionist Herbert Bentwich, kosher food, she prepared smelts stuffed with lobster.

Running into Wise, Lindheim asked if he would accept her as a special student at the Institute. His enthusiastic response led her to pause in her work for Zionism and to enroll at the Institute in October 1922, beginning a three-and-a-half-year period of intensive study. As with her earlier work for the Motor Corps and Zionism, Lindheim threw herself wholeheartedly into her studies. She sent her children out of the city to the family's twenty-two-room mansion in Glen Cove, Long Island, and set up a small studio apartment a block from the Institute. She then devoted herself to ten-hour days of classes and study, pausing only to cook dinner in the evenings for her husband and to spend weekends with her family.

Lindheim succeeded in school as she had elsewhere. She was accepted for a special graduate course at Columbia University, taught by the influential educator John Dewey, despite the fact that she lacked the bachelor's degree necessary for admission. Both the faculty and the students voted her best in scholarship two years in a row, she later claimed.

By February 1923, Lindheim determined to change her status from that of special student and petitioned the faculty to admit her as a regular student in the rabbinical program. At first the professors decided that the lack of proper facilities, such as dormitories, obviated against the admission of women to the Institute. Worried that the question of women's ordination might add to the burden of establishing the Institute on a firm ground and sensing that many of the present students lacked "seriousness," which would be more easily developed without the presence of women, the faculty voted to admit women only as auditors to Extension courses— what today we would call adult education classes—while allowing the three women already enrolled in Institute classes (including Lindheim), to remain. But the discussion continued. In March, the faculty again debated the question. At a third meeting, in May, the faculty changed its mind and unanimously recommended the admission of women to the Institute on the same basis as men. While the Institute's original catalogue described it as a school for training men for the Jewish ministry, its 1923 charter of incorporation stated that it had been founded "to train, in liberal spirit, men *and women* for the Jewish ministry, research and community service" (italics mine).[24] Much later, Lindheim wrote of her ambition: "It was not that I had any plan to function as a rabbi. I simply believed, in a time of women's gradual emergence as individuals in their own right, that if I prepared myself in accordance with the requirements of being a rabbi, the door would be opened for other women, should they wish and have the gift to minister to congregations."[25]

In the midst of her studies, in March 1924, the personal crisis that had tested her family since her husband's trial and conviction in 1920 came to a climax. Norvin Lindheim, whose conviction on conspiracy would be subsequently overturned, was called to serve his jail term. The month in jail and the long haul of the legal battle took its toll on the Lindheims. The seemingly unflappable Irma Lindheim sagged under the burden. In 1925, on the verge of collapse, she was ordered by her doctor to rest. The change of scenery he prescribed led her to make her first trip to Palestine, a journey recorded in the letters she wrote home and published as *The Immortal Adventure*.[26] When at last Lindheim returned to New York, she decided that she could no longer indulge herself in the luxury of being a student, that she had to act upon what she had seen and learned. Later she wrote that Wise was disappointed that she would not complete her final year at the Institute and become a rabbi but that as a devoted Zionist he understood that it was more important for her to work for Palestine than to receive ordination.

With renewed energy, Lindheim once again threw herself into Zionist work. In 1926, she succeeded Henrietta Szold as National President of Hadassah and was reelected to a second term in 1927. As its president, she traveled around the country, speaking from synagogue pulpits, both Reform and Conservative, and meeting with rabbis and lay leaders. She and others, including Wise, were angered by what they deemed to be the disastrous leadership of the Zionist Organization of America (ZOA) under Louis Lipsky. They were especially bothered by its refusal to grant Hadassah women, which was a constituent agency of the ZOA, representation on its committees commensurate with their numbers; she became embroiled in a public controversy to reorganize the ZOA, which spilled over onto the pages of the *New York Times*. In the midst of that campaign, in the spring of 1928, her husband died at the age of forty-seven. Lindheim refused reelection as Hadassah president and turned once again to Palestine to recover her spirit. In 1933, she settled there, eventually selling the family mansion in Glen Cove to join Kibbutz Mishmar Hae-mek and turn to Labor Zionism.

Yet she retained her passionate interests in American Jewish life. In her later years, she tried to push Hadassah to develop a Jewish youth farm experience modeled on her work with the Volunteer Land Corps during World War II; to sell copies of her autobiography, *Parallel Quest* (1962); and to develop "Gram-sie's Hour," a program of Jewish education she created to train Jewish mothers and grandmothers to imbue their children with a sense of Jewish identity. She died in 1978.[27]

Lindheim's story, although of interest in and of itself, must be set in context and compared to the accounts of others who attempted to crash the barriers for women in the rabbinate. Doing so will reveal how her history illuminates a number of themes common to those women who challenged the male hegemony over the rabbinate from the bottom up.

The first common thread concerns the seriousness with which her efforts to be admitted to rabbinical school were met. Martha Neumark saw Hebrew Union College faculty, administration, Board of Governors, and alumni in the Central Conference of American Rabbis respond thoughtfully to her raising of the question of women as rabbinical students; Lindheim's challenge was similarly deemed worthy of serious deliberation. Undoubtedly, the timing of the raising of this question explains in part the consideration both Neumark and Lindheim received. The early 1920s heralded an era of great expectations concerning the emancipation of women. In the wake of the passage of the suffrage amendment, many believed all other barriers to women's emancipation would easily fall. The fact that they did not revealed, as William Chafe has shown, that "discrimination against women remained deeply rooted in the structure of society—in the roles women and men played and how those roles were valued."[28] Despite all the attention given to the new jobs open to women—attention shared by the Anglo-Jewish press—career women in the 1920s remained clustered in traditionally female occupations rather than breaking down barriers to professions excluding them.

Yet equally important to the regard that both Neumark and Lindheim received was their position as insiders to their seminary communities. Neumark was the daughter of Hebrew Union College Professor David Neumark. The Lindheims not only belonged to Stephen Wise's Free Synagogue but were apparently long-standing supporters of Wise and the Institute. Norvin Lindheim was one of the Institute's trustees and presumably, as trustees elsewhere do, supported the school financially.[29] It was one thing to dismiss another Institute student of the 1920s, Dora Askowith, who held a doctorate from Columbia University and taught history at Hunter College, as unsuitable for the rabbinate. It was quite another to refuse admission to the wife of a trustee—even when she lacked the formal academic credentials requisite for admission.[30]

Finally, what Lindheim did after her years at the Institute reveals just how firmly entrenched male and female roles were for the Jewish community. Perhaps she was right when she wrote in her autobiography that Wise was disappointed that she did not become a rabbi. But until the 1970s the Jewish Institute of Religion never ordained a woman. When Helen Levinthal (the daughter and granddaughter of prominent rabbis and thus another insider) completed the curriculum in 1939, she received a Master's of Hebrew Letters degree, not ordination.

Instead, as Lindheim's story shows, Jewish women, gifted with knowledge and education and skilled in leadership, were to serve American Jewry, but they were to do so as "professional" volunteers. That was their calling. If they reached high office, that was their ordination. Lindheim understood this. In writing to Henrietta Szold of her nomination to the national presidency of Hadassah, of the call to lead its thirty thousand women, she claimed: "If, at the Convention, the decision of the National Board is confirmed, I shall feel that I have been ordained, more truly so, even, than had I been confirmed as a rabbi."[31]

Lindheim's journey from rabbinical school to volunteer service would be matched by some of the other women who tried to crash the barriers to the rabbinate. Only in a new era when a resurgence of feminism began in the late 1960s to spill over into American Jewish life would the battle fought by Lindheim and the other pioneers end in victory. After nearly a century of debate and discussion Jewish women would at last have the choice—of serving their community as volunteers and as rabbis.

NOTES

1. Mary Roth Walsh, *"Doctors Wanted: No Women Need Apply": Sexual Barriers in the Medical Profession, 1835–1975* (New Haven: Yale University Press, 1977), xi.

2. In addition to Walsh, *"Doctors Wanted,"* see Joan Jacobs Brumberg and Nancy Tomes, "Women in the Professions: A Research Agenda for American Historians," *Reviews in American History* 10 (June 1982): 275–96; Margaret W. Rossiter, *Women Scientists in America: Struggles and Strategies to 1940* (Baltimore: Johns Hopkins University Press, 1982); Karen Berger Morello, *The Invisible Bar: The Woman Lawyer in America, 1638 to the Present* (New York: Random House, 1986); Penina Migdal Glazer and Miriam Slater, *Unequal Colleagues: The Entrance of Women into the Professions, 1890–1940* (New Brunswick: Rutgers University Press, 1987); Lynn D. Gordon, *Gender and Higher Education in the Progressive Era* (New Haven: Yale University Press, 1990).

3. Emily C. Hewitt and Suzanne R. Hiatt, *Women Priests: Yes or No?* (New York: Seabury Press, 1973); Priscilla and William Proctor, *Women in the Pulpit: Is God an Equal Opportunity Employer?* (Garden City, NY: Doubleday, 1976); Virginia Lieson Brereton and Christa Ressmeyer Klein, "American Women in Ministry: A History of Protestant Beginning Points," in *Women of Spirit: Female Leadership in the Jewish and Christian Traditions,* ed. Rosemary Ruether and Eleanor McLaughlin (New York: Simon and Schuster, 1979), 301–32.

4. In 1915, the influential educator Abraham Flexner characterized a profession as a brotherhood; cited in Glazer and Slater, *Unequal Colleagues,* 175.

5. Carl N. Degler, *At Odds: Women and the Family in America from the Revolution to the Present* (New York: Oxford University Press, 1980), 189.

6. The following examples highlight landmark dates for women's entrance into the professions. They reveal first the gradualness of the movement of women into the professions over the course of the nineteenth century. Second, they demonstrate the various paths women pursued to enter the professions, first engaging in apprenticeships and then as professional education and licensure became more formalized, gaining admission to institutions granting the required degrees. In 1835, the sisters Harriot K. and Sarah Hunt completed their medical apprenticeships. Elizabeth Blackwell was the first woman to graduate from medical school (1849); Walsh, *"Doctors Wanted,"* 1. In 1853, Antoinette Brown was ordained a Congregationalist minister at Oberlin College; Barbara Miller Solomon, *In the Company of Educated Women: A History of Women and Higher Education in America* (New Haven: Yale University Press, 1985), 34–37. In 1870, Lemma Barkaloo became the first woman to graduate from law school; Morello, *The Invisible Bar,* 44. At Mount Holyoke, the "shift from the nineteenth-century faculty of pious, Christian ladies to the twentieth-century faculty of productive scholars and intellectuals" began in the 1890s; Glazer and Slater, *Unequal Colleagues,* 27. In 1904, Jessica Blanche Peixoho became the first female faculty member appointed at the University of California at Berkeley; Gordon, *Gender and Higher Education,* 62–63.

7. In 1847, Harriot Hunt applied unsuccessfully to Harvard Medical School; Walsh, *"Doctors Wanted,"* xiv. In 1868, Lemma Barkaloo applied to Harvard Law School; Morello, *The Invisible Bar,* xiii.

8. Anna Quindlen, *Living Out Loud* (New York: Random House, 1988), xvii.

9. Sally Jane Priesand, "Toward a Course of Study for Reform High School Youth Dealing with the Historic and Changing Role of the Jewish Woman," Rabbinic thesis, Hebrew Union College-Jewish Institute of Religion, 1972. This was subsequently published, with some revisions, as *Judaism and the New Woman* (New York: Behrman House, 1975). The date for Regina Jonas's ordination comes from Ellen M. Umansky, "Women's Journey towards Rabbinic Ordination," paper presented at the conference "Exploration and Celebration: An Academic Symposium Honoring the Twentieth Anniversary of Women in the Rabbinate," Hebrew Union College-Jewish Institute of Religion, January 31, 1993, and is based on the work of Katharina Kellenbach.

10. Ellen M. Umansky has published a number of articles touching on this subject, beginning with "Women in Judaism: From the Reform Movement to Contemporary Jewish Religious Feminism," in *Women of Spirit,* 333–54. Among her other works touching upon the same theme are "Spiritual Expressions: Jewish Women's Religious Lives in the Twentieth-Century United States," in *Jewish Women in Historical Perspective,* ed. Judith R. Baskin (Detroit: Wayne State University Press, 1991), 265–88; "Piety, Persuasion and Friendship: A History of Jewish Women's Spirituality," in *Four Centuries of Jewish Women's Spirituality. A Sourcebook,* ed. Ellen Umansky and Dianne Ashton (Boston: Beacon Press, 1992), 1–30.

11. Pamela S. Nadell and Rita J. Simon, "Sisterhood Ladies and Rabbis: Women in the American Reform Synagogue," in *Women in Jewish Culture: An Active Voice,* ed. Maurie Sacks (Urbana: University of Illinois Press, 1995).

12. I am indebted to Professors Michael Meyer and Jonathan Sarna for suggesting the term "functional equivalents" at a seminar during my fellowship at the American Jewish Archives in May 1989. Examples of these functional equivalents were Beatrice Sanders, who succeeded her husband Gilbert as president of Trinidad, Colorado's Temple Aaron in 1952 and for more than two decades conducted its weekly and High Holiday services; Lenell Goodman Ammerman, president of Washington, DC's Temple Sinai from 1965 to 1967; the Cleveland Jewish educator Libbie Braverman; and Paula Ackerman who, in 1950, succeeded her husband, William Ackerman, as rabbi of Beth Israel in Meridian, Mississippi.

13. Jewish Historical Society of Maryland, Microfilm #3/1 Hebrew College, Letters from Henrietta Szold, 1866–1944. Henrietta Szold to her mother, December 2, 1904.

14. Jewish Theological Seminary of America, Joseph and Miriam Ratner Center for the Study of Conservative Judaism. Jewish Theological Seminary Records, RG 3A, Faculty Minutes, Box 2, 1940–41, January 8, 1941, 16.

15. Jewish Theological Seminary of America, Joseph and Miriam Ratner Center for the Study of Conservative Judaism. Jewish Theological Seminary Records, RG IM, Box 153, Letter from Gladys Citrin to Dr. Finkelstein, May 20, 1957; Letter from Louis Finkelstein to Miss Citrin, May 28, 1957.

16. For a discussion of aspects of this, see Nadell and Simon, "Sisterhood Ladies and Rabbis."

17. In 1956, the Central Conference of American Rabbis (CCAR), Reform Judaism's rabbinical association, began to study once again the question of women's ordination. In 1963, at its fiftieth anniversary convention, the women of Reform Judaism at the biennial conference of the National Federation of Temple Sisterhoods resolved in favor of having the College and the CCAR take up the matter once again.

18. American Jewish Archives, Nearprint. Special Topics: Rabbis, Women. Jacob R. Marcus, "The First Woman Rabbi," Press Release, 1972; Samuel S. Cohon, "The History of the Hebrew Union College," *American Jewish Historical Quarterly* 40 (1950–51): 25–26;

the assessment is Michael A. Meyer's in "A Centennial History," in *Hebrew Union College-Jewish Institute of Religion at One Hundred Years,* ed. Samuel E. Karff (n.p.: Hebrew Union College Press, 1976), 18.

19. Those who completed an additional four years in the Collegiate Department, along with attendance at the University of Cincinnati, were ordained rabbis. For two different assessments of Ray Frank, see Reva Clar and William M. Kramer, "The Girl Rabbi of the Golden West: The Adventurous Life of Ray Frank in Nevada, California and the Northwest," *Western States Jewish History* 18 (1986): 99–111, 223–36, 336–51; Umansky, "Women's Journey towards Rabbinic Ordination."

20. Umansky, "Women's Journey towards Rabbinic Ordination."

21. Meyer, "A Centennial History," 137–69. The Jewish Institute of Religion merged with Hebrew Union College in 1950.

22. Irma L. Lindheim, *Parallel Quest: A Search of a Person and a People* (New York: Thomas Yoseloff, 1962), 106.

23. This and what follows are taken from Lindheim, *Parallel Quest;* 106–14 cover her years at the Institute.

24. American Jewish Archives, Mss Collection, #19, 9/7, Faculty Meetings, Minutes 1922–1951, February 2, 1923, March 7, 1923, May 4, 1923; *Jewish Institute of Religion Preliminary Announcement, 1923–1924, 6; Jewish Institute of Religion Catalogue 1946–47, 1947–48, 24.*

25. Lindheim, *Parallel Quest,* 112.

26. Lindheim, *The Immorial Adventure* (New York: Macaulay, 1928).

27. On the controversy with Lipsky, see Hadassah Archives, RG #4 Zionist Organizations and Zionist Institutional History, Box 1, Folders 3, 4, 7. On her later activities, see Hadassah Archives, Microfilm Reel #16 Zionist Political History, Hadassah President's Correspondence Series, RG #7 Irma Lindheim Correspondence, July 26, 1943–August 1, 1963, January 16, 1964–February 10, 1977.

28. William H. Chafe, *The Paradox of Change: American Women in the Twentieth Century* (rev. ed. of *The American Woman,* 1972; New York: Oxford University Press, 1991), 44, 100. On the Jewish press's celebration of Jewish women in new roles, see, for example, Libbian Benedict, "Jewish Women Headliners—XLVIII: Clarice M. Baright—Magistrate," *American Hebrew,* January 1, 1926; "Business Women in Industry," *American Hebrew,* November 5, 1926.

29. Ralph Marcus, "In Memoriam: Norvin R. Lindheim," *Jewish Institute Quarterly* 4, 2 (January 1929; misdated January 1928).

30. Jewish Institute of Religion, Faculty Meeting Minutes, Vol. 1 (September 1922–July 1928); 2 (September 1928–July 1932); 3 (1933–43). Askowith, who entered the Institute in its first year, is discussed in a number of meetings. The faculty concluded that Lindheim's lack of a bachelor's degree was more than made up for by her "background of information and culture" and her work at the Institute that warranted admitting her as a regular student; December 11, 1924.

31. Lindheim, *Parallel Quest,* 201.

Chapter Twelve

Budgets, Boycotts, and Babies
Jewish Women in the Great Depression

Beth S. Wenger

The Great Depression elicited many powerful portraits of American women. During the worst period of the economic crisis, Eleanor Roosevelt called upon the country's women to shoulder the burdens of the Great Depression. "It is [women's] courage and determination," she insisted, "which, time and again, have pulled us through worse crises than the present one."[1] The Great Depression saw women portrayed as selfless and sacrificing, struggling to support their families in hard times. The photographer Dorothea Lange provided perhaps the most enduring image of Depression-era women with her picture of the "Migrant Mother," which captured both the utter despair and the inner strength of a female tenant farmer.[2] But, for most Jewish women, the Great Depression was an event experienced not on the farms or in the Dust Bowl but rather in America's cities and urban neighborhoods. Like other urban women, Jewish women negotiated the challenges of rents, landlords, and grocery bills, using their particular skills as household managers and employing the familiar immigrant traditions of political activism. Within their families and neighborhoods, Jewish women often provided the first line of defense in times of economic crisis.

In order to understand the role of Jewish women, it is important to recognize the particular position of Jews within the Depression-era economy. Jews, as a group, fared better in the Depression than many other Americans because they worked in specific sectors of the economy. Jew's concentration in white-collar and skilled occupations resulted in less severe joblessness for them than was experienced by groups employed predominantly in manual and unskilled positions. Despite their overall economic profile, many Jewish families nonetheless experienced unemployment, downward mobility, and economic insecurity. Moreover, the sharp rise in job discrimination and the very recent attainment of businesses and employment positions by immigrant Jews and their families gave them ample cause for concern in the 1930s. For American Jews, the 1930s were not only a period of economic adversity but also a decade that marked a generational transition. During the 1930s, American Jewry became for the first time a predominantly American-born, rather than an immigrant population.[3] In most Depression-era Jewish households, immigrant mothers were raising American-born daughters. For Jewish women, the Great Depression reflected the intersection of generations. Throughout the economic crisis, Jewish women relied upon the scrupulous budgeting and bargaining techniques that had carried immigrant families through lean years long before the Depression. At the same time, the Depression hastened the arrival of new family patterns, as the daughters of immigrants made their decisions about marriage and childbearing. As a transitional moment for American Jews, as well as a period of economic insecurity, the Great Depression revealed both the enduring necessity of immigrant women's survival strategies and the beginning of new family choices and gender sensibilities among the emerging generation of Jewish women.

Depression-era Jewish households depended upon the collective contributions of all family members. Jewish wives and mothers contributed to the family economy in many ways, ranging from wage-labor to penny-pinching. Jewish women in America typically abandoned wage employment once they married, working for wages at a significantly lower rate than married women of other ethnic groups.[4] Jewish families generally chose to send unmarried daughters, rather than wives, to work outside the home.[5] During the Depression, the work patterns of Jewish families were not measurably altered. Yet, although Jewish wives of the 1930s continued to seek paid employment far less frequently than their non-Jewish counterparts, some Jewish women returned to the labor force when economic need demanded it.[6]

When husbands lost their jobs or the family needed extra income, Jewish women sometimes sought paid employment. The work of married women was usually described as supplemental, both by family members and by Jewish working wives themselves. "I didn't have good jobs, or make a lot of money," one Jewish woman explained about her Depression-era employment, "but I always had a job. If I didn't help out, we couldn't have managed at all."[7] Jewish wives frequently viewed their employment as "helping out," rather than as a legitimate occupation. When asked whether she had worked during the Depression, Rebecca Augenstein initially answered that she had not but later added that she had held a part-time job in a bakery. Augenstein lived with her husband and small children in the Bronx, and, like many Jewish wives, she provided income when her husband lost his job in the fur industry. Augenstein worked half the day until her children returned from school, earned meager wages, and clearly did not regard her job as full-fledged employment. However, she admitted, "I needed that eighty-five cents an hour very badly at that time."[8] In her account of Jewish immigrant women's lives, Sydney Weinberg observes that "daughters remembered, above all, their mothers 'managing' in hard times, when 'managing' frequently meant earning enough money to keep the family together."[9] During the 1930s, Jewish wives moved in and out of the labor force, taking jobs when finances were strained. Although women may have viewed their paid labor as supplemental, their contributions remained crucial to family stability during the Depression years.

By the 1930s, most Jewish families had begun to accept and to internalize American cultural norms that scorned employment outside the home for married women. "My husband never wanted me to work," one Jewish woman explained, "but it was a necessity, so I had to."[10] During the Depression, Jews struggled to balance the need for married women's wages with the desire to attain middle-class respectability. Even the socialist *Jewish Daily Forward*, the leading Yiddish daily, which advocated working-class concerns, wavered in its support for married women's work. Some Forward articles, notably written by women, argued strongly in favor of women's right to remain in the labor force after marriage. "Women have learned to be independent people," wrote one female *Forward* reporter. "They do not consider marriage as a medium to liberate them from work."[11] Echoing those sentiments, another reporter insisted that "married women have exactly the same right to hold their jobs as married men."[12] However, other editorials portrayed wage work by married women as a step backward. Deploring the depths to which impoverished Jewish wives had sunk in order to support their families during the Depression, one *Forward* author lamented,

> Poor Jewish women now look for all kinds of ways to make a living. They peddle; they take in boarders; they raise other people's children. Still others return to the factory. Fifteen years ago, they . . . dreamed that they would ultimately find their destined [mate] and be free of the factory. Now they have their mates, but after fifteen years' time, they must go back to the factory.[13]

In this article, as in many similar statements from the period, the need for married women to work during the Depression came to symbolize the unfulfilled expectations of a generation of immigrants. The image of the full-time housewife whose husband supported the family exerted a powerful influence even within families in which husbands were not the sole breadwinners. Many Jewish families simply could not conform to middle-class notions of proper gendered behavior in marriage. Feeling the weight of cultural norms, most Jews justified married women's work as a temporary necessity during difficult financial periods but never considered it an ideal situation.[14]

When economic necessity demanded that Jewish wives contribute income to the household, they usually chose those jobs that were the least disruptive to the ideal of American domesticity. Factory jobs and other full-time employment carried a stigma for married women, so Jewish wives often performed less visible wage-earning labor. Stanley Katz, who grew up in a middle-class Brooklyn family, re-membered that, during the Depression, his mother began working at home as a seamstress. "She had a small sewing room [in the apartment] and a Singer sewing machine." Working out of the home, she earned extra money, which Katz explained "was an important supplement to the income of the family." Ida Barnett and her husband struggled to make a living during the Depression years, and she regularly worked alongside her husband in the family's Bronx candy store.[15] For many women, the experience of working in the family business offered an acceptable alternative to other forms of wage labor. By working at home or in the family business, Jewish wives were able to earn money for the household while maintain-ing, as much as possible, their domestically centered roles.[16]

More often than they worked for wages, Jewish wives sustained the family economy through careful supervision of the household budget. "You had to buy just so much, had to be careful how to spend the money," explained Tillie Spiegel.

During the Depression, Spiegel's husband had steady employment as a clerk in a government office, and the couple lived on the Grand Concourse, a stylish, upper-middle-class Bronx neighborhood, but nevertheless she prudently monitored expenditures. "I cooked dairy," Spiegel elaborated, "I never skimped on my kids . . . [they also] had steak, meat, liver . . . you had to be economical, that's all."[17] The tasks that Jewish women performed as household managers varied widely, depending on the family's economic fortunes. In middle-income households, women could afford to feed their families well-balanced meals as long as they handled the budget carefully. Serving regular meals became more difficult in poorer families or when family members lost their jobs. In her memoirs, Kate Simon recalled that, during the Depression, "my father was never out of a job; we had fresh rolls and generous helpings of meat and chicken, and my mother bought her soup greens fresh and perky." Food remained inexpensive throughout the Depression, so lower-income families were able to provide regular meals. In Simon's working-class home, her father's steady earnings kept food on the family's table. She reported a much different scenario, however, at a friend's home where the father had long been unemployed. At her friend's table, she ate "two- or three-day-old bread that was bought cheaply at a local bakery and the improvisations on bones, stock of wilted soup greens, beans, and homemade noodles." The mother "saved a little [of the stock] each time to use as the base for the next invention, which might be a stew of carrots, onions, and potatoes, strengthened by another bone or two wheedled from the local butcher."[18]

In times of economic distress, Jewish wives had to become resourceful household managers, learning to shop for and cook foods that were both substantial and inexpensive. Rebecca Augenstein remembered that, during the Depression, she "learned to cook things that were nutritious and that lasted." Taking a lesson from "how my mother fed us in Europe," Augenstein described the content of her family's diet:

> There was a lot of potatoes; eggs were a very nutritional thing, beets—you made a borscht that lasted . . . and [served] chopped meat and chicken only when we had enough money . . . and only for Shabbat, Friday night to bring the Sabbath in.[19]

Jean Margolies, who grew up in one of the poorest sections of the Lower East Side, remembered that her mother refused to buy the cheapest grade of food that local markets sold at reduced prices. "She couldn't afford to give us nice portions," Margolies explained about her mother's marketing strategy. "She said, instead of buying cheap grade that was already half rotten, she'd get more quality and we'd all get small portions, and that's how she managed." When Margolies's father died, her mother struggled to feed the family on an extremely limited income. "She would shop every day for fresh milk and vegetables. . . . She always did her own baking. She even used to churn her own butter." Although the family ultimately applied for government assistance, Margolies remembered that "relief was only enough for bare necessities" and that it was her mother's ability to extend scarce resources that sustained the family during the worst years of the Depression.[20]

Federal relief investigators were often incredulous at women's ability to devise household strategies that stretched the family dollar. One investigator, assigned to review the welfare application of the Berger family, did not believe that the family of four could possibly manage on the five dollars a week that they claimed constituted the household food budget. Although the investigator stated that "there seemed to be little more than potatoes" when he examined the kitchen cupboard, he asked Mrs. Berger to keep a daily record of her food expenses. Three weeks later, the investigator reported:

> Mr. Berger presented a diet list kept by his wife. The family seems to have been living on a diet which excludes milk, meat, or fish. They use potatoes, evaporated milk, canned fish, etc. . . . Mrs. Berger . . . managed with what she had on hand.[21]

After reviewing the evidence, the relief investigator questioned the truthfulness of the Bergers' statement and turned the case over to the staff nutritionist for a final decision. Rejecting the Bergers' application, the nutritionist claimed that "the family could not have lived on this budget for any length of time without seriously impairing their health."[22] Such encounters between trained investigators and Jewish housewives revealed the wide gulf that existed between professional attempts to regulate the family diet and the daily realities of stretching the food budget.

In addition to applying prudence and imagination to the purchasing and preparation of food, Jewish women also found other ways to extend the family dollar. Jean Margolies recalled that her mother scrupulously monitored the family's use of electricity. "My mother was very careful. She made sure that we turned the lights off early at night. . . . She was frugal; she had to be." Margolies also reported that, in order to save five cents, her mother regularly restocked the ice box by carrying the heavy ice to the apartment on her back. Ice delivery cost ten cents, but the same product could be purchased "cash and carry" for only a nickel.[23] When welfare investigators questioned the Berger family, Mrs. Berger "explained that she watches every penny; that her husband takes his lunch with him and that her boy walks to school because they do not have the carfare to give him."[24] In order to clothe her family inexpensively during the Depression, Lillian Gorenstein scoured Coney Island's bargain stores for cloth remnants that she then stitched into garments "all by hand, since I had no sewing machine." In the worst years of the crisis, her husband, Saul, used cardboard inserts to preserve old pairs of shoes. Only after Saul Gorenstein found a secure government job did the family begin resoling shoes and purchasing more expensive clothing.[25] Jewish women's daily efforts to stretch limited resources carried their families through the difficult years of the Depression. Many immigrant women had years of experience supporting their families through slack seasons and periodic unemployment and brought their proven budgeting strategies to the challenges of the Great Depression. Whether working for wages, feeding the family, or extending the household budget, immigrant Jewish women provided vital, though often unrecognized, contributions to the family economy.

Jewish women's Depression-era activities became more visible when they reached beyond the home to the neighborhood streets. Since the early twentieth century, immigrant Jewish women had been central players in neighborhood rent strikes and consumer protests. When deteriorating economic conditions rekindled local Jewish activism in the 1930s, Jewish women once again took a leading role in neighborhood protests. During the Depression, working-class Jewish districts became frequent scenes of eviction resistance, rent strikes, and consumer boycotts. As in earlier protest movements, Jewish women emerged as preeminent political actors in the Depression-era campaigns that took place within their neighborhoods. In 1932, when Jewish residents of the Bronx organized a series of rent strikes that resulted in several evictions, Jewish women stood on the front lines of the often violent demonstrations. At Allerton Avenue, where approximately one thousand residents protested the eviction of twelve families, the *New York Times* reported that a "swarm of women" surrounded and threatened police officers until a mounted division arrived to disperse them.[26] Another New York newspaper noted that, even after the police had cleared the block and begun moving furniture into the street, "many residents of the house, mostly women, leaned from the windows of their apartments, hissing and jeering at the marshal and his crew."[27] Unlike the English-language newspapers, which tended to describe female activists as hysterical and irrational, the Yiddish press was more sympathetic to the strike cause and expressed greater approbation for women's contributions. "The strike is organized by the men but it is led by the women," explained the *Jewish Daily Forward*. "Such is the way in all the rent strikes that are going on today in greater New York. The women are the fighters, the pickets, the agitators. A remarkable bravery and battle-cheer is displayed by the women in the rent strikes."[28] Strikers often capitalized upon the emotional and strategic value of placing women on the front lines. At one demonstration, protesters implored, "We need women to come out and sock the cops."[29] Whether fighting to lower the cost of food or defending evicted tenants, women were at the heart of the political crusades brewing in Jewish neighborhoods.

Married and middle-aged women, often removed from party politics and trade unions, led the public campaigns in Jewish neighborhoods. Describing the protesters, the *Forward* pointed out that "some of them are housewives from large families, mothers with small children that in a normal time could not go out of the house for a minute, but now they stand half the day in the picket line [and] attend strike meetings."[30] Not all Jewish wives committed their energies to the cause. Kate Simon, who grew up in the Bronx co-ops, recalled that "My mother never responded [to the strikers call to protest]. She said the women who did were '*mishigoyim*' looking for excitement, anything to get away from their sinks and kids."[31] Yet, those women who chose to participate in the strikes often maintained informal neighborhood support networks that helped care for their families during the protests. During the demonstrations, women cooperated with child care and cooked meals for one another's families. When one woman was arrested on a Friday morning, the other women in her building took over Sabbath preparations for her family. The neighborhood context of rent strikes both motivated women to fight for their homes and families and provided the support networks that enabled them to do so.[32]

For working-class Jewish women, the high cost of rent and food constituted a direct threat to their roles as wives, mothers, and household managers. For example, in 1935, when the price of kosher meat became too inflated for Depression-era wages, Jewish women initiated a citywide kosher meat boycott, calling for a ten-cent-a-pound reduction in prices.[33] The high price of kosher meat had plagued Jewish consumers for years, precipitating sporadic consumer boycotts for more than three decades. Inflated meat prices were particularly devastating to household economies during the Great Depression. As the *Forward* explained, "With the small wages that workers bring home today, it is absolutely impossible for their wives to buy what is needed at home."[34] By the 1930s, Jewish women had gained a generation of experience in leading consumer protests and brought their seasoned talents to the 1935 campaign.[35] Under the banner of the City Action Committee against the High Cost of Living, Jewish women conducted a persistent meat boycott that in less than a week closed an estimated three thousand to 4,500 New York butcher shops. Beginning in the activist neighborhoods of Brooklyn and the Bronx, the protests spread quickly throughout the city. Violence erupted on several occasions as strikers assaulted "scabbers," people seen purchasing meat during the boycott.[36] The 1935 meat boycott ultimately achieved limited success. After being closed for a week, retail butcher shops gradually began reopening, despite the ongoing protests. Some shops reduced poultry prices by as much as nine cents a pound, but the Meat Trust remained a powerful force. Nevertheless, the meat boycott demonstrated women's evolving political roles and indicated the far-reaching consequences of their responsibilities as household managers. Throughout the Great Depression, Jewish women's abilities to budget, bargain, and, if necessary, engage in public protest sustained Jewish families in times of economic hardship.[37]

While immigrant Jewish wives and mothers relied upon proven survival strategies to carry their families through the vicissitudes of the Depression, Jewish daughters also played an important economic role within the family. During the Depression, unmarried daughters were still expected to contribute to the family economy, and most continued to work for wages. Their mothers had labored in the factories before marriage, but, by the 1930s, Jewish daughters gravitated toward clerical employment, rather than factory work. A 1935 survey conducted by the Welfare Council of New York City revealed that almost three-quarters of young Jewish women had received some vocational training, most in bookkeeping and stenography.[38] Clerical workers fared better during the Depression than factory and unskilled laborers, so Jewish women were often able to secure employment even in hard times. The *Forward* noted that a young woman could "find a job more quickly than a boy her age."[39] Because young women sometimes found employment more easily and because many families allowed sons to remain in school longer, Jewish daughters retained their role as family wage-earners during the Great Depression.

In many cases, daughters abandoned schooling to look for work so that sons could continue their educations. The combination of birth order and gender expectations generally determined work and educational patterns within Jewish families. The Welfare Council survey documented several cases in which Jewish daughters worked while their brothers furthered their educations. One typical case history reported: "A family of five, the oldest a Jewish youth of twenty and an eighteen-year-old girl, were the children of a Polish Jew, who owned a grocery store in lower Manhattan. The boy was in his last year in college, while the girl was a clerk at fifteen dollars a week in a dress factory."[40] Women were more likely to pursue education if they had older siblings. The third of five children, Anna Kfare described a typical situation: her two older sisters worked in the millinery industry, while the two younger brothers remained in school. With two sisters earning regular wages, Kfare completed the eighth grade but then enrolled in a commercial school, "because that was a lead to earning a living." After getting a job, Kfare pursued her education at night and earned a diploma from Morris Evening High School in 1935. The demands of full-time work clearly derailed her intellectual aspirations. "I went to high school at night," she recalled. "I thought I would go to college . . . but I was missing some credits . . . and I was working and so I gave up."[41]

Young Jewish women of the Depression era often served as family breadwinners for an extended period of time, postponing marriage during the economic crisis. Like other American youth, the children of Jewish immigrants responded to the uncertainty of the Depression and the scarcity of employment by rethinking decisions about marriage and childbearing. During the 1930s, the national marriage rate declined precipitously, falling from 10.1 marriages per thousand in 1929 to 7.9 during the worst year of the Depression, in 1932.[42] Unemployment, lack of financial resources, and monetary obligations to the family forced many Americans to postpone or cancel marriage plans. In the Welfare Council survey, 32 percent of men and 21 percent of women over the age of eighteen indicated that the Depression had interfered with their intentions to marry.[43] Jewish youth tended to marry at an even lower rate than their non-Jewish counterparts, a statistic that the Welfare Council attributed to their remaining in school longer. Although more than 12 percent of non-Jewish youth between the ages of sixteen and twenty-five had married by 1935, only 8 percent of young Jewish men and women had chosen to marry.[44] Marriage rates plummeted across the nation during the worst years of the Depression, but Jews demonstrated a particular tendency to avoid marriage in the wake of the economic crisis.

Obligations to the family contributed to the postponement of marriage. The *Jewish Daily Forward,* which covered the declining rate of Jewish marriage with great concern, chronicled in some detail the many economic constraints that kept young Jews from marrying. In 1933, the *Forward* reported:

> Nowadays there are thousands and thousands of families where only one family member earns anything and brings a few dollars to the household. The ten or fifteen or thirty dollars a week that one [family member] earns must maintain the whole family. If that one is a boy or a girl of marriageable age, he or she cannot think about getting married.[45]

Even when they were not the only wage earners in the family, many young Jews described similar feelings of household obligation. "My father is without work, and I must help out my family with my earnings," one young Jewish woman explained. "I have a young man who I would like to marry, but, under such circumstances, I can no longer think about getting married."[46]

The deteriorating economy not only made children's earnings particularly important to the family but also seriously hampered a young couple's ability to establish financial independence. "A lot of fellas didn't make a living," Jean Margolies recalled, so marriage seemed impractical.[47] Louis Kfare, a Bronx native who reached his twenties during the Depression, remembered that he and his girlfriend considered marriage. However, Kfare explained, "I realized that how could I have a wife, with what? I was earning peanuts. . . . How will I support a wife? How will I pay rent?" Kfare conceded that the couple probably could have managed somehow, "but I was too yellow, too scared."[48] Given the dearth of employment opportunities and the lack of job security, many young Jews believed that it was impossible or at least inadvisable to start their own families. Of course, young Jews did marry during the Depression years. After reaching its lowest point in 1932, the marriage rate gradually rebounded. Alfred Kazin remembered that, despite economic conditions, "many of my friends were getting married and moving in with the wife's family."[49] The combination of family obligations, lack of secure employment, and uncertain future prospects delayed many wedding plans, but postponement rather than cancelation of marriage characterized the experience of most Jewish couples.[50]

Young Jewish women of the 1930s not only married later than their mothers but also expressed a desire to modify the family patterns constructed by their immigrant parents. Young Jews who had been reared and educated in an American environment brought a variety of new expectations to their marriages and families. Jewish sons and daughters had come of age in a culture that celebrated romantic love, and they envisioned the family not only as an economic unit but also as a source of personal happiness and fulfillment.[51] Unlike many of their parents, young Jews often underscored the primary importance of attraction and romantic feelings when choosing their mates. "So far as I knew, love was not an element in my parents' experience," Alfred Kazin recalled, noting that immigrant couples "always had the look of being committed to something deeper than *mere* love. Their marriages were neither happy nor unhappy; they were arrangements."[52] Like other Americans their age, young Jews looked for love and companionship, even as the Depression forced them to view marriage pragmatically.

Once they chose their mates, young Jews reformulated Jewish family patterns. Young Jewish women of the Depression era postponed childbearing and had fewer children than their mothers had had in an earlier generation. The national birthrate fell from 21.3 live births per thousand in 1930 to 18.4 by 1933.[53] But the Jewish birthrate dropped even more precipitously than the national average. Even before the Depression, Jews had demonstrated a lower birthrate than the rest of the country. Since the early twentieth century, Jewish fertility had been low in absolute numbers, as well as in comparison to other American ethnic groups.[54] The economic crisis and the decrease in marriages during the 1930s only accelerated that trend. In 1930, Jews had sixty-nine births for every one hundred births among white Americans. Between 1920 and 1940, the decline in Jewish fertility was twice that of the native white population.[55]

The Yiddish press carefully monitored the falling Jewish birthrate and expressed great concern about the Depression's effect upon Jews considering parenthood. "In the past, women used to have as many children as 'God had given,' " declared one *Forward* reporter, nostalgically altering the history of Jewish fertility. The

Depression, he lamented, "has terrified parents about having children. Now, when one has only a few children, it is difficult to give them a means of support."[56] Like other Americans, second-generation Jews adjusted their decisions about childbearing according to changing economic circumstances. Although Jewish family size had been decreasing before the onset of the Depression, the economic crisis prompted more Jewish couples to postpone parenthood and to have fewer children.

As the lower birthrate indicates, Jewish women also demonstrated a greater tendency to control their fertility through contraception and family planning. By the 1930s, the birth control movement had gained momentum in America, fueled by growing popular support and fewer restrictions on the distribution of contraceptives.[57] The country as a whole grew more accepting of birth control during the Depression years, but American Jews relied upon contraception and family planning to a greater extent than other Americans. One Jewish demographer observed that Jewish fertility followed the overall trends of the general population, "but patterns of response to period societal change were relatively earlier, sharper, and faster as appropriate to a nearly perfectly contracepting population."[58] A study of the Bronx women who attended Margaret Sanger's Birth Control Clinical Research Bureau in 1931 and 1932 confirmed such assertions. The clinic, which served a largely white-collar population, reported that its Jewish clients used contraception far more frequently than women of other religious groups.[59] Corroborating previous findings about the prevalent use of birth control among Jews, the authors of a 1939 study concluded that, "Regardless of economic or educational status . . . urban American Jews constitute the most ardent birth controlling group in the population."[60]

Delayed marriages and fewer children were obvious signs of change for Jewish women coming of age in the 1930s, but the Depression years also brought the first tentative steps toward redefining gender roles within Jewish families. During the Great Depression, a fierce debate about married women's work swept the country. Throughout the economic crisis, women were accused of taking jobs from men and working only for "pin-money."[61] A 1936 Gallup poll reported that 82 percent of Americans believed that wives should not work if their husbands were employed.[62] As previously noted, the Jewish press expressed a range of opinion about work for wages by married women. Some critics considered married women's employment a sign of newfound independence, while others viewed it as a temporary necessity at best and a deviation from the ideal family structure. Since, during the Depression, the number of Jewish wives in the labor force remained relatively small, the discussions about married women's paid employment within the Jewish community were largely a mirror of the broader debate taking place throughout the country, as well as a reflection of gender expectations in Jewish families. Within the immigrant Jewish community, some support for the right of married women to work could be heard, but most Jews aspired to the American middle-class ideal, which prescribed that husbands be the sole breadwinners. The children of immigrants also aspired to that ideal, yet, interestingly, when young Jewish men and women articulated their opinions about married women's wage labor, they expressed attitudes about gender roles in marriage that differed somewhat from those of their immigrant parents.

On a practical level, Jewish youth of the Depression era understood that economic pressures placed new demands on both husband and wife. Moreover, young Jews often claimed to hold more progressive views about women and to reject the subservient role assigned to Jewish women in the traditional Jewish family. In 1931, the Yiddish newspaper *The Day* sponsored an essay contest, directed toward Jewish youth, that offered ten dollars to the contributor who best discussed the question of whether a "fifty-fifty marriage" was preferable to a traditional marriage arrangement. *The Day's* editors explained that, in a "fifty-fifty marriage," both the husband and wife worked for wages and provided equal economic contributions to the family. (Sharing household responsibilities was never mentioned.)[63] Almost half of the contest entrants advocated a marriage of equals. "The men have as their ideal a girl with the ability to handle two life jobs—career and home," reported the editors.[64] One young man's letter demanded, "Why cannot the woman with her newly found economic freedom help her husband in productivity so that their aims and ideals may be mutually attained?"[65]

Yet, while many letters supported a "modern" approach to marriage, most indicated that the "fifty-fifty" arrangement should be temporary, terminating once the couple had children. The young man who had argued fervently in support of a marriage of two employed partners added that "I am not speaking of the mother. The proper care of a child consumes all the time and energy that a mother can give."[66] The prize-winning essay, written by a young Jewish woman, unequivocally rejected the traditional Jewish marriage arrangement in which the woman "was merely a puppet" with no outlet for independence. She also acknowledged the difficult economic constraints that weighed upon Jewish couples and advocated shared economic responsibility within the family, but only until the birth of children:

> The man may not be in a position financially to establish and keep up a home so that the woman is forced to continue working to assist him. This may be a very satisfactory arrangement for a short time but, certainly, to keep it up would be to defeat the fundamental purpose of marriage,—that of bringing into the world, and rearing children.[67]

Young Jews, *The Day* explained, had "respect for women's integrity as an individual over and above her biologic role" and approved of a childless married woman's work, but they retained traditional notions about motherhood.[68] Given the hostility toward paid employment for married women, the views expressed by Jewish youth in the contest were rather progressive. Nevertheless, although most of the entrants described their attitudes as a modern rejection of their parents' values, they reflected less a departure from immigrant family models than an acceptance of middle-class American norms. Much like the opinions offered by an older generation of Jews, most of the contest letters portrayed married women's work as a temporary necessity and generally condemned mothers who worked. The younger Jewish generation, familiar with the rhetoric and accomplishments of the women's movement and the suffrage campaign, did articulate a new respect for women's abilities and independence, but they proposed only a modest reformulation of gender roles.

The emerging generation of Jews did not radically revise gender roles in marriage. Yet, young Jewish women of the 1930s came of age in households very different from those they would create in later years. Jewish daughters of the Depression era waited longer to marry, postponed having children, and chose to limit the size of their families—patterns that continue to define American Jewish families to the present day. The economic realities of the Depression hastened the demographic changes in Jewish women's lives, but gender roles evolved more gradually. Young Jewish women who had been reared and educated in an American environment brought new gender expectations to their marriages, but they continued to define themselves primarily by their familial roles as wives and mothers.

The Great Depression was not a watershed event for American Jewish women but rather a window that revealed the gradual changes in Jewish women's lives. The Depression arrived at a generational crossroads, requiring the economic survival strategies of immigrant mothers and modifying the family patterns of their daughters. The economic upheaval of the 1930s advanced the generational transition, producing a sharp alteration in marriage and childbearing decisions, yet the Great Depression was less a decisive turning point for Jewish women than a temporary crisis that furthered the steady evolution of Jewish women's identities and gender roles in America.

NOTES

Portions of this chapter are taken from my book, *New York Jews and the Great Depression: Uncertain Promise* (New Haven, CT: Yale University Press, 1996).

1. Eleanor Roosevelt, *It's Up to the Women* (New York: Frederick A. Stokes, 1933), ix.

2. For reproductions and discussions of Lange's "Migrant Mother," see Lawrence W. Levine, "The Historian and the Icon: Photography and the History of the American People in the 1930s and 1940s," 16–17, and Alan Trachtenberg, "From Image to Story: Reading the File," 68–70, in *Documenting America, 1935–1943,* ed. Carl Fleischhauer and Beverly W. Brannan (Berkeley: University of California Press, 1988).

3. Lloyd P. Gartner, "The Midpassage of American Jewry," in *The American Jewish Experience,* ed. Jonathan D. Sarna (New York: Holmes and Meier, 1986), 230; Abraham G. Duker, "Socio-Psychological Trends in the American Jewish Community Since 1900," *YIVO Annual of Jewish Social Science* 9 (1954): 167; Arthur Hertzberg, *The Jews in America: Four Centuries of an Uneasy Encounter: A History* (New York: Simon Schuster, 1989), 280; J. B. Maller, "A Study of Jewish Neighborhoods in New York City," *Jewish Social Service Quarterly* 10, no. 4 (June 1934): 272, 274.

4. In 1911, only 1 percent of married Jewish women in New York worked for wages, as opposed to 36 percent of Italian wives. Between 1910 and 1925, the percentage of Jewish women in the labor force declined as Jewish men attained a higher socioeconomic status and Jewish women came to accept American behavioral norms that celebrated married women's role within the home. For more on the East European tradition of married women's work and the role of Jewish wives in the American labor force, see Paula Hyman, "Culture and Gender: Women in the Immigrant Jewish Community," in *The Legacy of Jewish Migration: 1881 and Its Impact,* ed. David Berger (New York: Brooklyn College Press, 1983), 157–68;

see also Hyman, "Gender and the Immigrant Experience in the United States," in *Jewish Women in Historical Perspective,* ed. Judith R. Baskin (Detroit: Wayne State University Press, 1991), 225–26; Thomas Kessner, *The Golden Door: Italian and Jewish Immigrant Mobility in New York City, 1880–1915* (New York: Oxford University Press, 1977), 76; see statistical comparison of several ethnic groups in Elizabeth H. Pleck, "A Mother's Wages: Income Earning among Married Italian and Black Women, 1896–1911," in *A Heritage of Her Own: Toward a New Social History of American Women,* ed. Nancy F. Cott and Elizabeth H. Pleck (New York: Simon and Schuster, 1979), 372.

5. For a detailed discussion of the economic contributions of immigrant Jewish wives and the tendency of Jewish daughters rather than wives to assume wage-work, see Susan A. Glenn, *Daughters of the Shtetl: Life and Labor in the Immigrant Generation* (Ithaca: Cornell University Press, 1990), 50–89.

6. Immigrant Jews inherited a cultural tradition that supported married women's work. In Eastern Europe, Jewish wives regularly contributed to the household economy. The Jewish cultural *ideal* celebrated Jewish women who worked as storekeepers or small businesswomen in order to enable their husbands to pursue religious study. Although very few Jewish men actually engaged in full-time Talmudic study while their wives supported the family, immigrant Jews had been raised in an environment that legitimated the role of married women as breadwinners. Hyman, "Gender and the Immigrant Experience in the United States," 224–25.

7. Rose S., cited in Sydney Stahl Weinberg, *The World of Our Mothers: The Lives of Jewish Immigrant Women* (Chapel Hill: University of North Carolina Press, 1988), 229.

8. Personal interview, Rebecca Augenstein, August 26, 1991, New Haven, Connecticut (Augenstein's recollection of earning eighty-five cents an hour in part-time wages may not reflect the actual amount of her wages at the time.)

9. Weinberg, *The World of Our Mothers,* 235. Weinberg also points out that Jewish women derived satisfaction from their work and sometimes pursued their careers because they enjoyed the experience of working.

10. Rose S., cited in ibid., 229.

11. *Jewish Daily Forward,* April 4, 1935, 9.

12. *Jewish Daily Forward,* April 12, 1933, 3; see also ibid.

13. *Jewish Daily Forward,* June 18, 1931, 8.

14. Susan Glenn briefly discusses the conflicts that daughters of immigrants felt about married women's work. Glenn, *Daughters of the Shtetl,* 238–240.

15. Personal interview, Stanley Katz, August 23, 1991, New Haven, Connecticut; Personal interview, Ida Barnett, September 1, 1991, New Haven, Connecticut.

16. Glenn, *Daughters of the Shtetl,* 240.

17. Personal interview, Tillie Spiegel, August 22, 1991, New Haven, Connecticut.

18. Kate Simon, *A Wider World: Portraits in an Adolescence* (New York: Harper and Row, 1986), 110, 109.

19. Interview, Rebecca Augenstein.

20. Personal interview, Jean Margolies, August 27, 1991, New Haven, Connecticut.

21. Eli Ginzberg, "Urban Jewish Immigrants: The Bergers," case history included in *The Great Depression,* ed. David A. Shannon (Englewood Cliffs, NJ: Prentice Hall, 1960), 162, 160–62.

22. Ibid., 162.

23. Interview, Jean Margolies.

24. Eli Ginzberg, "Urban Jewish Immigrants: The Bergers," 161.

25. Lillian Gorenstein, unpublished memoirs, in possession of the author. Thanks to Arthur Goren for providing me with his mother's rich reminiscences of the Depression.

26. *New York Times,* February 9, 1932, 18. For an account of earlier Jewish women's political activism within the neighborhood, see Jenna Weissman Joselit, "The Landlord as Czar: Pre-World War I Tenant Activity," in *The Tenant Movement in New York City, 1904–1984,* ed. Ronald Lawson (New Brunswick, NJ: Rutgers University Press, 1986), 39–50; Paula E. Hyman, "Immigrant Women and Consumer Protest: The New York City Kosher Meat Boycott of 1902," *American Jewish History* 70 no. 1 (September 1980): 91–105.

27. *Bronx Home News,* January 29, 1932, 3; for a variety of accounts of the Allerton Avenue rent strike, see *Jewish Daily Forward,* January 29 1932, 1, 9; February 2, 1932, 1, 10; *New York Times,* January 30, 1932, 19; February 9, 1932, 18; *Bronx Home News,* January 29, 1932, 3; February 8, 1932, 3; see also Mark Naison, "From Eviction to Rent Control: Tenant Activism in the Great Depression," in Lawson, ed., *The Tenant Movement in New York City,* 103–5.

28. *Jewish Daily Forward,* January 21, 1932, 3; the *Forward* article went so far as to suggest that men involved in the strike should learn from the example of commitment and militancy set by the women.

29. *New York Times,* February 27, 1932, 17.

30. *Jewish Daily Forward,* January 21, 1932, 3.

31. Simon, *A Wider World,* 13.

32. Interview, Anna Taffler, January 8, 1978, Oral History of the American Left Collection, Tamiment Library, New York University. Reports of arrests, carried in virtually every newspaper report, showed that women were regular, even predominant, participants in neighborhood protests. Newspaper reports also included the ages of those arrested and showed that protesters ranged from adolescents to middle-aged men and women. Jewish women's informal networks had been crucial to neighborhood politics since the early twentieth century. See Hyman, "Immigrant Women and Consumer Protest."

33. For a few of the many accounts of the meat boycott, see *Jewish Daily Forward,* May 15, 1935, 4; May 26, 1935, Section I, 12; May 27, 1935, 1, 9; May 28, 1935, 1, 3, 6, 14; May 29, 1935, 1, 13; June 1, 1935, 16; *The Day,* May 25, 1935, 2; May 29, 1935, 1, 5; May 31, 1935, 1; June 1, 1935, 1, 6; *New York Times,* May 28, 1935, 27; May 31, 1935, 17; June 1, 1935, 8; *Bronx Home News,* May 23, 1935, 1; May 24, 1935, 3; May 25, 1935, 3; May 28, 1935, 3; May 29, 1935, 3; May 31, 1935, 3.

34. *Jewish Daily Forward,* May 28, 1935, 14, 3. Jewish women perceived the boycott as a distinctly female political activity and even suggested that women were more capable and committed to the campaign than men. In a letter to the *Forward,* one woman implored Jewish men to stand firm in boycotting meat, expressing absolute certainty that women would never waver in their resolve. See ibid.

35. For examples of previous kosher meat boycotts, see Hyman, "Immigrant Women and Consumer Protest"; Dana Frank, "Housewives, Socialists, and the Politics of Food: The 1917 New York Cost-of-Living Protests," *Feminist Studies* 11 (summer 1985): 255–86; Joselit, "The Landlord as Czar," 41–42.

36. For a few examples of arrests, see *The Day,* May 31, 1935, 1; *Jewish Daily Forward,* June 6, 1935, 14; *Bronx Home News,* May 31, 1935, 3; *New York Times,* May 31, 1935, 17.

37. *Jewish Daily Forward,* May 28, 1935, 1, 3, 6, 14; May 27, 1935, 1, 9; *The Day,* May 29, 1935, 1, 7; *New York Times,* May 27, 1935, 3; May 28, 1935, 27; *Bronx Home News,* May 25, 1935, 3. While Jewish women had engaged in consumer boycotts long before

the Depression, the 1935 campaign did differ in many important respects from earlier protests. The boycott that began in kosher butcher shops quickly spread to nonkosher shops, as well. The strike also gained support in non-Jewish neighborhoods, particularly in Harlem, as working women united to combat a shared consumer problem. Jewish women initiated and predominated in the campaign, but the City Action Committee was an umbrella organization that included women's groups from the African American community and Communist and Socialist associations, as well as settlement houses and mutual benefit societies. In transcending ethnic boundaries and linking the grass-roots efforts of several neighborhoods, the 1935 boycott exhibited a breadth of organization not evident in earlier protests.

For more on the activities, composition, and accomplishments of the City Action Committee against the High Cost of Living and of women's activism in the 1930s, see Annelise Orleck, *Common Sense and a Little Fire: Women and Working-Class Politics in the United States, 1900–1965* (Chapel Hill: University of North Carolina Press, 1995), 234–40. Orleck suggests that women's activism in the 1930s reflected more sophisticated political strategy, in part because the women involved had participated in the garment industry strikes and unionization movement during the first decades of the twentieth century, as well as in earlier neighborhood protests.

38. Nettie Pauline McGill, "Some Characteristics of Jewish Youth in New York City," *Jewish Social Service Quarterly* 14, no. 2 (December 1937): 259.

39. *Jewish Daily Forward,* November 12, 1930, 6.

40 Nettie Pauline McGill and Ellen Nathalie Matthews, *The Youth of New York City* (New York: Macmillan, 1940), 28.

41. Personal interview, Anna Kfare, August 18, 1991, New Haven, Connecticut.

42. Milkman, "Women's Work and the Economic Crisis: Some Lessons from the Great Depression," in Cott and Pleck, eds., *A Heritage of Her Own,* 523.

43. McGill and Matthews, *The Youth of New York City,* 30.

44. McGill, "Some Characteristics of Jewish Youth in New York City," 255–56.

45. *Jewish Daily Forward,* February 28, 1933, 4. For other examples of articles about declining marriage rates, see *Jewish Daily Forward,* January 18, 1931; May 28, 1934, 3; July 24, 1931, 4.

46. Ibid., May 28, 1934, 3.

47. Interview, Jean Margolies.

48. Personal interview, Louis Kfare, August 26, 1991, New Haven, Connecticut.

49. Alfred Kazin, *Starting Out in the Thirties* (Boston: Little, Brown, 1965; rep. ed., Ithaca: Cornell University Press, 1989), 78.

50. John Modell, *Into One's Own: From Youth to Adulthood in the United States, 1920–1975* (Berkeley: University of California Press, 1989), 132–40. Modell offers interesting insights into the different marriage patterns among various occupational groups. See also his provocative discussion about the development of the notion of engagement during the Depression years, 140–53.

51. Lois Scharf, *To Work and to Wed: Female Employment, Feminism, and the Great Depression* (Westport, CT: Greenwood Press, 1980), 145–46.

52. Kazin, *A Walker in the City,* 56, 55.

53. Susan Ware, *Holding Their Own: American Women in the 1930s* (Boston: Twayne, 1982), 7.

54. Calvin Goldscheider and Alan S. Zuckerman, *The Transformation of the Jews* (Chicago: University of Chicago Press, 1984), 177.

55. Arthur A. Goren, *The American Jews: Dimensions of Ethnicity* (Cambridge, MA:

Belknap Press, Harvard University Press, 1980), 76; Sidney Goldstein, "Jews in the United States: Perspectives from Demography," in *American Jews: A Reader,* ed. Marshall Sklare (New York: Behrman House, 1983), 58–59, 63, 70.

56. *Jewish Daily Forward,* May 28, 1934, 3.

57. A 1936 Gallup poll reported that 63 percent of Americans approved of both the teaching and the practice of birth control; a *Ladies Home Journal* survey rated women's endorsement of contraception at 79 percent. Moreover, birth control became more widely available as a result of both the growing commercialization of contraceptives and a 1936 federal appeals court decision that removed all previous federal bans on their distribution. By 1938, more than three hundred birth control clinics were operating across the nation. Ware, *Holding Their Own,* 7; John D'Emilio and Estelle B. Freedman, *Intimate Matters: A History of Sexuality in America* (New York: Harper and Row, 1988), 244–46; Linda Gordon, *Woman's Body, Woman's Right: A Social History of Birth Control in America* (New York: Penguin, 1976), 301–40. See also Gordon's discussion of the ideological and tactical shift in the birth control movement during this period.

58. Sergio Della Pergolla, cited in Goldstein, "Jews in the United States: Perspectives from Demography," 70.

59. Regine K. Stix and Frank W. Nottestein, *Controlled Fertility: An Evaluation of Clinic Service* (Baltimore: Williams and Wilkins, 1940), 10–12, 28–29.

60. Raymond Pearl, *The Natural History of Population* (New York: Oxford University Press, 1939), 242–43. During the Depression, Jewish women organized to demonstrate their support for the birth control movement. In 1933, the National Council of Jewish Women (NCJW) opened the first birth control clinic operating under explicitly Jewish auspices. Located in Brooklyn, the Mother's Health clinic provided advice and information about birth control to a very select population. The Clinic served only married women referred to the office by a social agency when they were unable to pay for medical services elsewhere. In addition, the NCJW indicated that the clinic provided contraceptive information only when the health of the woman was at stake. Despite the limited clientele served by the clinic, its Jewish sponsorship represented a significant formal endorsement of birth control on the part of Jewish women. *Jewish Daily Bulletin,* March 9, 1933, 2.

61. Scharf, *To Work and to Wed,* 43–65. Disapproval of married women's work gained government support in the so-called married persons clause contained in Section 213 of the National Economy Act of 1932. The legislation, which prohibited more than one family member from working in the federal civil service, came to symbolize nationwide condemnation of married women's employment. Scharf presents a detailed discussion of this legislation and other issues surrounding women's labor force participation in the Great Depression.

62. Ware, *Holding Their Own: American Women in the 1930s,* 27.

63. *The Day,* February 1, 1931, 8; March 1, 1931, 8.

64. *The Day,* March 1, 1931, 8; see also *The Day,* April 3, 1932, 8; October 18, 1930, 16.

65. *The Day,* March 8, 1931, 8.

66. Ibid. The majority of letters argued that a mother should not work for wages. However, there were notable exceptions. For a letter written by a Jewish woman that supported a mother's right to work, see ibid., April 3, 1932, 8.

67. *The Day,* March 1, 1931, 8.

68. Ibid.

Chapter Thirteen

Angels "Rewolt!"
Jewish Women in Modern Dance in the 1930s

Julia L. Foulkes

In the late 1920s, the modern dancer and choreographer Doris Humphrey noted that the "piles of Jewish girls" in her company "moved like angels."[1] Dancing in such works as Martha Graham's "Heretic" (1929) and Humphrey's "Life of the Bee" (1929), which dramatized Maurice Maeterlinck's 1901 study on the hierarchical authority of the queen bee and the pitiless duties of worker bees, Jewish women quickly put themselves in the middle of a dance revolution. Although the leaders of modern dance in the 1930s—Martha Graham, Doris Humphrey, Charles Weidman, and Hanya Holm—were not Jewish, Jewish women filled modern dance classes, companies, organizations, picket lines, and concert audiences. Teachers, such as Blanche Talmud and Edith Segal, taught performers, such as Lily Mehlman and Lillian Shapero; performances by choreographers, such as Anna Sokolow and Sophie Maslow, were reviewed by critics, such as Edna Ocko; while organizers, such as Helen Tamiris and Fanya Geltman, hassled labor unions and the federal government for increased attention to dance. These efforts in substantiating a new art form have been overlooked because our view of the arts tends to focus on a few stars, emphasizing individual genius rather than collective momentum and organizational drive. Jewish women shaped the foundation of modern dance, and in the mid-1930s their impact was well enough known that the eminent social commentator Fanny Brice could unleash her satire on the subject, playing Martha Graham in a sketch entitled "Modernistic Moe," in which she cried "Rewolt!" in a Yiddish accent.[2]

Modern dance attracted Jewish women because it sought to expose the serious expressiveness of body motion, distinguishing itself from the comic antics of vaudeville, showy kicks of Broadway chorus dancing, and ethereal fantasies of European-imported ballet. Like artists of other genres in the era, modern dancers steeped themselves in the social, political, and aesthetic issues of the day, emboldened by the aim to make artworks responsive and relevant to everyday life. One way modern dancers did this was by constructing an American art form. Children of immigrants, Jewish women battled anti-Semitism and politicized dance at a time when Americans were particularly concerned with expressing ideals of social justice and national renewal in their art.[3]

In this achievement they realized the goal of Mordecai Kaplan, who embraced American art and culture, including dance, as a means by which to explore and affirm Jewish identity and American citizenry. Believing that the diaspora was permanent for most Jews, Kaplan's Americanism rivaled his Judaism.[4] Disavowing the rigidity of the Orthodox tradition and the individualism of Reform, Kaplan advocated a variety of cultural activities, rather than just religious rituals to create and strengthen communal bonds. His entreaty to rejuvenate American Judaism this way paralleled other calls to find "an American way" in art and politics in the midst of the fearful times of the Great Depression. In 1934 Kaplan elaborated his views with the publication of *Judaism as a Civilization;* that same year, John Dewey and Ruth Benedict explored similar themes in *Art as Experience* and *Patterns of Culture*. These books emphasized the communal, ethical elements of American culture, a vision that modern dancers sought to put on stage. In their experimentation with movement, confrontational style, and passion for basics, American modern dancers played out in bodily form the experiential, pragmatic thrust of an American branch of philosophy. In their attempts to choreograph episodes in the American past and to identify and incorporate indigenous American dance traditions, they sought to give dance in America wider social impact just as the burgeoning field of anthropology was doing for other societies. And, in their active participation in a secular art form, Jewish modern dancers made modern dance a social and cultural movement, creating new roles for themselves in American society.[5]

To forge a larger ethnic cultural community, Kaplan embraced many different kinds of art because they were examples of secular activities that could be infused with an American Jewish flavor, and he specifically included dance in the list of arts to be taught. "The gamut of artistic expression must be widened to include poetry and song, music, drama, dance, painting, sculpture, and architecture," Kaplan wrote in *Judaism as a Civilization*.[6] At a time when most of America did not yet consider dance, even ballet, to be a serious art form, Kaplan and other Jews placed dance on par with other artistic genres. The psychologist Israel Strauss put dance on the same footing as classical music when he warned Jewish parents in 1931 against fostering anxieties in their children, saying, "[Parents] frequently carry their desires to excess in having the child exhibit his powers—whether he can play the Rachmaninoff Prelude at ten; whether she can dance as Isadora Duncan at eleven."[7]

Strauss's comment sanctioned the artistic worthiness of talent in dance but also reinstated different gender models in the arts. Women overwhelmed all dance forms at this time as a realm which featured the visual spectacle of bodies and ranged from ethereal pictures of idealized femininity in ballet to the bawdy sexual tease in burlesque.[8] The sexual appeal inherent in dance that most often produced women on stage with men watching them came from the medium of the art form: the movement of bodies. From Judeo-Christian thought through Western philosophy, women dwelled on the body side of a mind-body dualism. Women's bodies had "natural" significance through childbirth; women's affinity for expression through bodies, through dance, was a logical corollary.

Dance may have been understood as women's natural artistic expression, but women modern dancers, conformed to neither the sensual play of social dance and burlesque nor the otherworldly fantasies of ballet. Modern dance solidified in the decade following the passage of women's suffrage in 1920 and manifested the influence of both the separatist, discriminatory strategy of the women's suffrage movement and the individualist ethos of the failed fight for an equal rights amendment that followed. The leadership of women in modern dance corresponded with a broadening of opportunities for most women. By the 1920s, white American women voted, attended college in record numbers, enjoyed urban nightlife, and worked as a larger percentage of the workforce than before. Many women felt that the battle for equal rights had been won, and the cohesion among some groups of white women which helped pass suffrage began to disintegrate in the wake of that accomplishment. A strong individualist ethos emerged, of which modern dance was a part. "There is only one thing to dance about: the meaning of one's personal experience and this experience must be taken in its literal sense as action, and not as intellectual conception," Doris Humphrey opined, and her statement reflected the spirit infusing many arenas in which women were involved in the late 1920s and into the 1930s.[9] In modern dance, women became creators as well as performers, using their own bodies as the medium of expression.

Dance was also a part of the burgeoning of physical exercise at the beginning of the twentieth century, exemplified by the boisterous activities of Teddy Roosevelt. Attention to dance for girls accompanied attention to sports for boys, and Jewish boys gravitated to basketball and boxing. The rise of the "muscular Judaism" movement, which paralleled the "muscular Christianity" movement, fortified religious zeal with masculine weight. Both movements sought to dispel associations with feminine weakness and softness, a stereotype which Sander Gilman has shown often accompanied Jews in general and not just devout believers. Zionists in particular advocated physical strengthening and sponsored gymnastics and sports clubs.[10] In much the same way, modern dancers eschewed feminine ideals of beauty in dance and created movement that was hard, angular, ugly. "Ugliness may be beautiful if it cries out with the voice of power," Martha Graham declared.[11]

Arms ending in fists, flexed bare feet, agonizing backward falls, and intense faces conveyed intellectual and emotional seriousness that was absent from folk, ritual, and social dance among Jews. Although dance had always been a part of Jewish celebrations, particularly weddings, births, and bar and bat mitzvahs, folk and ritual dancing primarily fostered community participation and embodied the vibrancy and joy of life. In the late nineteenth and early twentieth centuries, dance was also a part of vaudeville and stage acts of Jewish performers. And, in the burst of dance halls and nightclubs in the 1910s and 1920s, young Jewish women flouted religious and parental concerns, dancing the turkey-trot and the Charleston. Modern dance, on the other hand, offered Jewish women a way to combine physical expression with the intellectual solemnity of Talmudic study denied to them.[12] Because of its newness and malleability, modern dance gave Jewish women an outlet to combine physical, political, and intellectual activities.

For many Jewish women, introduction to dance began in the settlement houses on the Lower East Side of New York City, particularly the Henry Street Settlement House, founded by the Jewish social reformer Lilian Wald in 1893. Like other settlement houses begun in the late nineteenth and early twentieth centuries, Henry Street provided needed services to immigrant neighborhoods. Believing that the environment in which people live shapes their actions, settlement house workers lived in poor neighborhoods, offering a model of domestication and behavior based on white middle-class ideals, such as restraint, cleanliness, and well-contained roles for girls and boys. Artistic activities were a vehicle for such instruction. Influenced by the ideas of the British artists and thinkers John Ruskin and William Morris, settlement house workers believed art could serve a social role by grouping people together in friendly ways and providing activity to enrich minds. Art could restore creativity and beauty siphoned off by industrial labor.[13]

Following these ideas, Alice and Irene Lewisohn ran the artistic activities at Henry Street, and Irene took particular interest in dance. American-born daughters of a German Jewish immigrant father, they directed their attention to the new influx of Eastern European Jews. Eastern Europeans quickly dominated the Jewish population in New York, and German Jews who had long resided in America hoped to instruct Eastern European Jews on how to fit into society. German Jews worried about certain traits that Eastern European Jews brought with them—Orthodox religious beliefs, political activism—and wanted to quell anti-Semitism that Eastern European Jews might provoke and by which German Jews might be harmed. To that end, the Lewisohn sisters promoted cultural rather than political activities and expected to bridge the different cultures by putting on street pageants, beginning in 1906, resplendent with the stories and costumes of homelands. They soon became more ambitious and in 1915 built a theatre, called the Neighborhood Playhouse, located just a few blocks from the Henry Street Settlement House. Their first production, "Jephthah's Daughter," based on the story in the Book of Judges, drew various responses. "The radically inclined were disappointed that the Old Testament was used as a source, rather than Andreyev or Gorky, and the conventionally minded were shocked at the bare feet of the dancers," Alice Lewisohn Crowley remembered.[14] The Lewisohn sisters incorporated Jewish traditions into the variety of productions the Neighborhood Playhouse sponsored.

In this maelstrom of varying values and beliefs, dance had a place as a form of expression and communication which did not require spoken language. Expanding on this idea, Henry Street offered a variety of dance classes, from folk to concert dance. Blanche Talmud became well known for her classes in "Interpretive Dancing," which followed Isadora Duncan's lead in stripping movement of stylized technique and letting bare feet and natural, gestural motions rule. This was the introduction to dance that influenced a number of Jewish women, including Edith Segal, Anna Sokolow, Sophie Maslow, Helen Tamiris, Lilian Shapero, Lily Mehlman, and Nadia Chilkovsky, most of whom were daughters of Eastern European Jewish immigrants. They received performance opportunities in the Neighborhood

Playhouse productions until the theatre closed in 1927. The School of the Neighborhood Playhouse continued at a midtown location, and Martha Graham taught classes in the new modern dance. Through the philanthropic help of the Lewisohn sisters and Rita Morgenthau, the Playhouse offered scholarships to many of Graham's students, giving free tuition and a stipend of fifteen dollars a week. From initial classes at Henry Street, daughters of Jewish immigrants found their way to classes by Graham, Humphrey, and others and then into their companies.

One of Talmud's students, Edith Segal, took modern dance from New York City into the summer camps of the Catskills. Throughout the 1930s Segal taught at Kinderland, a camp in Dutchess County devoted to promoting secular Jewish culture fused with radical politics. One of the most politically active modern dancers, Segal added classes on socialism at the Rand School to her dance classes from Talmud and Graham. She was a mainstay at New York Communist Party functions in the 1920s and 1930s, with her Red Dancers Group performing in various pageants. At Kinderland she created programs such as "Immigrants All! Americans All!" in the summer of 1939, which heralded the variety of people in America as the basis of American democracy.[15]

Jewish women trained at Henry Street and Kinderland were, in general, the dancers who promoted modern dance as a political art form open to the masses. Initially, a concern with the masses translated into adding dance to Communist Party activities. Segal choreographed "The Belt Goes Red," which recreated an assembly line, for the 1930 Lenin Memorial at Madison Square Garden. Dancers in "stiff, straight postures" represented the machine and, at the triumphant end, overtook the machine, covering it with a red cloth.[16] "They took it because they had built it," Segal proclaimed.[17] The New York Workers International Relief housed a Workers School of Music and the Dance; begun in September 1930, it offered dance classes to workers for ten cents and employed Segal, Lily Mehlman, and Nadia Chilkovsky, all trained at the Henry Street Settlement House.[18] Mehlman also led the International Workers Organization Dance Group, and Chilkovsky, under the pseudonym Nell Anyon, wrote articles about how best to make modern dance revolutionary. These women believed that everyone should and could participate in culture and art, they created dance works which held a political message, and they made a movement of modern dance with proliferating organizations and a unified purpose.

In 1932, the Workers Dance League and the New Dance Group were born with the more specific intention of blending the aesthetics of modern dance with an adherence to political goals that went beyond party propaganda. After the death of Harry Simms, a young union organizer shot and killed by the police in New Jersey in 1932, dancers who marched in a parade commemorating his death decided to create the New Dance Group.[19] "The philosophy we agreed on was to provide dance instruction for everybody, for the masses," recalled Chilkovsky, a founding member.[20] From Communist Party functions, Segal, Chilkovsky, Anna Sokolow and Miriam Blecher formed the Workers Dance League at a *Daily Worker*-sponsored May Day celebration and Recognition Rally of the Friends of the Soviet Union at the Bronx Coliseum in 1932. They planned to provide an umbrella organization for different performing troupes with the aim to increase communication among groups and create a larger place for dance within workers' movements. Their goal: to use "dance as a weapon in the class struggle."[21]

Miriam Blecher was a leading figure in both these groups who occasionally choreographed works on Jewish themes. Blecher, the daughter of an observant Jewish tailor who had immigrated from Austria-Hungary, became fascinated by the teeming world around her on the Lower East Side. She included "Two Jewish Songs" (1937) with "East Side Sketches" (1937) and dances to Negro poems in her concert works. Blecher was unusual, too, in choreographing a dance specifically about women. One review praised Blecher's portrayal of female sensuality in "The Woman" (1934), claiming that this was "the sort of woman that a worker comes home to."[22]

In Blecher's inclusion of Jews with African Americans, if not women, she followed the suggestion of Naum Rosen, a critic writing in a 1934 issue of the *Dance Observer* who advocated that the Jew be added to Martha Graham's famous declaration that called on modern dancers to utilize two indigenous traditions, those of "the Indian and Negro," in constructing their American art form.[23] Rosen argued that the Negro, Indian, and Jew had an active presence in society, but, more important, each had a long past on which to draw. Rosen claimed that increased interest in Jewish dancing stemmed from the successes of the Moscow Habima Theatre production of "The Dybbuk" in 1926 in New York and the Yiddish Art Theatre's production of "Yoshe Kalb" in 1933. In these theatrical productions, dance played a prominent part. Benjamin Zemach emerged as a master of Jewish folk dances in "The Dybbuk," and Lillian Shapero, a member of Martha Graham's group, choreographed dances for "Yoshe Kalb." For Rosen, the universal element underlying each religious tradition of the Jew, the Negro, and the Indian, as well as the geographical convergence and longevity in the United States of these three groups, determined their Americanness.[24]

Most Jewish women in modern dance, however, did not follow the path advocated by Rosen and picked up on by Blecher and Shapero. Following the trajectory of the Yiddish Art Theatre, which emerged in 1918, flourished in the 1920s, and faltered in the 1930s, modern dancers moved from their Jewish roots on the Lower East Side and at Henry Street to broader political movements and artistic ventures. The rise of the 92nd Street YMHA in the 1930s mirrored this change. In 1934, under the new leadership of Dr. William Kolodney, born in Minsk and raised in New York since the age of five, the Y took on a new role as a smaller cultural home for the arts for the whole city to enjoy. Modern dance, rather than Jewish folk dancing, immediately took up residence. In 1935, a subscription series for dance concerts started, and soon thereafter classes, lecture-demonstrations, and public interviews with dancers and choreographers followed.[25]

Helen Tamiris, the most influential Jewish modern dancer of the era, combined an attention to the politics that concerned Blecher, Segal, and Chilkovsky with an advocacy of secular American arts for Jews that Mordecai Kaplan and the 92nd Street Y promoted. Born Helen Becker in 1902 to Russian Jewish immigrants, Becker grew up amidst the poverty, squalid living conditions, and endless work of garment sweatshops of the Lower East Side. The early death of her mother, when Helen was three, added to the family's difficulties. Along with two of her four brothers, Becker found solace in creativity. One brother was an artist, another a sculptor, while Helen began her dance career in classes at the Henry Street Settlement House.[26]

Becker received the name Tamiris from a South American writer and boyfriend who retrieved it from a poem about an ancient Persian queen: "Thou art Tamiris, the ruthless queen who banishes all obstacles."[27] She would try to live up to this honorific by working to make modern dance permanent through forming organizations, including unions, promoting collaborative productions, and searching for funding. In 1930, Tamiris was the motivating force behind The Dance Repertory Theatre, which formed to combat the almost insurmountable costs of theatrical productions. Her idea was to have the leading modern dancers rent a theatre for a week and perform on alternating nights. In one week of performances competition for audiences, theatres, and dates would be avoided, costs shared, and Louis Horst's talents as accompanist utilized by all.[28] In 1930, Tamiris, Doris Humphrey, Charles Weidman, and Martha Graham performed; in 1931, Agnes de Mille joined them. The Dance Repertory Theatre did not last beyond that season, but Tamiris's organizing energy did not diminish, and in November 1934 she headed and helped organize the Dancers Union to find work for unemployed dancers. Claiming that dancers were overlooked in relief programs, the Dancers Union demanded that jobs be reserved in the newly formed Civil Works Administration for teachers and performers.

Modern dancers, led by Tamiris, also protested mightily to obtain a Dance Project from the federally funded Works Progress Administration (WPA), which began its Arts Projects in 1935. A Dance Project emerged under the auspices of New York City's Federal Theatre Project but was riddled with internal disputes. The "always embattled dancers," as they came to be called by the director of the Theatre Project, Hallie Flanagan, walked picket lines, staged a sit-in after a performance and remained in the theatre all night, and even made trips to Washington to voice their concerns to Flanagan.[29] Tamiris and Fanya Geltman became the notable spokespeople of the Dance Project. Called the "long and the short of it" because of Tamiris's height and Geltman's lack thereof, they stormed Federal Theatre offices in Washington, D.C., and New York City, protesting a variety of issues, including audition policies, the poor administrative work of the director of the Dance Project (which eventually caused his ousting), and the continuing decrease in funding for the WPA.[30] Geltman and another young Jewish woman, Paula Bass, became the dance representatives of the City Projects Council, the active union of WPA workers.

As the troubles of the Federal Theatre Project increased, dancers turned their attention to organizing a National Dance Congress, which met for the first time in May 1936 in New York City at the 92nd Street Y. The apex of the organizational drives of dancers of the era, the congress included days of talks and nights of performances with each night devoted to a different kind of dance: folk, modern, ballet, experimental, and theatre. The congress was led almost exclusively by modern dancers, many of whom were Jewish women also involved in leftist politics, including Tamiris, Anna Sokolow, Edna Ocko, and Miriam Blecher. Two leading dance critics attacked the political activism of the congress, which they felt distorted its activities. John Martin, of the *New York Times,* and Margaret Lloyd, of the *Christian Science Monitor,* condemned the leftists, with Lloyd warning, "And if the left-wingers continue to run the whole show, as they did this one, they will only succeed in turning the remaining liberals into fascisti."[31] Battles within the dance world raged and often mixed differing political views with dance issues. At a lecture entailed "Ballet Today," Lloyd coyly stated that Anatole Chujoy, the lecturer, "was nearly mobbed by objections not always closely related to the subject."[32] Modern dance radicals assailed ballet for its elitist stature and escapist purposes and heralded modern dance as inclusive, democratic, and full of serious significance.

The criticism of the overt politics of modern dance may have masked antisemitism. In modern dance as in other areas in the 1930s, anti-Semitism persisted, even if in covert ways. For some leading modern dancers, Jews were clearly not American, and their presence led to problems in creating an American art form. In 1928, Ruth St. Denis, a leading dancer in the 1910s and 1920s and a teacher and inspiration to the modern dancers of the 1930s, wanted to re-form her company with Ted Shawn, which was called Denishawn. It had lost popularity, and they hoped to remove the taint of vaudeville from their past, jobs which they had felt required to take for the money. In a crucial meeting to reorganize the school and company, St. Denis declared that she intended to make "all units of school or production . . . 90 percent Anglo-Saxon (so as to insure the art is American and is recognized by other countries as American)." She sought to maintain "the same percentage of foreign blood in their organization as the U.S. does in its government, that is, 8 to 10 percent," probably a general reference to the immigration quotas enacted in 1924. In a letter to her parents recounting the event, Doris Humphrey suggested that this was an attempt to limit the number of Jewish women in the company and noted St. Denis's hypocrisy that, after "spouting about Anglo-Saxon art," St. Denis "invited the Jewish girls to take part in the [Lewisohn] Stadium performance."[33]

St. Denis was a mystic Christian who had combined her Protestant upbringing with Eastern religious traditions. Her anti-Semitism refracted different personal religious beliefs into national terms: that is, an American art form required a dominant majority of 90 percent Anglo-Saxons. John Corbin, a theatre critic, expressed similar reservations about the number of Jews in drama who provided creativity and talent but also pulled the American theatre from its "Anglo-Saxon heritage."[34] The irony is that St. Denis's insistence on Anglo-Saxon art hastened the crumbling of Denishawn, which fell apart by 1930. Humphrey left Denishawn because of this demand and requests to yield "individuality to the good of the institution."[35] Gertrude Shurr, a Latvian Jewish immigrant raised in Brooklyn since she was nearly two years old, recalled that many of the Jewish women at Denishawn left to join Humphrey and Charles Weidman in their new company because "they stuck up for us."[36] In fact, both Humphrey and Graham praised the "emotional intensity belonging to the Jewish race," as Humphrey put it, which they felt particularly suited Jewish women for the new, dramatic modern dance.[37]

This positive interpretation still came from stereotyped understandings of the "Jewish race," however. When Humphrey remarked on the "piles of Jewish girls" in her classes, she added telling qualifications: "but they have their good qualities" and "you can be sure your school is a success in New York when the Jews come, because they're always sure of getting the best for their money."[38] Judgments of "emotional intensity" vied with miserliness and bled into the ways in which Jewish dancers were seen. St. Denis's comment that the art form needed to be recognized by other countries as American implied that Jews had a visual, physical identity which would not fit into a picture of America (as also, though unstated but clearly understood, African Americans would not).[39] Seemingly more important than an American way of moving was simply a particular type of static, physical appearance. Whether referring to facial characteristics or darker hair or skin, St. Denis's picture of America undoubtedly resembled her own fair-skinned and high-cheekboned features.[40]

Similarly, a former member of the Humphrey-Weidman group of the 1930s remembered hearing Humphrey and Weidman comment on the audition of a beautiful Jewish woman who "didn't have a WASP face." They reportedly said, "what do we do with a face like that?" Despite this reservation, they accepted her into the company.[41] Thus, modern dance may have been more welcoming to Jews than other realms of society, such as higher education with its quota system, and Humphrey, Weidman, Graham and others did not act on the anti-Semitic beliefs they may have held, as Ruth St. Denis and Ted Shawn did.[42] Modern dancers did employ many Jewish women. But distinctions between Jews and others remained, some particularly based on physical characteristics. "You could be Jewish [and have an easier time] if you didn't look Jewish," summarized another Jewish modern dancer of the Humphrey-Weidman group.[43]

Beyond the internal politics of the dance world, leading modern dancers stood up against Hitler and the rise of fascism in Germany and other parts of Europe. In 1936, the German government planned an International Dance Festival to accompany the Berlin Olympics, and leftist modern dancers formed a committee, with Lily Mehlman as one of the leaders to boycott the festival. The boycott successfully stopped American dancers from participating. In March 1936, Martha Graham decried the persecution of German artists and found it "impossible to identify [herself], by accepting the invitation, with the regime that has made such things possible. . . . Some of my concert group would not be welcome in Germany," she wrote, acknowledging the Jewish members of her company.[44] Humphrey and her partner Charles Weidman followed suit. They were joined by many Jews active in the dance field, including Miriam Blecher, Lincoln Kirstein, Anna Sokolow, Tamiris, and Benjamin Zemach.[45] In a December 1935 concert, Mehlman presented "Fatherland," which concerned "the shame and degradation of German fascism."[46] The critic Edna Ocko went further than boycotting the festival in berating the leading German dancers Mary Wigman and Rudolf von Laban for their participation in and willingness to organize the festival.[47] Other American dancers joined the protest against their seeming complicity with Nazi policy, which prompted Wigman's American proponent, Hanya Holm, to change the name of her school from the

Mary Wigman School to the Hanya Holm School in November 1936. Both politically active Jewish women and the leading modern dancers made significant pronouncements against artistic censorship and anti-Semitism in Europe.

Modern dancers also vehemently spoke out against the Franco regime in Spain. The subject of dances by Graham, Sokolow, Tamiris, and others, the Spanish Civil War brought out the humanitarianism of most artists and intellectuals in the mid-1930s. Anna Sokolow's "Excerpts from a War Poem" (1937) contained no battle scenes, melodrama, or preaching, but its five sections, organized around lines from a poem by the Italian poet F. T. Martinetti, contrasted the heroics of war celebrated in the poem with the chaos, despair, and suffering caused by war. To the lines "because it realizes the long-dreamed-of metalization of the human body," Sokolow choreographed a picture of physical contortion in the third section of the piece. Dancers moved spasmodically, crumpled by pain, frantic in chaos. A critic praised the choreographic picture of distortion "in which human values are crushed by the very symbols which pretended to idealize those values." Sokolow had created "a final stern and passionate indictment of the madness bred by fascism."[48] And, in one of the last works of the Federal Theatre Project, "Adelante," Tamiris choreographed a piece inspired by poetry written in Spain during the war about a peasant soldier who was executed and which ended "with a courageous, spirited, triumphal march of the peasantry."[49]

Joining writers, painters, and musicians, modern dancers danced in benefits to raise awareness and money for the fight against Franco. The American Dance Association, led by Tamiris, sponsored two concerts entitled "Dances for Spain," where a percentage of the proceeds went to the Medical Committee to Aid Spanish Democracy. Edna Ocko, head of the Dancers Committee of the Theatre Arts Committee, which was formed to aid victims of fascism, raised money for ambulances for Spain. Instead of debating practical policy points, artists championed humanitarianism and highlighted the human destruction inevitable in war. But nationalist elements still entered this universalist impulse. Fascism was nationalism gone awry; in response, modern dancers held up America and its version of democracy as the ideal. Ocko, the radical dance critic, succinctly summed up the importance of the fight against fascism in 1938: "by fighting fascism outside our own country we are defending democracy within our borders."[50]

By the late 1930s, modern dance had solidified as a movement and incorporated Jewish women into its ranks. The growth of fascism in Europe unified political passions under the banner of heralding American democracy. The unity was short-lived, however, as dance activities diminished drastically during World War II, with men and funds diverted toward the war effort. Prominent Jewish choreographers went separate ways. Anna Sokolow journeyed to Mexico and stayed there from 1939 to 1943, choreographing a number of works on Mexican themes, including "Homage to Garcia Lorca" (1940). Sophie Maslow left the Graham company and formed a trio with Jane Dudley and William Bales. Maslow created two of her most famous works in this period, "Dust Bowl Ballads" (1941) and "Folksay" (1942), to songs by Woody Guthrie, and placed herself, a Jewish, urban, radical woman, in the midst of American folk songs and stories of the Midwest.[51] Tamiris choreographed works for the U.S. Department of Agriculture, "It's Up to You" (1943), and Franklin D. Roosevelt's campaign, "The People's Bandwagon" (1944), before turning her energy to Broadway, where she had many successes in the 1940s and 1950s, including "Annie Get Your Gun" (1946), "Touch and Go" (1949), and "Plain and Fancy" (1955).

Most modern dancers and choreographers shifted emphasis in the post–World War II period, turning from communal hopes and patriotic Americanism to explorations of their own psyche. Martha Graham's large works of the 1940s and 1950s based on stories of Greek mythology, such as "Errand into the Maze" (1947) and "Clytemnestra" (1958), exemplified the change. This psychological turn took a different shape for Jewish modern dancers, who gravitated to more specific Jewish themes and stories in the aftermath of the Holocaust. Anna Sokolow, Sophie Maslow, and Pearl Lang all created works which drew from Jewish tradition, such as Sokolow's "Kaddish" (1945), a prayer of mourning at the end of World War II with Sokolow wrapped in a tefillin. Sophie Maslow returned from the American Midwest to the Russian shtetl of her ancestors in "The Village I Knew" (1949).[52] And Pearl Lang, who danced with Martha Graham's company from 1941 to 1955, choreographed her first of many works on Jewish themes, "Song of Deborah," in 1949. These women continued to choreograph topics inspired by Jewish traditions and history throughout the 1950s and saw their work performed by the Batsheva Company, a modern dance troupe founded in Israel in 1962 by Martha Graham's former patron, Bethsabee de Rothschild.

The attention to Jewish themes in the postwar era rippled beyond modern dance to a renewed consideration of folk dance. A 1944 article in *The Reconstructionist* by Dvora Lapson, an educator and expert on Jewish dance, advocated the use of dance in synagogues and religious schools by referring to biblical passages that mentioned the role of dance. Lapson ended by berating the support of Jewish centers and Ys for concert dance and their neglect of "Jewish dance."[53] At the same time, William Kolodney, at the 92nd Street Y, contemplated similar issues. In 1947, Kolodney engaged Fred Berk, an Austrian-born Jew who had fled to the United States via England and Cuba, to develop a "Jewish dance division" at the Y, and Israeli folk dancing grew under his inspiration and energy, burgeoning into annual Israeli Folk Dance Festivals beginning in 1952.

In 1950, a book appeared which drew together Jewish interests in dance. *Jewish Dances,* with an introduction by Mordecai Kaplan, gave detailed descriptions of the stories, music, and movement of folk dances from Eastern Europe. The author, Ruth Zahava, was the Dance Director of the Jewish Centers Association of Los Angeles and ran both modern dance and folk dance ensembles. In his introduction, Kaplan recognized that dance still played a limited role in Jewish culture and that it was the "art least generally thought of as a medium of Jewish self-expression," a reflection perhaps of the continuing stereotype of Jews as people of the book rather than of the body that also indicated a lack of attention to the activities of Jewish women. Kaplan went on to fortify the place of dance in the history of the Jewish people, from the Levites to Hasidism. Ultimately, dance represented the "great heights to which the human spirit may rise" and "possesses certain characteristics that render it uniquely adapted to become an entering wedge that would make way for all the other arts in Jewish life." In its engagement of the entire being, expressing thought and emotion often beyond words and therefore open to the widest possible audience, dance was well suited to stimulate communal and artistic fervor.[54]

In the 1950s, folks dances had an easily defensible place in community activities with a political message more aligned to Zionism, and Jewish modern dancers followed this trend, exploring Jewish traditions rather than questioning American politics. Tamiris's political alliances, in fact, began to haunt her by the late 1940s and especially in the 1950s. Although little evidence exists to elaborate this claim, Jane Dudley, another leftist dancer who was not Jewish, remembered that Tamiris "got clobbered" for involving herself with Communist affairs.[55] Tamiris herself in a letter from the early 1960s referred to the "cruel McCarthy period."[56] The hearings of the House Committee on Un-American Activities of the late 1940s and early 1950s identified her participation in many suspected Communist activities and Communist-front organizations. Tamiris was the most often cited dancer, even though others—such as Edna Ocko and Edith Segal—had much larger roles in the Communist Party. The attention to Tamiris attested to her talent, organizing ability, unwavering social conscience, and commitment to political and social change.

The alliance of Jewish women with leftist politics led to subtle dismissals of their work as mere political propaganda and eventually to their virtual exclusion from the annals of dance history, to which they are only recently being restored.[57] Tamiris, again, is a case in point. Although one of the most important modern dancers in the 1930s, she was left out of the Bennington College Summer School of the Dance, begun in 1934, which grouped together the stars of modern dance. She was excluded from most books about modern dance written in the 1930s, which precipitated her omission from histories of the movement written since then.[58] Many later recalled that her active political participation in leftist causes may have led to her exclusion.[59] More significant, our understanding of art forms most often focuses on their leading creators, ignoring the vast amount of organizational work and support that undergirds the emergence of a few artists. Tamiris's planning and rallying efforts, if not her choreographic ingenuity, have suffered from this bias, and this same mishap has concealed the contributions of many other Jewish women, as well.

It is also worth reconsidering Kaplan's wide embrace of cultural activities which recognized a place for modern dance alongside more traditional ethnic customs, such as folk dance. Arguments over the "Jewishness" of activities at Jewish institutions are long-running and important, and such discussions still shape the dance program at the 92nd Street Y.[60] Kaplan proposed casting a wider net in determining what could be a part of Jewish heritage and community activities, and modern dance fit into his proposal because of its malleability as a form of expression that could be utilized to further religious, political, or collective concerns. Now, however, modern dance also needs to be recognized in Jewish programs for the historical roles that Jewish dancers, philanthropists, religious philosophy, and institutions have had in its development. The judgment of Jewishness should measure not only the content of activities but the range of endeavors in which Jews have been involved. By this latter measurement, modern dance is a rightful part of American Jewish heritage.

Ultimately, Jewish participation in modern dance in the 1930s was a part of the larger attempt to define America in new cultural terms. Predominantly as children of immigrants, Jewish women displayed their Americanness on stage often at the expense of their Jewish tradition. But their roots molded their impact, primarily in giving modern dance its political base. They transformed a new art form into a value-laden movement that emphasized the communal, ethical elements embedded in the American traditions of pluralism and democracy. Creating an ephemeral but evocative art, Jewish women found in modern dance a rare artistic medium open to them that could be molded to absorb their past and their future in a fluid, fully alive moment where they could be both angels and revolutionaries.

NOTES

1. Doris Humphrey to her parents, October 20, 1927, Folder C268, and March 29, 1928, Folder C269, Doris Humphrey Collection, Dance Collection, New York Public Library of the Performing Arts (hereafter referred to as DH Collection and DC/NYPL).

2. Herbert G. Goldman, *Fanny Brice: The Original Funny Girl* (New York: Oxford University Press, 1992), 167; Barbara W. Grossman, *Funny Woman: The Life and Times of Fanny Brice* (Bloomington: Indiana University Press, 1991), 219.

3. The role of Jews in dance has just begun to receive attention. See *Jewish Women in America: An Historical Encyclopedia*, s.v. "Dance, Performance"; Naomi M. Jackson, "Converging Movements: Modern Dance and Jewish Culture at the 92nd Street Y, 1930–60," Ph.D. diss., New York University, 1997, esp. ch. 8.

4. For a view of Kaplan's tie to American nationalism, see Allan Lazaroff, "Kaplan and John Dewey," in *The American Judaism of Mordecai M. Kaplan*, ed. Emanuel S. Goldsmith, Mel Scult, and Robert M. Seltzer (New York, New York University Press, 1990), 173–96, and other essays in the same volume. Ira Eisenstein, in his book condensing Kaplan's *Judaism as a Civilization* entitled *Creative Judaism* (1936; repr., New York: Jewish Reconstructionist Foundation, 1941), writes: "In America, the Jews must be Americans first, and Jews second" (80). For a general biography of Kaplan, see Mel Scult, *Judaism Faces the Twentieth Century: A Biography of Mordecai M. Kaplan* (Detroit: Wayne State University Press, 1993).

5. For an overview of this general transition see Deborah Dash Moore, *At Home in America: Second Generation Jews* (New York: Columbia University Press, 1981); and Henry L. Feingold, *A Time for Searching: Entering the Mainstream, 1920–1945* (Baltimore: Johns Hopkins University Press, 1992).

6. Kaplan, quoted in *Dynamic Judaism: The Essential Writings of Mordecai M. Kaplan*, ed. Emanuel S. Goldsmith and Mel Scult (New York: Schocken, 1985), 209. For other views on art, see also Mordecai Kaplan, "Jewish Art," *S.A.J. Review* 6 (February 11, 1927): 6–7, 11; and Ira Eisenstein, "Art and Jewish Life," *Reconstructionist* 3 (February 11, 1938): 6–9.

7. Strauss, quoted in Jenna Weissman Joselit, *The Wonders of America: Reinventing Jewish Culture, 1880–1950* (New York: Hill and Wang, 1994), 86.

8. For a detailed account of the ties between notions of femininity and dance, see Linda J. Tomko, *Dancing Class: Gender, Ethnicity, and Social Divides in American Dance, 1890–1920* (Bloomington: Indiana University Press, 2000); Ann Daly, *Done into Dance: Isadora Duncan in America* (Bloomington: Indiana University Press, 1995); and my *Modern Bodies:*

Dance in American Modernism in the 1930s (Chapel Hill: University of North Carolina Press, 2001).

9. Doris Humphrey, "What Shall We Dance About?" *Trend* 1 (June–July–August 1932): 46.

10. Gail Bederman, *Manliness and Civilization: A Cultural History of Gender and Race in the United States, 1880–1917* (Chicago: University Chicago Press, 1995); Sander Gilman, *The Jew's Body* (New York: Routledge, 1991), 63; Paula E. Hyman, *Gender and Assimilation in Modern Jewish History: The Roles and Representations of Women* (Seattle: University of Washington Press, 1995), 142–46. For the best synthesis of the different roles for Jewish men and women, see Hyman and also Naomi Shepherd, *Price below Rubies: Jewish Women as Rebels and Radicals* (London: Harvard University Press, 1993), who argues that Jewish women participated in secular culture and political action more than Jewish men.

11. Graham, quoted in Merle Armitage, *Martha Graham: The Early Years* (New York: M. Armitage, 1937), 97.

12. It has been difficult to determine how devout these women were. In a letter to her parents, Doris Humphrey mentioned that "this being Yom Kippur or something like that I come in for a holiday from classes along with the Jewish girls." So, it seems certain observances were maintained. The quote also reveals Humphrey's lack of attention to Jewish holidays, since the letter was written in April when Passover was the holiday being celebrated. Doris Humphrey to her parents, April 12, 1933, Folder C330.8, DH Collection, DC/NYPL.

13. Tomko, *Dancing Class*, chs. 3–4, 86–88, on the influence of Ruskin and Morris; Linda Gordon Kuzmack, *Women's Cause: The Jewish Woman's Movement in England and the United States, 1891–1933* (Columbus: Ohio State University Press, 1990), ch. 4 on settlement reformers, 99–105 on Wald.

14. Alice Lewisohn Crowley, *The Neighborhood Playhouse: Leaves from a Theatre Scrapbook* (New York: Theatre Arts Books, 1959), 41. Biographical material on the Lewisohn Family, mainly photocopies of newspaper articles collected by Florence Lewisohn, American Jewish Archives, Cincinnati, Ohio.

15. Paul C. Mishler, *Raising Reds: Young Pioneers, Radical Summer Camps, and Communist Political Culture in the United States* (New York: Columbia University Press, 1999), 92–93. Segal's inspiration and title for the dance probably came from a series of radio programs in 1938–39, "Americans All . . . Immigrants All," that showcased the contributions of various ethnic groups; Philip Gleason, "Americans All: World War II and the Shaping of American Identity," *Review of Politics* 43 (October 1981): 483–518.

16. Reminiscences of Edith Segal (February 27, 1981), Oral History of the American Left, Tamiment Library, New York University (hereafter referred to as OHAL/NYU); Segal quoted in Stacey Prickett, " 'The People': Issues of Identity within the Revolutionary Dance," in "Of, by, and for the People: Dancing on the Left in the 1930s," *Studies in Dance History* 5 (spring 1994): 15.

17. Reminiscences of Edith Segal (January, February 1991), DC/NYPL.

18. For more detailed information on the connections between the revolutionary left and modern dance, see Ellen Graff, *Stepping Left: Dance and Politics in New York City, 1928–1942* (Durham, NC: Duke University Press, 1997) and, for a more theoretical account, Mark Franko, *Dancing Modernism/Performing Politics* (Bloomington: Indiana University Press, 1995).

19. Anne Betts, "An Historical Study of the New Dance Group of New York City," Master's thesis, New York University, 1945, 7.

20. Reminiscences of Nadia Chilkovsky, May 25, 1978, Works Projects Administration Oral Histories, Special Collections and Archives, George Mason University (hereafter referred to as WPA/GMU).

21. This slogan appears on a June 4, 1933 program of the Workers Dance League, DC/NYPL. The program was the first Workers Dance Spartakiade, a kind of competition among dance groups, held at The New School for Social Research in New York.

22. *New Dance* (January 1935).

23. Martha Graham, "The Dance in America," *Trend* I (March 1932): 6.

24. Naum Rosen, "The New Jewish Dance in America," *Dance Observer* I (June–July 1934): 51, 55.

25. Jackson, "Converging Movements"; William Kolodney, "History of the Educational Department of the YM-YWHA," Ed.D. diss, Teachers College, Columbia University, 1950, in the Archives of the 92nd Street YM-YWHA; Doreen A. Lanes, "The History of the 92nd Street YM-YWHA 1934–1953," term paper, 1978, DC/NYPL.

26. The best sources on Tamiris are a draft of her autobiography, a published chronology of her career, and primary sources of the Helen Tamiris Collection, DC/NYPL. Helen Tamiris, "Tamiris in Her Own Voice: Draft of an Autobiography," trans., ed., and annotated by Daniel Nagrin, *Studies in Dance History* I (fall/winter 1989): 1–64; Christena L. Schlundt, *Tamiris: A Chronicle of Her Dance Career, 1927–1955* (New York: New York Public Library, 1972). See also Pauline Tish, "Remembering Helen Tamiris," *Dance Chronicle* 17 (1994): 327–60.

27. Tamiris, "Tamiris in Her Own Voice," 18.

28. *New York Times,* November 10, 1929.

29. Hallie Flanagan, *Arena: The History of the Federal Theatre* (1940; repr., New York: Arno Press, 1980), 52. For information on the Dance Project and dance within the Theatre Project see Marian Roet, "Dance Project of the WPA Federal Theatre," Master's thesis, New York University, 1949; Kathleen Ann Lally, "A History of the Federal Dance Theatre of the WPA, 1935–1939," Ph.D. diss., Texas Women's University, 1978; Graff, *Stepping Left,* ch. 4.

30. Reminiscences of Fanya Geltman Del Bourgo December 16, 1977, WPA/GMU.

31. *Christian Science Monitor,* June 2, 1936.

32. Ibid.

33. Doris Humphrey to her parents, July 2, 1928, Folder C270.10a, DH Collection, DC/NYPL.

34. John Corbin, "Drama and the Jew," *Scribner's Magazine* 93 (1933): 295–300. Anti-Semitism in the arts has not received enough scholarly attention. For an account of anti-Semitism in theatre which includes a discussion of the above remark, see Ellen Schiff, "Shylock's 'Mishpocheh': Anti-Semitism on the American Stage," in *Anti-Semitism in American History,* ed. David A. Gerber (Urban: University of Illinois Press, 1986), 79–99. One of the best understandings of its effect in the painting world is James Breslin, *Mark Rothko: A Biography* (Chicago: University of Chicago Press, 1993). For a contemporary perspective on whether the issue of being Jewish affects art, see Harold Rosenberg, "Jews in Art," in *Art and Other Serious Matters* (Chicago: University of Chicago Press, 1985), 258–69. Jonathan Miller, a British comic and author, makes this provocative but still largely unproven comment on the large numbers of Jews in the performing arts: "I suspect that if Jews are overrepresented in these areas it's probably because they're portable talents. They're professions or industries or activities which are not respectable, therefore not heavily guarded at the entrance by white Anglo-Saxon Protestant custodians": quoted in Israel Shenker, *Coat of Many Colors: Pages from Jewish Life* (Garden City, NY: Doubleday, 1985), 279.

35. Doris Humphrey to her parents, July 2, 1928, Folder C270.10a, DH Collection, DC/ NYPL.

36. Don McDonagh, "A Conversation with Gertrude Shurr" *Ballet Review* 4 (1973): 19.

37. Draft of a letter from Doris Humphrey to Ted Shawn and Ruth St. Denis [early 1928?], DH Collection, Folder C272.1 DC/NYPL. For an indication of Graham's view, see McDonagh, "A Conversation," 19–20.

38. Doris Humphrey to her parents, October 20, 1927, Folder C268, DH Collection, DC/NYPL.

39. See my *Modern Bodies* for the ways in which African Americans interacted with and affected the development of modern dance. For the relationship between Jews and African Americans in movies during this period, see Michael Rogin, *Blackface, White Noise: Jewish Immigrants in the Hollywood Melting Pot* (Berkeley: University of California Press, 1996).

40. For general work on the physical attributes of anti-Semitism which persist throughout history see Gilman, *Jew's Body; People of the Body: Jews and Judaism from an Embodied Perspective,* ed. Howard Eilberg-Schwartz (Albany: State University of New York Press, 1992); Robert Singerman, "The Jew as Racial Alien: The Genetic Component of American Anti-Semitism," in Gerber, *Anti-Semitism,* 103–28. How these physical stereotypes affected Jewish women still needs further attention.

41. Miriam Raphael Cooper, interview with the author, New York City, December 8, 1994.

42. For accounts of anti-Semitism in the 1930s in higher education, see Marcia Graham Synnott, "Anti-Semitism and American Universities: Did Quotas Follow the Jews?" in Gerber, *Anti-Semitism,* 233–71.

43. Lee Sherman, interview with the author, New York City, December 16, 1994.

44. *New York Times,* March 13, 1936.

45. *New Theatre* (May 1936): 37.

46. *New Masses 18* (January 7, 1936): 28.

47. *New Theatre* (November 1936): 17.

48. *Dance Observer* 4 (April 1937): 41.

49. Henry Gilfond, "Adelante," *Dance Observer* 6 (May 1939): 218.

50. *Dance Bulletin* [1938], a publication of the Dancers' Federation of Los Angeles, gift of Sue Nadel, WPA/GMU.

51. For an extended discussion of Maslow, see Graff, *Stepping Left,* 139–51.

52. For an extended analysis of these dances see Jackson, "Converging Movements," 299–311.

53. Dvora Lapson, "The Jewish Dance," *Reconstructionist* 10 (May 26, 1944): 13–17.

54. Ruth Zahava, *Jewish Dances* (Los Angeles: Kilography, 1950), 7, 9.

55. Reminiscences of Jane Dudley (1981), OHAL/NYU.

56. Tamiris to Daniel Nagrin [1965?], correspondence, Helen Tamiris Collection, DC/ NYPL.

57. *See Jewish Women in America;* Jackson, "Converging Movements"; Graff, *Stepping Left;* Tomko, *Dancing Class.*

58. Daniel Nagrin, "Helen Tamiris and the Dance Historians," *Society of Dance History Scholars Proceedings, 12th Annual Conference* (1989): 15–43.

59. For example, see the oral histories of the Bennington Summer School of the Dance housed in the Columbia University Oral History Project, particularly those of Louise Allen Haviland, Dorothy Bird Villard, Welland Lathrop, and Faith Reyher Jackson. In his oral

history for the Bennington project, Lee Sherman brings up the possibility of anti-Semitism lying behind Tamiris's exclusion without prompting from the interviewer: "you could say it might be anti-Semitic, but I don't think it was."

60. For some historical perspective on this from the current director of dance at the Y, see Joan Finkelstein, "Doris Humphrey and the 92nd Street Y: A Dance Center for the People," *Dance Research Journal* 28 (fall 1996): 49–99.

Part IV

Fierce Attachments

American Jewry emerged from World War II the largest Jewish community in the world. By 1990, there were 5.5 million Jews in the United States; half were female.[1] These years, to borrow the critic Vivian Gornick's phrase, were ones of "fierce attachments" for American Jewish women, to their American and to their Jewish identities. Now, as she writes: "The world made sense, there was ground beneath our feet, a place in the universe to stand." But the places American Jewish women stood were exceedingly diverse. A "hungry energy" marked their "fierce attachments"[2] to their families and Jewish homes; to their synagogues, Jewish communities, and Israel; to politics and art.

In "The 'Me' of Me," Joan Jacobs Brumberg surveys the transitions to the postwar era—from the immigrant mothers of "old-world origins," to the first generation of American Jewish women "deeply invested in modernity," to the teenage daughters they were raising in the 1950s. Her prism is the diary. Inspired by *The Diary of Anne Frank,*[3] Jewish girls began keeping their own diaries in the 1950s. But Brumberg finds little specific Jewish content in the "identity struggles" of these teens. Instead, their diaries, filled with how "to be pretty, personable, and most of all popular," revealed the ease of Jews in the postwar middle class. The rare diary of a Jewish girl in the 1920s provides "a stark contrast." Although Helen Landis never set foot in a synagogue until she was fifteen, Jewishness defined her adolescence. Her diary "evokes the struggle of countless other minority girls who shaped their self-image in a mass culture that did not include representations of their 'own kind.' "

Yet, as Riv-Ellen Prell shows, the pervasive postwar stereotypes of the Jewish mother and the Jewish American Princess (JAP) presented "symbolic representations of [the] American Jewish experience," even if the 1950s diary writers Brumberg read did not notice them. In "Rage and Representation," Prell places these images, popularized by Jewish men, at the core of the paradox of postwar American Jewish culture. "To be an American and a Jew," she writes, "necessitates relinquishing one or another of these identities." She thus finds that the stereotypes say a great deal about "Jewish men's distress about becoming American men" and about changes in American Jewish life, including anxieties over increased possibilities for assimilation and intermarriage.[4]

Even as American Jewish men shaped the gendered stereotypes of American Jewish culture, American Jewish women led in constructing another aspect of that culture, its foodways. In " 'From the Recipe File of Luba Cohen,' " Marcie Cohen

Ferris shows how "southern Jewish women shaped their cultural identity through food." When Luba Cohen cooked "Fanny Weinstein's matzoh balls," "Chicken Chop Suey," and "Mother's Best Hush Puppies," she laid open her life—her years as a "Russian child, a New York immigrant, and finally a southern housewife." In cooking foods remembered from the past, in exchanging recipes with far-flung friends and neighbors, southern Jewish women not only maintained Jewish identity but also sustained networks among Jewish southerners. And when they added fried chicken and sweet potato pie to the gefilte fish of their holiday tables, these women created a unique southern Jewish identity. That culture crossed boundaries of race and class, for Black cooks and domestics played central roles.

Political activism provides another prism for considering the intersection of race and class in American Jewish women's history. As Debra L. Schultz shows in "Going South," northern Jewish women risked violence and arrest as they fought for racial equality in the Deep South in the 1960s. Schultz understands how some women turned away from the conformity of the postwar Jewish suburbs, where Brumberg's diary writers lived, out of their "hunger for meaningful action." They found that the civil rights movement "gave life a focus and a meaning beyond those expected for daughters of the rising white middle class at the time."[5]

In these years, American Jewish women were also swept up in the second wave of American feminism. In "Jewish Feminism Faces the American Women's Movement," Paula E. Hyman considers the emergence of the Jewish feminist movement. While many of the early leaders of American feminism were in fact Jews, transforming Judaism was not their concern. Instead, Jewish feminism emerged among a group of young women who simply "could not deny the centrality of Jewishness in their identity." Applying the feminist critique to Judaism, they called for "the full, direct, and equal participation of women at all levels of Jewish life." But, as they discovered, Jewish feminism diverged from American feminism. Jewish feminists decried the latter's portrayal of "mothers simply as drudges" and were deeply concerned that the American women's movement embraced anti-Semitism cloaked as anti-Zionism. In recent years, Hyman observes, as Jewish communal institutions have embraced gender equality, secular feminists of Jewish birth have come to engage their Jewishness.[6]

NOTES

1. Assessing the American Jewish population is extremely complex; for a fuller discussion see Sidney Goldstein, "Profile of American Jewry: Insights from the 1990 National Jewish Population Survey," *American Jewish Year Book* 92 (1992): 77–173, esp. 107, 44, table 2.

2. Vivian Gornick, *Fierce Attachments* (New York: Touchstone Book, 1987), 106.

3. Anne Frank, *Anne Frank: The Diary of a Young Girl,* trans. B. M. Mooyaart (1952; rpt., New York: Pocket Books, 1972).

4. For a fuller discussion, see Riv-Ellen Prell, *Fighting to Become Americans: Jews, Gender, and the Anxiety of Assimilation* (Boston: Beacon Press, 1999).

5. This comes from the introduction to Debra L. Schultz, *Going South: Jewish Women in the Civil Rights Movement* (New York: New York University Press, 2001).

6. On the impact of Jewish feminism, see Sylvia Barack Fishman, *A Breath of Life: Feminism in the American Jewish Community* (New York: Free Press, 1993).

Chapter Fourteen

The "Me" of Me

Voices of Jewish Girls in Adolescent Diaries of the 1920s and 1950s

Joan Jacobs Brumberg

In March 1955, fifteen-year-old Sandra Rubin wrote in her private diary: "Often as I open this book . . . I wonder, what is to become of all this writing? Some is silly, some serious and meaningful. Will it all be on the bottom of an aged cedar chest in the attic? Or will it be read by a few close friends? Or will I become important enough to have it published? Or will it be destroyed in a war? How I wonder and dream about my diaries! They are so meaningful! They show so well the 'me' of me."[1]

Just like many other middle-class Jewish girls in her generation, Sandra regarded her personal diary as her "most treasured possession," and she appreciated its usefulness as an important emotional outlet: "Without you, O my dearest of books, without you as a companion I should be so lonely, so inhibited, so tightly bottled up." Because she understood the ways in which she had inscribed herself on its pages, Sandra Rubin fantasized about threats to the diary and proclaimed her loyalty to it. "I swear that the first thing I will save in any crisis will not be money, nor clothes, nor jewels, but you!" she assured the inanimate little book. Sandra's conviction that her diary captured her true self, what she called "the 'me' of me," suggests a great deal about the continuing emotional needs of girls, needs that transcend time, place, and ethnicity but are also shaped by those same considerations.[2]

But diary keeping was not something that either Sandra's mother or her grandmother did. In the 1950s, for the first time, large numbers of American girls began to keep diaries, just as their gentile sisters had done since the nineteenth century.[3] Until the post–World War II era, diaries were, by and large the expressive vehicle of well-educated white Protestant girls, and the personal voices of Jewish adolescents were muffled and hard to discern. But in the 1950s, Jewish girls found a satisfying vehicle for describing and reflecting on the process of growing up. These diaries now provide historians and psychologists with an opportunity to assess the relationship between popular culture and self-image, particularly the ways in which Jewish girls did (or did not) internalize messages from the mainstream gentile culture.

Why this expressive form was generally delayed until the 1950s is a complex matter that reflects the changing nature of Jewish life in America. Although I have searched long and hard for the manuscript diaries of ethnic girls, no group—whether African American, Italian American, Asian American, Latino, or Jewish—seems to produce a sizable cohort of adolescent diarists until they are substantially middle class or at least until they are driven by bourgeois imperatives and expectations for self-expression and personal happiness. Obviously, opportunities to express oneself in adolescence are structured by social class, a reality that makes both the existence and the content of diaries an important barometer of the acculturation process.

By the 1950s, more and more American Jewish families had achieved middle-class status, and, as a result, their daughters were emotionally and materially privileged in ways that earlier generations were not.[4] This generation—the grandaughters of immigrants—had the time, space, and inclination to contemplate "private" thoughts and write them down. They lived at home, and they did not work for wages except for occasional jobs that provided them with their own "spending money." Girls like these also had their own rooms, where they wrote in their diaries without parental surveillance, surrounded by clothes, cosmetics, stuffed animals, and phonograph records, all of which were linked to their sense of identity. Diary writing in this generation was further stimulated by the fact that adolescents could purchase, with their weekly allowance, small leatherette volumes embossed in gold and provided with a lock and key.[5]

After the American publication of Anne Frank's diary in June 1952, many adolescent girls, Jewish and gentile alike, began to think about the value of a private journal.[6] Anne Frank represented all the Jews who were murdered in the Holocaust, but she also epitomized the normal difficulties of adolescent girls, especially anxieties associated with sexual development and learning to assert one's individuality in the context of family life. Anne Frank's diary was an immediate publishing sensation: the first printing was sold out on publication day; by the end of the summer of 1952 it had become a staple on national best-seller lists. By 1957, there was both a Broadway play (starring Susan Strasberg) and a Hollywood film (starring Millie Perkins). By 1959, the diary had sold over 3.5. million copies.[7]

In this way, Anne Frank became a fixture of American popular culture in the 1950s. Middle-class Jewish parents reinforced the idea that Anne was a model of the spirit and resiliency of the youthful Jewish female by giving the diary to their daughters, either as a special gift or simply to read after the adults had finished it. Although few Jewish girls actually cited Anne Frank as the reason for starting a diary, many mentioned that they had read or seen the story of her life in the Secret Annex, and they used this experience to reflect on their own diaries and on the differences in their situations.

In 1959, after seeing the Preminger movie at a Saturday matinee in Queens, New York, thirteen-year-old Ruth Teischmann wrote: "I know I can't make this diary like hers because there's no Hitler (thank G-d), but I'll try. I'd rather there would be no Hitler and a fair diary than Hitler and a great diary." Ruth felt that her life as a teenager was less interesting than Anne's because of the freedom she had as an

American Jew, but she reveled in the high emotions generated by the film: "It was fabulous. Every minute [the Franks] thought the Nazis would find them, my heart beat so fast. I thought everyone around me would hear it." Ruth's reading of that awful moment when the Franks were discovered and taken from the Secret Annex demonstrated how Hollywood priorities and adolescent sensibilities combined to turn the story into a romance: "At the end, when the Nazis finally did come I was so sad because Anne and Peter were in love, and they would have to *split up,* but I didn't cry" (my emphasis).[8]

For Lynn Saul, another Jewish teenager growing up in the 1950s, Anne Frank's diary also provoked comparison. "I certainly hope and pray my diary never will serve the purpose hers did. The purpose of my diary is to tell all the happenings of my daily life which I simply would boil over with if I couldn't tell something about them."[9] Lynn Saul clearly regarded her diary as an important outlet in her emotional life, but she also understood that her daily writing—done in the comfort and security of her suburban Pittsburgh bedroom—probably was no testament to history, the way Anne's was. For girls like Ruth and Lynn, reading and thinking about Anne Frank was a way to explore and affirm the value and privilege of being a Jewish girl in a country where it was possible to feel safe and unthreatened.

Despite their familiarity with Anne Frank and the specter of European anti-Semitism, adolescent diarists in the 1950s rarely wrote about their Jewishness as an issue or influence in their personal development. This is not to say that Jewish identity had disappeared among daughters of middle-class Jews in postwar America; these girls went to "services," attended seders, and sometimes reported on the rabbi's sermon. In general, however, religious identity took a backseat to concerns about appearance, social life, and heterosexual identity. In the 1950s, the core subject matter of most adolescent diaries was remarkably formulaic, regardless of religion or locale. Driven by powerful protocols for popularity, Protestant, Catholic, and Jewish girls alike filled their diaries with rapturous reports about "sighting" desirable boys, the contents of important telephone conversations, and wistful thoughts about perfect hairdos and prospective dates. Being Jewish gave some structure to these possibilities—usually in terms of whom to date or which parties to go to—but it was rarely mentioned as a factor in defining the self, and it appeared only occasionally as an issue in high school when real dating began. Instead of classic issues of adolescent sturm und drang, girls' diaries in the 1950s seem preoccupied with the trivial.

The personal diaries of the postwar cohort reflected images of women in American popular culture. These girls wanted to be pretty, personable, and, most of all, popular.[10] When they represented themselves to themselves in their private journals, they worried more about their individual social success than they did about patterns of exclusion because they were Jews. In effect poor grooming or an awkward social style [was] treated as [a] greater liability than being Jewish. Although these girls clearly understood anti-Semitism, it did little to limit their aspirations. Almost all wanted good grades and looked forward to college, an expectation that marked them as a watershed generation in the history of American Jewish women.[11]

The absence of Jewish content in the identity struggles of girls in the 1950s and their concentration on the details of adolescent social life provide a stark contrast to the experience of Jewish girls who came of age in the 1920s. These two generations of adolescents, the 1950s and the 1920s, are linked not only by their common experience of postwar prosperity but also by their familial and emotional relationship to one another: many girls who were adolescent in the 1920s became the mothers of girls who were teens in the 1950s. Because of the exigencies of life during the Great Depression and the fact that many young people did not have jobs, marriages were delayed throughout the 1930s; opportunities for higher education also evaporated, particularly for girls.[12]

Jewish girls who were daughters of immigrants rarely kept diaries, a reality that makes the reconstruction of their experience in the 1920s more difficult than for the prolific and well-documented 1950s. Although I looked persistently for manuscript diaries by adolescents in the second generation, I had little success until I discovered a rare diary that provides a revealing contrast to the "assimilationist" voices of the 1950s. This diary, the personal journal of Helen Labrovitz, provides an invaluable window into the thoughts and experiences of a Jewish girl in the 1920s, one who came of age in a distinctive New England environment that was decidedly different from either the *shtetls* of the Old World or the urban ghettos of the New World. Being Jewish was inextricably tied to how Helen represented herself, and her words and thoughts on this subject prefigure themes of popular fiction writers of the 1950s, such as Herman Wouk and Philip Roth, who created female characters who saw themselves as forever marked and different because of their Judaism.[13] Helen Labrovitz's diary is a firsthand account of the particular difficulties of being Jewish in the 1920s, but it also evokes the struggle of countless other minority girls who shaped their self-image in a mass culture that did not include representations of their "own kind."

Helen Labrovitz was born in 1907 in Amherst, Massachusetts, to Russian immigrant parents; she was the fourth child in a family of eight that included three girls and five boys. Helen had one older sister, Rose, born in 1900, and one younger sister, Edith, born in 1909. Until after World War I, the Labrovitzes were the only Jewish family in Amherst, although there were a growing number of Jewish boys who were students at the area's colleges and universities.[14]

Helen's father, Isaac, was apprenticed as a tailor in his native Odessa, and he spent a year in London before his arrival in the "Golden Medina," where he took advantage of every economic opportunity. In short order he moved away from New York's East Side to Northampton, Massachusetts (where he had family), and then to nearby Amherst, where he turned his talents with needle and cloth into a successful collegiate haberdashery business that rented caps, gowns, and tuxedos but also sold clothing geared to the tastes of male students in a flourishing college town. In Amherst, the growing Labrovitz family lived above the store, and all the children attended local schools. By the early 1920s, when Helen entered high school, the business was prospering, and its proprietor had changed his name from Labrovitz to Landis, an alteration that he hoped would save his children from discrimination and also make for a shorter, snappier business sign.[15]

Although Helen enjoyed hanging around "the store" because it provided her with an opportunity to flirt with attractive Amherst College freshmen, she was sometimes embarrassed by her father's behavior there. Whether he was Landis or Labrovitz, Papa was less refined than she wanted him to be, a fact that galled Helen in her adolescent years: "Felt how foolish papa was to talk to customers in his absurd manner which is terrible. This isn't the first time I realized [sic] it but I can't believe it." Her father's "absurd manner," which was designed to entertain and sell merchandise, included "telling dirty jokes" and being "abjectible" (sic), both of which did little to win the heart of a teenage girl who was attuned early in life to the politics of gentiles and gentility in a town dominated by a Congregationalist elite.

In this environment, Helen learned and came to embrace popular distinctions about "good" and "bad" Jews. In the early 1920s, when Harvard publicly announced its intention to impose a Jewish quota, the policy was often justified on the grounds that the university did, after all, accept good ones; it simply had no responsibility for the others: "No one objects to the best Jews coming but the others make much trouble especially in the library." Even the liberal and sympathetic editors at the *Nation,* a magazine that took a strong stand against institutional anti-Semitism, admitted that there were "disagreeable Jews, the product of a race in transition."[16]

Distinctions between good and bad Jews were operative for Helen because they were useful in establishing her own identity in adolescence, but they also explain some of her impatience with her father. Although she did not mind that her parents sometimes spoke privately to one another in Yiddish, when she was mad at Papa she was not above casting him as old-fashioned and uncouth. And when she saw the 1922 silent film *A Five Dollar Baby,* about an orphaned Irish waif adopted by a kindly Jewish pawnbroker named Ben Shapinsky, she was pleased that it was about "good Jews." Helen developed early an acute sensitivity not only to how her "own kind" were portrayed but also to how they behaved.

Because her mother was so busy with younger siblings, Helen's older sister, Rose, became her guide to what was right in American clothing, education, and social behavior. As in many large families, the Landis siblings grouped themselves into older and younger cohorts, and Helen forged a special relationship with Rose, the second oldest child, who was a home economics major at the State Agricultural College in Amherst when Helen began keeping her diary in 1922 at the age of fifteen. By this time, Rose was living in a nearby dormitory, where Helen could drop in to chat and even spend the night with her sister. As a result of her enthusiasm for her older sister's collegiate life, Helen had little patience for her younger sister, Edith, the only other girl at home. They had frequent disagreements, which Rose tried to mediate from afar but with little effect. "Fight with Edith," Helen noted summarily in October 1922. "How terrible I am. For that I get another pimple."

Because she was the oldest girl at home, Helen had a considerable amount of domestic work throughout her high school years. As a fifteen-year-old she regularly cleaned the house, ironed clothes, did the dishes, and cared for her younger brothers, but not without resentment. "I washed the floors, like a good little girl," Helen reported sarcastically. On the other hand, Helen clearly understood her role in the family economy, and she worked hard at a number of menial jobs that many middle-class girls would not do by the 1920s: she cleaned regularly at the Ginsburgs' boardinghouse, and in the summer of 1922 she joined Rose in the White Mountains of New Hampshire, where they both worked as waitresses at the Crawford Notch House. It was hard serving and clearing three meals a day when you were just fifteen, and there were some unhappy moments when Helen overheard nasty comments at her tables "about Jews and the oatmeal." Still, it was extremely lucrative, and she made enough money to send most of it home to her parents in the form of money orders written at the local post office. When she returned to Amherst, she had another job, providing child care for the son of an Amherst College faculty member. A significant portion of Helen's earnings was set aside for college tuition.

For Helen and for her entire family, the educational institutions in and around Amherst were a natural stimulus to think about higher education. The Landis boys swam in the Amherst College pool and belonged to the Boys Club led by college students; the girls attended basketball games at the State Agricultural College, now the University of Massachusetts, and went to lectures. Although they were well aware that "Aggies" lacked the social status of Amherst or Smith students, the elder Landis children were quick to take advantage of the free tuition at the state college. When Edward went there to study horticulture and Rose to major in home economics, the family made an important step into the middle class.

In this collegiate environment, both Rose and Helen developed tastes and aspirations for the life-style of middle-class, educated New England women. Their mother, Sarah, supported the Yankee ambitions of her girls: as early as her sophomore year in high school, Helen was encouraged by her mother to think about Smith (rather than "Aggie" or one of the state normal schools) despite its hefty tuition and upper-class ambiance. When Helen actually saw the Smith campus for the first time, she wrote: "It's wonderful. I'd like to be rich and go there." When sister Rose graduated from "Aggie" and went off to Cornell University to study for an advanced degree in dietetics, she urged her little sister to follow her to Ithaca. Neither Smith nor Cornell was exactly a plebeian place in the 1920s, and neither attracted many girls who still ate kreplach, borscht, and gefülte fish in their homes, as Rose and Helen Landis did.

At Amherst High School, where there were only a few other Jewish students, Helen worked hard to achieve academic and social success. Like any adolescent girl, regardless of religion or race, Helen wanted to be well liked and popular, and she assumed that if she did well and also looked good, friends would come her way. Her diary reveals a young woman who was constantly concerned about receiving high grades and who often prayed for assistance in that realm: "Had English exam which I hope God will help me through with an A." But when Helen made the honor roll, she proudly linked that achievement to her Jewish identity: "Mr. Brown read my name on the [sophomore] honor roll. . . . Edith and I were the only Jewish kids. Was happy because [I] deserved it after hard work. Even Emily Lockwood congratulated me."

Helen's blonde, blue-eyed good looks and petite figure also won her numerous compliments, which she recorded in great detail: "Mr. Novick thinks I am pretty. I wonder who else does." And "Ade Henry said I was the best looking girl in the sophomore class and Maxie [her brother] said I was beautiful but selfish." At fifteen, Helen was attractive enough to generate constant compliments even from gentiles, but she was just as often confused as she was exhilarated by this admiration: "[Steven] Witt told me I was pretty. Can it be true?"

Despite all the compliments and her solid school record, Helen remained convinced that being Jewish had a negative effect on her status at Amherst High. In her mind, Judaism was a burden that inhibited her popularity. On a number of different occasions, she told her diary what she told some of her teachers and a few of her peers: "the girls do not like me because I am a Jew." When she announced this in English class, she got a negative reaction and came home frustrated: "now they hate me worse." Although she spoke to one of her teachers about her feelings, the issue was never resolved, and Helen remained on edge about it, sometimes turning to her closest friend, Sadie Ginsburg, for empathy and long "chats about [our] Jewishness." These conversations were clearly about social identity, not about religion, however. The Landis family owned no Bible, Helen knew no Hebrew, and she attended a synagogue for the first time in her life when she was fifteen.[17]

Yet being Jewish clearly defined the shape of Helen's adolescence: although she mixed with Protestant and Catholic youngsters in school, extensive interactions with non-Jewish boys were discouraged if not prohibited. In October 1922, when she had an interest in a gentile boy from Amherst, Helen wrote: "Saw McLead— Dear boy is lucky [that I like him] but he is not Jewish." Discrimination based on religion was an operative principle in the 1920s, and family names, such as Labrovitz or even McLead, were often a basic impediment to acceptance by mainline Protestant groups. When a college student told Helen about the systematic exclusion of both Catholics and Jews in Theta Chi fraternity, she responded: "Ah what a world that a nation should be held in shame for their names."

Like many girls, Helen worried about peer acceptance, but her concerns were intensified by an undercurrent of anti-Semitism, which gave normal adolescent anxieties an even more painful edge. Although she never used the term "anti-Semitism" or offered any thoughts about its sources, she did recognize the unpleasant pattern in her life and reported direct harassment in a matter-of-fact way. In the spring of 1922, following an after-school session with her French teacher, Helen complained that she had to stand "belittlement for I am Jewish." A few weeks later, she reported meeting Hop Eldridge, a local Amherst boy, who called her "a female Jew" as he drove away on his bicycle. This made Helen "awfully mad" and caused her to comment in her diary that it was "a cursed world."

But, most of the time, Helen's discomfort was generated by feelings of exclusion, rather than by name-calling or taunts. When a song she wrote failed to be published in the *Graphic Board*, the school newspaper, she responded to the rejection note with this quip: "A Jew has no place unless he works hard." And when she longed for the leading role in the prestigious Junior Play, she asked God to give her the part in exchange for "being a Jew": "Yes, God I have been disappointed enough in my life. Make me get in [the] play. Please." Helen failed to get the role she coveted, but she considered herself lucky, given her religion, to get any part at all. Over and over she felt the pain of exclusion in Amherst and admitted to feeling "jealousy" and "hatred" toward "those terrible Christians." A set of troubled interactions with classmates prompted her to write: "After school talked with the girls. I can feel the curse of those Gentiles in my Jewish blood and so I wish I could go to Springfield and live with Tante Edith and go to Springfield High School."

In 1924, when she was seventeen, Helen Landis got her opportunity to attend college and also to enter a larger, more Jewish world. Because Rose (now twenty-four) was working as a dietitian for the Federation of Jewish Charities in Baltimore, Helen went there to live with her sister and attend Goucher College, formerly the Women's College of Baltimore.[18] Although Goucher did not have the panache of Smith or Cornell, it was well regarded, and the sisters' consolidated living arrangements made it possible to pay the tuition and launch Helen on a collegiate career.

Although Helen loved the idea of being a college girl, the experience did little to resolve the anxieties she felt about being Jewish. In fact, the first few years in Baltimore exacerbated her uneasiness because she became profoundly sensitive to social class distinctions both within and outside the Jewish community. In Baltimore, Helen was exposed to more varied forms of Jewish life: the squalid tenements of East Baltimore with its newly arrived Russian immigrants; the lively social organizations and noisy entertainments of young Jewish working people; and the ample, well-managed homes and private clubs of the city's successful German Jewish elite. Although the house she shared with Rose and two other unmarried Jewish social workers provided her with access to many young Jewish professionals, including a sizable pool of eligible young men in medical and law school, Helen was not terribly happy because she still felt that she did not fit in.

At Goucher, Helen felt like an outsider again, only this time it was worse. Not only was she Jewish, now she had an occasional "flunk slip" to deal with, and she felt poor by comparison with classmates who lived in the dormitories. Helen rarely even got invited there, and, when she did, it was notable: "spent some time in the girls' college room—it's nice to be rich, Oh boy!" Helen also felt different because she had no real family, as did the other commuting students, most of whom lived at home with their parents. "I'd love to have a home here [in Baltimore]," she wrote. "Why should my life be so different from the millions of other girls in this world?" Some of the "city girls" did invite Helen for dinner or bridge at their homes, where she got a taste for a more affluent, bourgeois Jewish life.[19] But her pleasure was tempered by her envy and an adolescent tendency toward exaggeration. After a visit to the home of a Goucher friend, Helen wrote: "I felt a sense of jealousy grip me for the people who live in real houses—and go around with their own type. . . . This is a thing I've been deprived of all my life. Something that can never be made up for—not even a case of lost time."

So, despite the opportunities Baltimore provided for lively entertainments, frequent dates, and numerous absorbing romances, Helen never felt like a real college girl, although she adopted all the collegiate lingo, such as "darling" and "row-did-dow" or "bummed" and "bunk." Helen's most gnawing concern was whether or not she could afford to continue being a college girl. Although she had saved the required $425 for the first year, she was uncertain as to how and where she would find the money to enroll for the second. This was particularly upsetting in the context of Baltimore, where she met all kinds of young Jewish men and women, some aspiring and preprofessional but many other poor and ignorant, and this forced her to realize how precarious her class status really was. Without college, she would be just an ordinary working girl like those she saw at parties and dances but did not like.

Given her admiration for New England culture and reserve, in Baltimore, Helen became particularly sensitive to the specter of "the kike."[20] Although she never cut herself off from the city's Jewish social clubs and enjoyed occasional Friday evening services at the Reform Synagogue on Eutaw Street, Helen sprinkled her diary with expressions of her distaste for ordinary Jews and their social life. In November 1925, she lamented having wasted "a good day of my life preparing and serving at . . . a true Jewish banquet. What fuss and business over nothing. How those Jews can talk." When Helen went to an event sponsored by the Council of Jewish Women, she came away with little feeling of sisterhood and declared instead: "Jewish girls . . . as a type do not agree with me." Her complaint was that they were "loud and flashy"; another time she wrote: "I dislike the average type of Jewish girl. She's so boisterous and flippy." Helen clearly saw herself as different: "the Jews here, I'm not used to them!" she exclaimed after a dance at the Young Men's Hebrew Association. A Phi Delta Epsilon fraternity dance prompted her to detail how she stood out: "Had a darling time. Feel as tho[ugh] I have poise and beauty among those heterogenous Jew girls."

Helen drew pride from her Yankee roots and her allegedly "non-Jewish" looks because they signified assimilation and suggested her status as a college girl. When a student at Johns Hopkins remarked that she "looked Jewish" and asked if she lived in East Baltimore (the Jewish section), Helen was deeply insulted. At this stage in her life, the highest compliment anyone could pay her was to say that she did not look or act Jewish. "I slept at Ann Robinson's house," Helen wrote when she was eighteen. "Had a nice time. They said I had lovely skin and looked like a Gentile." In the fall of 1925, Helen was equally delighted when Morris Davidson, an artist who was one of Rose's friends, told her that she was not only "sophisticated for a girl of eighteen" but that she also acted differently from most Jewish girls. *"I don't act Jewish,"* she wrote pointedly and excitedly, underlining Davidson's welcome affirmation of her identity. At another point she stated bluntly: "Revelled in the fact that I am not an average Jewish type." (In effect, Helen prided herself on her ability to "pass" in much the same way that light-skinned African Americans did.)[21]

But Helen had to work in order to remain a college girl, and that was an unpleasant and disappointing reminder of how close she really was to the mass of young Jewish working women. Her sister announced that in her sophomore year she would expect Helen to begin paying five dollars a week toward her board, a request that Helen considered "just" but provoked her to ask: "My God, how will I do it?" As a result, at the end of the spring term of 1925, Helen did not go home to Amherst but began to work five days a week as a salesclerk in the lingerie department at Hochschild, Kohn and Company, a flourishing Jewish-owned department store in the heart of Baltimore's shopping district, where she had worked before as a "contingent" just on Saturdays. During the summer, Helen tolerated the work because she was able to combine it with an active social life and frequent jaunts, even during the week, to a cottage on the Middle River, where she could swim and row in the evening after work. Moreover, she was anticipating her fall return to Goucher and a swift conclusion to her stint as an urban working girl.

But on a hot sticky day at the end of August, Helen heard from Rose that she must continue working throughout the month of September, right up until school started, or return to Amherst and go to "Aggie." This turn of fortune took Helen by surprise and became a focus for outbursts of unhappiness and a general moodiness. "[I] realize how much I am ashamed of working when others about me of my intelligence and career don't have to," Helen admitted candidly. But understanding her resentment did not stop her from deliberately "playing the college girl" at work and belittling the "plain" and "illiterate" working girls who were her colleagues at the store: "I feel right[ly] superior towards the average sales girl. She is ignorant, selfish, and unwilling to help fellow workers." Store policy fueled Helen's distance from the other salesgirls; because she had college credentials, she was paid more for the same work.

Although Helen had some good days at work, in her diary she represented September 1925 as a tragic interlude that entailed great suffering: "Realize how much I hate work and everything in Life. Hate the people around me and the life I am leading." Late in September, when some girls were already back on campus, Helen lamented her class position: "I don't realize [understand] why I have to work when other girls who attend Goucher with me are so wealthy and well-dressed. Why is it my fate to work, to toil, and suffer? What have I done to deserve the miserable lot I have to take? Life—what has it in store for me . . . ? I am told I have a beautiful face and perfect form! I can swim, row, dive to perfection. [Nothing] is beyond my power to do and comprehend, except that I am unhappy." By late-September, when there was still no assurance that she could return to Goucher, Helen became extremely nervous and fearful. To convince Rose that she would do anything to remain, Helen promised to be responsible for cleaning the house they shared with two of Rose's friends. Privately, Helen was willing to act as a domestic to ensure that she could be a college girl.

Helen's return to Goucher in October was a great relief, and she looked for assurance that the tribulations of September and her temporary loss of status had had no long-term effect. "Felt as much like a college girl as they did," she pronounced happily after seeing some classmates from the year before. The first week of classes provided Helen with a time to revel in collegiate life and its obvious privileges: "It sure does seem good to be back again among the college friends of mine. These girls and this environment is so different from that of the average working girl. Oh how thankful I am to be among the 'intelligentia' [*sic*]:" Helen repeated this theme many times, as if repetition would solidify her status: "Love to feel like one of the college girls—to sit among them and imbibe the same things and be in their environment. After all I am one of them." College, she said, "elevate [d] [her] feelings and thoughts on the cosmic things in life."

Yet Helen Landis's remaining years at Goucher continued to be marked by emotional oscillations rooted in her feelings of class insecurity, rather than absorption in her schoolwork. "I had an inferiority complex all day," she noted as a junior when Goucher seemed threatening and inhospitable; a week later she felt positive about her ability to adapt to the college's tony environment: "Felt very important and acted like one of the Goucher girls." However flexible and successful she was, the Goucher experience generated in Helen a deep awareness of the prerogatives of wealth and social class: "How little one is worth after all if they have no money," she wrote in 1927. With the help of her older sister, she began to acquire some of the outward, costly trappings of her collegiate status. In her junior year, she had her hair bobbed in what she called a "panjola," and Rose bought her a raccoon coat so that she would feel stylish and truly collegiate.

Even though Helen's diary entries revolved around boyfriends and social anxieties, she did have some meaningful intellectual experiences at Goucher that were critical in shaping her adult life. As a result of readings and discussion in her social science classes, as well as a number of inspiring chapel sermons about the value of social work, the class-conscious young woman in the raccoon coat began to accompany friends who were social workers on their visits to poor families in East Baltimore, exactly the social address she longed to avoid.[22] In 1928, Helen Landis graduated from Goucher with a degree in sociology and became a social worker, living in and working out of the Neighborhood Center, a settlement house in the pushcart section of Philadelphia run by the Federation of Jewish Charities.[23] During the Depression, she worked with the Department of Homeless Men and later with the County Relief Board; she also married (a Jewish attorney, Milton Mitchell Bennett) and raised two sons.

In maturity, Helen Landis Bennett became a competent and caring social work professional who empathized with the plight of the poor and also felt a strong identification with Judaism and humanitarian causes. But as an adolescent girl who longed for social acceptance, she was often unhappy, and she articulated in her private diary some of the most painful and intimate aspects of growing up female in the second generation of American Jews. Although her concerns about popularity, autonomy, and identity were (and are) characteristic of most American adolescent girls, these concerns had a particular edge for the daughters of immigrants who lived in a non-Jewish world, such as Amherst, Massachusetts, or Goucher College.

As Helen did the normal developmental work of separating from parents, establishing an individual identity, and mapping a future, she also had to cope with the difficulties of being Jewish and female in a fast-paced society, where sexual mores were in flux, her parents were "greenhorns," and her religious identity was a real liability. Although Helen attributed many of her high school problems to prejudice, she felt relatively secure and happy as long as she remained in Amherst, where there were only a few Jews and she knew them all. But, in Baltimore, where she saw the full range of Jewish experience, including the rough, illiterate, and avaricious, she began to internalize some of the worst aspects of popular anti-Semitism. Increasingly, her self-definition and self-esteem rested on her ability to separate herself from the mass of her own people, a pattern often described as Jewish self-hatred.[24]

Because she was a truly modern girl, one who understood the critical linkage between good looks and female success, Helen focused her energies on looking and acting like a "college girl," a status that somehow neutralized both her Judaism and her tenuous class position. By attending Goucher and also looking gentile, Helen hoped to distance herself from the mass of working-class Jewish girls whose dark hair and eyes, common clothing, and boisterous behavior were a reflection and a reminder of her roots. But Helen's reliance on negative differentiation was not unusual at her stage of life: most adolescents find it easier to articulate what they do not want to be, rather than what they admire or are.

In her diary, Helen Landis represented herself to herself as a girl who was doing something original. Like most young people, she regarded herself as authentic and unique. Of course, in some ways she was: her perspective was shaped by the experience of her particular family, their special location in Amherst, her subsequent move to Baltimore, and her individual psychological makeup. But her personal diary also stands as testimony to the anguish and the rewards of the assimilation process for an entire generation of Jewish women. With its frank admission of envy of others and disgust for her own, Helen captured the pressures experienced by Jewish girls who were both bright and confident enough to pursue higher education in an environment that provided them with enormous new opportunities but failed to welcome them with open arms. For these girls, growing up Jewish required that they cope with a range of normal developmental burdens as well as their difference, difference from their classmates and also from their own mothers, whose old-world origins provided inadequate preparation for raising daughters who were so deeply invested in modernity.[25]

How young women of the second generation traversed adolescence had real consequence for the kind of mothers they became, which in turn affected the daughters they raised and encouraged to keep diaries in the 1950s. Those who were "outsiders" in their youth, such as Helen Landis, made serious investments in helping their teenage daughters "belong," be popular, and look good in ways that were sanctioned and encouraged by postwar educators, doctors, and beauty experts. This was the first generation of Jewish parents able to buy their daughters unblemished skin (with dermatologic treatments), perfect teeth (with orthodonture), and better looks (with contact lenses).[26] And because of Anne Frank and the legacy of the Holocaust, Jewish mothers in the 1950s probably aided and abetted their daughters' immersion in teenage culture because it seemed so "normal" and they felt so fortunate.

Ultimately, the diaries of Jewish girls in the 1950s stand as a powerful symbol of security and middle-class expectation. Their numbers, compared to the 1920s, and their formulaic content demonstrate how potent the ideals of youth culture had become and how cultural imagery is internalized by young girls as they struggle to define and understand the self in their adolescent years. Although the material circumstances of Jewish life in America had certainly improved, adolescent girls in the 1950s seemed no more able than their mothers to resist powerful imperatives about beauty and feminine behavior. The irony may be that the hard-won economic and social success of postwar Jewry and the legacy of Anne Frank combined to make them even more vulnerable to the seductions of mass culture.

NOTES

1. The diary of Sandra Rubin (pseudonym), b. 1939, in the collection of the author.

2. This dynamic—the interplay of the biological, psychological, and cultural—is central to the history of female adolescence described in my book *The Body Project: An Intimate History of American Girls* (New York: Random House, 1997). I am particularly interested in how relatively fixed developmental imperatives, such as the biological processes of adolescent development, are shaped by different social and cultural settings.

3. Adolescent girls in the United States first began to keep diaries in large numbers as part of the evangelical revivals associated with the Second Great Awakening. For a history of trends in girls and diary keeping, see Joan Jacobs Brumberg, "Dear Diary: Continuity and Change in the Voices of Adolescent Girls" (Gannett Lecture, Rochester Institute of Technology, Rochester, NY, January 1993). On American girls and diary keeping at the end of the nineteenth century, see Jane Hunter, "Inscribing the Self in the Heart of the Family: Girlhood and Diaries in Late Victorian America," *American Quarterly* 44 (March 1992): 51–81.

4. For an excellent description of the history of American Jews in the period preceding, see Henry L. Feingold, *A Time for Searching: Entering the Mainstream, 1920–1945* (Baltimore: Johns Hopkins University Press, 1992).

5. The growth of the personal diary industry is reflected in Thomas's *Register of American Manufacturers* for the years 1910–1960. In the 1950s, the largest supplier probably was the Samuel Ward Manufacturing Company in Boston. Over 70 percent of the commercial diaries that I have read, by girls in the 1950s, were produced by this company.

6. *The Diary of a Young Girl,* written by Anne Frank, appeared in Dutch in 1947 and in Germany and France in 1950. In the United States, the first printing was sold out on the first day, and fifty thousand copies were sold within a week. See *Publishers Weekly,* June 5, 1952; August 2, 1952. Popular coverage of the Anne Frank story developed again in 1957 when the movie, produced by Twentieth Century-Fox, appeared.

7. See *Publishers Weekly* for the 1950s. According to Alice Payne Hackett and James Henry Burke, *80 Years of Best Sellers, 1895–1975* (New York: R. R. Bowker Co., 1977), *The Diary of a Young Girl* had sold over five million copies by 1975, making it fifty-ninth in the list of best-sellers.

8. Diary of Ruth Teischmann (pseudonym), b. 1946, entry for September 26, 1959, Schlesinger Library, Radcliffe College, Cambridge, MA.

9. Unpublished diary of Lynn Saul, b. 1945, entry for October 1960, in the collection of the author.

10. See Wini Breines, *Young, White and Miserable: Growing Up Female in the 1950s* (Boston: Beacon Press, 1992).

11. Beginning in the 1920s, American Jewish girls went to college in disproportionately higher numbers than did other ethnic groups, but only in the post–World War II era did the percentage of Jewish women in college approximate or exceed 50 percent of the eligible age group. On the history of Jewish girls in college, see Ruth Sapinsky, "The Jewish Girl at College (1916)," reprinted in *The American Jewish Woman, 1654–1980*, ed. Jacob Rader Marcus (Cincinnati: American Jewish Archives, 1981); Bernard J. Weiss, ed., *American Education and the European Immigrant, 1840–1940* (Urbana: University of Illinois Press, 1982), 46–55; Abraham Lavender, "Studies of Jewish College Students," *Jewish Social Studies* 39 (winter-spring 1977): 37–175; Alfred Jospe, "Jewish College Students in the United States," in *The American Jewish Yearbook*, ed. Morris Fine and Milton Himmelfarb (New York: American Jewish Committee, 1964), 131–45. See also Sydney Stahl Weinberg, *The World of Our Mothers: The Lives of Jewish Immigrant Women* (Chapel Hill: University of North Carolina Press, 1988), 175.

12. This is my own story and another reason that I gave this essay the title "The 'Me' of Me." On the effect of the Depression on adolescents and young adults, see Glen Elder, *Children of the Great Depression* (Chicago: University of Chicago Press, 1974).

13. See, for example, Herman Wouk, *Marjorie Morningstar* (Garden City, NY: Doubleday, 1955); Philip Roth, *Letting Go* (New York: Random House, 1962); and Roth, *Portnoy's Complaint* (New York: Random House, 1969).

14. All of the quotations that follow are from the manuscript diaries, 1922–27, of Helen Landis, now in the possession of the author. There were actually ten children born to Sarah Browdy Laprovitz; Lewis died at his bris in 1906, and Florence died of rheumatic fever at age eleven, when Helen was eight. For an interesting account of growing up in Amherst as the son of immigrants, see Edward Landis, "An Immigrant Boyhood in Amherst, 1904–28," in *Essays on Amherst's History* (Amherst, MA: Vista Trust, 1978), 270–80.

15. What Isaac Landis and others did not realize, however, was that name changes were often transparent in America and that some educational institutions, such as Harvard, ferreted out students with Jewish origins by asking on preliminary admission forms if the applicant's father had ever changed his name. See "What Was Your Father's Name," *Nation* 115 (October 4, 1922): 332.

16. Ibid.

17. The synagogue was in Springfield, Massachusetts, the home of Helen's father's younger brother. Springfield had a sizable Jewish community in the 1920s, a synagogue, and kosher restaurants.

18. Goucher was founded in 1885 by the Baltimore Conference of the Methodist Episcopal Church. See Anna Heubeck Knipp and Thaddeus P. Thomas, *The History of Goucher College* (Baltimore: Goucher College, 1938).

19. Almost all of the Jewish students at Goucher were commuters in this era; as of 1910, there were only seventeen Jewish graduates of the Women's College of Baltimore. See Isidor Blum, *The Jews of Baltimore* (Baltimore: Historical Review Publishing Co., 1910), 55.

20. For a definition, see H. L. Mencken, *The American Language*, 4th ed. (New York: Knopf, 1960), 295. It is relevant to note that Mencken lived in Baltimore and probably heard the same vocabulary as Helen Landis. Baltimore was a city whose Jewish population had long been divided into Uptown (German) and Downtown (Russian) Jews; Henrietta Szold initiated the first night schools and Americanization efforts for the Russian Jewish immigration, beginning in the 1880s and continuing unabated well into the 1910s and even early 1920s. See Blum, *The Jews of Baltimore*; Naomi Kellman, *The Beginnings of Jewish Charities in Baltimore* (Baltimore: Jewish Historical Society of Maryland, 1970); and Isaac M. Fein,

The Making of an American Jewish Community: The History of Baltimore Jewry from 1773 to 1920 (Philadelphia: Jewish Publication Society, 1971).

21. Passing is a theme in fiction by Nella Larson, James Weldon Johnson, William Dean Howells, and Mark Twain. For discussions of passing among African Americans, see Joel Williamson, *New People: Miscegenation and Mulattoes in the United States* (New York: Free Press, 1986); Juda Bennett, *The Passing Figure: Racial Confusion in Modern America* (New York: Peter Lang, 1996); and Cheryl Wall, "Passing for What? Aspects of Identity in Nella Larsen's Novels," *Black American Literature Forum* XX (spring–summer 1988).

22. Sociology was extremely popular in American colleges and universities in the 1920s; see Dorothy Ross, *The Origins of American Social Science* (Cambridge: Cambridge University Press, 1991). Helen took classes in "social origins" and "social theory," among others.

23. On the history of women in social work, see Penina Glazer and Miriam Slater, *Unequal Colleagues: The Entrance of Women into the Professions, 1890–1940* (New Brunswick, NJ: Rutgers University Press, 1987).

24. See, for example, Sander Gilman, *Jewish Self Hatred: Anti-Semitism and the Hidden Language of the Jews* (Baltimore: Johns Hopkins University Press, 1986).

25. This is a theme in Weinberg, *World of Our Mothers,* as well as in the fiction of Anzia Yezierska.

26. On middle-class investments in the skin, teeth, and beauty of adolescent daughters, see Brumberg, *The Body Project,* ch. 3.

Chapter Fifteen

Rage and Representation
Jewish Gender Stereotypes in American Culture

Riv-Ellen Prell

Jewish mothers, for more than fifty years, and Jewish princesses for the past decade, are well-known and pervasive stereotypes of Jewish women held by Jews, as well as by many other Americans. In combination, the two stereotypes provide opposing, if related, images of women who overwhelm men, respectively, by excessive nurturance or acquisitiveness.

According to these stereotypes, Jewish mothers give too much, whether it is food or demands for success. They suffer and induce guilt in their ever disloyal children, particularly sons. They behave like martyrs and constantly deny their own needs and wishes. The Jewish mother's character is captured well by the ethnic variant on the light bulb jokes of the 1970s.

> How many Jewish mothers does it take to change a light bulb?
> None, "I'll sit in the dark."[1]

Martyred, willing to sacrifice, yet miffed at those who neglect her and forget her sacrifices, the stereotypical Jewish mother exaggerates all forms of maternal nurturing, only to invert them by her demand to be compensated through the constant love and attention she will never directly request.

By contrast, Jewish American Princesses (JAPs) require everything and give nothing. In jokes about them, they are completely focused on themselves and their overwhelming needs. They do not nurture but require others to meet their constant demands. They do not take responsibility, or cook, or clean for their families. They are particularly obsessed with their physical attractiveness, although not in the interest of sexual pleasure. A widely circulating joke about JAPs conjures up the stereotype.

> How do you get a JAP to stop having sex?
> Marry her.

In this essay, I examine pervasive Jewish gender stereotypes held by Jewish men about Jewish women. They appear in popular, widely circulated jokes, as well as in canonized literature written by American Jewish men. These gender stereotypes are changing. Jewish mothers are yielding to Jewish American Princesses, and a male stereotyped persona, the Jewish American Prince, is appearing on the scene for the first time. Stereotypes, then, change because they are sensitive to changing issues of relations between ethnic and majority groups. I will argue that the changing humor and stereotypes reveal the conflicts experienced by Jewish men as they negotiate their difference from and continuity with American culture.

These stereotypes certainly reveal a particular form taken by Jewish men's ideas and anxieties about women. What is less apparent is that the women of these jokes may also symbolize many facets of American Jewish life for men. The culture that gave rise to and nurtured these widely known gender images communicated powerful constructions of what constituted success, Americanization, loyalty, and Jewishness. Gender and ethnicity are linked in this humor because how Jewish men think about Jewish women may well reveal how they think about themselves as Americans and Jews.

Scholars of ethnicity, normally committed to the study of boundaries and differences, in this case between Jews and Christians, systematically overlook the *intra*group differentiation between men and women who share an ethnic group. Gender and ethnicity are rarely and have been only recently considered together. Men and women, for example, may be joined by ethnic ties, but they often experience the consequences and meaning of their ethnicity differently. Feminist anthropologists, historians, and sociologists have demonstrated the significance of these differences in a variety of cultures and historical periods.

Gender is significant not only because it forms the basis of social relationships within ethnic groups but also because it frequently symbolizes the ethnic group for its members, as well as outsiders. Long suffering, nurturing mothers and distant fathers are each gender-coded symbols, which may represent an entire ethnic group in the mass media and to its members. Interpreting these stereotypes provides clues for understanding what links gender to ethnicity and how that link operates to establish differentiation both from outsiders and within groups.

Gender can be made to represent ethnic experience because it is so closely associated with relationships—self and other, child and parent—that quite explicitly portray one's place in a group. Gender, then, can be linked to intimacy or outsiderhood, or versions of both, and is a powerful symbolic vehicle for constructing, and reconstructing, the significance of ethnicity for minority men and women within a dominant culture.

Stereotyping is inevitable when groups, differentiated by a variety of factors, meet within a single social system. Stereotypes simplify and concretize difference. Sometimes humans admire others from afar, creating positive stereotypes, but more often stereotypes denigrate and differentiate groups to the advantage of those who hold these ideas. In neither positive nor negative cases are stereotypes accurate depictions of reality. Rather, they are representations of others, created sometimes out of limited shared experiences and sometimes out of fears projected on others one may know well. Gender stereotypes are more likely the latter. In combination with ethnicity, gender stereotypes may be decoded to understand how difference is expressed not only between groups but within them, as well.

Jewish stereotypes, like all other cultural stereotypes, rely on broad social categories. For example, both European and American Jewish humor have employed culturally significant categorical differences, such as social class, region of origin, and level of religious and secular education. Contemporary American Jewish humor, however, particularly since the 1960s, seems singularly focused on gender. The Jewish mother is the most prominent figure of contemporary Jewish humor,[2] and jokes about her began before the Second World War. Jokes about Jewish American Princesses developed in the 1960s and flowered in the 1980s. As a result, the joke repertoire about Jewish women includes wives and potential marriage partners, as well as mothers. As Susan Schnur wrote about students, Jewish and non-Jewish, whom she taught at Colgate University in 1987, "I had been raised on moron jokes; *they* had been raised on JAP jokes."[3] Jokes about Jewish women have become a common coin of American life, as well as the central province of American Jewish humor. The subjects and numbers of jokes about women are expanding, but the images are redundant. The Jewish mother and princess reflect one another. The jokes often rest on simple inversions of characterizations thought to be ridiculous.[4]

Gendered jokes have dominated American Jewish humor, but women rather than men are consistently the subjects of these jokes. There are no Jewish father jokes, and the Jewish American Prince is just developing as a stereotype, not yet the subject of a series of jokes. Both the prominence of women in the humor and the absence of men from it require explanation as much as the roles (mother and princess) that are featured, to the exclusion of any other type of woman. Gender stereotypes, and the humor that makes use of them, seem neither random nor idiosyncratic. They depend on a narrowed, yet consistent set of messages and ideas. Jewish women are, for example, associated with a number of roles and activities, as well as social movements that range beyond mother and potential wife. The presence of Jewish women in unions, Socialist movements, and contemporary politics from feminism to antiwar activism conceivably could have yielded a stereotype of a political activist. Many Jewish women have, like their middle- and upper-class counterparts in the larger society, been active participants in voluntary and charitable associations, but no stereotype of a "society lady" has emerged. Linking Jewish women to men through these two stereotypes is an issue to be understood rather than assumed.

Marilyn Strathern, an anthropologist who writes about New Guinea, has put the problem of gender stereotypes well by differentiating between "the ideal" and the "actual,"[5] urging us never to read from stereotype to behavior, or from idealized images to actual social relations, because representations are not actualities. Gender stereotypes are symbolic representations of the sexes, underpinning formal relations of authority or power. While typifications may tell us about many features of a society, how women and men actually function in a particular social system cannot be predicted by the stereotype alone. In Strathern's research among New Guinea Hageners, men and women may well be associated with either gender stereotype. Stereotypes must be "read" for cultural notions and then interpreted in light of how men and women behave. The inevitable inconsistencies can aid our understanding of cultural prescriptions, as well as the realities of social existence.

In a pluralistic and literate society, the matter of stereotypes is more complex.

Stereotypes are often written into literature, which is then read by members of the subculture, as well as by those outside it. Inscribed in print, these stereotypes take on reality for people inside and outside a subculture. At the same time, male and female stereotypes may stand as cultural symbols for a series of relationships between opposites. They may also symbolize intrapsychic conflicts about belonging and rejection, associating women, for example, with negative ethnic group qualities, such as aggression, and distancing males from these associations. All of these possibilities only underscore Strathern's caution that gender stereotypes cannot be read literally but must be understood in a series of contexts.

Strathern's insight is crucial for understanding American Jewish gender stereotypes. The popular and scholarly studies of these stereotypes consistently discuss whether or not they are "true" or "provable." While Jews have long been engaged in combatting anti-Semitic stereotypes, their encounter with gender stereotypes is of a different order. Jewish gender stereotypes are largely held among and generated by Jews themselves. They tend, then, to articulate internally held constructions. Yet, they bristle with the hostility and degradation that are associated with anti-Semitism. To read the stereotypes as actualities moves us away from the task of understanding what they mean.

Some argue that the stereotypes are untrue, others that they are true, and others still that they are both true and untrue.[6] Those that argue they are untrue claim, by way of sociological and quantifiable studies that, for example, Jewish mothers are not measurably more protective than others, or that Jewish college-age women are not different from their peers.[7] They claim, particularly in the cases where these stereotypes are also held in the wider society, that these caricatures are codes for anti-Semitic accusations masked by gender.[8] And, indeed, some suggest that gender slurs seem to function to overshadow the transparent anti-Semitism.[9]

Nevertheless, there are those who argue that the stereotypes are based on accurate descriptions of behavior, and link their "truth" to cultural and historical developments. They explain that a history of uncertainty and oppression creates a preoccupation with safety, hence the Jewish mother with her suffocating behavior.[10] Others argue that a long religious tradition of sexual repression leads to certain attitudes toward the body and pleasure, hence the Jewish woman characterized as the frigid Jewish princess.[11] Or, as the folklorist Alan Dundes suggests, more recent Jewish American Princess stereotypes suggest a rejection of middle-class norms that idealize complicit women devoted to denying their own needs in order to satisfy those of their families.[12]

Finally, there are those who write that the stereotypes are *both* true and untrue. For example, several writers who have looked at the stereotypes of Jewish women's sexuality suggest that Jewish men may denigrate women's sexuality out of their fear of inadequately competing with gentile men.[13] Others argue that these stereotypes constitute a Jewish internalization of anti-Semitism expressed by the larger culture. This more profoundly psychological analysis recognizes the complex process by which minorities represent themselves to themselves as outsiders in a majority culture. These typifications involve internalized negative stereotypes held by others about one's own group. The very popularity of the JAP jokes with some non-Jews may well support this point. The implicit anti-Semitism of JAP jokes means one thing within the Jewish community and another outside it, but both associate Jews with an unfair and undeserved affluence.[14] Indeed, the JAP humor of the late 1980s is more hostile and, by implication, violent than previous decades.

> What is the difference between a JAP and a vulture?
> Painted nails.
> What do you call 48 JAPs floating face down in a river?
> A start.[15]

Jokes, such as these, wish the death of people who are both women and Jews. The graffiti about JAPs reported on college campuses suggests that these stereotypes share much in common with racist ones. The line between "self-hate" and anti-Semitism is becoming harder to draw.

My point is not to support or deny these analyses of stereotypes. Rather, it is to suggest that virtually all approaches to the study of Jewish gender stereotypes invoke an unexpectedly positivist base that assumes they are capable of being accurate reflections of reality, or at least partially true, or generated from seekers of truth. What is missing in this conversation is some sense of these gender stereotypes as symbolic representations of American Jewish experience, and any inquiry into why relations between men and women are a medium for constructing Jews' relationships to other Jews and to American culture.

The humor, as I read it, suggests a fundamental incompatibility at the core of American Jewish culture. To be an American and a Jew necessitates relinquishing one or another of those identities. Social class, career aspirations, styles of interaction and sexuality—separately and together—are codes for and symbols of how one is American. I suggest that the stereotypical suffocating mother or whiny and withholding wife express ideas about how Jewish men understand their own place in American society. These stereotypical women represent the anxiety, anger, and pain of Jewish men as they negotiate an American Jewish identity. Jewish women, in these stereotypes, symbolize elements of "Jewishness" and "Americanness" to be rejected. Jewish women represent these features precisely because of their link to Jewish men, whom they do and do not resemble. Like a distorted mirror, Jewish men see Jewish women as inaccurately reflecting themselves. These stereotypes suggest that women may be represented as "too Jewish" or "too American," through their pattern of sexuality, nurturance, and consumption. Because gender and ethnicity are about sameness and difference, these stereotypes associate certain features of American and Jewish life with women that Jewish men fear and wish to abandon.

American Culture and the Jewish American Princess

No one is certain where this stereotype began, but a princess-like character appears in Herman Wouk's novel *Marjorie Morningstar*[16] and in the character of Brenda Patimkin in Philip Roth's short story "Goodbye Columbus" some years later.[17]

Both works of fiction were made into popular films. This stereotyped young woman is a figure of postwar American Jewish affluence, whose key features concern consumption and sexuality, activities that figure as structural opposites in the humor and stereotype. The JAP is as rapacious and eager a consumer as she is unwilling to engage with her husband in an animated and mutually satisfying sexual relationship. When she is sexually active, it is as a lure to entrapment.

The JAP can be both a wife and a daughter in the humor, and both relations make possible her insatiable desire to consume through acquiring expensive things and going to expensive places. Perhaps the most often told "consumption joke" asks, "What is a JAP's favorite wine?" The punch line ranges from "Take me to Florida" to "Buy me a mink." The answer not only may interchange various luxury consumer items for one another but can vary depending on the person to whom it is directed. Some versions specifically include "Daddy, take me to. . . ." in the joke. Such jokes use consumption to link a woman to her husband and her father as vehicles for achieving her desire. JAP jokes about sexuality link only husband and wife and assume her to be withholding and uninterested or portray the JAP as sexually active because she is an unmarried woman. One JAP joke makes the complex links disturbingly clear. "How do you give a JAP an orgasm? Scream 'Charge it to Daddy'."[18] There is no mutuality in any of these relations. The JAP takes but does not give. She takes because she is dependent and may give only to create dependence.

What is particularly striking about the humor as Jewish humor is how it portrays the butt of the jokes. Jewish humor in Europe and America typically has been iconoclastic. It is antiauthoritarian, mocking all authorities, including God. Jews have often used their sharp humor to puncture the authorities within and without their community, who could not otherwise be criticized. Little people tended to emerge triumphant by the punch line of the joke.[19] This humor often ridicules the grandiose as offending a fundamentally democratic spirit. By contrast, the JAP, almost always the butt of the joke, is a whiner and a consumer, but she is neither powerful nor authoritative. Paradoxically, she, not the males who support her, is open to ridicule. As American Jewish humor focuses on gender, its sharp edge is directed at a relatively powerless figure. If the JAP is grandiose, the others in her world of affluence are free of ridicule and not the butt of the joke.

JAP jokes are atypical Jewish humor for a second reason. They are unmarked by any specific Jewish characteristics. There is no Yiddish in the jokes, or even dialects, both of which have been essential features of many generations of American Jewish jokes. The JAP has few qualities in common with other Jewish characters in Jewish humor. She is neither the fool nor a clever deceiver. There is only a small measure of parody in the humor and some irony. If there is one humorous device, it is, of course, exaggeration, but little else.

JAP jokes are constructed around completely American figures in American settings, behaving like Americans, in other words: consumers. Indeed, even the name of the stereotype, the JAP, is interesting because of the position of "American" in it. "Jewish mothers," or "German Jews," or "rabbis," or "schnorrers" (hangers on) never carried a cultural designation specific to the United States. The JAP stereotype is overwhelmingly marked by the American experience, the postwar American experience in particular. Although there is evidence in earlier immigrant novels of vulgar bourgeois women, in Yezierska's *Bread Givers*[20] and Gold's *Jews without Money*,[21] they were neither young nor on the verge of marriage. Even married JAPs do not have children. Brenda Patimkin's mother in Roth's "Goodbye Columbus" was a woman of the suburbs, but she was not a princess, for all her wealth and attractiveness. The JAP, then, has no accent, and no history marred by suffering, hunger, or want, all typical of immigrant experiences. She not only is fully American but epitomizes American success; she is affluent.

The Construction of the JAP Stereotype

The JAP is in every way American, and yet she is the butt of contemporary Jewish humor. What, then, is funny about the Americanness of the JAP? The answer lies in part in understanding from whose perspective the JAP is constructed. The JAP is a different type of Jew and American from the teller of the joke. The folklorist Alan Dundes's analysis of the JAP implies that Jewish women have created the image as a protest. He writes, "For women, the JAP joke cycle pinpoints what's wrong with the traditional roles women were expected to accept cheerfully in the American upwardly mobile middle class."[22] However, these jokes are not told from the point of view of women. They are always told *about* women. Women are the butt of the jokes.[23] Although women may tell these jokes, they tend to tell them about others. Although some women may call themselves "JAPs" or wear gold necklaces that say "JAP," they are typifying themselves from another's point of view.

Dundes draws a peculiar conclusion about the JAP joke from the point of view of women when he insists that the disinclination of women to engage in oral sex is because it "presumably give(s) primary pleasure to males."[24] Nowhere do the jokes suggest that any form of sex is pleasant for women. And Dundes also argues that the humor portrays autonomous women because the JAP is free to shop and beautify herself. This conclusion is hardly convincing if we are to believe that this joke cycle appeals to middle-class women as an expression of protest against their lack of autonomy and self-expression.

In JAP jokes, women are passive, except for engaging in those activities done for the purpose of making themselves attractive—shopping, staying thin, and beautifying themselves—which depend on leisure and affluence. A greeting card that consists of JAP jokes portrays a JAP: she is standing, dressed in tennis whites. She wears high-heeled shoes, drapes a mink coat over her shoulder, and wears a long strand of pearls at her neck, and a Diet Pepsi with a straw stands before her. The diet beverage and tennis attire suggest a preoccupation with staying thin, but the portrayal of her as a physically active or competent woman, even for leisure, is undermined by the presence of jewelry, mink coat, and, above all, high-heeled shoes. Affluence and consumption undermine her physical vigor.

These stereotyped women are emulating culturally prescribed standards of beauty associated with the highest social strata. Whether this form of beauty—

obsessively thin and highly styled—is directed toward men may be debatable. Nevertheless, this appearance depends on affluence and leisure, the combination of which is most likely acquired through marriage.

The jokes and images present women as nonsexual and narcissistic. More to the point, they make men victims of prey of women because men finance consumption but get nothing in return. In the jokes, JAPs withhold sex and victimize men. These jokes, their images, their anger, and their exaggeration, are constructed by males about women. The perspective of the joke teller and the butt are quite straightforwardly differentiated by gender. What appears to be funny about the jokes, what constitutes a "protest" in the humor, is that men saddled with demands for producing economically to finance consumption reveal their true oppressors. The message of the humor is that Jewish wives or potential wives are slave drivers and ridiculous in their unceasing consumption. For all of their apparent beauty, JAPs are frauds, sexless and childish. Men tell these jokes as an apparent protest against their fate with these women.

Paul Cowan's memoir about his journey to become a Jew articulates a related perspective.[25] He wrote about events that occurred decades before he became committed to feminism and Judaism. Consequently, we must read this passage about his relationship to Jewish women as a young man in light of his "new" consciousness. In the memoir, he describes why he avoided young Jewish women after reading *Marjorie Morningstar*. In this novel he discovered "Shirleys," stereotyped Jewish women feared by the novel's initially appealing male character, Noel Airman, who wants a career in theater. For Wouk and Cowan, the "Shirley"—a predecessor of the JAP—had the potential to ruin a man's life. Cowan writes:

> I feared that Jewish women would imprison me. It left me feeling scared that my idealized version of my adult self as a latter day James Agee or John Dos Passos would be stifled by some Shirley who outwardly encouraged me to adventure but who privately planned to trap me in a stifling suburban home. By contrast, the blondes to whom I was attracted were golden girls who would help me act out my journalist's version of the frontiersman's dream. They would provide me with protective coloration.[26]

Cowan makes explicit that the JAP stereotype is a gender stereotype held by Jewish men about Jewish women. It is constructed by a Jewish man in opposition to his immediate world. He does not want to exist within his family's expectations. He does not want to be forced to work or live like his father, who achieved affluence for the family. He does not want to be constrained by the expectations or narrowed vistas of American Jews hurtling themselves toward suburban success.

Precisely as the Jewish male rejects the Jewish American Princess as the embodiment of middle-class Jewish life, he does so with another woman and another life in mind. I would argue that JAPs are always constructed in contrast to a concealed stereotyped Christian woman whom Lenny Bruce called "the shiksa goddess," or Philip Roth portrayed as "the monkey" in *Portnoy's Complaint*.[27] If Jewish women consume, then there is an unnamed stereotyped woman who does not. If the JAP avoids oral sex, as in the singleminded preoccupation of JAP jokes, there is a

stereotyped woman who apparently delights in it. Cowan implies this general opposition between Jewish and gentile women when he writes of the "protective
coloration" of the "golden girl," who is decisively not Jewish. If the JAP is accessible
and the expected partner of the Jewish man, the shiksa may be interesting in part
because she, like many aspects of American culture, may not be attainable.

In the published text of a performance piece, "The Last Jew in America," Susan
Mogul reflects Cowan's and Wouk's construction of Jewish men's attitudes toward
Jewish women by dramatizing a Jewish woman's view of this relationship in the
following monologue:

> My mother said, "You know, Susan, you could be the last Jew in America, with the
> way all your brothers and sisters are intermarrying." I thought I owed it to my
> research, at least to try to go after a Jewish guy and see what it's like. Who knows?
>
> Anyway, I went out to the Beverly Hills singles bars one night, and I had absolutely
> no luck. Christian guys would come up and we talked, but no Jewish action whatso-
> ever. So I called up my friend Carol Mike on the phone and I said, "You know, Jewish
> men just don't want to date Jewish women, I'm convinced of it. We'll conduct a
> scientific experiment. I'll prove I'm right."
>
> I went down to Woolworth's and I picked up this cross for $5.95, and, of course, I
> scratched the words "not really" on the back to protect myself from the wrath of my
> father and of God, as well. (She hangs the cross around her neck.)
>
> Well! You would not believe the action. You think I'm exaggerating, but really. I'd
> never gotten so much attention from Jewish men *in my life,* or from men at all.[28]

Cowan and Mogul both reveal a construction of Jewish gender relations in which
Jewish men reject Jewish women. A woman is not essentially attractive or unattrac-
tive. What makes a woman attractive to a Jewish man is that she is identifiably
non-Jewish. As a non-Jew she will not be focused on consumption, her husband's
productivity, and success, either because she already has it or because she is so poor
and undemanding she cannot imagine it.

The asymmetry of the identifiers "American" (desirable) and "Jewish" (undesir-
able) reflects a second asymmetry between male and female. What is constructed in
these male-generated Jewish gender stereotypes is not a simple, more familiar mirror
image. We do not find oppositions, such as male is to female as strong is to weak
or aggressive is to passive. Rather, we find a triangulated relationship. Jewish men
are to Jewish women are to Christian women as successful is to demanding is to
acquiescent, or as sexual potency is to frigidity is to sexual desire. The third term is
ever present but always invisible. It is the JAP's Jewishness and its relationship to
her Americanness that the stereotype and humor feature. Jewishness is what she
shares with the constructor of the stereotype. As he seeks his counterpart, he must
construct two females, one like him and one unlike him, rejecting the Jewish woman
and their shared qualities in favor of the American woman. Frederic Cople Jaher
argues that, in American Jewish fiction, Jewish protagonists are inevitably punished
for their liaisons with gentile women. He writes that "Jewish boys who forsake
Jehovah and virtuous women of their own faith for Dionysius and gentile tempt-
resses inevitably get punished."[29] Jewish gendered humor, as well as the stereotype
itself, demonstrates that Jewish men also perceive themselves as punished for liai-

sons with "virtuous women of their own faith." The punishment results from associating Jewish women with the American economic success that deprives men of the sexual rights associated with gentile women.

Consumers and Consumed: The Refiguring of American Affluence

The JAP stereotype describes married but apparently childless women, or women in search of a marriage partner at the age of marriageability. Like the princess of fairy tales, the JAP always stands on the threshold of womanhood. The JAP's link to marriage is the most salient feature in her portrait as entrapper. Middle-class American Jewish men, not unlike most American men in the middle class, see adult status, ambition, career, and marriage as linked. Mainstream American Jewish culture has successfully encouraged its young adults to make choices that lead to careers that guarantee, at minimum, a middle-class life. The American Jewish family has made this career pattern for men its highest priority since immigration, certainly emphasizing education and success over religious observance and Jewish education. Not only are American Jews economically successful ethnics, they have achieved their success through education leading to a limited number of professional and career choices. They do so with remarkable loyalty to their ethnic group, demonstrated by their choice to live among Jews and maintain Jewish friendships. This pattern is particularly true of second and subsequent generations of men, who have been in the workforce for a longer time than Jewish women and whose careers are determinative of family social class status.[30] Although as a group Jewish women are well educated, until recently they stayed at home with their children and entered the labor force much later, if at all.[31] These Jewish patterns are, of course, shared with the white middle class. Major demographic studies of New York, Boston, and Rhode Island demonstrate that Jewish success and Jewish identification, although not religious adherence, have been achieved.[32]

In American culture, success is associated with and symbolized by consumption, particularly since the Second World War. Jokes centering on JAPs' preoccupation with consumption, T-shirts that proclaim "I live to shop," and all the caricatures of spending to excess are the products of this pervasive American pattern. Warren Susman[33] and William H. Whyte,[34] among others, have written about the transformation of American society to a consumption-rather than a production-oriented culture. Nothing characterizes the suburban family more completely than shared consumption. And Elaine May's recent book on the postwar family maintains that consumption was a critical element in maintaining families against divorce in the 1950s.[35] Indeed, her discussion of the Nixon-Khrushchev debates in the 1950s demonstrates that even global policy was argued on the grounds of who had better consumer items and would be likely to maintain them over time.

The JAP stereotype, then, articulates the epitome of middle-class life and family-oriented consumption, whether owning the proper designer labels, spending a great deal of time in restaurants, or redecorating a home. The humor moves back and forth in its portrayal of the JAP as American (focused on consumption) and Jewish (narcissistic, sexually withholding, and manipulative). The jokes in no overt sense differentiate Jewish and American, but the humor depends on identifying against the JAP. The ironic juxtaposition of consumption and frigidity make clear that the JAP is the consummate consumer who cannot herself be consumed. A series of jokes, in fact, juxtapose shopping and sex.

> How does a JAP fake an orgasm?
> She thinks of going shopping.
> What's a JAP's favorite position?
> Bending over credit cards.
> What's a JAP's favorite position?
> Facing Neiman-Marcus (or Bloomingdale's).[36]

All that has been achieved by American success has been showered on the JAP, who inexplicably resists the sexual relationship that assures her continued affluence. This stereotype-driven humor, of course, does not *describe* Jews' social class, women's shopping habits, or sexual relations. Rather, it *represents* Jewish men's distress about becoming American men. Jewish women are portrayed as a barrier to adult male life because they withhold sex and demand production. Men are victimized by both demands and refusals. What appears to be the normal steps to adult life—education, career, marriage—in jokes and stereotypes are perilous steps on the way to disaster because of who waits in the wings as the appropriate marriage partner. Marriage will not ensure sexuality and will lead to a career that will drive one toward giving and receiving nothing in return. JAP jokes are only peripherally about women. Rather, women's demands and refusals symbolize what will become of men as they enter adulthood, only to be deprived of their dreams.

Links and Spaces between Jewish Mothers and Jewish American Princesses

To understand these key elements of the stereotype—consumption and the refusal to be consumed—requires reconsidering the older, more conventional female gender stereotype of the Jewish mother. Dundes's discussion of this stereotype attempts to generate the new acronym JAM, Jewish American Mother, but it is his invention and has not yet caught on in the culture. The Jewish mother has no geographic specificity. Novak and Waldoks, in their *Big Book of Jewish Humor,* suggest that the humorous figure of the Jewish mother appears only after migration to America.[37] This view is only partially correct. There has always been a Jewish mother or "Yiddishe mama," but she was not a butt of humor until the second generation of immigrant society. Henry Roth's *Call It Sleep*[38] and Michael Gold's *Jews without Money* both enshrine a perfect mother. She is present everywhere in the immigrant experience, from music to theater and from film to novels. But she is the representation of the lost world, the fantasy perfect mother, who is characterized above all by total and complete self-sacrifice for others, particularly her sons. Indeed, Novak and Waldoks argue that it is the Jewish mother's changing economic role that is responsible for her becoming a figure of ridicule. In Europe, she was a productive member of the family. In America, she no longer actively contributed to its economic survival. Rather, her inactivity became a sign of the financial success of her husband.[39]

These changes may well contribute to the stereotype. Nevertheless, it is not her financial dependency but her preoccupation with her children and concern for them, the very aspects of the once romanticized Jewish mother, which are the subjects for ridicule. Her characteristics change less than the perceptions of them held by her sons. By the second generation, she became the butt of humor because Jewish men were now the products of families focused on acculturation, and these sons rendered self-sacrifice as suffocation. Jewish men did not want to sacrifice and could not bear the sacrifices apparently implied by their mother's behavior. The all-giving mother was revealed as the all-demanding mother.

Ironically, for all of their differences, mother and princess present the same dangers to Jewish males. The Jewish mother cannot give her children enough food. The classic JAP joke about her ability to nurture states that what she makes best for dinner is "reservations." Over a period of a mere two decades, the stereotype of the Jewish woman became two stereotypes: a nurturer and a person unable to cook, feed, or care for her family, particularly her husband. Jewish mothers were separated from Jewish wives. The Jewish mother, however, bears a partial resemblance to the "shiksa" who gives all and asks nothing. The difference between "shiksa" and "mother" is that there are hidden demands in the mother's gift and that the mother is not gentile, American, or mainstream. Shiksas are not associated with food, and they are less nurturant than undemanding. Ultimately, then, what unites the Jewish mother and the Jewish princess is that each is a threat to the Jewish male: son and potential husband. These women are entrappers and seducers. Neither will give without asking for something in return. They are also bound to each other by their relationships to men.

Are Jewish mothers represented as having special alliances with Jewish princesses? Are these gender representations linked? I would suggest not. In literature, humor, and folklore, Jewish mothers are tied primarily to their sons. Jewish princesses seem to be made by their fathers in the humor I have reviewed. In all types of literature, humor, and folklore, there is an ever present sexual antagonism between men and women of the same generation, and an overattachment across generations. What cannot or will not be expressed between men and women of the same generation is played out between parents and opposite-sex children as intimacy without a sexual component. Mothers indulge their sons, and fathers indulge their daughters. Mothers hold out high aspirations for their sons, apparently expecting them to be different from the men they married. Fathers withdraw from their wives and delight in creating a royal daughter, despite the fact that they are never portrayed as kings.[40] The father-daughter link portrayed in JAP humor and stereotypes reflects the sudden affluence of many Jews following a major economic depression and World War II.[41]

Acculturation and Its Costs

In these gender stereotypes we see at work both the representations of profound contradictions in American Jewish life and the process of transmitting those very contradictions. In these stereotypes one finds consumption and success bought at the price of lost sexuality. We see women who demand and never reciprocate, leaving men successful yet betrayed. We see men feeling themselves under constant threat of annihilation, in the person of either the suffocating mother or the parasitic wife. The success that makes consumption possible satisfies the mother but does not provide the avenue for adult sexuality or mutuality. The promises of American culture pay off only in liaisons with the other, the shiksa or gentile, who then makes it impossible to continue Jewish life.[42]

The cultural costs and implications of an economic system in which men produce and women consume is well-documented. From Thorsten Veblen to the feminist Barbara Ehrenreich, social critics have noted the inevitability of men's resentment and women's portrayal as parasites built into this division of labor.[43] Elisa New's analysis of a recent book about the trial of a husband who murdered his wife because she was a "Jewish princess" effectively argues that Jews have collapsed American Jewish culture with American success, to such an extent that they have become indistinguishable.[44] Female representations among Jews—mother and princess—then clearly share much in common with other middle-class representations of women as narcissistic and sexually withholding.

These analyses do not, however, address other implications for male-female opposition within the family. In the case of American Jews, the Jewish family is associated with the continuation of the Jewish people. To marry a Jewish partner is increasingly seen as the most certain insurance for transmitting a culture and history. Sociologists have documented thoroughly the fact that when they form families, American Jewish adults become synagogue members and ritual participants. The center of Jewish life has moved from community to family to the individual. The individual is the center of gravity for Judaism. The choices leading to economic success and endogamous marriage are the most powerful promise for a continuing Jewish people.

The individualism of the American Jew, however, is rather different from the individualism of American culture, which idealizes the freedom to move anywhere, unfettered by any past. Unlike the quintessential American communities of the 1970s described by Frances FitzGerald, American Jews do not make up their lives free of a history.[45] The American Jew is, of course, no longer closely tied to a community bound by shared religious obligations and a single status hierarchy, as was the case for many centuries for Jews throughout the world. American Jews do not deny one another a place in their communities if they desecrate the Sabbath or violate various laws of purity. Nevertheless, neither are they free of a past nor do strongly identified Jews hope that their children will set out in search of an uncharted future. American Jews' persistent identification with Judaism despite their nonobservance of Jewish religious practice makes clear to their children that they should continue to be Jews. Individuals are autonomous and free to make their own choices. But these choices include the proper marriage partners, having children who understand that they are Jews, and being successful. These choices are expected, even overdetermined. They seem to be the minimum requirement for remaining within the normative Jewish community. Approval, love, and acceptance, qualities often associated with Jewish families, are typically withdrawn when individuals exercise their "autonomy" to make the wrong choices. Undeniably, American Jewish families emphasize these issues as they raise their children, and it is these cultural demands that are represented in the humor.

To be free of JAPs is to assert one's freedom from obligation, responsibility, and productivity, but it is also to negate the Jewish people, the family, and hence the self. To be linked to a JAP is to undermine the self linked to community. The Jewish mother who nurtures, protects, and rewards makes one Jewish and successful. The JAP takes and withholds and is constructed as the poisoned reward for success. This terrible dilemma is normally associated with the "wrong" choices made by Jewish men who are attracted to the forbidden outsider, the shiksa, who symbolizes an unambiguous Americanization. Intermarriage, however, implies abandoning one's own family and people. The stereotypes that are increasingly apparent in the 1980s suggest that Jewish men construct Jewish women as representations of a vision of American success associated with their parents' dreams for them. In this sense, the JAP is another version of the Jewish mother, bent on blocking access to unfettered autonomy precisely because she represents American expectations for consumption and success. This culturally acceptable union continues the Jewish people by both promoting the achievement of success and producing another generation. Obviously, men share these cultural norms, or the choice would not entail such conflict and agony. Marriage, women, and gender relations all symbolize this generationally transmitted conflict between the Jewish man's wish to enter adulthood and reproduce the Jewish people and a fear of that course as destroying his development as an autonomous male.

Jewish gender images, then, represent the tension between reproducing Judaism, maturing and assuming responsibility, and pursuing one's destiny. That men were trained for careers and women for marriage was one common pattern for success that appears to evoke this inevitable tension. However, stereotypes are not sociological road maps for describing how American Jews became who they are. Rather, they symbolize, through one gender's perspective, the association of sexuality, acculturation, family, and consumption, the key themes of American Judaism in the postwar period. These could not be European or immigrant stereotypes because they assume affluence; they reflect and construct choices and possibilities unavailable until the period of increasing assimilation. Indeed, Jewish intermarriage skyrocketed in the 1960s when these stereotypes were just taking shape.[46] They speak most centrally to the association of Judaism and suburban success and the projection of that desire for success onto women. Americanization as a middle-class aspiration appears to be feared by men, who associate Americanization with Jewish women. The other, the gentile woman, remains a counterbalance fantasy partner for freedom from this connection, but at the cost of a future.

Are There Princes in the Royal Family?

I have emphasized female stereotypes in this chapter. I emphasize the perspective of the stereotype because it provides the key to understanding why these gender representations appear when they do and in the form that they do. There are stereotypes about Jewish men, but few are named. There is no Jewish father, for example, although there is the pervasive stereotype of the Jewish male as passive. Only recently has a defined stereotype of the Jewish prince emerged. The writer Nora Ephron describes him in her book *Heartburn*. He wants attention and service lavished upon him. She writes,

> You know what a Jewish prince is, don't you? If you don't, there's an easy way to recognize one. A simple sentence, "Where's the butter?" Okay. We all know where the butter is, don't we? The butter is in the refrigerator. . . . But the Jewish prince doesn't mean "Where's the butter?" He means "Get me the butter." He's too clever to say "Get me" so he says "Where's." And if you say to him (shouting) "in the refrigerator" and he goes to look, an interesting thing happens, a medical phenomenon that has not been sufficiently remarked upon. The effect of the refrigerator light on the male cornea. Blindness. "I don't see it anywhere." . . . I've always believed that the concept of the Jewish princess was invented by a Jewish prince who couldn't get his wife to fetch him the butter.[47]

The Jewish prince is simply the son of the Jewish mother. He has become the butt of the joke and stereotype. The presence of this stereotype simply inverts the mirroring images of one male and two women, one Christian and one Jewish, for one woman and two males.

These direct inversions—prince and princess—emerge as stereotypical parallel figures as Jewish mother and father did not. The culture generated a marked Jewish mother and left Jewish males entirely unmarked. Perhaps the newest gender stereotypes speak to a change in family relations, in part created by the fact that both men and women are likely to be employed. Changing family relations are unlikely, however, to be the sole explanation for these stereotypes. Gender representations continue to express the tensions and conflicts surrounding assimilation, acculturation, and success which continue to be associated with one's family of origin and choice of marriage partner.

I have argued that Jewish gender stereotypes are a strategic site for the analysis of American Jewish culture. I suggest that the focus of American Jewish humor on gender relations requires that we understand why these relations effectively symbolize how Jews attempt to remain Jews and live in the American mainstream. Understanding that the point of view of the stereotype is male, I have argued that Jewish women are associated with the desire for prestige, consumption, the continuity of the Jewish people, and the absence of erotic desire. Gender stereotypes are a rich vein to be mined for understanding American culture and the ways in which social class, ethnicity, gender and culture guide the construction of American lives.

These stereotypes suggest that Jewish men and women do not experience their Judaism in precisely the same way. Both are clearly affected by the association of Judaism with social class, but women, until recently, were dependent on husbands' and fathers' successes to achieve Americanization and mobility. Men reacted to that dependence in the portraits they made of wives and mothers as demanding and suffocating. The link of class and ethnicity is a close one for American Jews, who seek success without assimilation. Since cultural uniqueness is guaranteed by marriage choice, it should not be surprising that the dangers and enticements of assimilation are expressed in representations of Jewish women, both young and mature, as dependent, insatiable consumers with devastating power.

NOTES

I appreciate the helpful, often witty, always insightful comments of Howard Eilberg-Schwartz, Sara Evans, Steven Foldes, Amy Kaminsky, Elaine Tyler May, Cheri Register, Anna Tsing, and Barbara Tomlinson on a previous draft of this chapter.

1. William Novak and Moshe Waldoks, *The Big Book of Jewish Humor* (New York: Harper and Row, 1981).

2. Ibid.

3. Susan Schnur, "When a J.A.P. Is Not a Yuppie? Blazes of Truth," *Lilith: The Jewish Women's Magazine* 17 (1987): 10–11.

4. Alan Dundes "The J.A.P. and the J.A.M. in American Jokelore," *Journal of American Folklore* 98 (1985): 456–75. Dundes has also noted the link between these two stereotypes; as I note, our approaches differ on several points.

5. Marilyn Strathern, "Self Interest and the Social Good: Some Implications of Hagen Gender Imagery," in *Sexual Meanings; the Cultural Construction of Gender and Sexuality,* ed. Sherry Ortner and Harriet Whitehead (Cambridge: Cambridge University Press, 1981), 166–91.

6. Dundes, "The J.A.P. and the J.A.M.," 466–68, addresses these issues of Jewish women's stereotypes and some of the literature on the stereotypes.

7. See Zena Smith Blau, "In Defense of the Jewish Mother," *Midstream* 13 (2): 42–49, and Sherry Chyat, "JAP-Baiting on the College Scene," *Lilith: The Jewish Women's Magazine* 17 (1987): 42–49.

8. Chyat, "Jap-Baiting," 7.

9. Francine Klagsburn, "JAP: The New Anti-Semitic Code Words," *Lilith: The Jewish Women's Magazine* 17 (1987): 11.

10. Charlotte Baum, Paula Hyman, and Sonya Michel, *The Jewish Woman in America* (New York: Plume, 1975), 242.

11. Susan Weidman Schneider, "In a Coma! I Thought She Was Jewish!: Some Truths and Some Speculations about Jewish Women and Sex," *Lilith: The Jewish Women's Magazine* (1979): 5–8.

12. Dundes, "The J.A.P. and the J.A.M.," 470.

13. Schneider, "In a Coma!"

14. Jewish gender stereotypes have captured some interest of late. Graffiti were found in 1986 at Syracuse University throughout the library slurring Jewish American Princesses. These incidents have been discussed by Chyat, "JAP-Baiting," Schnur, "When a J.A.P. Is Not a Yuppie?," and Judith Allen Rubenstein, "The Graffiti Wars," *Lilith: The Jewish Women's Magazine* 17 (1987): 8–9.

15. Cited in *Lilith* 17 (1987).

16. Herman Wouk, *Marjorie Morningstar* (Garden City, NY: Doubleday, 1965).

17. Philip Roth, *Goodbye Columbus* (New York: Houghton Mifflin, 1959).

18. From Noble Works Greeting Card.

19. Novak and Waldoks, *Big Book of Jewish Humor,* xx–xxi.

20. Anzia Yezierska, *Bread Givers: A Struggle between a Father of the Old World and a Daughter of the New* (1925; repr., New York: Persea Books, 1975).

21. Michael Gold, *Jews without Money* (1930; repr., New York: Avon Books, 1965).

22. Dundes, "The J.A.P. and the J.A.M.," 470.

23. The significance of gender for the perspective of the joke is also noted by Gladys Rothbell, "The Jewish Mother: Social Construction of a Popular Image," in *The Jewish Family: Myths and Reality,* ed. Steven Cohen and Paula Hyman (New York: Holmes and Meier, 1986), and E. Fuchs, "Humor and Sexism," in *Jewish Humor,* ed. (Tel Aviv: Papyrus Publishing House, 1986).

24. Dundes, "The J.A.P. and the J.A.M.," 470.

25. Paul Cowan, *An Orphan in History: Retrieving a Jewish Legacy* (Garden City, NY: Doubleday, 1982).

26. Ibid., 112.

27. Philip Roth, *Portnoy's Complaint* (New York: Random House, 1969).

28. Susan Mogul and Sandy Nelson, "The Last Jew in America: A Performance by Susan Mogul," *Images and Issues* 4 (1984): 22–24.

29. Frederic Cople Jaher, "The Quest for the Ultimate Shiksa," *American Quarterly* 35 (1983): 529.

30. See Steven M. Cohen, *American Assimilation or Jewish Revival?* (Bloomington: Indiana University Press, 1988); and Calvin Goldscheider and Alan S. Zuckerman, *The Transformation of the Jews* (Chicago: University of Chicago Press, 1984).

31. Sidney Goldstein and Calvin Goldscheider, *Jewish Americans: Three Generations in a Jewish Community* (Englewood Cliffs, NJ: Prentice Hall, 1966).

32. See Steven M. Cohen, *American Modernity and Jewish Identity* (New York: Tavistock, 1983), Cohen, *American Assimilation,* and Goldstein and Goldscheider, *Jewish Americans.*

33. Warren I. Susman, *Culture as History: The Transformation of American Society in the Twentieth Century* (New York: Pantheon Books, 1984).

34. William H. Whyte, *The Organization Man* (Garden City, NY: Doubleday, 1956).

35. Elaine Tyler May, *Homeward Bound: American Families in the Cold War Era* (New York: Basic, 1988).

36. Dundes, "The J.A.P. and the J.A.M.," 464. In the third joke, an obvious reference is made to Jews facing east when they pray in remembrance of their allegiance to ancient Israel and Jerusalem, which was the center of worship. In the joke, shopping is associated with prayer and sex is stimulated by facing a substitute sacred center.

37. Novak and Waldoks, *Big Book of Jewish Humor,* 268.

38. Henry Roth, *Call It Sleep* (1934, repr., New York: Avon, 1976).

39. Novak and Waldoks, *Big Book of Jewish Humor,* 268.

40. Patricia Erens's study of the portrayal of Jews in American films demonstrates that in the 1920s the patriarchal father was the source of power and villainy in films. He grows weaker and virtually disappears from films as the mother grows more powerful and suffocating. See *The Jew in American Cinema* (Indiana University Press: Bloomington, 1984), 256–57.

41. Writers about eastern European Jewish life have emphasized the very powerful link between sons and mothers. Some have suggested a link between daughters and fathers, as

well, but in general the father is characterized as remote. Both the mother-son attachment and son-mother-in-law hostility are articulated in folklore, but far less exists around the daughter-father tie. See Marc Zborowski and Elizabeth Herzog, *Life Is with People: The Culture of the Shtetl,* 8th ed. (New York: Schocken Books, 1971).

42. In a related argument regarding Roth's *Portnoy's Complaint,* Alan Segal notes that Portnoy can escape his condition only by "shedding" a Jewish identity which dominates and controls him. His means of escape is "sex with the goyim" or "shikses" on "a compulsive scale which both emancipates and imprisons him because its pleasure derives from it being forbidden." Segal focuses not on Roth's female contemporaries but only on the Jewish mother. Alan Segal, "Portnoy's Complaint and the Sociology of Literature," *British Journal of Sociology* 22 (1971): 267.

43. *The Hearts of Men: American Dreams and the Flight from Commitment* (New York: Doubleday, 1983).

44. "Killing the Princess: The Offense of a Bad Defense," *Tikkun* 2 (1989): 17.

45. Frances FitzGerald, *Cities on a Hill: A Journey through American Cultures* (New York: Simon and Schuster, 1986).

46. Cohen, *American Assimilation.*

47. Nora Ephron, *Heartburn* (New York: Knopf, 1983).

Chapter Sixteen

"From the Recipe File of Luba Cohen"
A Study of Southern Jewish Foodways and Cultural Identity

Marcie Cohen Ferris

Luba Tooter traveled from Odessa to America in September 1912. Hers is a tale familiar to scores of other Jewish immigrants who made similar journeys from Europe between 1881 and 1924 in the wake of Russian and Polish pogroms. Less familiar but equally important is Luba's life in Arkansas and the letters and recipes she left behind, which reveal a compelling, significant network of women's friendships. These friendships surface in recipes, letters, and cookbooks where they reveal how foodways shaped networks of community, family, and sisterhood.[1]

With their parents, Harry and Mollie Tooter, Luba and her brothers, Milton, Maurice, Edward, Joseph, Albert, and George, traveled in a horse-drawn wagon for over two months. Claiming that they were going to a family wedding, the Tooters packed just enough baggage to appear that they were leaving for vacation, rather than making a permanent exodus from Russia. After an arduous journey to Rotterdam that required an illegal crossing of the Austro-Hungarian border, the family boarded the *America* and squeezed into small steerage compartments for their ten-day journey to New York. At the age of ninety-two, Luba's youngest brother Joe still remembers a small cubicle on the ship where Jewish passengers gathered to observe Rosh Hashanah and Yom Kippur.[2] Their cousin, Minnie Issacson, met the family after they were cleared through Ellis Island and took them to an apartment she had rented in Brooklyn.[3] Luba was fifteen years old when her family arrived in New York. Eight years later she married Samuel Joseph Cohen, a Russian Jew who had emigrated from Minsk in 1912. They soon moved from New York to Blytheville, Arkansas.[4]

When Luba died in 1985 at the age of eighty-eight, she left in her Arkansas home a wooden recipe box and the rolling pin with which she made noodle dough as her mother had done in Odessa. Stuffed into the box was a disorderly collection of recipes written on scraps of paper, note pads from her husband's construction company, stationery from the Statler Hotel in New York and the Peabody in Memphis, bits of wallpaper, backs of envelopes, recipes clipped from the Memphis

Commercial Appeal, and her personal cards with the inscription "from the recipe file of Luba Cohen" printed across the top.

When Luba arrived in Arkansas in 1920 as a young bride, she brought both recipes of her native Russian foods and those of American dishes she discovered during her seven years in New York City. She soon blended these recipes with southern recipes in Blytheville where she quickly developed friendships with her predominantly non-Jewish neighbors. Their cards for "Mrs. Thornton Scott's cocoon cookies," "Julia's jam cake," and "May Dixon's 'Cook While You Sleep' cookies" filled her recipe box, along with cut-out newspaper recipes for peach jam, pecan tarts, "Brer' Rabbit" molasses cookies, crabapple jelly, grasshopper pie, and "Mother's Best Hush Puppies" removed from the back of a corn meal package. Luba's recipes for food favorites from the 1950s such as tutti-fruitti rolls, "perfect tuna casserole," Chinese egg rolls, veal scallopini, and gelatin molds suggest how she acculturated by incorporating popular American dishes and entertaining styles.

Luba also had recipe cards from her Jewish friends who lived in Blytheville and nearby small towns in northeastern Arkansas and in the "boot heel" of Missouri, where their husbands were merchants, doctors, engineers, and manufacturers. By 1947, these families had raised funds to build Temple Israel in Blytheville. Because her husband, Samuel Joseph Cohen, known as "Jimmy," had little interest in the temple and Jewish life, Luba remained on the edge of the Jewish community. A constant exchange of recipes with her "temple friends" for dishes like "Fanny Weinstein's matzoh balls," "Lillian's strudel," "Lena's mandelbrodt," and "Minnie's honey cake" unconsciously preserved her cultural identity in a place where there were few connections to distant family and Jewish memory.* After 1946, recipes from Huddy Horowitz and her mother, Lena, appear in Luba's box. Huddy married Luba and Jimmy's son, Jerry, in 1946 and moved with him to Blytheville. Reared in an active, traditional Jewish community in New London, Connecticut, Huddy embraced the small Jewish community at Temple Israel in Blytheville, where deep friendships developed through temple activities and the preparation of food for holiday meals and special events. Huddy explained that "The Temple was our connection to our close friendships, our place of worship and identity. It held us all together, and the support was enormous."[5]

One well-used recipe in Luba's box was "Chicken Chop Suey or Chow Mein," the dish she prepared when entertaining her family. Why did she cook a dish so "un-Jewish," so foreign to her Russian roots? Chow mein was a dish she had discovered in New York. Living in Brooklyn from 1912 to 1920, she and many other eastern European Jews first encountered Chinese restaurants, where they enjoyed this inexpensive food that did not mix milk and meat, as proscribed by kosher law. And pork, a forbidden food for Jews who kept kosher, was minced too small to recognize. Chinese cuisine featured garlic, celery, onion, overcooked vegetables, chicken dishes, eggs, sweet and sour dishes, and hot tea, tastes that an eastern European palate appreciated.[6] While Chinese people called their noodle dumplings

*For a description of foods, see the Appendix to this essay. Certain spelling variations may occur.

won tons, Jews looked into the same steaming bowls of chicken broth and saw kreplach.

On Luba's kitchen shelves was *Tried and True Recipes,* a guidebook to southern cooking published in 1922 by the Alabama Division of the United Daughters of the Confederacy. There was also the small, spiral-bound *Art of Chinese Cooking,* published in 1956. Luba's recipes, cookbooks, and Russian rolling pin reveal her experiences as a Russian child, a New York immigrant, and finally a southern housewife.

Luba Cohen's life suggests how southern Jewish foodways reveal a cultural history. We are what we eat, and the foods people enjoy as well as those they avoid reveal their cultural identity. Charged with the preparation of their family's meals, southern Jewish women shaped their cultural identity through food.[7] Their history survives in nontraditional sources such as recipes, menus, letters, journals, and cookbooks. Consider the letter written by a friend to Luba Cohen on Peabody Hotel stationery: "Dear Luba, Received the chocolate nut cookie recipe from Rebecca today. Meant to bring this copy to you tonite. She said to pass the recipe on to you and Florence. I'm afraid I'll misplace same if I don't copy this tonight. I'm not too sleepy— here goes."[8] While it is unclear whether the friend was Jewish, whether the recipe was for every day use or for a Jewish holiday, the letter reveals a powerful connection between four women, separated by distance, who communicated through foodways. Recipes must be read carefully to understand how women relate to family, friends, community, and their creation of cultural identity. This essay explores these recipes and how they reveal southern Jewish identity, foodways patterns, acculturation, women's networks, and the interaction between African American and southern Jewish women. The essay concludes with a brief case study of Natchez, Mississippi, and a 1998 survey of southern Jewish foodways.[9]

Don Yoder is the first folklorist who noted the connection between food and cultural identity. In 1972, Yoder introduced the term "folk cookery."[10] This phrase, subsequently replaced by the term "foodways," embraced the study of food, its preparation and preservation, social and psychological functions of food, and its connections to other aspects of folk culture.[11] Yoder views regional and national cuisine as "a culinary hybrid, with an elaborate stratification of diverse historical layers."[12] Charles Camp later argues that food shapes culture because "ordinary people understand and employ the symbolic and cultural dimensions of food in their everyday affairs."[13] Food, explains Camp, "is one of the most, if not the single most, visible badges of identity."[14] People turn to traditional foodways when their culture is at risk because food communicates human values that are both publicly and privately held.[15] Theodore and Lin Humphrey define foodways as communication between people, the "way that people express themselves."[16] And Susan Kačik views foodways as performance, "in which statements of identity can be made—in preparing, eating, serving, forbidding, and talking about food."[17]

Examples of these theories abound in southern Jewish foodways. Sally Wolff King was born in Dumas, Arkansas, in 1954, and remembers a recipe for "Romanian Eggplant Salad" that she inherited from her Romanian grandmother. "The recipe reminds me of our roots in the old country and the power of tradition.

Whenever I make this dish, I think about my parents, grandparents, and great grandparents."[18] D. D. Rudner Eisenberg (b. 1947) was raised in Memphis, Tennessee, and recalls "rolling matzah balls with my Mom. This was my mother's mother's recipe. The kids would visit and roll matzah balls with my mother. Every trip to Memphis, my mother makes this soup for me and for my children."[19] Gerry Barkovitz of Hayti, Missouri (b. 1923), described her grandmother's house, where "Eastern Europe was absolutely palpable." Both of her grandmothers passed on their recipes, but "Neither of them ever measured anything. Grandma, how do you make this? Well, you shick arein a bissel dis and a bissel dos [Yiddish for 'put in a little of this and a little of that'], and you taste."[20] Gerry's daughter, Ellen Barkovitz O'Kelley (b. 1949), wrote, "In our family, food is such an important thing that it is really the underpinnings of our traditions. Most of my memories of my grandmother are related to food."[21] In Tyler, Texas, Maurine Genecov Muntz (b. 1927) remembers "black-eyed peas, turnip greens, and cornbread, fried chicken, barley and beans cooked with short ribs on Friday nights [Shabbat]. Also, we had okra fried with tomatoes and fried or candied yams."[22] Leslie Koock Silver (b. 1942), who grew up in Birmingham, Alabama, explains that foodway "traditions are my threads that came across the Atlantic Ocean to Ellis Island and are now settled in Vicksburg, Mississippi."[23]

For folklorists, these foodways stories are expressions of cultural history and identity, communication, and performance. Foodways clearly show how the southern Jewish community chose to address its diverse cultural roots. Evocative tastes and smells link southern Jews to past experiences, to faraway places, and to people distantly remembered.[24] Living in small communities where there were so few Jews, in many cases only a single family, Jewish southerners from the early nineteenth century to the present developed networks with one another that sustained them both socially and spiritually. This networking is common among southern Jews, who use the term "Jewish Geography" to refer to conversations that focus on regional name-swapping and the familiar question, "do you know . . . ?" Leanne Lipnick Silverblatt (b. 1949), of Indianola, Mississippi, describes a gathering of Jewish friends and family at the Delta Jewish Supper Club, begun in the 1970s, which continues this tradition of Jewish socializing:

> We meet sporadically in different towns all over the Delta. Of course, the biggest "Jew Meet" is the Delta Jewish Open Golf Tournament. [An annual benefit in Greenville, MS for the Henry S. Jacobs Camp in Utica, MS.] My parents belonged to the YJPL (the Young Jewish People's League, [c. 1940s]). They met every month or so to eat— Jewish couples from all over the Delta belonged. Our family enjoyed all Jewish holidays with extended family and friends in Greenwood, Grenada, and Ruleville, Mississippi.[25]

Jewish women's emphasis on food preparation and shared recipes remembered from mothers and grandmothers who had died or lived far from the South remains vital to maintaining Jewish identity. Foodways sustain networks between Jewish southerners, and, to understand their community today and the evolution of its foodways, one must understand its roots in the colonial South.

From the mid-eighteenth century to the early decades of the twentieth century, Jews in the South encountered Anglo-Americans and African Americans with their respective roots in the British Isles and Africa. They lived together in the most isolated, predominantly Protestant region in the country.[26] Southern Jews discovered a creolization of foodways, as black southerners combined African okra and yams with the cornbread and pies of the white South. How to respect Jewish dietary laws in the earliest years of settlement in a region that consumed bacon, ham, pork shoulder, lard, head meat, chitterlings, pig feet, salt pork, fatback, side meat, white meat, pot likker, pig ears, and "even the squeal" at every meal was a challenge.[27] Joe Gray Taylor noted, "So long as he had pork, the Southerner ate it everyday and at nearly every meal."[28]

During the colonial period, Jewish immigrants to the South who tried to keep kosher had to either learn to slaughter their animals in the ritual manner or go hungry.[29] Joan Nathan notes a letter sent to Mordecai Sheftall, of Georgia, from his Christian friend, John Wereat, in 1788, that counsels, "Don't forget to bring your sharp knife with you. And then you shall not fast here unless 'tis your own fault, as I am putting up some sheep to fatten."[30] By the eighteenth century, Sephardic Jews sought religious tolerance as well as economic opportunity in the newly developing markets of the coastal South. Many settled in Savannah, Georgia, and Charleston, South Carolina, where they were joined by a smaller number of Ashkenazic Jews.[31] Their Sephardic cuisine was shaped by Mediterranean traditional foods such as almonds, olive oil, dates, chickpeas, fava beans, grapes, and pomegranates.[32] Stewed fish and fish fried in olive oil, beef and bean stews, almond puddings, and egg custards are among the Sephardic foods that were eaten in colonial America.[33]

Although their foodways differed from those of other southerners, Jewish immigrants and their descendants in the South found much that was familiar to their own tastes. They appreciated the nineteenth-century southern table where "big eating" included fried and boiled meats, overcooked vegetables, pickled vegetables and fruits, sweets and hot breads.[34] Both Jewish immigrants and native southerners viewed food as a way to celebrate daily life and to share with others. Jews also embraced the southern notion of hospitality. According to John Egerton, "serving large quantities of good things to eat to large numbers of hungry people, of sharing food and drink with family and friends and strangers, proved to be a durable tradition in the South, outliving war and depression and hunger."[35] Such hospitality was a concept with which Jewish people strongly identified.

Between 1820 and 1880, a second wave of Jewish immigration to America occurred, and Ashkenazic Jews from central and western Europe, including the Germanic states, France, Hungary, and Poland came south.[36] Single Jewish men sought economic opportunity and political rights, and women came for similar reasons and to "make a good match." Jews who had been peddlers and traders in their countries of origin sought similar work in the South. To keep kosher while on the road, a peddler carried food supplies for his journey. Cherokee Indians referred to Jewish peddlers as "egg eaters" because they kept hard-boiled eggs in their pockets and ate them with either dried beef sausages or pickled herring that they roasted in newspaper over an open fire.[37] As they prospered and expanded their operations, peddlers purchased wagons and eventually settled in towns and cities. German Jews built stores throughout the South and became integral members of their communities. Merchants wrote home to family in Germany requesting suitable brides. These Jewish women brought their foodways with them as a welcome taste of home for their husbands. Chicken and vegetable soups, roasted goose, duck, and chicken, stewed and baked fish dishes, sweet and sour tongue, kugels, cakes, breads, and tortes were basic foodstuffs in the German and Alsace-Lorraine Jewish kitchen.[38]

These Jews gathered for religious services in temporary locations like a merchant's store or a Masonic Hall. Once enough Jewish families settled in a town, a familiar pattern of Jewish community development followed. They created a *chevra kadisha* and a *chevra nashim*. Benevolent societies were organized to administer Jewish community philanthropy, and permanent places of worship were constructed.

Gradually these Jews shaped an identity that focused on ethical principles more than Jewish ritual and ceremonial practices. It was important to fit into the larger society, and, in many homes, Jewish dietary laws were dropped because of the community's small numbers and the difficulty of obtaining kosher foods.[39]

The foodways of twentieth-century descendants of central European immigrants reveal the evolution of their cultural identity.[40] Kathryn Loeb Wiener (b. 1929), a native of Montgomery, Alabama, described "Matzah charlotte at Passover and matzah balls. The rest was strictly assimilated southern."[41] Bettye Lamensdorf Kline (b. 1939), of Vicksburg, Mississippi, remembers, "Almost no Jewish food was prepared in my home. I only remember matzah balls at my grandmother's. I did not eat Jewish food until I was married."[42] Also from Vicksburg, Minette Switzer Cooper (b. 1937) recalls "only matzahs; we were not into 'Jewish.' Holiday food for us was usually fried chicken, rice and gravy, string beans, salad, and ice cream. We [now] celebrate Passover here at the house. I make up my own charoses [sic]* — pecans, apples, apricots, sweet wine, and honey."[43] Cathy Samuel Wolf (b. 1944) grew up in New Orleans, where her family "had no Jewish traditions or experiences. . . . Sometimes we ate Aunt Maud's matzah balls, swimming in butter, on Wednesday nights when our family ate at my Grandmother Samuel's, who lived with Aunt Maud."[44] Suzanne Schwarz Rosenzweig (b. 1925) was raised in Wheeling, West Virginia, where her "southern grandmother observed the Sabbath by not eating bacon."[45] Amelie Banov Burgunder, of Baltimore, Maryland (b. 1927), explained that

> Our family was fairly traditional about holidays. Meals with relatives and lots of cooking. Strudel, kuchen, and lots of foods made with only cream and butter. The tradition was more German, than southern. No root vegetables—too peasanty [sic]. I, of course, love them. Passover foods included matzah dumplings with lemon sauce, prunes and chestnuts, and flourless sponge cakes. One of my aunts made schnecken (sticky buns) so great that she sold them locally.[46]

Southern Jews effectively adapted their religious practices, while holding on to the tenets of their faith. They could think and believe Jewish thoughts while they

*See *haroses* in the Appendix.

dressed and acted like southerners. English was substituted for Hebrew, choirs and organs were introduced into the service, mixed seating was allowed, the rabbi preached much like the Protestant clergy, the yarmulke and tallit disappeared, and a quiet, dignified decorum was encouraged during worship.[47] Even the architecture of the new synagogues was modeled after churches, de-emphasizing the Jew's Old World roots in a country increasingly resentful of outsiders.[48] Southern Protestants strongly related to the piety and Old Testament traditions of Jews in their communities.

Central European Jews had barely transformed themselves into Americans when they were followed by a massive immigration of Jews from Russia, Romania, Galicia, Silesia, Czechoslovakia, and Russian-held Poland.[49] As a direct result of the flood of immigrants to America in the late nineteenth century, both German Jews and the newly arrived eastern European Jews faced a growing anti-Semitism. Jews who were already settled saw themselves as vulnerable and believed it was in the best interest of all Jews to quickly assimilate the newly arrived immigrants and direct attention from their "foreign-ness." Tensions quickly developed between these new immigrants and the already established Jews due in part to significant differences in worship styles. Eastern European Jews created separate subcommunities in small towns where German Jews already lived.[50] In larger cities, eastern European Jews built their own synagogues and followed Orthodox religious practices.

Unlike the German Jews before them, many eastern European Jews clung tightly to *kashrut* and the traditional foodways they had known in their countries of origin, such as bagels, borscht, chicken soup, stuffed cabbage, cholent, tsimmes, herring, kreplach, and tongue. Rosa Poliakoff, who was born in Union, South Carolina, in 1914, describes her family's commitment to keeping kosher in the South and how the Jewish community helped to make it possible:

> There was this place in Atlanta called S. J. Gold and they shipped kosher meat all over the South. When I went to college in Atlanta, my mother wrote to 'em and told them I was coming. She didn't want me to eat any chometz on Passover. . . . They were so busy shipping Passover orders all over the southeast, they stayed up all night the night before Passover to be sure everybody got their [orders]. They would drive out to Agnes Scott College to get me every night to eat supper at their house, so I could keep Pesachdicke.[51]

Oscar Fendler (b. 1909), whose mother and father came to Manila, Arkansas, from Cracow, Poland, via New York, in 1908, remembers:

> Dad would take me for high holidays to the synagogues in Little Rock, Memphis, or St. Louis. They could not keep kosher in a town such as Manila, but they did their best. We never had pork in our home during all the time Dad and Mother lived. We never had any catfish in our home. That food was not considered proper. We had lots of crappie, perch, buffalo, and carp. Some of the best-tasting crappie was fried in animal fat. It was a delicacy for breakfast and was served with hot biscuits. At times, when we had been to Memphis, Dad would buy herring at a delicatessen.[52]

Like the Fendlers, eastern European and other Jewish families made frequent trips to cities with larger Jewish populations to purchase both kosher and kosher-style ['Jewish,' but not kosher] foods. Most American delicatessens were run by non-Jewish Germans and Alsatians until the late nineteenth century, when Jews came into the businesses.[53] At the delicatessen, defined as the American "Jewish eating experience," one could grocery shop for kosher foods, fresh meats, salads, fish, bread, pickles, knishes, and other "Jewish" products or sit at the counter or tables to enjoy a gargantuan corned beef sandwich or piece of cheesecake.[54] Although centered in New York, where there were over five thousand delis by the mid-1930s, these institutions quickly spread across the United States.[55] For many years Irving and Judy Feldman, owners of the Old Tyme Delicatessen, which opened in Jackson, Mississippi, in the early 1960s, were the only source of kosher meat in Mississippi. They sent frequent shipments to Jewish customers throughout the region. In Hot Springs, Arkansas, the Forshberg family has operated Mollie's Restaurant since 1955, serving delicatessen fare to the small number of Jews in town, the Jewish tourists that once came to enjoy the area's curative waters, and now a non-Jewish clientele that has learned to love kreplach and corned beef. Atlanta, Georgia, had many delicatessens, including those owned by members of the Sephardic community such as Nace Amato's The Roxy and Victor Papouchado's Victor's, both located on Peachtree Street in the 1920s. An Atlanta newspaper reporter described Victor's: "There is no place in New York or Washington that surpasses Victor's Delicatessen in beauty of appointments or great variety of good things to eat."[56]

Examples of southern Jewish delicatessen memories abound. Bess Seligman, who grew up in Shaw, a small town in the Mississippi Delta, remembers getting supplies for Passover: "I was the delivery boy. I went to Memphis and took everybody's order and brought back the meats and the perishable foods. The matzah, the flour, the potato starch, and all that, we would ship by bus or by train, because we couldn't put it all in a car. Don't you remember the wonderful smoked goose legs that we got from Cincinnati!"[57] Eli Evans (b. 1936) explains that, in Durham, North Carolina, the *shochet* also performed as the cantor and *mohel.* "He ran a small deli with a few tables, where he served corned beef sandwiches, brisket, etc."[58] Joan Levy (b. 1942), of Savannah, recalls that "Gottlieb's Deli and Gottlieb's Bakery were very popular from the 1930s."[59] Roberta Schandler Grossman's (b. 1943) father "had the Pickle Barrell in Asheville, North Carolina, until his death. Before him, grandpa had kosher meats and groceries."[60] Helene Markstein Tucker (b. 1943) and other Birmingham natives enjoyed "Brody's Delicatessen in Mountain Brook, Alabama, a family-run grocery store that was the only place to buy food on Sunday."[61]

In downtown Savannah, Jane Guthman Kahn (b. 1933) wrote, "my husband's aunts ran Hirsch's Delicatessen during the 1930s and early 1940s. It always smelled of pickles. My husband would attend afternoon Hebrew School, then walk over there for a free oversized corned beef sandwich."[62] Mary Lynn Alltmont (b. 1943), of Memphis, described Halpern's Delicatessen, which advertised, "Say it with food." She remembers "going there with my mother and grandmother, buying bread, smoked whitefish, and herring."[63] In Columbia, South Carolina, the "Five Points Delicatessen was a regular stop after Sunday school classes" for Jack Bass (b. 1934) and his family.[64]

Another reliable source for Jewish foods was the northern relative who frequently traveled to the South beginning in the 1940s and 1950s, laden with Jewish supplies. Vicki Reikes Fox (b. 1952), of Hattiesburg, Mississippi, recalls how her "grandparents visited yearly from New York and they always brought bags full of lox, bagels, whitefish, rye bread, and farmer's cheese from the city. When they arrived, no matter what time, we always sat down to enjoy a meal of this New York deli food."[65]

Following the eastern European immigration, a second wave of Sephardic Jews came to the South early in the twentieth century. Jews from Turkey and the Isle of Rhodes settled in Montgomery, Alabama, and Atlanta, Georgia, where they found jobs as fruit peddlers, butchers, storekeepers, grocers, tailors, hatters, and shoemakers. Like eastern European Jews before them, they settled where synagogues were established and by the 1920s built their own places of worship, Congregation Or VeShalom in Atlanta and Congregation Etz Ahayem in Montgomery. Social functions, organizational affiliations, cultural events, the Ladino language, and Mediterranean foodways characterize these Sephardim. Miriam Cohen, a long-time member of the Montgomery Sephardic community, reflected on her food traditions from the 1920s to the 1990s: "You know, when I cook pink rice, my son says, 'This is Jewish soul food!' It is, you know."[66] Regina Piha Capilouto (b. 1920), who was born in Montgomery and whose parents and grandparents came from the Isle of Rhodes, remembers childhood dishes of "baked noodles, spinach, and cheese, stuffed grape leaves, rice with tomato sauce, rojaldes, and boyos. For Passover dishes: fried chicken, turnip greens, fish with Creole sauce, sweet potatoes with brown sugar and butter, and baklava."[67] Congregation Or VeShalom's sisterhood is famous for its annual Sephardic food bazaar, which inspired the sisterhood to publish a cookbook, *The Sephardic Cooks*, now in its fourth edition.[68] While the cookbook is filled with traditional Sephardic recipes for dishes like arroz con pollo, albondigas, dolmas de calvasa, and pastelles, the congregation's southern sense of place intermingled with Ashkenazic tastes, as seen in recipes for fried chicken, black-eyed peas, macaroni and cheese, pecan balls, matzo balls, brisket, kugel, and mandel bread.

In *Jewish Cooking in America*, Joan Nathan explains that Jews always carry the foodways of their home countries with them and adapt these traditions to those of the local culture.[69] Southern Jews brought with them foodways from their countries of origin: from Germany, kuchens, strudels, breads, roasted goose, matzah balls, and gefilte fish; from the Mediterranean, feta, olive oil, fish, rice dishes, and filo dough pastries; from eastern Europe, chopped liver, kishke, stuffed cabbage, roasted chicken, kreplach, and herring; from Alsace and Lorraine, tortes, kuchens, pastries, breads, onions and garlic, cheeses, baked and stewed fish dishes.[70] Recipes were copied into journals, written on cards, and brought by memory to the South. Jewish women continued to cook the foods remembered from their Old World homes and modified the ingredients, methods, and occasions for eating these foods as a result of southern influences. The informal communication network between Jewish women allowed the recipes to pass within and between families and friends, changing as each person made the particular dish her own. For second- and third-generation southern Jews, the foods of everyday meals in the Old World became special foods for holidays.[71] Chopped liver, gefilte fish, salami, and rye bread are known as "Jewish" foods because they are so closely tied to the Old World that the foods became a symbol of the group itself.[72]

As their southern Jewish identities evolved from the eighteenth century and through the early twentieth century, some women kept their southern and Jewish dishes separate, while others chose to blend the cuisines by adding pecans, fresh tomatoes, okra, butter beans, and sweet potatoes to their holiday menus and substituting regional specialties such as fried chicken, gumbo, and beef ribs for the traditional roasted chicken at Friday evening Sabbath suppers. In present-day southern kitchens, Jewish women effectively blend and distinguish southern and Jewish foods in ways that celebrate the distinctive foodways of both the region and their Jewish culture. Miriam Graeber Cohn (b. 1925) describes her "food guides": "My mother came from Austria; my husband's grandmother came from France; an aunt from Cajun Country; and my mother-in-law from Port Gibson, Mississippi. Some recipes came from our beloved servants, relatives, and friends."[73] Bert Fischel (b. 1940) grew up in Vicksburg, Mississippi, where his grandmother Mama Stella "lived with us, as was the custom for most families at the time. It was Mama Stella's kitchen, not my mother's, because Mama Stella had a passion for the kitchen, where she spent hours each day directing Mamie, our cook."[74] Mama Stella's Alsatian roots were reflected in her rich cakes and meringues, her love for strong cheese, sauerkraut, and white asparagus, and her predilection for ham. In Lexington, Mississippi, Phyllis Berkower Stern (b. 1924) blends southern and Jewish foodways in her Rosh Hashanah dinner as she prepares her mother-in-law "Big Momma" 's kreplach, brisket, butter beans from her garden, squash casserole, rice and gravy, and turnip greens.[75] Paula Ross Hoffman (b. 1939), of Baton Rouge, Louisiana, explains how her husband, Harvey, and daughter, Julie, make the gefilte fish for Passover using sea trout and "goo," an abbreviation of gasper goo: "Pike and whitefish aren't available around here. We call matzah brei 'lost matzah' after the New Orleans term for French toast, 'lost bread,' or 'pain perdu'; eating hamantaschen and wearing the costume I had worn for Mardi Gras are my memories of Purim."[76] Ann Zerlin Streiffer (b. 1954), of New Orleans, makes jambalaya by substituting kosher chicken and kosher sausage for the customary ham and shrimp.[77]

Leanne Lipnick Silverblatt (b. 1949), of Indianola, Mississippi, explained that "Southern foods were always a part of our holiday meals. We often had fried or barbequed chicken on Jewish holidays. Pecan pie, lemon meringue pie, and peach cobbler were favorite desserts for holiday meals."[78] Judith Weil Shanks (b. 1941), of Montgomery, Alabama, also remembers holiday foods, including "pickled shrimp, smoked turkey, ham, always biscuits, fried chicken, 'chopped' chicken liver, like a mousse. The Jewish country club (mainly German Reform) had [an] Easter egg hunt, Fourth of July with pork barbeque."[79] Bobbie Scharlack Malone (b. 1944), who was raised in San Antonio, Texas, says, "We tend to eat southern *or*

Jewish, but not at the same meal. That's how we ate growing up, too—fried chicken and biscuits at one meal; challah and baked chicken at another."[80] Suzanne Ginsberg Kantziper (b. 1936) grew up in Savannah, Georgia, where "my parents' home was kosher, so we had traditional foods for the holidays. We also ate okra and tomatoes, grits and fried chicken, black-eyed peas, zipper peas, squash, collard greens, turnips, but that was for everyday fare."[81] Shirley Ettinger Orlansky (b. 1931), raised in Alexandria, Louisiana, has made "cornbread oyster dressing with smaltz [sic]"*for the past eighteen family Thanksgivings.[82] Some southern Jewish families serve Old World recipes, such as German lebkuchen, at Thanksgiving and Christmas holiday celebrations. Peggy Kronsberg Pearlstein (b. 1942) remembers how "Friday night dinners were always dairy. My father hated chicken; growing up on Tilghman's Island on the Eastern Shore of Maryland, it was hard to obtain kosher meat and the family ate chicken, and more chicken. My paternal grandmother made sweet potato pies for each of her sons' families for Friday night dinner. Sunday brunch was grits, kippers, fried tomatoes, and fried corn."[83]

Shulamith Reich Elster (b. 1939), of Norfolk, Virginia, recalls, "Southern fried chicken—cold for Shabbat summer [dinners] and always watermelon for dessert."[84] Jack Bass (b. 1934) grew up in North, South Carolina, and remembers fried salt herring served with grits for breakfast and, on holidays, sweet potatoes substituted for the carrots in tsimmes.[85] Carolyn Lipson-Walker (b. 1951) describes Mississippi recipes for gefilte fish that use nonkosher catfish and a Texas Jewish family that barbeques matzah balls on the grill.[86] Marion Wiener Weiss (b. 1936) of Shreveport, Louisiana, remembers: "Pecans in haroses, smothered chicken and/or beef tongue. For Shabbat, southern food. Always home-made soup first. Sunday brunch: smothered chicken livers and biscuits. Sometimes during Passover, we had matzah pancakes for breakfast with mayhaw jelly or matzah fritters with apples and raisins and lemon sauce."[87]

From the 1930s to the early 1950s, many eastern European and German Jewish families in the South vacationed at inns and small resorts in the mountains of North Carolina and at coastal beaches that catered to Jews and to their taste for traditional Jewish foods. Esther Rosenbaum Buchsbaum (b. 1936) remembers a Jewish resort, the Lake Osceola Inn, in Hendersonville, North Carolina, where "I first tasted potato knishes to die for."[88] Also in Hendersonville, the Jack Bass family stayed at the "Horowitz Kosher Inn—southern Catskills with lots of eating and rocking chair activity."[89] Eli Evans's family met at the Cavalier Hotel, at Virginia Beach, Virginia, and the Maison Sur Mer Condominium, in Myrtle Beach, South Carolina: "the nick-name for Maison Sur Mer was 'the Kibbutz.' "[90] Joan Levy (b. 1942) describes a beach club at Tybee, a resort on the Atlantic Coast, where the Reform Jews of Savannah vacationed.[91]

Reva Schneider Hart (b. 1924), of Winona, Mississippi, writes about the Henry S. Jacobs Camp, in Utica, Mississippi: "It's not a resort, but close to it!"[92] Although a center for Jewish youth in the summers, the Henry S. Jacobs Camp has provided

*See schmaltz in the Appendix.

year-round adult education for Jewish families from Arkansas, Louisiana, Mississippi, Tennessee, and Alabama since June 1970. Fried chicken and biscuits is a Friday-night Shabbat tradition at the camp.

While Jewish camps like Henry S. Jacobs, delicatessens, summer resorts, and northern urban families were sources for Jewish food outside the home, most Jewish foods were prepared in the home by mothers, aunts, grandmothers, and the cooks they supervised. Although most southern Jewish women used recipes passed to them from mothers and grandmothers, they were equally dependent on nationally popular sources such as the *Settlement Cook Book* and *"Aunt Babette's" Cook Book, Foreign and Domestic Receipts for the Household.* In 1901, Lizzie Black Kander, founder of the Milwaukee Jewish Mission, published the *Settlement Cook Book* as a fundraiser to benefit the organization. Based on the mission's cooking school curriculum, the cookbook offered basic information on household and kitchen management and one hundred nonkosher American and German Jewish recipes.[93] One of the most successful cookbooks ever published, forty editions have sold over 1.5 million copies.[94]

The *Settlement Cook Book* remains a classic in southern Jewish women's kitchens. Its mix of American classics like waffles and brownies with decidedly nonkosher delicacies like shrimp à la Creole, fried oysters, and creamed crabmeat particularly appealed to southern Jewish women. Anne Bower suggests that women authors like Lizzie Kander asserted themselves as upper-middle-class, assimilated Americans, "comfortable acknowledging the German aspect of their German Jewish background, but worried that their Jewishness . . . could undo their secure lives," because of growing anti-Semitism at the beginning of the twentieth century.[95] The large number of nonkosher recipes reflected the Americanizing mission of the *Settlement Cook Book.* Kander saw no place for kosher dietary laws in the modern Jewish home, and her recipes and cooking classes emphasized American tastes, although she did include several recipes for traditional German dishes such as kugels, kuchens, tortes, and "filled fish" or gefilte fish. She taught her readers to eat and entertain like middle-class Americans with nonkosher meat and potatoes, salads, seafood, and German-style desserts fed to Jewish and non-Jewish guests alike. "In the Cohn family," writes Miriam Graeber Cohn, of Vicksburg, Mississippi, "the only cookbook I saw was the *Settlement Cook Book.*"[96]

Another favorite in American Jewish kitchens, *"Aunt Babette's" Cook Book, Foreign and Domestic Receipts for the Household,* was published in 1889 by the Bloch Publishing and Printing Company in Cincinnati, "the oldest Jewish printing company in the United States."[97] *"Aunt Babette's"* was passed down through generations of American Jewish women, southerners included, who turned to this quietly Jewish cookbook more for its charlotte russe and escalloped oysters than for its matzah balls. Janice Rothschild Blumberg's (b. 1924) 1891 edition was originally owned by her great-grandmother, Sophia Weil Browne, who lived in Columbus and Atlanta, Georgia, and was married to Rabbi Edward Benjamin Morris Brown, who officiated at Atlanta's Hebrew Benevolent Congregation between 1877 and 1881. Mrs. Browne appreciated the cookbook's many German recipes, as well as its lenient view of *kashrut*.[98] "Aunt Babette," the pseudonym of Mrs. Bertha F. Kramer, wrote "nothing is trefa [*sic*]* that is healthy and clean."[99] A section of Passover recipes was titled "Easter Dishes, Cakes, Puddings, Wines, Etc., How to Set the Table for the Service of the Sedar [*sic*] on the Eve of Pesach or Passover." Menus and instructions for "Kaffee klatch," "Pink Teas" [a novelty party at which everything was pink], "Thanksgiving Dinner," "Plain Sunday Dinner," "Lunch Parties," and "Portable Luncheons" gave southern Jewish women the tools they needed to shape an acceptable Jewish identity in their predominantly Christian community. Barbara Kirshenblatt-Gimblett explains that "Treyf cookbooks like that of *'Aunt Babette's'* reveal how Jewish identity was constructed in the kitchen and at the table through the conspicuous rejection of the dietary laws and enthusiastic acceptance of culinary eclecticism."[100]

From the early 1900s to the 1950s, American Jewish women were encouraged to blend food, interior design, religious practice, and daily values to create the model Jewish home, "a bond in sanctity" between Jewish religion and family life.[101] Jenna Weissmann Joselit describes this phase of American Jewish domestic culture as a time concerned with the spiritual and emotional properties of the home that differed from an earlier era where domestic reformers like Lizzie Kander focused on hygiene, contagious disease, and Americanization.[102] This new form of Jewish identity, known as "domestic Judaism," became a way for Jews to "recapture and revivify a sense of connection."[103] Temple sisterhoods reinforced this ideology with congregational cookbooks that equated food preparation with making a Jewish home. To raise funds, virtually every synagogue in the country published a cookbook that mixed its members' regional specialties and their family's heirloom Jewish recipes. Some popular southern examples include Savannah, Georgia's Congregation Mickve Israel's *Shalom Y'all Cookbook;* Atlanta, Georgia's Congregation Or Ve-Shalom's *The Sephardic Cooks;* New Orleans, Louisiana's Gates of Prayer's *Everyday and Challah Day Cooking;* Dallas, Texas' Temple Emanu-El's *Five Thousand Years in the Kitchen;* Baton Rouge, Louisiana's Liberal Synagogue's *Matzo Ball Gumbo;* and cookbooks published by southern chapters of Hadassah, B'nai B'rith Women, and the National Council of Jewish Women.

The influence of African American cooks and domestics is central to the lives of southern Jewish families. Like their white Protestant neighbors, Jews were intimately associated with black nannies, cooks, housekeepers, drivers, gardeners, and workers who cared for them from cradle to grave. Eli Evans recalls how he "was raised Southern-style—by the maid."[104] Having "black help" was common, and Jews who did not hire black domestics were in the minority. In a recent survey of southern Jewish foodways, more than half of the 117 respondents mentioned black female domestic workers who either did all the cooking or provided part-time assistance in their childhood homes. The generational differences between Jewish women who hired black cooks and those who did their own cooking suggests that acculturation and class influenced the increased hiring of black domestics. In many southern Jewish households, grandmothers who lived with their grown children

Trayf: nonkosher.

oversaw the kitchen and black cooks, while their daughters and daughters-in-laws participated in Jewish organizational activities outside the home.

Today many African Americans still work for Jewish families. Members of southern synagogues have lifelong relationships with black southerners who open their buildings and who turn out the lights after services. In Natchez, Mississippi, Eula Mae Demby, a long-time employee of Temple B'nai Israel, visits the synagogue almost every day and has given as many tours of the building as its Jewish members. Jewish southerners frequently mention relationships with black men and women who cooked for them, served family meals, catered parties, and cleaned their houses. Jane Guthman Kahn (b. 1933), who grew up in Savannah, recalled a black woman who cooked for her aunt for more than forty years: "Her recipes are the ones I remember most fondly."[105]

Cultural traditions and foodways passed back and forth between black women cooks and their Jewish employers. Black women brought sweet potato pies and biscuits to their Jewish "families" and went home at the end of the day with chopped liver and corned beef. Dale Grundfest Ronnel (b. 1939) grew up in the Mississippi Delta and recalls Georgella Green, a black cook who worked for her grandmother from age seventeen to retirement. Mrs. Green learned to cook from Ronnel's grandmother and "cooked Jewish-style even in her own home."[106] Anne Grundfest Gerache (b. 1933), of Vicksburg, Mississippi, recalled that "black women were good cooks who grew up preparing traditional southern food. They could improvise and adapt, and Jewish food was just one more facet of their experience."[107] This ability was seen in many southern households where black women learned how to "cook Jewish" on Friday nights and on Jewish holidays. Eli Evans explains that, once black women had learned to cook for a Jewish family, they were assured of constant and secure employment in the Jewish community.[108] Nan Dattel Borod (b. 1943), of Rosedale, Mississippi, experienced this in her own family: "We had a cook, Geneva Jones, who worked for our family for forty years and cooked every meal. My maternal grandmother, who lived with us, taught her how to cook."[109]

Kathryn Loeb Wiener (b. 1929) remembered that her German grandparents took their black housekeeper with them on a visit to Germany in 1903: "Eula went to Germany to visit my great-grandparents, and she learned German and the cooking at their home."[110] This story suggests how important it was for the older generation to maintain their German foodways and language, so much so that they brought Eula to learn from German cooks, the most direct and knowledgeable source. Ethel Hargraves, Eli Evans' family's black cook, sometimes found a southern inspiration for her "Jewish" recipes. Evans described the "Atlanta Brisket" made by Hargraves and explained her secret recipe was to marinate the brisket in Coca Cola overnight.[111] Dorothy Goldner Levy (b. 1912), of Birmingham, Alabama, recalls that "our maid picked the feathers off the fresh killed chickens, grated the fresh horseradish, scraped the scales off the fresh fish, fried the 'gribbenes'."[112] Saul Krawcheck was born in 1926 in Charleston and spoke of the interbraided Jewish and Low Country cuisines that were shaped by his family's black cook:

Our home was kosher, presided over by a colored woman named Agnes Jenkins, who came from the country and only had one job in her life and that was being my mother's cook. . . . One day you'd get a typical southern dinner of fried chicken and rice and okra gumbo—and the next day, the appetizer would be pickled smoked salmon and then a bowl of lentil soup and then potato latkes or potato kugel or tsimmes.[113]

In some homes the Jewish wife oversaw a division of labor in which she prepared the Jewish foods for special occasions, and the black cook took charge of southern food that was eaten every day, while in others black cooks prepared all the food. Miriam Graeber Cohn, of Vicksburg, Mississippi, recalls that "our maid cooked the regular food—fried chicken and all southern foods, but mother liked to have the holiday meal just perfect. They did prepare our meals, but nothing Jewish, which Mother did."[114] In New Orleans, Judith Page (b. 1951) described the black housekeeper who worked for her grandparents. When Page's grandparents died, the housekeeper came to work for Judith's family: "The housekeeper knew how to cook all Jewish foods, even though she cooked soul food and Creole at home."[115] Esther Rosenbaum Buchsbaum (b. 1936), of Atlanta, Georgia, explained, "My mother's parents worked in their grocery store. They always had a black maid who made corn bread, cooked with collards, turnip greens, and other vegetables from the store, but kosher, not with meat as usual southern-style dictates."[116] Jill Reikes Bauman (b. 1954) and Vicki Reikes Fox (b. 1952) grew up in Hattiesburg, Mississippi, and have strong memories of Willie Mae Boucher. Vicki recalls, "She was a wonderful southern cook and she became a real Jewish cook. She called herself 'the only black Jew!' " Jill remembered that "she cooked mostly 'southern,' but also cooked 'Jewish,' according to Mom's recipes and directions."[117] In Blytheville, Arkansas, Richie Lee King was the black housekeeper who worked for the Cohen family from 1955 to the early 1980s. Huddy Horowitz Cohen (b. 1926) prepared the Jewish dishes, and Richie handled southern specialties like fried chicken for Shabbat, cornbread, vegetable stew, and sweet potato pie. Richie helped at the annual Rosh Hashanah and Yom Kippur dinners at the Cohen home, greeting the visiting student rabbi with a big hug and a 'Good Yontuf, Rabbi.' " Southern black and Jewish worlds mixed and merged, shaped by shared personal relationships, sense of place, and family connections.

Black southerners also worked for Jews in food-related businesses such as Robert Zalkin's (b. 1925) grandfather's kosher butcher shop in Charleston, South Carolina. Sam Coaxum, a black man who worked at the butcher shop, learned Yiddish so he could speak with eastern European Jewish women that traded there. Zalkin would join Coaxum on his delivery rounds, often stopping at the black man's home, where the Jewish child intimately absorbed southern black life.[118]

The Jewish community of Natchez, Mississippi, exemplifies small-town southern Jewish life and the ways in which ethnic foodways and southern traditions intertwine in the South. Elaine Ullman Lehmann's German great-grandfather, Samuel Ullman, was a founding member of Natchez's Temple B'nai Israel, which was dedicated in 1872. Temple records describe how Ullman's fellow congregant Isaac

Lowenburg went home to Germany in the summer of 1870 and came back with a Torah given by the Jewish community at Hechingen. In 1994, Elaine Lehmann helped plan the Natchez Jewish Homecoming, a seminar sponsored by the Museum of the Southern Jewish Experience that celebrated the history of Temple B'nai Israel.[119] The weekend attracted hundreds of people with ties to the Natchez Jewish community, as well as scholars, rabbinic leaders, and the president of the National Trust for Historic Preservation. The food for the event symbolized Natchez's culinary expertise, the community's noted hospitality, and, above all, the heritage of the Jewish community of Natchez.

Choosing the menu for the weekend meals was complicated by the age-old questions of Jewish ritual observance versus the celebration of southern traditions. How could you have an event in Natchez without serving the city's famed "ham biscuits," tiny buttery biscuits filled with thin slices of salty ham? But how could you serve ham biscuits with Rabbi Alexander Schindler, the leader of the American Reform movement, at the front of the buffet line? The compromise was to serve plain biscuits at one end of the table and ham biscuits at the other. The temple sisterhood made hundreds of petit fours, and Eula Mae Demby, the temple's black housekeeper, oversaw the silver tray logistics. At lunch, seminar participants had a choice of nonkosher catfish or, for the more observant participants, fried chicken, while all were entertained by the New Orleans Klezmer All-Star Band.

The Natchez Jewish Homecoming was rich with stories about family history and Jewish acculturation in the South. Although Elaine Lehmann and her Vicksburg-born mother, Mildred Ullman Ehrman (b. 1896), employed cooks for their households, Lehmann remembered the cooking skills of earlier generations. Elaine's grandmother, Sara Gross Ehrman, and Sara's sister, Mamie Gross Loeb, were born in Canton, Mississippi, in the mid-nineteenth century. Their families came from Alsace, and both were excellent cooks. Elaine's family saved Mamie's personal cookbook journals, which are filled with recipes from family, friends, and African American cooks.[120] Like Luba Cohen, Mamie Loeb stuffed her cookbooks with loose recipes written on scraps of paper and stationery from the Mississippi State Senate and the Hotel Monteleone in New Orleans. Handwritten names—Cousin Carrie, Bertha Loeb, Tilly, Alma, Hatty, Mrs. Marx, Pauline, Neva, Mrs. Jeffers, Lizzie—and places—New Orleans, Louisiana, Portsmouth, Virginia, Uniontown, Alabama, Canton, Mississippi—reveal Mamie's foodways. Part of a letter from Elaine's mother, Mildred Ehrman, describes a recipe for "Delmonico Pudding." Penciled on the back, she wrote "How are Bud and Lillian? Hope they are both improving. Mamma feels fairly well, nothing to brag on. I didn't know a thing about Memphis when you wrote, but received a letter from their Sisterhood President."[121] The cookbook journals reflect the dual southern and Alsatian Jewish identities of Mamie and Sara Gross, who collected recipes for forty cakes, three kinds of barbeque, four versions of biscuits, bourbon balls, five types of cheese straws, matzah griddle cakes, matzah ball soup, matzah meal cake, matzah charlotte, mint juleps, nonkosher deviled crabs—*nine versions*—Oysters Rockefeller,

Shrimp Creole, shrimp mousse, cream curry shrimp, ham soufflé, and five types of lebkuchen, including "Mama's."[122] Mamie and Sara's lives clearly revolved around family meals, Jewish holidays, and frequent entertaining.

The preparation of traditional Jewish foods, as well as blended southern and Jewish fare, is still one of the most important ways that southern Jewish women create Jewish homes. This pattern is evident in responses to a questionnaire on southern Jewish foodways conducted in the fall of 1998, which provided extensive information on the history of family foodways, contemporary traditions, recipes, holiday menus, and meal memories. Responses came from 111 women and six men from fourteen different states. Sixty-seven of the respondents had eastern European roots, twenty-six had German and Alsatian roots, two had Sephardic roots, and twenty-two had both eastern and western European roots. Most of the respondents were born between 1918 and 1949.[123]

When asked to list Jewish foods they remembered from their childhoods, those with eastern European roots listed the largest numbers of food items: 103; those with German/Alsatian roots listed thirty; those with mixed eastern and western European roots listed thirty-nine foods. From the eastern European list, the most frequently mentioned in order of popularity were: gefilte fish, chopped liver, matzah ball soup, potato latkes, noodle kugel, kreplach, stuffed cabbage, borscht, brisket, strudel, and tsimmes. More than 50 percent of the participants wrote that black cooks assisted in the preparation of Jewish foods in their childhood homes.

The respondents continue to prepare 'Jewish' foods in their kitchens today. Examples include Ann Grundfest Gerache's "Mamaw's Slip and Slide Cake" [a Passover meringue torte filled with strawberries, ice cream, and whipped cream], Suzanne Schwarz Rosenzweig's mandelbrodt with pecans, Joan Levy's Alsatian lemon stew fish and pflauman kuchen, Amelie Banov Burgunder's brod torte, Riki Saltzman's Hungarian coffeecake, Dale Grundfest Ronnel's "Birdie Tenenbaum's Shaum Torte," Elaine Ullman Lehmann's lebkuchen, Huddy Horowitz Cohen's apple noodle kugel, Regina Piha Capilouto's boyos, and Deborah Lamensdorf Jacob's Passover Brownies. These recipes recall foodways traditions from Germany, Alsace-Lorraine, eastern Europe, Turkey, and the Isle of Rhodes, as well as the influence of American-style dishes and ingredients.

The survey confirms that preparing, eating, and remembering traditional Jewish foods remains one of the most compelling ways that women create Jewish homes and maintain Jewish family identity within the American South. Barbara Antis Levingston's (b. 1948) meal memory from Cleveland, Mississippi, illustrates the intricate web of family relationships tied to food and cultural identity:

> Rosh Hashanah is the only holiday I host. We used to have my husband's parents and relatives, the Jerry Sklars and Ron Sklars [from] Memphis, Uncle Ben Sklar [from] Ruleville, Mississippi, Aunt Sylvia Sklar, Jerry and Ron's mother, and Ben's wife, who died ten years ago. For years, she had all of the family to her home in Ruleville for the holidays—Rosh Hashanah, Chanukah, and Passover. She was the matriarch of the Levingston family. After her death, Jerry and his wife, Louise, took over Chanukah; Ron and Linda took over Passover; my mother-in-law, Vivian Levingston, took over Rosh Hashanah. I started doing it six years ago.[124]

This memory evokes the essence of Jewish life in a small southern town, of the Jewish home filled with memory, ritual, extended family, congregational friendships, holiday celebrations, traditional foods, and hospitality.

In southern Jewish homes from the mid-nineteenth century to the early twentieth century, women were responsible for maintaining traditional foodways and, as a result, controlled one arena of the family's acculturation to the South. Husbands and children might express their wishes about ritual practice and food tastes, but it was women who decided whether or not their kitchens were kosher as they prepared holiday food and incorporated traditional foodways into the family's weekly menus. Women defined this world for themselves and for their families. Their experiences suggest the importance of studying southern Jewish women and the influence of foodways in shaping cultural identity, community, and sisterhood. It is equally important to study the relationships between southern Jewish and black women and the dynamic of race and class that surrounds housework and the preparation of food.

Luba Tooter Cohen's journey from Odessa to New York to Blytheville is evoked by the foods she prepared. As she and other southern Jewish women shared their recipes and cookbooks, they created complex networks that extended across the South. Their foodways allow us to chart a map of the southern Jewish experience and its rich history of acculturation. Sephardic, central European, and eastern European Jews each brought their foodways to the South, and each generation hence has adapted these traditions to reflect their steadily evolving southern Jewish identity. Their country of origin, their date of immigration, the communities where they settled, and their attitudes toward assimilation are all reflected in what they eat. While food has nurtured southern Jews, it has also linked them to Jewish heritage, to southern places, and to their northern brethren as well. Carolyn Lipson-Walker, a folklorist who grew up in Alabama in the 1950s and 1960s, captures this dynamic in the emotions she felt when she received a gift of warm sugared pecans in honor of her son's bar mitzvah in September 1998:

> The Sunday afternoon before the bar mitzvah an older woman from Vincennes delivered the pecans to use for the Oneg Shabbat and hospitality room. The smell of those pecans brought back so many emotions. I remember I was alone in the house and I put them on the counter and wept—not because I was sad, but I was so grateful for the gift that called up so many childhood memories. . . . The pecans brought back memories of sitting on my grandmother's back porch in Marks [Mississippi] and shelling pecans from their trees.[125]

The gift between two Jewish women of southern food for a Jewish rite of passage recalled memories of Carolyn's grandmother in Marks, Mississippi. Southern networks, recipes, memories and identity all bond through food. Together they communicate the southern Jewish experience, who they are today, their pasts, and the people they hope to become.

APPENDIX
DESCRIPTION OF FOODS

albondigas—meat balls

arroz con pollo—chicken with rice

bagel—boiled and baked roll with a hole

baklava—filo pastry layered with honey and nuts

blintz—thin pancakes filled with cheese or potato

borscht—beet soup

boyos—spinach and cheese pie

brisket—cut of beef from the front quarters of the steer

brod torte—cake made with bread crumbs and grated nuts, instead of flour

buffalo—a southern, freshwater fish

challah—braided egg bread

charlotte russe—sponge cake filled with whipped cream, garnished with fresh fruit

chitterling—pig intestines

cholent—Sabbath luncheon stew, made with beans, onions, garlic, and meat

chopped liver—pate of chopped chicken livers, chicken fat, and eggs

collards—southern greens

crappie—a southern, freshwater fish

dolmas de calvasa—stuffed yellow squash

fat back—pig fat

gasper goo—a southern, freshwater fish

gefilte fish—poached, minced fish ball (usually whitefish, pike or carp) with filler of bread crumbs or matzah meal

gribenes—"cracklings" or fried bits of chicken fat

hamantaschen—triangular-shaped butter cookie dough with prune or poppy seed filling, associated with holiday of Purim

haroses—traditional Passover dish made from fruits and nuts

jambalaya—Creole tomato-based stew made with ham and shrimp

kippers—salted or smoked herring

kreplach—noodle dough with meat filling

kuchen—coffee cake

kugel—noodle or potato baked dish; noodle kugels often enriched with sour cream, cottage cheese, apples, jam, raisins, and cinnamon

latkes—fried, grated potato pancakes

lebkuchen—iced gingerbread

lox—smoked and salted salmon

mandelbrot—twice-baked almond cookies

matzah—unleavened bread eaten during Passover

matzah ball—a dumpling made of matzah meal, usually served in chicken broth or soup

matzah brie—matzah soaked in milk and egg batter and fried in butter

matzah charlotte—baked dessert of matzahs, egg whites, sugar; can include apples, raisins

mayhaw—southern berry

pastelles—meat pies

pink rice—rice simmered in tomato sauce, Sephardic-style

pflaumen kuchen—plum coffee cake

pot likker—liquid from vegetables cooked with bacon or salt pork

rojaldes—filo turnovers

schmaltz—rendered chicken fat

schnecken—sweet rolls or sticky buns

shaum torte—meringue cake made with egg whites and sugar

tsimmes—baked dish of carrots, prunes, apricots, root vegetables; can include short ribs

NOTES

1. Recipe collections like these, plus community cookbooks and women's compiled cookbooks, are the subject of study in *Recipes for Readings: Community Cookbooks, Stories, Histories,* edited by Anne L. Bower (Amherst: University of Massachusetts Press, 1997). This collection of essays by scholars from a variety of disciplines examines how community cookbooks and recipes, described as "nonliterary print documents," reveal the stories of women and their networks of friendship. Because the authors were unknown women, posi-

tioned in the private, domestic sphere, these fragmentary historical sources have been trivialized and considered unworthy of serious study by traditional scholars. Recently, feminist scholars in English literature, history, and women's studies have noted the value of nontraditional texts as examples of women's self-expression, social interaction, and evidence of how they shape the communities around them. The author would like to thank Bill Ferris, Leah Hagedorn, John Vlach, and Joan Nathan for their time and thoughtful advice regarding earlier drafts of this article. Additionally, the author is grateful to the staff of the Museum of the Southern Jewish Experience for their assistance with the Southern Jewish Foodways Survey.

2. Luba Tooter Cohen interview, conducted by Joseph Tudor, Washington, DC, April 9, 1978, 17. Luba Tooter Cohen was born in Odessa, Russia, in 1897 and was the author's grandmother.

3. Joseph Tudor interview, conducted by Marcie C. Ferris, Washington, DC, September 11, 1998, 11.

4. Jerry Cohen telephone interview, conducted by Marcie C. Ferris, March 17, 1999.

5. Huddy Cohen, New London, CT/Blytheville, AR, Southern Jewish Food Survey (SJFS), November 1998.

6. Gaye Tuchman and Harry Gene Levine, "New York Jews and Chinese Food: The Social Construction of an Ethnic Pattern," *Taste of American Place: A Reader on Regional and Ethnic Foods,* ed. Barbara G. Shortridge and James R. Shortridge (Lanham, MD: Rowman and Littlefield, 1998), 171–72.

7. In a recent article on Savannah, Georgia's Jewish women from 1830 to 1900, the historian Mark Greenberg writes about the ways wives and mothers, who fostered Jewish identity through their control over the kitchen where they maintained a kosher kitchen, created the ritual foods that accompanied Jewish holidays and observed the Sabbath and Jewish festivals. Miriam Moses Cohen's nineteenth-century recipe book contained recipes for Passover "soup dumplings" and "koogle." In the 1860s and 1870s, Lavinia Florence Minis baked "Haman's ears" for her family's Purim celebrations and sent Passover matzahs to her son, Jacob, when he was away attending a university. Mark I. Greenberg, "Savannah's Jewish Women and the Shaping of Ethnic and Gender Identity, 1830–1900," *Georgia Historical Quarterly* 4 (winter 1998): 760.

8. Unsigned letter to Luba Tooter Cohen, n.d., possession of author.

9. For the purposes of this study, the South is defined as a cultural area, rather than a geographical region based on the eleven states of the former Confederacy (Alabama, Arkansas, Florida, Georgia, Louisiana, Mississippi, North Carolina, South Carolina, Tennessee, Texas, and Virginia). Because southern foodways patterns bleed into neighboring regions and are equally shaped by those regions and the movement of people, the boundaries for a foodways study are not sharply defined. I have used the definition from the *Encyclopedia of Southern Culture,* eds. Charles Reagan Wilson and William Ferris (Chapel Hill, NC: University of North Carolina Press, 1989), xv: "The South is found wherever southern culture is found . . . ," and thus includes states such as Missouri, Maryland, and Delaware.

10. Don Yoder, "Folk Cookery," *Folklore and Folklife,* ed. Richard Dorson (Chicago: University of Chicago Press, 1972), 325.

11. Ibid., 325.

12. Ibid., 334.

13. Charles Camp, *American Foodways: What, When, Why, and How We Eat in America,* American Folklore Series (Little Rock: August House, 1989), 23, 29.

14. Ibid.

15. Ibid.

16. Theodore C. Humphrey, Sue Samuelson, and Lin T. Humphrey, "Introduction: Food and Festivity in American Life," in *"We Gather Together:" Food and Festivity in American Life* (Ann Arbor: UMI Research Press, 1988), 5.

17. Susan Kalčik, "Ethnic Foodways in America: Symbol and the Performance of Identity," in *Ethnic and Regional Foodways in the United States: The Performance of Group Identity,* ed. Linda Keller Brown and Kay Mussell (Knoxville: University of Tennessee Press, 1984), 54.

18. Sally Wolff King, Dumas, AR/Atlanta, GA, Southern Jewish Foodways Survey (SJFS), November 1998.

19. D. D. Rudner Eisenberg, Memphis, TN/Washington, DC, SJFS, November 1998.

20. Gerry Barkovitz, St. Louis, MO/Hayti, MO, SJFS, November 1998.

21. Ellen Barkovitz O'Kelley, Hayti, MO/Overland Park, KS, SJFS, November 1998.

22. Maurine Muntz, Tyler, TX, SJFS, November 1998.

23. Leslie Koock Silver, Birmingham, AL/Vicksburg, MS, SJFS, November 1998.

24. Kalčik, "Ethnic Foodways in America," 49.

25. Leanne Silverblatt, Indianola, MS, SJFS, November 1998. The Delta Jewish Open Golf Tournament celebrated its twelfth year in October 1999.

26. James R. Curtis, "Ethnic Geography," *Encyclopedia of Southern Culture,* ed. Wilson and Ferris, 541.

27. John Egerton, *Southern Food* (New York: Knopf, 1987), 21.

28. Joe Gray Taylor, "Foodways," *Encyclopedia of Southern Culture,* ed. Wilson and Ferris, 614.

29. Joan Nathan, *Jewish Cooking in America* (New York: Knopf, 1994), 10.

30. Ibid.

31. Ibid., 42. Organized in 1735, Savannah's Congregation Mickve Israel was officially chartered by Governor Edward Telfair in 1790. (Congregation Mickve Israel, *Shalom Y'all Cookbook,* ed. Arlene Belzer, Becky Civjan, Elaine Erlich, Diane Kuhr, Joan Levy, Margie Levy, and Sue Ruby (Savannah, 1995), intro. In 1697, Charleston, South Carolina, had only four Jewish settlers. By 1775, its congregation had grown to more than fifty families. Construction for a permanent place of worship began in 1792, and Beth Elohim was dedicated in 1794. In both Charleston and Savannah, the first Jewish settlers were merchants who were connected to an extensive network of trade up and down the east coast and across the Atlantic. (Eli Faber, *A Time for Planting: The First Migration, 1654–1820, The Jewish People in America,* 1 [Baltimore: John Hopkins University Press, 1992], 41–42.)

32. Nathan, *Jewish Cooking in America,* 10–11.

33. Ibid., 11.

34. Taylor, "Foodways," *Encyclopedia of Southern Culture,* 614.

35. Egerton, *Southern Food,* 38.

36. Hasia Diner, "German Immigrant Period," *Jewish Women in America: An Historical Encyclopedia,* ed. Paula E. Hyman and Deborah Dash Moore (New York: Routledge, 1997), 502.

37. Bobbie Malone, "A History of Jews in the South," Mississippi Humanities Council and Museum of the Southern Jewish Experience Lecture, Meridian, MS, 1993, and Nathan, *Jewish Cooking in America,* 12.

38. Nathan, *Jewish Cooking in America,* 13.

39. Isaac Mayer Wise, the organizing leader of the Reform movement in America, encouraged his brethren to reconsider the relevance of ritual. This heated discussion culminated

at the July 11, 1883, "Treyfa Banquet," a graduation dinner for the first class of American rabbis in Cincinnati and their two hundred guests, who were served nonkosher little neck clams, soft-shell crabs, shrimp salad, and frogs' legs with cream. Several shocked guests left the room, insulted by the absence of respect for the Jewish dietary laws. This episode, plus the long history of dissension regarding ritual within the movement, led to a permanent split within American Jewry. At the 1885 Pittsburgh conference, a platform was defined that emphasized the Classical Reform principles that distinguished the movement from other Jewish groups. That a food-centered issue should cause such turmoil suggests the powerful connection between food, cultural identity, and the basis of Jewish religious practice. (Nathan, *Jewish Cooking in America,* 15, and Gerald Sorin, *A Time for Building: The Third Migration, 1880–1920,* 3 [Baltimore: John Hopkins University Press, 1992], 172.)

40. Barbara Kirshenblatt-Gimblett, "Kitchen Judaism," *Getting Comfortable in New York: The American Jewish Home, 1889–1950,* ed. Susan L. Braunstein and Jenna Weissman Joselit (New York: Jewish Museum, 1990), 80.

41. Kathryn Loeb Wiener, Montgomery, AL/Jackson, MS, SJFS, November 1998.

42. Bettye Lamensdorf Klein, Vicksburg, MS, SJFS, November 1998.

43. Minette Switzer Cooper, Vicksburg, MS/Norfolk, VA, SJFS, November 1998.

44. Cathy Samuel Wolf, New Orleans, LA/Washington, DC, SJFS, November 1998.

45. Suzanne Schwarz Rosenzweig, Wheeling, WV/Hot Springs, AR, SJFS, November 1998.

46. Amelie Banov Burgunder, Baltimore, MD/Bethesda, MD, SJFS, November 1998.

47. Louis E. Schmier, "Jewish Religious Life," *Encyclopedia of Southern Culture,* ed. Wilson and Ferris, 1290.

48. Ibid.

49. Sorin, *A Time for Building,* 1, 2, 12.

50. Lee Shai Weissbach, "East European Immigrants and the Image of Jews in the Small-Town South," *American Jewish History* 85 (September 1997): 242.

51. Rosa From Poliakoff interview, May 1, 1995, Jewish Heritage Collection, College of Charleston, Charleston, SC (hereinafter cited as Jewish Heritage Collection).

52. Oscar Fendler, Blytheville, AR, SJFS, November 1998.

53. Nathan, *Jewish Cooking in America,* 185.

54. Ibid.

55. Jenna Weissman Joselit, *The Wonders of America: Reinventing Jewish Culture, 1880–1950* (New York: Hill and Wang, 1994), 203.

56. Sol Beton, ed., *Sephardim and A History of Congregation Or VeShalom* (Atlanta: The Congregation, 1981), 229–230.

57. Bess Seligman interview, conducted by Marcie C. Ferris, Museum of the Southern Jewish Experience, Jackson, MS, 1993.

58. Eli N. Evans, Durham, NC/New York, NY, SJFS, November 1998.

59. Joan Levy, Savannah, GA, SJFS, November 1998.

60. Roberta Schandler Grossman, Asheville, NC/Johnson City, TN, SJFS, November 1998.

61. Helene Markstein Tucker, Birmingham, AL/Chevy Chase, MD, SJFS, November 1998.

62. Jane Guthman Kahn, Savannah, GA, SJFS, November 1998.

63. Mary Lynn Alltmont, Memphis, TN/La Place, LA, SJFS, November 1998.

64. Jack Bass, North, SC/Atlanta, GA, SJFS, November 1998.

65. Vicki Reikes Fox, Hattiesburg, MS/Los Angeles, CA, SJFS, November 1998.

66. Miriam Cohen interview, conducted by Marcie C. Ferris, Montgomery, AL, Museum of the Southern Jewish Experience, Jackson, MS, November 1994.

67. Regina Piha Capilouto, Rhodes, Greece/Montgomery, AL, SJFS, November 1998.

68. Congregation Or VeShalom Sisterhood, *The Sephardic Cooks,* ed. Emily Amato, Blanchette Ichay, and Marcy Franco (Atlanta: Sisterhood, 1992), and Beton, *Sephardim,* 210.

69. Nathan, *Jewish Cooking in America,* 3.

70. Ibid., 4.

71. Ibid.

72. Ibid.

73. Miriam Graeber Cohn, Port Gibson, MS/Shreveport, LA, SJFS, November 1998.

74. Bert Fischel, Vicksburg, MS/Dallas, TX, SJFS, June 1999.

75. Phyllis Berkower Stern, Tottenville, NY/Lexington, MS, SJFS, November 1998.

76. Paula Ross Hoffman, Baton Rouge, LA, SJFS, November 1998.

77. Ann Zerlin Streiffer, New Orleans, LA, SJFS, November 1998.

78. Leanne Lipnick Silverblatt, SJFS.

79. Judith Weil Shanks, Montgomery, AL/Washington, DC, SJFS, November 1998.

80. Bobbie Scharlack Malone, San Antonio, TX/Madison, WI, SJFS, November 1998.

81. Suzanne Ginsberg Kantziper, Savannah, GA, SJFS, November 1998.

82. Shirley Ettinger Orlansky, Alexandria, LA/Greenville, MS, SJFS, November 1998.

83. Peggy Kronsberg Pearlstein, Charleston, SC/Silver Spring, MD, SJFS, November 1998.

84. Shulameth Reich Elster, Norfolk, VA, SJFS, November 1998.

85. Jack Bass, SJFS.

86. Carolyn Lipson-Walker, " 'Shalom Y'all': The Folklore and Culture of Southern Jews," Ph.D. diss, Indiana University, 1986, 286–87.

87. Marion Wiener Weiss, Shreveport, LA, SJFS, November 1998.

88. Esther Rosenbaum Buchsbaum, Atlanta, GA/Tybee Island, GA, SJFS, November 1998.

89. Jack Bass, SJFS.

90. Eli Evans, SJFS.

91. Joan Levy, SJFS.

92. Reva Hart, Winona, MS, SJFS, November 1998.

93. Joan Nathan, "Food," *Jewish Women in America: An Historical Encyclopedia,* ed. Paula E. Hyman and Deborah Dash Moore (New York: Routledge, 1997), 460.

94. Kirshenblatt-Gimblett, "Kitchen Judaism," 96.

95. Anne L. Bower, "Bound Together: Recipes, Lives, Stories, and Readings," *Recipes for Reading: Community Cookbooks, Stories, Histories,* ed. Anne L. Bower (Amherst: University of Massachusetts Press, 1997), 3.

96. Miriam Graeber Cohn, SJFS.

97. Mrs. Bertha F. Kramer, *"Aunt Babette's" Cookbook, Foreign and Domestic Receipts for the Household* (Cincinnati: Bloch, 1891), back page.

98. Janice Rothschild Blumberg interview, conducted by Marcie C. Ferris, Washington, DC, November 2, 1998, 17.

99. Kramer, 452.

100. Kirshenblatt-Gimblett, "Kitchen Judaism," 80.

101. Ibid., 77.

102. Joselit, " 'A Set Table': Jewish Domestic Culture in the New World, 1880–1950," 45.

103. Joselit, *The Wonders of America,* 171.

104. Eli N. Evans, *The Provincials: A Personal History of Jews in the South* (New York: Atheneum, 1973), 255.

105. Jane Guthman Kahn, SJFS.

106. Dale Grundfest Ronnel, Cary, MS/Little Rock, AR, SJFS, November 1998.

107. Anne Grundfest Gerache, Cary, MS/Vicksburg, MS, SJFS, November 1998.

108. Evans, *The Provincials,* 256.

109. Nan Dattel Borod, Rosedale, MS/Boston, Massachusetts, SJFS, November 1998.

110. Kathryn Loeb Wiener, SJFS.

111. Eli N. Evans, SJFS.

112. Dorothy Goldner Levy, Birmingham, AL, SJFS, November 1998.

113. Saul Krawcheck interview, July 6, 1995, Jewish Heritage Collection.

114. Miriam Graeber Cohn, SJFS.

115. Judith Page, New Orleans, LA/Jackson, MS, SJFS, November 1998.

116. Esther Rosenbaum Buchsbaum, SJFS.

117. Vicki Reikes Fox, SJFS, and Jill Reikes Bauman, Hattiesburg, MS/Little Rock, AR, SJFS, November 1998.

118. Robert Zalkin interview, July 14, 1995, Jewish Heritage Collection.

119. The Natchez Jewish Homecoming, sponsored by the Museum of the Southern Jewish Experience and Temple B'nai Israel, Natchez, MS, May 1994.

120. Camp, *American Foodways,* 99. Charles Camp describes the importance and poignancy of compiled cookbooks like these: "A cook's records are the records of how regularly social worlds—special occasions, friends, family—and the world of food—recipes, instructions, mementoes—converge, and how much the records of one world stand for the other." He speaks of the "wholeness" of these collections, the overlap of holiday recipes and souvenirs, recipes from people and the local newspaper, and the juxtaposition of private and public worlds.

121. Mrs. Max Ullman, letter, n.d., Natchez, MS, property of Elaine Ullman Lehmann.

122. Cookbook journals, v. 1, 2, property of Elaine Ullman Lehmann.

123. The survey was primarily sent to female Jewish southerners, but several male Jewish southerners also responded, or were given copies of the survey by a family member or friend.

124. Barbara Antis Levingston, Cleveland, MS, SJFS, November 1998.

125. Carolyn Lipson-Walker, Tuscaloosa, AL/Bloomington, IN, SJFS, November 1998.

Chapter Seventeen

Going South
Jewish Women in the Civil Rights Movement

Debra L. Schultz

Fighting Back

As a child in California, Vivian Leburg Rothstein (b. 1946) saw blue numbers that had been tattooed onto adult arms and heard the mournful, bitter stories of concentration camp survivors. She contrasted the romantic life her artistic parents had led in Europe with her mother's struggle to raise two children as a single parent and woman refugee. For Leburg, "[T]he Holocaust was the defining fact of my childhood. I was raised totally in a community of refugees. That's what propelled me into oppositional politics. I was used to being outside the mainstream. That made it easier to be critical and to identify with the oppression of Blacks."[1] Tired of being "a follower and not a leader" in the Berkeley Free Speech Movement, sophomore Leburg signed up to register Black voters in Mississippi for the summer of 1965.

Gertrude "Trudy" Weissman Orris (b. 1916) joined her husband, a military doctor, in Germany, at the end of World War II. As Orris recounts, "Whenever I met anybody German, I would say to them, 'What did you do during the war?' " One evening, a German musician said to her, "If you're asking me if I was a coward, I was a coward. I knew what was happening, but I couldn't do anything about it. My best friend was taken away. Now let me ask you something—what are you going to do when your turn comes?" Stunned, Orris recalls, "I stopped. I couldn't answer him. I said I didn't know what I would do but I would hope that I would do the right thing." The man said, "What you hope and what you do are two different things."

"When I came back to the United States," notes Orris, "I was a different person. I felt that the most important thing that I could do is to work in the Black movement. If anything happened, then somebody didn't have to say to me, what did you do?"[2] In addition to going south several times for freedom rides and major demonstrations, Orris would help bring national attention and resources to the southern movement as one of the founders of New York Parents of the Student Nonviolent Coordinating Committee (SNCC).

At age six, racism became a personal issue for Faith Holsaert (b. 1943). When

Holsaert's parents divorced, her mother and Charity Bailey, Holsaert's African American music teacher who rented a room in her parents' Greenwich Village apartment, became a "couple," raising Holsaert and her sister. This family, highly unusual by 1950s standards, endured constant taunts on the street and more subtle forms of racism, sexism, and homophobia from their communities. Yet even this couple balked twelve years later when eighteen-year-old Holsaert announced in December 1961 that she was going south for the first time to get arrested at a sit-in in Christfield, Maryland. Despite the fact that Holsaert's decision was a product of her upbringing in their household, her mother and Charity Bailey expressed ambivalence and fear. When several churches were burned in southwest Georgia in the summer of 1962, Holsaert had to find the inner strength to take the next step on her own—to go south as one of the first white women to join the volatile Albany, Georgia, movement.

Whether they knew it or not at the time, the decision to go south for, go south for civil rights would ultimately transform the lives of these Jewish women. As the women describe their various motivations, distinctive patterns and themes emerge. The stories recounted here are primarily those of northern women connected to the Student Nonviolent Coordinating Committee because, in the South, SNCC (founded in 1960 by Black students) was the most grassroots and democratic organization accessible to white volunteers. SNCC provided a home for white antiracist activists at a time when the very notion of white antiracism was all too rare to most Americans, despite the existence of a white antiracist tradition.[3]

What Vivian Leburg Rothstein, Trudy Weissman Orris, and Faith Holsaert had in common was personal experience with the effects of fascism and racism. The civil rights movement gave them the opportunity to fight back and they seized it. Jewish women had many motives for going south, but their primary impetus was clearly to be part of a democratic movement to combat racial injustice. Like many young people of their generation, they sought to hold the United States to its democratic ideals. Yet, they made their decision to join the movement from a more specific historical location: as women in mid-twentieth-century American Jewish life.

Rothstein, Holsaert, and most other northern Jewish women who went south were part of a transitional generation. Born between 1935 and 1946, the Great Depression and the end of World War II, the core group of women grew up in families intimately familiar with struggle. They were the daughters and granddaughters of Jewish immigrants striving to succeed in the United States. They had direct experiences with working-class Jewishness even as the American Jewish community began its extraordinary socioeconomic climb. At formative ages, many had moved from the warmth and tumult of urban extended family life to the more affluent alienation of the suburbs. For many, family deviations from the 1950s cultural norm (such as divorce, the early death of a parent, physical disability, or parental radicalism) made them feel different and helped them identify with others who were different. Their "in-between-ness" facilitated the decision to go south and their ability to cross boundaries of various kinds.

The act of going south required them to traverse geographic, racial, gender, ethnic, class, and political boundaries. Risking their lives for democratic ideals, they had little time to reflect on what these aspects of their "identities" might mean to them. Yet, Jewish women civil rights activists present an interesting example of women with multiple and contradictory identities. They were relatively privileged, well-educated northern students who chose to go south to work in a social justice movement; still, they often felt slightly outside the mainstream. They were Jewish women from families and a culture that both encouraged and limited their life choices. They were the children of Jews struggling to assimilate into American culture without losing their Jewish connection entirely. They were white women in a movement led most visibly by Black men. They were competent and experienced, willing to take action before the feminist movement made it legitimate to do so. They were secular Jews in a Black Christian movement working in the anti-Semitic and virulently racist South. As such, they began to see their own experiences and those of African Americans from a variety of perspectives. This raised many challenging questions that would inform their complex responses to future movements based on identity politics. These movements led many groups to organize politically around a single facet of identity, such as race, gender, or ethnicity.

What did being Jewish mean, if anything, for the women who went south? Though most of the women interviewed did not identify strongly as Jewish while in the movement, "Jewishness" nevertheless played an important role in the development of their political, antiracist consciousness. Despite varying degrees of alienation and/or identification with Judaism, Jewish backgrounds, traditions, politics, and values did shape their worldviews and commitments. Though less directly than Rothstein and Orris, almost all the women interviewed had absorbed a sense of World War II and the Holocaust at young ages. Nightmares about Nazis and fantasies of joining the Resistance haunted their dreams. The Holocaust permeated their consciousness before the Jewish community could talk about it openly. Many, asking themselves how they would have responded if they had been in Europe, welcomed the chance to answer that question for themselves, to "resist" in a fight that was less obviously about their own survival.

Though the struggle was not directly about Jewish survival, it was not unrelated to Jewish identity.[4] In a range of ways, these women were exposed to a liberal Jewish moral framework of social justice that made involvement in the civil rights movement almost irresistible. As a number comment, once they heard about the movement, "I just knew I had to be there." For many, involvement in the civil rights movement was a creative application of a primary message of their parents' generation: to embrace both American and Jewish identity.

Some but not all were children of Old Left families. For these women, activism was in keeping with family values. Not surprisingly, those with roots in Left politics (Trudy Weissman Orris, Harriet Tanzman, Dorothy "Dottie" Miller Zellner) articulated the strongest connection between a Jewish cultural identity and their politics. Others who came from liberal Democratic families retained a sense of *tikkun olam* (Hebrew for "repair of the world"). For those politically disinclined toward Zionism as a nationalist movement, the civil rights movement before 1966 provided an opportunity to fight for both "American" and "Jewish" social justice ideals.

The stories of Jewish women activists in the civil rights movement prompt us to think about the meanings of Jewishness for Jews (particularly Jewish women) in antiracist and other social justice movements. The forces of tradition, history, and Jewish politics legitimize religion as the ultimate expression of Jewishness. Yet, this focus often obscures other complex relationships to Jewishness that do not fit the mold.[5] Despite a Talmudic tradition that invites dissent and multiple perspectives on any given issue, organized Judaism historically has alienated a number of questioning people who were born Jewish. It is perhaps a tribute to the power and tenacity of the Jewish tradition that so many rebels have struggled so hard to relate to it. Hegemonic definitions of Judaism impoverish our collective culture by not including a fine tradition of radicals, dissenters, and visionaries.

Antiracist activism is one expression of a universalist concern with justice that has roots in Jewish history, ethics, and political radicalism. For these women, one link between Jewishness and future activism came through lessons learned in their families. Most of the Jewish women activists grew up with a nonpolitical, culturally based Jewish social justice imperative to "do the right thing." Although their families did not identify as "political," the message they sent certainly was.

As the women matured and sought to shape lives that would have an impact, their diverse Jewish backgrounds informed their decisions to take action. Once in the southern movement, their Jewish identities would mean different things in different contexts.

Stepping into History

While routes to movement involvement came in many forms, catalytic events in the South often propelled northern Jewish women into action. Some who came from political families or were already involved in local civil right protests recognized this as the moment to step into a fight that would change the course of American history.

On February 1, 1960, four Black college students in Greensboro, North Carolina, ignited the sit-in movement by taking seats at a whites-only Woolworth's lunch counter. Images of their quiet dignity as local racists screamed at them and poured flour over their heads rocked the world. Within two months, Black students were demanding the right to be served at segregated lunch counters in seventy southern cities.[6]

By the end of the spring of 1960, students at one hundred northern colleges had mobilized in support of the actions in the South. Among them was Barbara Jacobs Haber (b. 1938), a self-described "bohemian-politico" at Brandeis University. After hearing a firsthand account of the Greensboro sit-ins from Brandeis graduate Michael Walzer, Jacobs was "absolutely galvanized. I'll just never forget what it was like to hear Michael tell in his very low-key way what was going on there and to feel that YES inside myself that I had to be part of this and not to think twice about it, just to do it."[7]

In 1960, this Black-initiated nonviolent but confrontational form of protest catalyzed the white-student movement's militant activism.[8] During the course of the next year, almost every campus across the country experienced some type of civil rights-related activity: support groups, freedom ride committees, local sit-ins and pickets, and travel to the South. At Brandeis, Harber says, "[W]e got a hundred students out picketing every week at different Woolworth's. I became totally involved in the civil rights movement." Later that year, she would go south to attend SNCC's founding convention.

After dropping out of graduate school (a class "sin" from a middle-class Jewish perspective), Jacobs took a job in Baltimore as a social worker, a helping profession deemed appropriate for women at that time, yet her increasing involvement with civil rights activism challenged gender stereotypes. Like many Jewish women who went south, she got her training with the Congress of Racial Equality (CORE), an interracial civil rights organization founded in 1942. A member of Baltimore CORE, she relished the challenge of desegregating bars or restaurants in mixed groups: "I was a very macho sort of young woman—and, in some ways, stupid. I just liked to go into these restaurants and bars and to be at the front, you know, in their face."

Dottie Miller Zellner (b. 1938) was another passionate young woman for whom the Greensboro sit-ins signaled the start of a journey on which she was eager to embark. A Queens College senior, she edited the student newspaper, as had Jacobs. A red-diaper baby attuned to world events, Miller was looking for a way to connect with the emerging civil rights movement as she graduated from college. That summer of 1960, she seized an opportunity to go south with CORE for training in nonviolent resistance. Miller went to Miami with thirty-five community leaders and was arrested immediately in a demonstration. In the segregated jails, Miller (the only white woman civil rights worker in the project) did her time with twelve white women criminals.

Confronting the culture of segregation was one of many adaptations the southern movement required. Though southern Blacks interacted with whites in various contexts, especially those related to work, they had separate social worlds. Even northern activists with impeccable civil rights credentials had to learn a whole new way of being when they crossed into the South. As Zellner notes, "Even though I had come from the Left all my life, this was my first real exposure to the whole Black social environment. It was my first exposure to Black culture, and certainly my first exposure to ministers and religious people." Cross-cultural communication proved to be one of the basic challenges in building these boundary-crossing alliances. Recalls Zellner, invoking her New York Jewish accent, "[T]hey couldn't understand me!"[9]

Despite these differences, Miller felt she was finally in the right place. Pleading with CORE organizers, "[D]on't send me home yet," Miller "wangled my way" to New Orleans for further movement work. Though it "was very nerve-wracking and scary," Miller also participated in the sit-ins there. Facing with great reluctance the prospect of returning home, she vowed to find a way back south. Her CORE colleagues told her, "[I]f you want to come back, the group to contact is SNCC." Though she did not know what SNCC was at the time, the organization would become her lifelong political reference point.

University of Chicago graduate Carol Ruth Silver (b. 1938) knew what she wanted: a year working in New York before going to law school. With a passionate interest in international relations, she talked her way into a clerk/typist job at the United Nations. Eager to learn, she manufactured excuses to watch proceedings of the Security Council. There, in January 1961, she saw Soviet premier Nikita Khrushchev bang his shoe on the table during his famous address declaring the Soviet Union's support for national liberation struggles in Cuba and Vietnam.

Witnessing Khrushchev's historic challenge to U.S. hegemony in international affairs broadened Silver's thinking. Thus, she became more receptive to critiques of domestic affairs, such as the persistence of racism. In May 1961, when Silver heard CORE's radio call for Freedom Riders, "I felt as if it was a call to me personally. I could not say no."[10] Within weeks, she was on one of the earlier buses heading south to challenge segregation in intrastate travel. In a letter to her mother from jail, Silver wrote, "Don't worry about me, please. This should be one of the most interesting experiences of my life bar none and certainly something which I will never again get a chance to do."

Sometimes the decision to go south needed to germinate. During the heyday of early sixties radicalism at the University of Wisconsin at Madison, history major Harriet Tanzman (b. 1940) was struggling over what to do with her life. A member of the W.E.B. Dubois Club, Tanzman was also working with the local CORE chapter (headed by future SNCC leader Silas Norman). She had considered going south after hearing some Freedom Riders speak in 1961: "I was too afraid to do it, but I was very affected by them." Early in 1963, Tanzman heard two powerful Black women leaders speak about the movement. Diane Nash, of SNCC, had pushed successfully for the continuation of the Freedom Rides despite the violence they encountered and the resistance of CORE leadership.[11] Gloria Richardson, a rare woman leader of the Cambridge, Maryland, movement, endured death threats and physical repression in a violent fight to end school segregation. Enormously moved by Richardson, Tanzman recalls, "She basically invited us. She said that there's this work to be done and you could participate." Throughout the summer and fall, Tanzman continued to study and organize locally, "trying to get myself to feeling like I could just go south, especially since I was studying something I didn't like—social work."[12]

Sitting in the lunchroom of her fieldwork placement at the State of Wisconsin's Youth Division of Probation, Tanzman looked up at a television screen and saw coverage of John F. Kennedy's November 1963 assassination. Her sense that "enormous things were happening out there, the assassination, the war, the strife in the South . . . just somehow gave me the oomph to quit the next day." Tanzman took her scholarship money and went directly to stay with friends in Atlanta. In the first of several "stints" in the southern movement, Tanzman "just showed up in the SNCC office." She helped do paperwork and participated in the revitalized Atlanta sit-in movement.

Breaking Free and Searching for Meaning

For some northern Jewish women, the decision to go south blended a search for meaning with a desperate desire to break free of the constraints of 1950s life, including American Jewish gender norms. From today's perspective, it is difficult to conceive of sending young women to college without any expectation of vocation except for marriage and motherhood.[13] As Wini Breines notes dryly in her study of growing up white and female in that decade, "[M]arriage, the only sanctioned goal for girls in the 1950s, does not lend itself to rational planning as does a career."[14] The college-educated, second- and third-generation Jewish women ran right into the dilemma of what to do with their lives when they realized they wanted more than marriage and family. "The concept of getting married, living happily ever after, and not doing anything after that always bewildered me," Janice Goodman (b. 1935) recalls. "I did a lot of housecleaning as a child. I did not see cleaning the house as an occupation."[15]

The need to escape confinement to the home was a recurrent theme. For these primarily urban Jewish women, images of suburban life symbolized the trap they sought to avoid. When asked what enabled young Jewish women like her to face the danger of going south, Rita Schwerner Bender replied firmly, "I did not see myself as saving anyone, but I did have a view of saving myself from a split-level house."[16]

During the postwar period when future civil rights activists were growing up, the development of Jewish suburbs epitomized rapid Jewish social and economic mobility (and its discontents). Jewish intellectuals criticized suburban Jewish life in general as bland, conformist, and materialistic and looked upon suburban Jews' religious practice (building and attending synagogues primarily to make their socioeconomic success as Jews visible in the community) as anti-intellectual, spiritually shallow, and vulgar.[17] Radical Jews of the 1960s and 1970s were the most bitter critics of Jewish suburbia. Irving Howe contended that assimilation there had extinguished some of the most distinctive qualities of the Jewish spirit: "an eager restlessness, a moral anxiety, an openness to novelty, a hunger for dialectic, a refusal of contentment, an ironic criticism of all fixed opinion."[18] Certainly, these qualities describe the Jewish women activists.

In Newark, New Jersey, housewife Jacqueline Levine (b. 1926) and her five-year-old daughter marched in an endless circle protesting Woolworth's segregated lunch counters. It was the late 1950s, before the Greensboro sit-ins galvanized a national civil rights movement. Not long before, Levine's husband had asked, "Are you just going to take care of the children and the house, or are you going to do something with your mind?"[19] Harkening back to her suffragist mother and grandmother, Levine stepped onto the picket line and into a forty-year career of volunteerism and leadership in the Jewish communal world.

Inspired by her mentor, Rabbi Joachim Prinz, she attended the 1963 March on Washington, which Prinz helped organize. Later, Levine flew in for the Montgomery rally at the end of the 1965 Selma-to-Montgomery march. Because there was a small contingent from the American Jewish Congress participating, she felt more comfortable going to Montgomery and proud to be there as a Jew. As a highly visible leader, Levine represents untold numbers of women in Jewish organizations who have pushed the Jewish community to live up to its social justice ideals in twentieth-century race relations.

Jewish women's hunger for meaningful action explains their tenacity in facing difficult movement experiences. After she describes a "horrible" 1963 jail experience in Albany, Georgia, that included a hunger strike, Miriam Cohen Glickman (b. 1942) explains why she stayed:

> I guess I need to be clear about my commitment. I had many horrible experiences. There wasn't anything else I could have been doing at the time that had anywhere near the pull that this did, of helping make the world a better place. I mean what were the alternatives? I could go back and get a 9-to-5 job somewhere. In those days, women were teachers, nurses, and psychologists/counselors. And Jewish women weren't nurses. So I had the other two to choose from. I would have stayed forever down there. I finally left because I was forced out. But all of us felt that what we were doing was the most important work that could be done. Nobody said this was a wonderful experience. If you find anybody that told you that, they've forgotten.[20]

Glickman's honesty demystifies the daily work of social-change movements. For Glickman as for other white women activists, including Jewish women, the work of the civil rights movement, while often very challenging, gave life a focus and a meaning beyond those expected for daughters of the rising white middle class at the time.

After Elizabeth Slade Hirschfeld (b. 1937) graduated from Cornell University in 1958, she worked in a genetics lab, at an Atomic Energy Commission lab located at Cornell, and at the Veterinary School. She also, in her words, "screwed around a lot." Although she didn't want to think about it, it was clear that "I wasn't getting married." Slade "was looking for a career or something compelling, something to commit to. The main career for women in the '50s was being a housewife and mother, and there were just no appropriate role models for me, certainly not in my family. I needed something to do that would be something for me. I didn't know what to do. So when the Freedom Rides came along, I felt it was a wonderful opportunity for me."[21]

Some Jewish women's decisions to go south seemed arbitrary on the surface but actually reflected an intuition that the movement experience would liberate them in unforeseen ways. Elaine DeLott Baker (b. 1942) exemplified this dynamic, crediting disgust with hypocrisy as her motivation.

A Radcliffe College junior, DeLott was staying at a friend's house in Cambridge over Christmas break, 1963. A group of friends came to visit, including "a guy who was part of our group and we ended up sleeping together. In that time, there was that kind of loose sexuality. In fact, we had never slept together before, and we never did again, but we slept together that night."[22] Breaking sexual taboos must have been both exciting and nerve-wracking for DeLott and her peers, who grew up in an era when even talking about sex publicly was taboo.[23] Despite the fact that the Pill liberated women of their generation to become more sexually active, young people's sexual expression was still subterranean and subject to social control in the early 1960s, as DeLott's story illustrates.

In the next room, also sleeping over, was a young girl who said she was a junior at M.I.T. When her uncle, a captain in the Cambridge police force, stormed in at five o'clock in the morning, they learned that she "was a townie, a junior in high school, a Catholic girl whose father was dead. Her mother sent the police to arrest her for being a willful child." The police arrested DeLott and her friends (only a few years older than the "willful child"), too, and charged them with fornication, lewd and lascivious behavior, and corrupting the morals of a minor—one misdemeanor and two felonies.

Paroled into the custody of the college and her Harvard-based dean, DeLott endured a humiliating talk designed to uplift her morals. The dean told her the story of his own daughter, whom "you might call a little wild. But she married someone who was a little boring but who didn't care about her past. Someday you will find someone who doesn't care about your past." After this enlightening talk, the school first expelled DeLott and then readmitted her. "I had to have a police escort to my exams because the court hearing was the same morning as my exams."

As a working-class woman who struggled to find her place at an elite institution, DeLott was incensed. "I felt shame for my parents who had to come. I felt indignation as a woman of the world. As an intellectual, you knew that this was bullshit. So I finished the academic year and said, 'This place is fucked—I'm getting out of here.' " When two Harvard doctoral student friends invited her to join them to teach at the summer session at Tougaloo College, DeLott literally jumped on the SNCC bus heading toward Jackson. That was the beginning of her antiracist education.

Doing What Needed to Be Done

Jewish women's ability and willingness to work—to handle a variety of necessary tasks—gave them access to the southern civil rights movement and legitimized their participation. Many Jewish women civil rights activists had direct proximity to Eastern European working-class Jewishness and to working mothers. They were aware of the traditional Eastern European Jewish gender division of labor: women managed family and business; men studied Torah. They internalized a culturally derived, gendered work ethic of doing what needed to be done.

Embodying this Jewish women's work ethic, some northern Jewish women, often slightly older professionals, went south when they saw they had skills the movement needed. Florence Howe (b. 1929) was already a professor at Goucher College in Baltimore by the time she first went south. Howe had involved her students in local civil rights protests in 1963 and 1964, and it was they who pushed her to deepen her commitment. She went to Mississippi in 1964, using her teaching and organizational skills to coordinate the Blair Street Freedom School in Jackson. In a much more dangerous assignment, she returned the following summer to work on school desegregation for a month in Natchez, a Klan stronghold.

During her internship at a Jewish hospital in Chicago, the British-born physician June Finer (b. 1935) began to understand American racism. "I began to be really upset by the level of illness of the Black people who would come in at death's door. Their health would be neglected until they were really, really, really sick. It became increasingly clear that the differences in class and income were making a big differ-ence in their health status."[24] Finer's relationship with the Jewish activist and physician Quentin Young reinforced her perceptions and opened up a world of radical activism in Chicago. She became part of a long-standing interracial organi-zation called the Committee to End Discrimination in Chicago Medical Institutions (CED). Finer headed south for the first time on a CED-chartered train to the 1963 March on Washington.

Providing care (a traditional women's role) in a nontraditional career for women at that time, Finer worked with the medical staff during the 1964 Mississippi Summer Project. She returned in the spring of 1965 to serve for five months as southern coordinator for the Medical Committee for Human Rights (MCHR). Finer managed and dispatched the many volunteer medical professionals who came south. MCHR literally bound up the wounds of SNCC activists on the front lines.

Not everyone who wanted to go south could do so at a moment's notice. Roberta Galler's priority was always to work where she was most needed, and for a long time that meant the North. On leave from the University of Chicago, Galler (b. 1936) became manager of the journal *New University Thought,* an early northern-student chronicler of events in the southern civil rights movement. In 1961, *New University Thought* hosted a SNCC fundraiser. As activists told their stories about the struggle in the South, Galler committed herself fully to the movement. She had planned to go back to school in the fall to finish her degree, but, as she puts it, "I forgot to."[25] She helped found Chicago Friends of SNCC and became its first executive secretary.

From her fundraising, organizing, and press outreach work in Chicago, Galler developed strong connections with many SNCC activists. Some would come to stay with her to recuperate from stress or injuries. Keeping in close touch with SNCC field offices on a daily basis, Galler made direct interventions that brought food, information, money, national attention, and personal support to SNCC centers across the South. Movements for radical social change (and organizations like SNCC) generally fight against great odds with limited resources. Women like Galler manage, protect, and preserve precious human and material resources. They func-tion as connective tissue—taking care of people's needs. The work of revitalizing activist communities through authentic personal connections sustains individuals and their collective vision.

In the fall of 1964, Lawrence Guyot offered Galler just such a challenging assignment. He invited her to come to Mississippi to open the first statewide office of the Mississippi Freedom Democratic Party (MFDP) at a moment when the entire staff was demoralized and burnt out. After the high of Freedom Summer, SNCC had to face the failure to seat the MFDP delegation at the Atlantic City Democratic National Convention. The next wave of voter registration work that Galler helped organize in Mississippi would empower both staff and local people.

SNCC was small and worked in dangerous Klan territory in several southern states. Therefore, it required keenly aware coordinators who knew the location of each field organizer at any given moment. A number of the Jewish women profiled played such roles for SNCC. This type of coordinating work called for the ability to deal with people across differences, to manage information, to run offices, to assess danger, and to handle multiple tasks amid chaos. These are also skills that women must develop to perform their traditional gender roles. The work performed by many of the women illustrates the different ways they protected the network they cherished as SNCC's "beloved community."

Parental Reactions

Once young Jewish women made up their minds to go south, they faced two hurdles: figuring out the organizational connections that would get them there and telling their parents. First, one had to be quite determined as a white woman to work for SNCC at any time other than the 1964 and 1965 Mississippi Summer Projects. Dottie Miller, Miriam Cohen, and Harriet Tanzman all wrote letters to the Atlanta office asking to work for SNCC. The letters went unanswered, probably because the office was understaffed and chaotic and there was no formal process for bringing white students into SNCC other than the Summer Projects.

Second, the women had to deal with a range of parental reactions when they announced their decision. Most Jewish women volunteers did not need parental permission to go south, but they certainly must have wanted their family's support.[26] Yet, those women who went, more often than not, confronted parental disapproval. Even women from progressive households had to face parental ambivalence.

The women's decision to put their bodies on the line to fight racism was a transgressive act on a number of levels. To begin with, it carried the potential to cross Jewish class boundaries. Throughout the twentieth century, American Jewish parents invested a great deal of energy and resources trying to protect their children and to ensure their children's future security. They saw higher education as leading almost inevitably to upward mobility and social safety. Activism threatened to disrupt this hard-won and privileged path.[27] Those who left college temporarily or permanently for the movement often widened the breach between generations.

For northern Jewish women, going south was also a transgression of Jewish gender norms. Women who had never rebelled before shattered their parents' perception of them as obedient daughters, nice Jewish girls. Jewish daughters were in training for marrying upward, building a family, maintaining Jewish continuity, and supporting a husband's and children's success. The primary injunction was not to make waves. Their job was to ensure that their family and the Jewish community would "make it" in the United States. Within twentieth-century American Jewish culture, the Jewish woman's body has been the medium for expressing the community's gender, race, and class issues. Specifically, Jewish women's bodies have symbolized Jewish ethnicity, but as an affluent, acculturating presence.[28] Jewish women civil rights activists resisted this symbolic function.

Making waves in more ways than one, many Jewish daughters who went south knew that their parents would not be pleased. While trying to respect parental fears, daughters were mindful that they were enacting values learned at home. When Carol Ruth Silver told her mother she was going south on one of the early Freedom Rides, Silver recalls that her mother said, " 'Oy, my heart, my heart.' My father said, 'Well, just be careful.' My mother said, 'You're going to kill me. You can't do this, it's dangerous.' I said, 'Mother, this is what you taught me to do and this is what you taught me to be. If I don't do it, then I will not be true to all that you have taught me.' She knew it was true, and she was legitimately frightened for me. Now that I'm the mother of kids who take risks, I know that feeling, but it's in kids' nature to do that to their parents."

Even the most engaged parents found it hard to watch their children risking violence for an ideal. This hit home for longtime labor and peace activist Trudy Orris when her sixteen-year-old son Peter insisted on going with her on a Freedom Ride to Gwynne Oaks, Maryland, in 1963. "My son wanted to be arrested," she relates, "and I wanted him to go to school." As the bus rolled southward down the East Coast, the entire group passionately debated whether Peter should get arrested. "People took sides, and the majority decided that he should not. He was very young." Whenever she wanted to go south for the movement, Orris had to balance delicately her activist and her mothering roles. This was a creative adaptation of Jewish gender roles.

Ambivalence was the best possible response Jewish daughters could expect when sharing their decision to go south. Because their daughters were usually acting in consonance with the values taught at home, parents had a hard time arguing against the morality of the impulse to take action. Still, naturally, they were frightened for their daughters' safety, and all the more so after the disappearance of the activists Goodman, Schwerner, and Chaney in Mississippi in June 1964.

Ilene Strelitz, editor of the *Stanford Daily* and a protégée of the former Stanford dean and liberal activist Allard Lowenstein, had a very stressful time with her mother during the training session for the 1964 Mississippi Summer Project at Oxford, Ohio:

> Every night, in complete fear and anguish, I waited to see my mother on the [TV] screen. She had sent me a telegram signed with my brother's name saying that she had had a heart attack and I must come home immediately (none of which was true). Telephone calls, with her screaming, threatening, crying until I hung up, came every day. Long vituperative letters came from her for me. After the phone calls I would disappear into the ladies' room, and cry out the engulfing rage and accumulated frustration. When I recovered, I desperately threw cold water on my face as it was rather well advertised that there were psychiatrists around looking for people showing signs of breaking down and who thus should be weeded out before they got to Mississippi. *Mississippi had nothing over a Jewish mother.*[29]

A number of the women had more trouble with their fathers than with their mothers. This often required them to break explicitly with patriarchal authority and values, including overt racism. Janice Goodman had been out of school for seven years and involved in sit-ins and progressive New York politics by the time she announced that she was going to Mississippi in 1964. Goodman's mother reacted with "a mixture of fear and pride" that her daughter was "doing this very exciting, meaningful, and important thing." On the other hand, Goodman's father (from whom her mother had been divorced for some time) took her out to dinner to try to talk her out of going. Goodman recalls: "He said, 'God, it's dangerous, aren't you worried?' And then when he was getting no place with that, he finally said, 'Don't you realize, Jan, that those people down there, they rape and ravage?' "[30]

Although Florence Howe was already a professor at the time she went south, her commitment also had repercussions for her relationship with her family. When Howe adopted Alice Jackson, a black teenager she met in Mississippi, her family "was very angry with me. More than angry. They just refused to see me with her. Same thing. My brother was an incredible racist. I didn't see my brother for about fifteen years over Alice and a couple of other things."[31]

Elizabeth Slade Hirschfeld's mother "was very proud of me. Real, real proud of me. Yeah, she loved it." However, before she left on the sixth bus of the Freedom Rides, she had a huge fight over the phone with her Republican (assimilated Jewish) father. He was furious and screamed at her, "You're a damn fool." Later, Hirschfeld notes, "my dad came around. In fact, after I was married and he had been out here once, he said, 'The problem with you all was that you didn't stay with it.' "

Despite memories of her own flight from Berlin to Amsterdam to New York, Vivian Leburg's mother supported her daughter's decision to go south; her refugee father did not. Opposed to the idea of sending young people into such danger, he tried to bring other volunteers' parents around to his point of view at an emergency meeting of the local Parents of SNCC group. In an August 8, 1965, letter responding to his daughter's youthfully militant letter from jail, Werner Leburg described this meeting, where, "I can assure you, I did not have an easy time when I talked against these professional speakers."[32] In the letter, Leburg's German-Jewish rationalism and moral intelligence warred with his emotions:

Dear Chicky:
    As far as I can remember, I never could have tried to tell you that what you are doing is wrong. This would by no means be in line with my social conscience or ethical philosophy.
    All what I tried to convey to you and as a matter of fact also to the parent committee was, that within my knowledge of so very many revolutionary movements in Europe and elsewhere I never came across a single fact where young girls have been sent into the front and fireline, except maybe for the so called "children's crusade" during the middle ages, which ended in a catastrophe.
    However, whatever the opinions are for ways and means to achieve results, risks have to match possibilities of results and you should not construct your parents' concern about your safety as a disapproval of your present activities.
    Chicky, do not take unnecessary risks and that is all we ask for, that is all we can ask for and if you even are able to do that we do not know and doubt it, but we hope so with all our heart. Keep well, Chicky, and good luck to you.

                                                                        All my love, Daddy

Werner Leburg's poignant letter speaks for all the parents who balanced concern for their daughters' vulnerability with pride in their courage to make the decision to go south.

Exploring the significance of that decision and chronicling the actions that followed, this study acknowledges the ordinariness and extraordinariness of northern Jewish women who went south. Their stories reveal how "ordinary" Jewish women found ways to contribute to the extraordinary fight for civil rights led by Black people in the 1960s. As Dottie Miller Zellner puts it, "The primary lesson I learned is that ordinary people can do the most extraordinary things." Although Zellner was speaking primarily of local Black people, who were the heart and soul of the southern movement, her statement also applies to many northern Jewish women like herself, who moved out of a relatively comfortable existence into an unfamiliar and often dangerous context in order to take action on principles in which they believed.

NOTES

1. Interview with Vivian Leburg Rothstein, June 26, 1994.

2. Interview with Gertrude Weissman Orris, January 21, 1994.

3. Herbert Aptheker argues that white antiracism, more common among the working classes, women, and those in direct contact with blacks, has been underestimated in U.S. history. Herbert Aptheker, *Anti-Racism in United States History: The First Two Hundred Years* (Westport, CT: Greenwood Press, 1992).

4. As the historian Hasia Diner has argued, the nature of twentieth-century Black-Jewish collaboration mixes altruism with self-interest. Identification with the plight of African Americans and efforts to "help" them enabled American Jews to explore and consolidate their own identities as Americans. Michael Rogin's linkage of Jewish civil rights workers with immigrant Jewish entertainers who wore blackface stretches the analogy too far. However, Naomi Seidman's analysis is more resonant with the experience of Jewish civil rights workers and contemporary Jewish progressives. She argues that "in the absence of a particularist Jewish political affiliation that could also satisfy the progressive universalist agenda with which Jewish politics has been historically linked, adopting the particularist position of another group paradoxically becomes a distinctly Jewish act." Thus, she "names" a "Jewish politics of vicarious identity," which, if conceptualized with respect for the real contributions of Jewish cross-cultural activists, helps illuminate the American Jewish progressive tradition. See Hasia Diner, *In the Almost Promised Land: American Jews and Blacks, 1915–1935* (Westport, CT: Greenwood Press, 1977); Michael Rogin, *Blackface, White Noise: Jewish Immigrants in the Hollywood Melting Pot* (Berkeley: University of California Press, 1996); and Naomi Seidman, "Fag-Hags and Bu-Jews: Toward a (Jewish) Politics of Vicarious Identity," in *Insider/Outsider: American Jews and Multiculturalism,* ed. David Biale, Susannah Heschel, and Michael Galchinsky (Berkeley: University of California Press, 1998), 261.

5. Jewish law defines any child of a Jewish mother as Jewish. Any group, particularly one as historically reviled as the Jews, must create boundaries to define who is a safe member of the community and who is a threatening outsider.

6. Aldon D. Morris, *The Origins of the Civil Rights Movement: Black Communities Organizing for Change* (New York: Free Press, 1984), 195.

7. Interview with Barbara Jacobs Haber, February 20, 1994. Michael Walzer went on to become a noted political philosopher and the author of many books, including *Exodus and Revolution* (New York: Basic Books, 1985), a meditation on the political meaning of the biblical Exodus story. Walzer has used his early civil rights experiences to reflect on contemporary Black-Jewish relations. See Walzer, "Blacks and Jews: A Personal Reflection," in Jack Salzman and Cornel West, eds., *Struggles in the Promised Land* (New York: Oxford University Press, 1997).

8. Morris, *Origins of the Civil Rights Movement*, 222.

9. Quoted in Fred Powledge, *Free at Last? The Civil Rights Movement and the People Who Made It* (New York: HarperCollins, 1992), 222.

10. Interview with Carol Ruth Silver, February 9, 1994.

11. Clayborne Carson, *In Struggle: SNCC and the Black Awakening of the 1960s* (Cambridge: Harvard University Press, 1981), 34.

12. Interview with Harriet Tanzman, October 15, 1993.

13. By 1956, one-fourth of all urban white college women married while still in college. Elaine Tyler May, *Homeward Bound: American Families in the Cold War Era* (New York: Basic Books, 1988), 79.

14. Wini Breines, *Young, White, and Miserable: Growing Up Female in the 1950s* (Boston: Beacon Press, 1992), 107.

15. Interview with Janice Goodman, October 21, 1993. The rebellion of daughters of the aspiring white middle class against the idea of being "the wife of a house" helped inspire the early moments of second-wave feminism. However, the failure to make visible the relationship between such aspirations and Black women's domestic work created tensions in the women's movement.

16. Telephone conversation with Rita Schwerner Bender, February 1994.

17. Edward S. Shapiro, *A Time for Healing: American Jewry since World War II* (Baltimore: Johns Hopkins University Press, 1992), 151.

18. Irving Howe, *World of Our Fathers,* cited in ibid., 152.

19. As recounted during interview with Jacqueline Levine, October 1993.

20. Interview with Miriam Cohen Glickman, February 11, 1994.

21. Interview with Elizabeth Slade Hirschfeld, February 10, 1994.

22. Interview with Elaine DeLott Baker, September 23, 1994.

23. John D'Emilio and Estelle Freedman, *Intimate Matters: A History of Sexuality in America* (New York: Harper and Row, 1988), 282.

24. Interview with June Finer, December 21, 1993.

25. Interview with Roberta Galler, December 10, 1994.

26. Doug McAdam, *Freedom Summer,* (New York: Oxford University Press, 1988), 65.

27. Some Jewish women civil rights veterans became lifelong radicals, just getting by with modest wages from progressive organizations.

28. Riv-Ellen Prell, "Why Jewish Princesses Don't Sweat: Desire and Consumption in Postwar American Jewish Culture," in *The People of the Body: Jews and Judaism from an Embodied Perspective,* ed., Howard Eilberg-Schwartz (Albany: SUNY Press, 1993).

29. Excerpt from Strelitz's unpublished memoir, cited in Mary Aickin Rothschild, "White Women Volunteers in the Freedom Summers," *Feminist Studies* 5, no. 3 (fall 1979): 475, emphasis added. Also, see William Chafe, *Never Stop Running: Allard Lowenstein and the Struggle to Save American Liberalism* (New York: Basic Books, 1993), for discussion of the Ilene Strelitz and other Allard Lowenstein civil rights protégées.

30. In recounting the story, Goodman said, "So hey, my father was a racist. You know,

in his heart of hearts, he ended up being a racist. Not an active racist because he was a jolly person and he was a basically decent person. On a one-to-one [basis], he wouldn't hurt anybody and was good natured. But as a political matter, he was basically a racist." Goodman's distinction between "active racism" and her father's "political racism" is an honest attempt to grapple with the difficult question of Jewish racism. Adrienne Rich also distinguishes forms of racism, (1) active domination and (2) passive collusion; Jews may participate in both forms, as well as in resistance to racism. Jewish racism has its own dynamics. It often derives from a sense of victimization and a consequent commitment to protecting oneself and one's family from harm, as with Goodman's father. See Adrienne Rich's classic essay, "Disloyal to Civilization: Feminism, Racism, and Gynephobia," in *On Lies, Secrets, and Silences: Selected Prose, 1966–1978* (New York: Norton, 1979).

31. Interview with Florence Howe, December 1, 1993.

32. I am very grateful to Vivian Leburg Rothstein for sharing her father's letter with me. She subsequently published parts of the letter in "Reunion," *Boston Review* (December/January 1994–1995): 8–11, a piece reflecting on her experience at the 1994 Mississippi Freedom Summer Project 30th Anniversary Reunion.

Chapter Eighteen

Jewish Feminism Faces the American Women's Movement
Convergence and Divergence

Paula E. Hyman

The Jewish feminist movement has transformed the public space of American Jewry. Distinct from American feminism, the "Jewish feminist movement" does not consist of the totality of women of Jewish origin who are active in American feminism. Nor does it have a single address. Rather, it is a loose construct of Jewish women who have brought feminist insights and critiques into the Jewish community and into the field of Jewish Studies in the American university. All have been influenced by the American women's movement, but all have dissented from some of its manifestations. It is the complex relation between specifically Jewish feminism and the American women's movement that this chapter explores.

The impact of Jewish feminism is readily apparent in any investigation of American Jewish life. Formerly relegated to the home, to synagogue sisterhoods, and to their own philanthropic organizations, in the past twenty-five years women have emerged as spiritual leaders in the synagogue and as lay leaders and professionals in the organized Jewish community. The first woman rabbi was ordained in 1972; now there are more than four hundred rabbis, graduates of Reform, Reconstructionist, and Conservative rabbinical schools, serving American Jewry. About 180 women cantors also serve in the American Jewish community.[1] Courses on the history of Jewish women and on women and Judaism have appeared on many American campuses, and gender has been tentatively incorporated as a category of analysis in Jewish Studies courses. Although there were no women among the twenty-five professors who established the Association for Jewish Studies in the late 1960s, women now constitute about 35 percent of its members and sponsor an active Women's Caucus. Even the conservative critic of many aspects of feminist ideology Jack Wertheimer, in his thoughtful survey of the state of Judaism in America in the last half of the twentieth century, has noted feminism's considerable impact on the American Jewish community and the source of creativity it has been.[2]

Like Zionism, Jewish feminism emerged from an encounter of Jews who were deeply concerned with the fate of their group with secular western culture.[3] The Zionist movement did not spring in an unmediated way from Jewish tradition;

indeed, it initially inspired hostility from the leaders of Orthodox Jewry in both western and eastern Europe. It took secularized Jews, influenced by the rise of modern nationalism in the latter part of the nineteenth century, to found a Jewish nationalist movement that gave a radically modern form to traditional Jewish longings. Jewish feminism, too, did not spring in an unmediated way from Jewish tradition; indeed, it initially inspired, and continues to elicit, hostility from the leaders of Orthodox Jewry. It took secularized Jews, influenced by the rise of feminism in America in the 1960s, to establish a Jewish feminist movement that provided a radically modern form to strivings for gender equality. Here the parallel between Zionism and Jewish feminism founders because the strivings for gender equality had not found direct expression in the male-produced classical Jewish texts as the yearning for restoration in Zion had. Still, Jewish feminists asserted, from their first public efforts in the early 1970s, that the demands of feminism were fully consonant with Jewish experience in the modern era, with Jewish self-understanding, and with traditional Jewish concern for the status of women. The conditions of the late twentieth century had simply provided a new concept, that of gender equality, that undermined the misogyny and "separate but equal" approach that characterized many rabbinic attitudes toward women, attitudes shaped by the social and ideological contexts of premodern times.

A Jewish feminist movement is inconceivable without the emergence of a robust American women's movement by the end of the 1960s. The second wave of twentieth-century American feminism, often dated from the publication in 1963 of Betty Friedan's The Feminist Mystique, had been institutionalized with the establishment of the National Organization for Women. American feminism provided the ideological framework and the social format for Jewish feminism.[4] Young Jewish women were found in large numbers in places quickly penetrated by feminist ideas: the civil rights and anti-Vietnam movements of the 1960s and the American university.[5] Because of their middle-class incomes, small family size, and cultural valorization of education in the years following World War II, 1970s Jewish families provided their daughters with higher education to a much greater percent than other white Americans. In 1970, more than half of American Jewish women of college age were enrolled in college.[6]

Many young Jewish women were introduced to feminist ideas on the campus, not in their college courses but in consciousness-raising groups that mushroomed in the first few years of the 1970s. These groups provided opportunities for women to share their experiences growing up female in the 1950s and sixties and to read feminist literature ranging from Simone de Beauvoir's classic The Second Sex to the radical new literature produced by young Americans, such as Kate Millett's Sexual Politics, Shulamith Firestone's The Dialectic of Sex, and Robin Morgan's collection entitled Sisterhood Is Powerful.[7] All three were available by 1970. As the historian Hester Eisenstein has pointed out, in its early years American feminism focused on "the socially constructed differences between the sexes" as the "chief source of female oppression. In the main, feminist theory concentrated on establishing the distinction between sex and gender and developed an analysis of sex roles as a mode of social control."[8] Liberation, then, necessitated severing the connection between gender and social function, the opening up of societal roles to all, irrespective of gender.

Despite the fact that Shulamith Firestone and Robin Morgan, as well as Betty Friedan, were of Jewish origin, none dealt specifically with Judaism or with the Jewish community. Betty Friedan asserted her Jewishness only a decade or so after the publication of her book, and in response to the United Nations' welcome of Yasir Arafat and her perception of the reemergence of anti-Semitism—a subject which I will address further.[9]

This avoidance of Judaism was characteristic of American ideological and political culture of the time. Within feminism, this reticence was reinforced by the presumption that gender trumped all other aspects of identity. American feminism proclaimed that all women were united, despite their differences of class, race, and ethnicity, because their gender invariably led to a subordinate status. Although many working-class and black women quickly dissented from a feminist agenda that overlooked their multiple allegiances and their solidarity with men of their own groups, Jewish women within the American feminist movement tended initially not to assert a Jewish dimension to their feminism or to bring the issue of gender equality to the Jewish community.

A specifically Jewish feminism emerged in America only when young women who had received a substantial Jewish education and participated actively in Jewish religious and cultural life concluded that they could not limit their feminist analysis to general American social conditions and institutions alone. Once they experienced the feminist "click," the realization that female inferiority was a cultural construct, that things did not have to be the way they were, Jewish women became acutely aware of the inequities women suffered in Jewish law, in the synagogue, and in Jewish communal institutions.[10] By 1974, articles analyzing the patriarchal nature of Judaism had appeared, a group called Ezrat Nashim had issued a call to the Conservative movement to count women in the *minyan* and to ordain women as rabbis, and the Jewish Feminist Organization had formed as a result of two successful conferences in New York City, held in 1973 and 1974 and attended by hundreds of women (and some men as well).[11] The conferences aimed to bring together secular and religious Jewish feminists to explore Jewish women's identities and needs. Speakers included Congresswoman Bella Abzug and the Orthodox feminist Blu Greenberg. As was the case with the American women's movement, Jewish feminists focused on prescribed sex roles as a mode of social control—specifically the ways in which women had been excluded from education and positions of power because of their gender. They dedicated themselves to achieving equal access of women to the realms from which they had been excluded.

The Jewish Feminist Organization, which was formally founded in April 1974, articulated the double goal that became characteristic of Jewish feminism: to achieve "the full, direct, and equal participation of women at all levels of Jewish life—communal, educational, and political" and "to be the voice of the Jewish feminist movement in the national and international movement."[12] From its early days, then, Jewish feminists presumed that they had particular issues to advance in the women's movement.

There were many Jews who participated in the American women's movement but relatively few who identified in the early 1970s with specifically Jewish feminist groups. Many feminists, Christians as well as Jews, had determined that their patriarchal religions were simply a source of oppression and hence irrelevant to their lives. Those who sought a vehicle for their own spirituality often turned to Eastern religions, such as Buddhism, or to the goddess-worshipping Wiccan tradition.[13] Or they determined to take the theologian Mary Daly's advice and create new religious traditions based on their own experiences as women. In 1973, in her widely read book *Beyond God the Father: Toward a Philosophy of Women's Liberation,* Daly, who had been raised as a Catholic and taught at a Catholic college, formulated a rationale for a woman-centered spirituality that would undermine the hierarchic thinking characteristic of patriarchy, thereby providing the basis for human liberation. She called on women to refuse to be co-opted by institutions, like the church (and by implication the synagogue), "whose sexism is direct and explicit (e.g., written into rules and by-laws) but whose ideologies, policies, and goals are not defined exclusively or primarily by sexism." [For her, the Catholic Church oscillated between this level-two category and the level-one category of antiwoman institution "whose ideologies, policies, and goals not only are directly and explicitly sexist but even are exclusively and primarily defined by sexism."] Instead, she suggested that women could resist cooptation by recognizing "that our own liberation, seen in its fullest implications, is primary in importance." Liberation would include the formation of exodus communities of women, founded on a covenant of sisterhood, that leave behind "the false self and sexist society." Women had the option, in Daly's words, to give "priority to what we find valid in our own experience without needing to look to the past for justification."[14]

Jewish feminists as I've defined them could not follow Mary Daly. They felt that their Jewishness was a fundamental aspect of their identity that transcended traditional Judaism's assumptions about women and specific constraints on women's access to religious education and to agency within Jewish law. They could not define themselves solely through their feminist ideology and affiliations. As Judith Plaskow wrote in *Standing Again at Sinai,* the only systematic feminist Jewish theology, "the move toward embracing a whole Jewish/feminist identity did not grow out of my conviction that Judaism is 'redeemable,' but out of my sense that sundering Judaism and feminism would mean sundering my being."[15] As Plaskow's statement indicates, Jewish feminists could not turn their back on the Jewish past, finding validity in their own experience alone, when the impress of the Jewish past on their very identity was so strong.

There were American feminists with whom Jewish feminists felt a special kinship. In battling sexism within their tradition and in exploring feminist interpretations of classical texts, Jewish feminists shared many of the perspectives of Christian feminists. They were aware of Protestant denominations that had ordained women as ministers and were intrigued by Christian feminist exegesis of the Adam and Eve story. Reflective of this sympathy was the reprinting of Phyllis Trible's essay "Depatriarchalizing in Biblical Interpretation" in the first Jewish feminist collection of essays, *The Jewish Woman: New Perspectives,* published in 1976.[16]

But, as Plaskow indicated, their Jewish identity was rooted in Jewish historical experience and culture as much as in belief. Just as black feminists felt that their experience and culture as members of a racial minority could not be subordinated to their gender without denying their essential being, so Jewish feminists (though clearly not all feminists of Jewish origin) felt they could not deny the centrality of Jewishness in their identity. This connection to Jewish history and culture, however vague its content, was not limited to Jewish women who were religiously affiliated. As the editors of *Lilith,* the new Jewish feminist journal which defined its constituency as secular as well as religious feminists, wrote, in their premiere edition in 1976, "As women, we are attracted to much of the ideology of the general women's movement; as Jews, we recognize that we have particular concerns not always shared by other groups."[17]

Aside from refusing to walk away from Judaism because it was a patriarchal culture, Jewish feminists also combated aspects of the American women's movement that they viewed as reflective of a tendency of some on the political left to delegitimate Jewish particularity and even to indulge in anti-Semitism. Jewish feminists sought recognition of their particularity within the American women's movement not only because they had specific issues to address but also because they were unwilling to suppress an important component of who they were in the name of feminism. In assuming that their experience and culture were normative, middle-class, white Christian women denied voices to those whose experience and culture differed from theirs, and particularly to those who had loyalties to a group that transcended their gender. Black women had written of this problem with eloquence. In 1980, the poet and activist Audre Lorde proclaimed, in a speech at Amherst College, "Refusing to recognize difference makes it impossible to see the different problems and pitfalls facing us as women."[18] Yet, black as well as white feminists did not recognize Jewishness as a legitimate source of identity and seemed oblivious to its erasure.

By 1980, Jewish feminists identified trends within the American women's movement that in the best light revealed anti-Jewish biases and at worst were themselves expressions of anti-Semitism. In the pages of *Lilith,* Judith Plaskow and Annette Daum, coordinator of the Reform movement's Department of Interreligious Affairs, attacked the tendency of Christian feminists to blame Judaism for the birth and survival of patriarchy, the cultural system that oppressed women. The traditional Christian claim of Judaism as inferior to Christianity and as the source of evil in the world was now clad in new feminist garb.

Plaskow pointed to the creation of a "new myth" in Christian feminist circles, that, before the ancient Hebrews came onto the historical scene, "the goddess reigned in matriarchal glory, and that after them Jesus tried to restore egalitarianism but was foiled by the persistence of Jewish attitudes within the Christian tradition."[19] One Catholic theologian, Leonard Swidler, published an article in 1971 with the title "Jesus Was a Feminist" and proclaimed in a later book that "feminism [was] . . . a constitutive part of the gospel, the good news of Jesus," while the rabbis were the central disseminators of misogyny within Western religious traditions.[20] As Plaskow pointed out, Christian feminists read the Jewish tradition selectively, highlighting only the negative passages about women. Most important, she noted, "Feminist research projects onto Judaism the failure of the Christian tradition unambiguously to renounce sexism. It projects onto Judaism the 'backsliding' of a tradition which was to develop sexism in a new and virulent direction. It thus allows the Christian feminist to avoid confronting the failures of her/his own tradition."[21] Similarly, Annette Daum saw the feminist attack on Judaism, by both Christians and pagan worshippers of the goddess, as a feminist reformulation of the traditional charge against the Jews of deicide in the crucifixion of Jesus.[22] Susannah Heschel, like Plaskow a scholar of religion, has continued to press the issue, asserting that Christian feminists have created a new theodicy "that blames the Jews for the suffering of women and the existence of violence." The Jews thus replace women in bringing about the Fall.[23] Heschel challenges Christian feminists to refrain from distorting Judaism in their attempts to deal with the problems of misogyny in their own tradition, problems that are, she notes, "ultimately . . . so similar to our own. Their problems will not be resolved through a manipulative ideology that projects Christian problems (or human problems) onto Jews."[24] By addressing the position of Jews and Judaism in feminist theology and in feminist reflections on patriarchy, Jewish feminists have focused attention on the (perhaps) unconscious continuation of anti-Jewish stereotypes which have a long history in Christian and secular Western thought. Because Jewish feminists are raising these issues from within feminist ranks, they have access to an audience that is unlikely to read rabbis' sermons or Anti-Defamation League press releases.

Jewish feminists also pointed out that much of the general American women's movement displayed discomfort with the issues of Jewish identity and antisemitism. Here Jewish lesbian feminists took the lead in expressing their dismay at the denial of difference that they found in the American women's movement. Although the women's movement seemed ready to respond to charges of racial and class bias, there was little discussion of the dismissal of Jewishness as a legitimate category of difference and of anti-Semitism as a form of oppression. Alienated from Jewish religious tradition because of its sexism and homophobia, Jewish lesbian feminism, in the words of activist Melanie Kaye/Kantrowitz, were "pulled back to the theme of danger as the shared Jewish identity."[25] They were also sensitive to issues of difference because of their sexual orientation; within the lesbian/feminist movement, they expected to find respect for the full complexity of their identities. Yet, they felt triply marginalized: as feminists within the Jewish community, as lesbians within the Jewish feminist movement, and as Jews within the lesbian community. The poet and lesbian activist Irena Klepfisz first articulated her sense of unease with the silence surrounding the subject of anti-Semitism in a letter she sent in 1981 to *Womanews,* a New York City feminist paper, a letter that resulted in an entire issue devoted to the topic. Klepfisz's contribution to that issue described the feelings of many Jewish feminists. Although few shared her sense that anti-Semitism was a serious phenomenon in American society, they did recognize with pain her encounter in the lesbian/feminist community of "an anti-Semitism either of omission or one which trivializes the Jewish experience and Jewish oppression."[26] Similarly, in an article published in 1985 in a general book of feminist thought, Judith Plaskow brought to American feminists an analysis of anti-Semitism as "the unacknowledged racism" of the women's movement. Jewish feminists, she recounted, heard anti-Semitic jokes and references to anti-Semitic stereotypes such as the "JAP" at women's meetings and yet were accused of paranoia when they complained of anti-Semitism.[27] By raising these issues, Jewish activists within feminist circles and Jewish feminist scholars who participate within Women's Studies programs have challenged the position that only persons of color have their own political goals that merit support or distinctive cultures worthy of study.

Most painful of all was the acceptance by some in the international feminist community of an anti-Zionist stance that descended into anti-Semitism. At the International Women's Conference in Mexico City and at the 1980 International Women's Conference in Copenhagen, both sponsored by the United Nations, Jewish feminists encountered not only opposition to Israeli policy but denial of Israel's right to exist. In Copenhagen, a Program of Action was adopted that called for the elimination of Zionism (i.e., the State of Israel), and delegates heard such statements as "The only way to rid the world of Zionism is to kill all the Jews." Although Jewish women formed a caucus to respond to the attacks and Bella Abzug spoke with her customary power and Jewish pride, the experience for Jews who were present was one of fear and vulnerability.[28]

Letty Cottin Pogrebin, who, like Abzug, bridged the general American women's movement and Jewish feminism, publicly brought the issue of anti-Semitism to the American feminist community in 1982 in the pages of *Ms.* magazine. Her article spoke eloquently about anti-Semitism on the Right and the Left, about feminists' failure to see the parallels between anti-Semitism and sexism, and about black-Jewish relations. Most important, she identified what she called the "three i's" that Jewish women experienced as anti-Semitism: "invisibility (the omission of Jewish reality from feminist consciousness)," "insult," and "internalized oppression (Jewish self-hatred)." Perhaps her most poignant question was "why [could] the Movement's healing embrace encompass the black woman, the Chicana, the white ethnic woman, the disabled woman, and every other female whose struggle is complicated by an extra element of 'outness,' but the Jewish woman [was] not honored in her specificity?"[29] Pogrebin's piece drew what the magazine called "one of the largest reader responses of any article published in *Ms.*" The editors added that "the overwhelming majority of the letters expressed support of Letty Pogrebin for taking on a topic of such complexity, gratitude for an analysis that challenged their own assumption, and relief that someone had named for them a problem that had brought pain to their own lives." Nonetheless, the magazine's editors, despite Pogrebin's objection—she was then an editor at *Ms.*—decided to publish only three long letters, all critical of her position.[30] Because of the prominence of *Ms.* magazine, however, Pogrebin's article lent legitimacy to Jewish women in the American feminist movement to name their discomfort with hiding their Jewishness and to reconcile their identification as both feminists and Jews. As Pogrebin reflected a decade later, the article and its responses also "exposed some feminists' anti-Semitic feelings and inspired movement activists to analyze this behavior constructively in workshops and conferences."[31]

Pogrebin was also a founder of a group called Feminists against Anti-Semitism, which included, among others, the writers E. M. Broner and Aviva Cantor, the psychologist Phyllis Chesler, Judith Plaskow, Susan Weidman Schneider, editor of *Lilith,* and myself. The group organized a panel, entitled "Anti-Semitism: The Unacknowledged Racism," at the 1981 meeting of the National Women's Studies Association. About three hundred women attended the session. The panel's five participants—Andrea Dworkin, Broner, Chesler, Plaskow, and myself—discussed contemporary manifestations of anti-Semitism in anti-Zionism and the links between anti-Semitism and anti-feminism.[32] A plenary session on racism and anti-Semitism, held at the 1983 conference and organized by the lesbian activist and scholar Evelyn Torton Beck, drew an audience of some 1,500 persons and resulted in the formation of a Task Force on Jewish Issues that established a Jewish Women's Caucus within the Association the following year. The Caucus asserted that Jews were "a cultural/religious minority within American society," a minority that was still "mocked, despised, feared, and scapegoated." It called for integrating the experience of Jewish women "as Jews" in feminist organizations. Already at the 1983 Women's Studies Association conference there were six additional sessions on Jewish women's history and literature.[33] The experience of anti-Semitism—an issue of what we might now label identity politics—thus brought together Jewish feminists who worked primarily in the Jewish community and Jewish feminists who worked primarily in the American feminist movement. Members of this alliance called attention to, and delegitimated, anti-Semitism within the women's movement and explained how it could be cloaked in the guise of anti-Zionism. In doing so, Jewish feminists sensitized a portion of the American Left, where the Jewish Establishment is disdained, to take seriously the legitimacy of Jewish particularity and Jewish concern for Israel. They also spurred the American Jewish Congress to found a National Commission on Women's Equality in 1984, with Betty Friedan as one of its co-chairs.

Jewish feminists rarely criticized the American women's movement except where anti-Semitism and anti-Zionism were concerned, but they often avoided themes that became prominent in general American feminism. They differed with American feminism in their attitudes to the family and with regard to essentialism, the assertion that women's biological and cultural differences should be celebrated and should become the basis of a separate women's culture. To be sure, some Jewish feminists have incorporated symbols and forms of women's spirituality from other, often pagan, religious traditions into their rituals in a form of syncretism, but they have had little impact on institutionalized Jewish religious life, with the exception of the Reconstructionist movement, which, however, has formally repudiated any reference to pagan gods.[34] As of now, these syncretistic rituals, which often focus on issues related to domestic life or with women's life cycle events, remain an aspect of what has been called "New Age" Judaism.

American feminists were widely perceived as elevating professional accomplishment and public activity over women's traditional domestic roles. Although feminists spoke about empowering women and giving them choices, in the early years of the women's movement they seemed to portray housewives and mothers simply as drudges. Many feminists depicted the nuclear family only as a source of women's oppression, failing to acknowledge the satisfactions it also offered to women (as well as to men). They made light of the stress experienced by women who sought to combine careers and family life. As Betty Friedan asserted in her 1981 book *The Second Stage,* because of their perceived hostility to the family, feminist ideologues were failing to reach the majority of American women, who were rooted in family life and connected their sense of self to their domestic roles. "The women's movement," she noted, "[was] being blamed . . . for the destruction of the family."[35]

Jewish feminists disseminated a different vision of the family. To be sure, they expressed concern about calls from communal leaders for Jewish women to have more children to compensate for the Holocaust or for the growing rate of intermarriage in America. They recognized that promoters of traditional Jewish family life often romanticized the past and blamed mothers for the perceived decline in Jewish identification among American Jews. Their concern was driven by the fact that the promotion of higher fertility in Jewish families was too often accompanied by attacks on feminism and was rarely followed by communal efforts to alleviate the high costs, particularly for large families, of raising Jewish children.[36] But Jewish feminists refrained from statements of radical individualism. They did not denigrate the family as such, for they were aware of its role as the central unit in Jewish communal life. As the writer Anne Roiphe later put it in an article offering a feminist perspective on the Jewish family, "A truly feminist position does not mock the family and a Jewish feminist position must by definition cherish the home and value the work that is done there."[37]

Jewish feminists, both male and female, did suggest, however, that Jews had embraced many family patterns throughout history, depending on socioeconomic conditions, and should expand their concept of family to respond to the actual Jewish families that made up the American Jewish population.[38] They noted that, like American families over the course of the past two generations, Jewish families have changed. There are now far more singles, single parents, and gay couples and parents among American Jews than ever before.[39] Serving the needs of all American Jewish families, including those who depart from the stereotype, Jewish feminists have argued, strengthens the Jewish community. Not only does an inclusive, welcoming policy draw otherwise alienated Jews into contact with Jewish institutions, but, as Martha Ackelsberg suggests with regard to gay and lesbian Jewish families, it provides opportunities for communal discussions of sexuality and of the ways in which nonparents can promote intergenerational Jewish continuity. Feminists conclude that serving the needs of families broadly defined is also rooted in Jewish concepts of communal responsibility.[40] This relative family friendliness on the part of Jewish feminism predated the reconsideration by mainstream American feminism of its attitude toward family life.

The emphasis of American feminism in the 1960s and 1970s was the identification of women's oppression and exclusion from power and the definition of strategies to secure self-empowerment and political change. Perhaps because most leaders of American feminism were white and middle class, their primary goal was for women to attain a fair share of the material wealth and status available to white men in American society. Jewish feminism mirrored this goal in its early articulation of an "equal access" platform, seeking equity for women in Jewish communal life and in the synagogue. In the late 1970s, American feminism began to highlight some of women's differences from men as positive attributes. To cite the historian Hester Eisenstein once more, "the woman-centered perspective located specific virtues in the historical and psychological experience of women. Instead of seeking to minimize the polarization between masculine and feminine, it sought to isolate and define those aspects of female experience that were potential sources of strength and power for women and, more broadly, of a new blueprint for social change."[41] Just as American feminists began to celebrate women's culture, as expressed in particular art forms or in styles of storytelling, so Jewish feminists began, in the early 1980s, to articulate the need for women's interpretation of classical Jewish texts and creation of liturgy that reflected the ways in which women named, and experienced, God. They struggled with the tension between the need to innovate, so that liturgy might reflect deeply felt spiritual beliefs, and the desire to remain attached to a liturgy whose authenticity was rooted in its age and communal usage.[42] As Judith Plaskow has noted of feminist reinterpretation of rituals and reworking of or creating new liturgy, "[W]omen are seeking to transform Jewish ritual so that it acknowledges our existence and experience. In the ritual moment, women's history is made present."[43]

This project of feminist-inspired change suggested that Jewish culture as a whole would benefit from the infusion of women's perspectives, that these could become a blueprint for change. And, in fact, feminists have stimulated much liturgical creativity, leading to the production of new prayer books by the Reform and Reconstructionist movements, feminist *haggadot* for use at family Passover seders or at special third feminist seders, and the publication, for example, of the poet and Hebraist Marcia Falk's innovative *The Book of Blessings*. Falk has pioneered in the creation of a Hebrew liturgy that incorporates feminist understandings of God.[44]

The validation of female culture within American feminism led some radical feminists to develop an ideology often called "essentialism," or "cultural feminism." As opposed to "liberal feminists," who see men and women as basically the same and seek therefore to rectify inequities in the treatment of women, essentialists argue that women and men are basically different. Women have a different way of speaking, of constructing reality, and of learning. Differences between men and women are not simply the product of their social conditioning, as liberal feminists would have it, but are inherent in their femaleness, in physiological distinctiveness. As opposed to adherents of Western cultural paradigms who see females as different and inferior, essentialists sees females as different and superior. To give just one example, according to essentialists, women must be free to design and administer their own schools, giving full recognition to women's nonlinear and nonrational styles of learning. Essentialists have inverted antifeminist presumptions, celebrating women's modes of being in the world as morally superior to men's.

Essentialism is virtually absent from Jewish feminism; Jewish feminists by and large still fall into the liberal camp. Although they believe that women may have a distinctive perspective to offer in the interpretation of Jewish texts and may display a different leadership style, they share Jewish cultural treasures with men and they seek to be partners with men in exploring the culture of the past and creating the culture of the future. They make no claim to female superiority. True, some Jewish feminists have rejected *tallit* and *tefillin* as male paraphernalia inappropriate to women and have suggested that women find more congenial garb for prayer. Some have reclaimed women's rituals linked to women's biological cycle, ranging from marking Rosh Hodesh, the beginning of the month, as a special day for women, to immersion in the *mikvah* (ritual bath) at the conclusion of their menstrual periods.[45] In both these cases Jewish feminists have reappropriated these rites as a way to link their own spiritual expressions to Jewish women of the past as well as to their own physiology. They have, however, adapted these practices to their own contemporary needs. They have created new ceremonies, often with a learning component, to mark Rosh Hodesh, which was acknowledged in the past as a half-holiday for women on which they might refrain from some of their household tasks but was not celebrated as such. And they have eliminated the negative elements that traditionally surrounded observance of the rules of family purity.[46]

Ironically, Jewish essentialists can be found more readily among ultra-Orthodox women than among feminists.[47] As Debra Kaufman found in her study of *ba'alot teshuva,* women who became Orthodox, those who affiliated with ultra-Orthodox sects saw themselves as sharing special qualities as women, such as a capacity for nurturing and a higher degree of spirituality. In their view, these natural, indeed divinely bestowed, qualities fit them for their roles as wives and mothers, responsible for their families, and justified the sex segregation and women's exemption from *mitzvot* (commandments) that characterizes ultra-Orthodox life. As Kaufman notes, "both newly Orthodox Jewish women and radical feminists see women's culture as the source for transformation of values for humankind."[48] However, unlike essentialist feminists who seek women's autonomy and power, Orthodox women accept the rules determined by men in a patriarchal system.

Despite its lack of a central address, Jewish feminism remains a vibrant voice, primarily within the various denominations of American Judaism. Like much of the American Jewish community, it seems to have turned inward. Jewish feminists participate in general feminist organizations, but they do so as individuals. Jewish feminist scholarship appears in general collections of articles in history, anthropology, and literature and is published by respectable university and trade presses. Yet most Jewish feminist scholars are more concerned with having an impact on the field of Judaic than on Women's Studies. Ideally, of course, they seek both. The inclusion of topics on Jewish women's history and literature at women's studies conferences and the explosion of work on women and gender in the annual conference of the Association for Jewish Studies has muted Jewish feminists' sense of isolation within the scholarly world. Although general feminist theory continues to proliferate, it has become so arcane and jargon-filled that it plays little role in the lives of most American women, whether secular or religious, Christian or Jewish.

In turning inward, the Jewish community and Jewish feminism as well reflect the fragmentation of society and culture in contemporary America. Jewish feminists are less concerned with making their voices heard as Jews in the institutions of the

American women's movement than they were in the past. Their experience of anti-Semitism in American and international meetings has declined. They have chosen to direct their attention to the institutions of the Jewish community to realize feminist visions of equality, not only in terms of equal access but also in terms of cultural revitalization.

So many Jewish feminist activists have declared, in one way or another, "Feminism enables me to be a Jew" or "Feminism has brought me back to my Jewishness." Because Jewish feminism has been successful in its efforts to end the exclusion of women from spiritual and communal leadership and to restore the experience of women to Jewish history, it has enabled many secular feminists of Jewish birth to find a place for themselves within the community of Jews. Letty Cottin Pogrebin recounts, in *Deborah, Golda, and Me,* how Jewish feminism provided her with an opportunity to overcome her alienation from Judaism, an alienation that dated back to her being excluded from reciting *kaddish,* the memorial prayer for the dead, after her mother's death when she was fifteen.[49] Only after she encountered anti-Semitism within the women's movement did Betty Friedan begin to reflect on the Jewish component of her identity. She traveled to Israel, joined a Jewish study group in America, and became involved with the organized Jewish community through the American Jewish Congress's Commission on the Status of Women. After the writer Anne Roiphe began a serious study of Jewish history and Talmud in the aftermath of the passionate negative responses to her *New York Times* article on celebrating Christmas as a secular Jew, she realized that she could join the Jewish community only if she found a synagogue to which she could take her daughters "without subjecting them to insults."[50] By the 1980s, when she was incorporating Judaism into her family's life, thanks to Jewish feminism, many egalitarian synagogues existed. The poet Adrienne Rich also turned to Judaism through her feminism. Born into a mixed Jewish/Christian household with its Jewish roots in the South, Rich was raised to deny her Jewishness. Her marriage to a Brooklyn-born Jew, of East European origin, in a ceremony at Harvard Hillel was in part a rejection of her parents' values. They recognized it as such and refused to attend the wedding. In a long poem written in 1960, she described herself as "Split at the Root, Neither Gentile nor Jew, Yankee nor Rebel."[51] When she came to the recognition of her lesbianism, she also affirmed her identity as a Jew and turned to Jewish feminist writings as resources. She has written poems on Jewish sources and was a founding editor of the Jewish feminist journal *Bridges.*[52]

In addition to prominent feminists whose encounter with anti-Semitism in the women's movement or with Jewish feminism led to an engagement with the meaning of Jewishness in their own lives, many women whose names are not known to us also use feminist ritual to connect with Jewish tradition. For example, the feminist seder organized by Ma'ayan, the Jewish Women's Project, in New York in 1996 attracted more than nine hundred women. Although this was a feminist celebration, it placed women's experience within a Jewish structure and within a Jewish time-frame. Adult women have also organized programs of study and have celebrated adult bat mitzvahs, marking their sense of full recognition as Jews.[53]

Although Jewish feminism developed under the impact of the American women's movement and diverged from it largely because that movement did not see Jewish women's specific concerns as of interest, Jewish feminism has developed a momentum of its own. Its adherents are aware of general feminist issues that transcend ethnic and religious lines, but their feminism is informed by Jewish communal concerns. With no central organizations, Jewish feminism depends on the energy of religious professionals and lay people to bring its issues to local institutions, both mainstream and what a generation ago would have been called countercultural. The fragmented nature of American Jewry and of American society suggests that Jewish feminism in America will continue to be diversified; the history of the movement demonstrates that a relatively small number of persons, attuned to the currents of social and cultural change, can have an influence beyond their numbers.

NOTES

1. Conversations with representatives of the Conservative, Reconstructionist, and Reform movements yield figures of seventy-eight females in the Conservative Rabbinical Assembly, seventy-three female graduates of the Reconstructionist Rabbinical College, and between 250 and three-hundred female Reform rabbis as of spring 1997. (The Reform Central Conference of American Rabbis claims not to take note of gender distinctions.) There is likely to be an overlap among rabbis since graduates of the RRC may join either the CCAR or the Rabbinical Assembly. The Conservative Cantors' Assembly has thirty-nine female members, and the American Conference of Cantors informed me that 40 percent of its 350 members were women.

2. Jack Wertheimer, *A People Divided: Judaism in Contemporary America* (New York: Basic Books, 1993), 21–22, 72–75.

3. Arthur Hertzberg, *The Zionist Idea* (New York: Antheneum, 1970); David Vital, *The Origins of Zionism* (New York: Oxford University Press, 1975).

4. Betty Friedan, *The Feminist Mystique* (New York: Norton, 1963).

5. On the countercultural background to radical feminism, see Alice Echols, *Daring to Be Bad: Radical Feminism in America, 1967–75* (Minneapolis: University of Minnesota Press, 1989).

6. Derived from figures provided in Moshe Hartman and Harriet Hartman, *Gender Equality and American Jews* (Albany: SUNY Press, 1996), 31–43. The data for their conclusions are drawn from the 1990 National Jewish Population Survey.

7. Kate Millett, *Sexual Politics* (Garden City, NY: Doubleday, 1969); Shulamith Firestone, *The Dialectic of Sex* (New York: William Morrow, 1970); Robin Morgan, ed., *Sisterhood Is Powerful* (New York: Random House, 1970). All three appeared in paperback editions by 1971.

8. Hester Eisenstein, *Contemporary Feminist Thought* (Boston: G. K. Hall, 1983), xi.

9. "Friedan at 55," *Lilith* 1, no. 1 (fall 1976): 11.

10. On the beginnings of Jewish feminism, see Sylvia Barack Fishman. *A Breath of Life: Feminism in the American Jewish Community* (New York: Free Press, 1993), 1–9, and Paula E. Hyman, "Ezrat Nashim and the Emergence of a New Jewish Feminism," in *The Americanization of the Jews,* ed., Robert M. Seltzer and Norman Cohen (New York: NYU Press, 1995), 284–95. For the most comprehensive recent study, with an emphasis on individual biographies, see Joyce Antler, *The Journey Home: Jewish Women and the American Century* (New York: Free Press, 1997), 259–308.

11. See Trude Weiss-Rosmarin, "The Unfreedom of Jewish Women," *Jewish Spectator* (October 1970): 2–6; Rachel Adler, "The Jew Who Wasn't There," *Davka* (summer 1971): 6–11; Paula E. Hyman. "The Other Half: Women in the Jewish Tradition," *Conservative Judaism* 26, no. 4 (summer 1972): 14–21; Judith Hauptman, "Women's Liberation in the Talmudic Period: An Assessment," *Conservative Judaism* 26, no. 4 (summer 1972): 22–28; Ezrat Nashim's "Jewish Women Call for Change," my personal archive; program of the second Jewish Feminist Organization Conference, April 1974, my personal archive.

12. The Jewish Feminist Organization, Statement of Purpose, April 28, 1974, my personal archive.

13. For example, the prominent Wiccan Starhawk (Miriam Simos), author of *The Spiral Dance: A Rebirth of the Ancient Religion of the Great Goddess* (San Francisco: Harper and Row, 1979), *Dreaming the Dark: Magic, Sex, and Politics* (Boston: Beacon Press, 1982), and *Truth or Dare: Encounters with Power, Authority, and Mystery* (San Francisco: Harper and Row, 1987), was born and raised a Jew.

14. Mary Daly, *Beyond God the Father: Toward a Philosophy of Women's Liberation* (Boston: Beacon Press, 1973), 55–59, 157–58. The first three citations are from 56, 55, and 59, respectively, the fourth from 158, and the fifth from 74.

15. Judith Plaskow, *Standing Again at Sinai: Judaism from a Feminist Perspective* (San Francisco: Harper and Row, 1990), xi.

16. *The Jewish Woman: New Perspectives,* ed. Elizabeth Koltun (New York: Schocken Books, 1976), 217–40.

17. "From the Editors," *Lilith* 1, no. 1 (fall 1976): 3.

18. Audre Lorde, "Age, Race, Class, and Sex: Women Redefining Difference," in her *Sister Outsider* (Trumansburg, NY: Crossing Press, 1984), 118.

19. Judith Plaskow, "Blaming the Jews for the Birth of Patriarchy," *Lilith,* 7 (1980): 11–12. The citation is from 11. Reprinted in *Nice Jewish Girls,* ed. Evelyn Torton Beck (Watertown, MA: Persephone Press, 1982), 250–54.

20. Leonard Swidler, "Jesus Was a Feminist," *Catholic World* 212 (January 1971): 177–83. The citation is from *Biblical Affirmations of Woman* (Philadelphia: Westminster Press, 1979), 164. Swidler's *Women in Judaism: The Status of Women in Formative Judaism* (Metuchen, NJ: Scarecrow Press, 1976) asserted the rabbinic source of the disparagement of women in western culture.

21. Plaskow, "Blaming the Jews." The citation is from 12.

22. Annette Daum, "Blaming Jews for the Death of the Goddess," *Lilith* 7 (1980): 12–13. Reprinted in *Nice Jewish Girls,* 255–61.

23. See, for example, Susannah Heschel, "Anti-Judaism in Christian Feminist Theology," *Tikkun* 5, no. 3 (May/June 1990): 25–28, 95–97. The citation is from 27.

24. Ibid., 97.

25. Melanie Kaye, "Some Notes on Jewish Lesbian Identity," in *Nice Jewish Girls,* 38.

26. Irena Klepfisz, "Anti-Semitism in the Lesbian/Feminist Movement," in *Nice Jewish Girls,* 45–51. The citation is from 46.

27. Judith Plaskow, "Anti-Semitism: The Unacknowledged Racism," in *Women's Consciousness, Women's Conscience,* ed. B. H. Andolson, C. E. Gudof, and M. D. Pollaner (Minneapolis: Winston Press, 1985), 47–65.

28. As cited in Letty Cottin Pogrebin, "Anti-Semitism in the Women's Movement," *Ms.* (June 1982): 48–49. The quotation was reported by a non-Jewish American activist. For a discussion of this issue, see Fishman, *Breath of Life,* 9–12.

29. Pogrebin, "Anti-Semitism in the Women's Movement," 45, 46, 48–49, 62, 65–66,

69–70, 73–74. The "three i's" are discussed on 65–66, 69–70. The essay is reprinted in abbreviated form in Pogrebin's *Deborah, Golda, and Me* (New York: Crown, 1991), 205–228.

30. *Ms.* (February 1983), 12. The three long letters that the magazine published criticized anti-Semitism but dissented from Pogrebin's understanding of Zionism and of the significance of anti-Semitism.

31. Pogrebin, *Deborah, Golda, and Me,* 204.

32. Minutes, Feminists against Anti-Semitism, January 22, 1981, February 22, 1981, my personal archive; Pogrebin, "Anti-Semitism in the Women's Movement," 46; Vivian J. Scheinmann, "Jewish Feminists Demand Equal Treatment," *New Directions for Women,* July/August 1981, 5, 16.

33. *Lilith* 11 (fall/winter 1983): 5 and Antler, *Journey Home,* 294. The quotation of the Caucus's statement is from Antler.

34. Nurit Zaidman, "Variations of Jewish Feminism: The Traditional, Modern, and Postmodern Approaches," *Modern Judaism* 16 (1996): 54. Zaidman considers Jewish feminism that has sought equality for women within the various denominations of American Judaism as "modern," while "postmodern" feminism includes self-conscious attempts to bring together eclectically symbols and rituals from a variety of traditions in order to remake Judaism. She provides an analysis of a postmodern feminist ritual, the burying of a baby boy's umbilical cord, placenta, and dried foreskin, 54–57.

35. See Betty Friedan, *The Second Stage* (New York: Summit Books, 1981). The citation is from 22.

36. See my "Looking for a Usable Past," *Congress Monthly,* October 1975, reprinted in *On Being a Jewish Feminist: A Reader,* ed. Susannah Heschel (New York: Schocken Books, 1983), 19–26.

37. Anne Roiphe, "The Jewish Family: A Feminist Perspective," *Tikkun* 1, no. 2 (1985): 71.

38. Steven M. Cohen, "The American Jewish Family Today," *American Jewish Yearbook* (1982), 136–54.

39. On the demographic changes among American Jewish families, see, ibid. and Steven M. Cohen, *American Modernity and Jewish Identity* (New York: Tavistock, 1983), 113–31.

40. Martha Ackelsberg, "Redefining Families: Models for the Jewish Future," in *Twice Blessed: On Being Lesbian or Gay and Jewish,* ed. Christie Balka and Andy Rose (Boston: Beacon Press, 1989), 107–17.

41. Eisenstein, *Contemporary Feminist Thought,* xii.

42. Rita Gross, "Female God Language in a Jewish Context," in *Womanspirit Rising: A Feminist Reader in Religion,* ed. Carol Christ and Judith Plaskow (San Francisco: Harper and Row, 1979), 167–73; Ellen Umansky, "(Re)Imaging the Divine," *Response* 41–42 (fall-winter 1982) and "Creating a Jewish Feminist Theology," in *Weaving the Visions: New Patterns in Feminist Spirituality,* ed. Judith Plaskow and Carol Christ (San Francisco: Harper and Row, 1989), 187–98; Susannah Heschel, "Introduction," in *On Being a Jewish Feminist: A Reader,* xii–xxxiii; Judith Plaskow, "The Right Question Is Theological," in ibid., 223–33; Martha Ackelsberg, "Spirituality, Community, and Politics: B'not Esh and the Feminist Reconstruction of Judaism," *Journal of Feminist Studies in Religion* 2 (1986): 109–20. The Women's Institute of Continuing Jewish Education, located in San Diego and directed by its founder, Irene Fine, has published a number of volumes of women's *midrash* (interpretation), including *Taking the Fruit: Modern Women's Tales of the Bible,* ed. Jane Zones (San Diego: Woman's Institute for Continuing Jewish Education, 1981), 2nd rev. ed., 1989; *On Our*

Spiritual Journey, A Creative Shabbat Service, ed. Jacquelyn Tolley (San Diego: Woman's Institute for Continuing Jewish Education, 1984); *San Diego Women's Haggadah,* 2nd ed., ed. Jane Zones (San Diego: Woman's Institute for Continuing Jewish Education, 1986); Irene Fine, *Midlife, A Rite of Passage/The Wise Woman, A Celebration* (San Diego: Woman's Institute for Continuing Jewish Education, 1988); *A Ceremonies Sampler: New Rites, Celebrations, and Observances of Jewish Women,* ed. Elizabeth Levine (San Diego: Woman's Institute for Continuing Jewish Education, 1991).

43. Judith Plaskow, "Standing Again at Sinai: Jewish Memory from a Feminist Perspective," *Tikkun* 1, no. 2 (1985): 33.

44. See the Reconstructionist *siddur, Kol Haneshamah,* ed. David Teutsch (Wyncote, PA: Reconstructionist Press, 1993); the Reform *Gates of Prayer for Shabbat,* and *Gates of Prayer for Weekdays and at a House of Mourning,* both edited by Chaim Stern (New York: Central Conference of American Rabbis, 1992); Marcia Falk, *The Book of Blessings: New Jewish Prayers for Daily Life, the Sabbath, and the New Moon Festival* (San Francisco: Harper/Collins Publishers, 1996).

45. See Peninah Adelman, *Miriam's Well: Rituals for Jewish Women Around the Year* (Fresh Meadows, NY: Biblio Press, 1986).

46. Many women no longer wait seven days after the end of their menstrual periods, and unmarried women, whose sexuality belongs only to themselves, are also using the *mikvah* (ritual bath).

47. Debra R. Kaufman first noted this parallel in her book *Rachel's Daughters: Newly Orthodox Jewish Women* (New Brunswick, NJ: Rutgers University Press, 1991), 149–54.

48. Ibid., 153.

49. Pogrebin, *Deborah, Golda, and Me,* 42, 48–52, 54–80, 236–56.

50. Anne Roiphe, *Generation without Memory: A Jewish Journey in Christian America* (New York: Simon and Schuster, 1981), 203–04.

51. Adrienne Rich, "Split at the Root," in *Nice Jewish Girls,* 67–84. The citation is from 67.

52. Antler, *Journey Home,* 301.

53. Ma'ayan brochure. On adult bat-mitzvah rituals, see Stuart Schoenfeld, "Integration in the Group and Sacred Uniqueness: An Analysis of Adult Bat Mitzvah," in *Persistence and Flexibility: Anthropological Perspectives on the American Jewish Experience,* ed. Walter Zenner (Albany: SUNY Press, 1989), 117–33; and Schoenfeld, "Ritual and Role Transition: Adult Bat Mitzvah as a Successful Rite of Passage," in *The Uses of Tradition: Jewish Community in the Modern Era,* ed. Jack Wertheimer (New York: Jewish Theological Seminary, 1992), 349–76.

Contributors

Joyce Antler, the Samuel Lane Professor of American Jewish History and Culture at Brandeis University, is the author of, among others, *The Journey Home: How Jewish Women Shaped Modern America* (1997), and editor of *America and I: Short Stories by American Jewish Women Writers* (1990).

Dianne Ashton is professor of religion and director of American studies at Rowan University. She is the author of *Rebecca Gratz: Women and Judaism in Antebellum America* (1997) and *Jewish Life in Pennsylvania* (1998) and co-editor, with Ellen Umansky, of *Four Centuries of Jewish Women's Spirituality* (1992). Her work on women in American Jewish life appears in many collections.

Joan Jacobs Brumberg is the author of *Fasting Girls: The History of Anorexia Nervosa* and *The Body Project: An Intimate History of American Girls.* She is Stephen H. Weiss Presidential Fellow and professor of history, human development, and women's studies at Cornell University.

Marcie Cohen Ferris is a Ph.D. candidate in American studies at George Washington University, where she is writing a dissertation on southern Jewish foodways. She has worked in the field of public history for more than twenty years, at the Norlands Living History Center, Colonial Williamsburg, Plimoth Plantation, Elderhostel, and the Museum of the Southern Jewish Experience. She is a native of Blytheville, Arkansas.

Julia L. Foulkes is a Core Faculty member at New School University in New York City, where she teaches history. She recently published *Modern Bodies: Dance and American Modernism from Martha Graham to Alvin Alley* (2002) and is a 2002–2003 fellow at the David C. Driskell Center for the Study of the African Diaspora at the University of Maryland.

Paula E. Hyman, Lucy Moses Professor of Modern Jewish History at Yale University, is the author of, among others, *Gender and Assimilation in Modern Jewish History: The Roles and Representation of Women* (1995) and co-editor, with Deborah Dash Moore, of *Jewish Women in America: An Historical Encyclopedia* (1997).

Jenna Weissman Joselit currently teaches American studies and Jewish studies at Princeton University. Her most recent books include *A Perfect Fit: Clothes,*

313

Character, and the Promise of America (2001) and *Immigration and American Religion* (2001).

Alice Kessler-Harris, Hoxie Professor of American History at Columbia University, is the author of, among others, *Out to Work: A History of Wage-Earning Women in the United States* (1982) and *In Pursuit of Equity: Women, Men, and the Quest for Economic Citizenship in Twentieth-Century America* (2001).

Pamela S. Nadell is professor of history and director of the Jewish Studies Program at American University. She is the author of *Women Who Would Be Rabbis: A History of Women's Ordination, 1889–1985* (1998), which was a finalist for the National Jewish Book Award, and co-editor, with Jonathan D. Sarna, of *Women and American Judaism: Historical Perspectives* (2001). She is also chair of the Academic Council of the American Jewish Historical Society.

Riv-Ellen Prell is professor of American studies at the University of Minnesota and the author of *Prayer and Community: The Havurah in American Judaism* (1989) and *Fighting to Become Americans: Jews, Gender, and the Anxiety of Assimilation* (1999).

Faith Rogow, Ph.D., author of *Gone to Another Meeting: A History of the National Council of Jewish Women* (1993), founded Insighters Educational Consulting in 1996 to help people learn from the media and from one another. She is the founding national president of the Alliance for a Media Literate America (www.AMLAinfo.org).

Jonathan D. Sarna is the Joseph H. and Belle R. Braun Professor of American Jewish History at Brandeis University and chairs the Academic Advisory and Editorial Board of the Jacob Rader Marcus Center of the American Jewish Archives. His many books include *Women and American Judaism: Historical Perspectives,* co-edited with Pamela S. Nadell (2001); *JPS: The Americanization of Jewish Culture* (1989); *The American Jewish Experience* (1986; rev. ed., 1997); *Jacksonian Jew: The Two Worlds of Mordecai Noah* (1981); and volumes dealing with the history of Jews in New Haven, Cincinnati, and Boston. He is currently completing a new history of the Jewish religion in America, to be published by Yale University Press.

Linda Mack Schloff is the director of the Jewish Historical Society of the Upper Midwest, in St. Paul, and the author of *"And Prairie Dogs Weren't Kosher": Jewish Women in the Upper Midwest since 1855* (1996).

Debra L. Schultz is the director of programs for the Open Society Institute (Soros Foundations Network) Women's Program and the author of *Going South: Jewish Women in the Civil Rights Movement* (2001).

Ellen Smith is associate director of the Gralla Fellows Program for Religion Journalists at Brandeis University, and principal of Museumsmith. She has curated over thirty exhibitions, including Facing the New World: Jewish Portraits in

Colonial and Federal America, and is the co-editor, with Jonathan D. Sarna, of the *Jews of Boston* (1995).

Shelly Tenenbaum is associate professor of sociology and Director of Holocaust and Genocide Studies at Clark University. She is the author of *A Credit to Their Community: Jewish Loan Societies in the United States, 1880–1945* (1993) and co-editor, with Lynn Davidman, of *Feminist Perspectives on Jewish Studies* (1994) and, with Judith Baskin, of *Gender and Jewish Studies: A Curriculum Guide* (1994).

Beth S. Wenger holds the Katz Family Chair in American Jewish History at the University of Pennsylvania and is the author of *New York Jews and the Great Depression: Uncertain Promise* (1996). She is also co-editor of *Remembering the Lower East Side: American Jewish Reflections* (2000).

Permissions

Ellen Smith, "Portraits of a Community: The Image and Experience of Early American Jews," edited and abridged. Reprinted by permission of the author, The Jewish Museum, New York, and Prestel-Verlag. Copyright © 1997 by The Jewish Museum, New York, under the auspices of The Jewish Theological Seminary, and Prestel-Verlag, Munich. This essay was previously published in the exhibition catalogue *Facing the New World: Jewish Portraits in Colonial and Federal America.*

Dianne Ashton, "The Lessons of the Hebrew Sunday School." Reprinted from *Rebecca Gratz: Women and Judaism in Antebellum America*, by Diane Ashton, by permission of the Wayne State University Press and by permission of the author. Copyright © 1997 by Wayne State University Press, Detroit, Michigan 48201. All rights are reserved.

Jonathan D. Sarna, "A Great Awakening: The Transformation That Shaped Twentieth-Century American Judaism," edited and abridged and reprinted by permission of the author from CIJE Essay Series, Council for Initiatives in Jewish Education. Another version appeared in *Religious Diversity and American Religious History*, ed. Walter H. Conser and Sumner Twiss (Athens: University of Georgia Press, 1997), 1–25. Copyright © 1997 by the University of Georgia Press.

Faith Rogow, "Gone to Another Meeting: The National Council of Jewish Women, 1893–1993." Reprinted from *Gone to Another Meeting: The National Council of Jewish Women, 1893–1993*, by Faith Rogow, by permission of the University of Alabama Press. Copyright © 1993 by University of Alabama Press.

Shelly Tenenbaum, "Borrowers or Lenders Be: Jewish Immigrant Women's Credit Networks," based in part on *A Credit to Their Community: Jewish Loan Societies in the United States, 1880–1945*, by Shelly Tenenbaum. Copyright © 1993 by Wayne State University Press. Reprinted by permission of Wayne State University Press.

Linda Mack Schloff, " 'We Dug More Rocks': Women and Work," from *"And Prairie Dogs Weren't Kosher": Jewish Women in the Upper Midwest Since 1855*, by Linda Mack Schloff. Copyright © 1996 Linda Mack Schloff. Reprinted by permission of the Minnesota Historical Society Press.

Index